o be returne

# A CULTURAL HISTORY
# OF THEATRE

VOLUME 5

**A Cultural History of Theatre**
*General Editors: Christopher B. Balme and Tracy C. Davis*

**Volume 1**
A Cultural History of Theatre in Antiquity
*Edited by Martin Revermann*

**Volume 2**
A Cultural History of Theatre in the Middle Ages
*Edited by Jody Enders*

**Volume 3**
A Cultural History of Theatre in the Early Modern Age
*Edited by Robert Henke*

**Volume 4**
A Cultural History of Theatre in the Age of Enlightenment
*Edited by Mechele Leon*

**Volume 5**
A Cultural History of Theatre in the Age of Empire
*Edited by Peter W. Marx*

**Volume 6**
A Cultural History of Theatre in the Modern Age
*Edited by Kim Solga*

# A CULTURAL HISTORY
# OF THEATRE

# IN THE AGE
# OF EMPIRE

## VOLUME 5

*Edited by Peter W. Marx*

Bloomsbury Academic
An imprint of Bloomsbury Publishing Plc

B L O O M S B U R Y
LONDON · OXFORD · NEW YORK · NEW DELHI · SYDNEY

**Bloomsbury Academic**

An imprint of Bloomsbury Publishing Plc

| 50 Bedford Square | 1385 Broadway |
| London | New York |
| WC1B 3DP | NY 10018 |
| UK | USA |

**www.bloomsbury.com**

**BLOOMSBURY and the Diana logo are trademarks of Bloomsbury Publishing Plc**

First published 2017

**British Library Cataloguing-in-Publication Data**

A catalogue record for this book is available from the British Library.

ISBN: HB: 978-1-472-58576-9
HB Set: 978-1-4725-8584-4

**Library of Congress Cataloging-in-Publication Data**

A catalog record for this book is available from the Library of Congress.

Series: Cultural Histories

Cover image: *Paris Opera* by Charles Fichot (1874). Courtesy of TWS.

Typeset by RefineCatch Limited, Bungay, Suffolk
Printed and bound in Great Britain

To find out more about our authors and books visit www.bloomsbury.com. Here you will find extracts, author interviews, details of forthcoming events and the option to sign up for our newsletters.

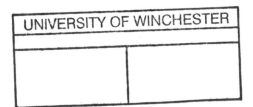

# CONTENTS

# LIST OF ILLUSTRATIONS

CHAPTER TWO

CHAPTER THREE

CHAPTER FOUR

## CHAPTER FIVE

## CHAPTER SIX

## CHAPTER SEVEN

## CHAPTER EIGHT

## CHAPTER NINE

# LIST OF TABLES

# NOTES ON CONTRIBUTORS

**Christopher Balme** holds the chair in Theatre Studies at LMU Munich. His publications include *Decolonizing the Stage: Theatrical syncretism and postcolonial drama* (1999); *Pacific Performances: Theatricality and Cross-Cultural Encounter in the South Seas* (2007); *Cambridge Introduction to Theatre Studies* (2008); *The theatrical public sphere* (2014). He is principal investigator of the ERC Advanced Grant 'Developing Theatre: Building Expert Networks for Theatre in Emerging Countries after 1945'.

**Tobias Becker** is a Research Fellow at the German Historical Institute London, where he works on the 'nostalgia wave' in the 1970s and 1980s. His research focuses on the history of popular culture and the popularization of history as well as on urban and theatre history. His publications include (with Daniel Morat, Kerstin Lange, Johanna Niedbalski, Anne Gnausch and Paul Nolte) *Weltstadtvergnügen. Berlin 1880-1930* (2016), *Inszenierte Moderne. Populäres Theater in Berlin und London, 1880-1930* (2014), and (ed. with Len Platt and David Linton) *Popular Musical Theatre in London and Berlin, 1890–1939* (2014).

**Jim Davis** is Professor of Theatre Studies at the University of Warwick. His major research interest is in nineteenth-century British theatre and his most recent books are *Comic Acting and Portraiture in Late-Georgian and Regency England* (2015) and *Theatre & Entertainment* (2016). He is also joint-author of a prize-winning study of London theatre audiences in the nineteenth century, *Reflecting the Audience: London Theatre-going 1840–1880* (2001). A two-volume edition of nineteenth-century dramatizations of Dickens (with Jacky Bratton) for Oxford University Press is currently in production. He is also an editor of *Nineteenth Century Theatre and Film*.

**Anselm Heinrich** is a Senior Lecturer in Theatre Studies at the University of Glasgow. He is the author of *Entertainment, Education, Propaganda. Regional Theatres in Germany and Britain Between 1918 and 1945* (2007), *Theater in der Region. Westfalen und Yorkshire 1918–1945* (2012), and he has co-edited a collection of essays on *Ruskin, The Theatre, and Victorian Visual Culture* with Kate Newey and Jeffrey Richards (2009). He is currently under contract from Routledge to write a book-length study on theatre in Europe under Nazi occupation during the Second World War. Other research interests include contemporary German theatre and performance, dramaturgy and cultural policy.

**Zoltán Imre** received his PhD from Queen Mary College, University of London (2005), and is now a reader at the Department of Comparative Literature and Culture, Eötvös University, Budapest. His publications include *Transfer and Translation: Intercultural Dialogues* (co-editor, author, 2002), *Theatre and Theatricality* (2003), *Transillumination: Hungarian Theatre in European Context* (editor, author, 2004), *On the Border of Theatre and Sociology* (co-editor, 2005), *Alternative Theatre Histories* (editor, author, 2008), *Staging Theatre – Theories, Histories, and Alternatives* (2009), *Staging the Nation – The Changing Concept of the Hungarian National Theatre from 1837 until Today* (2013), and various articles on Hungarian and European theatre.

**Nic Leonhardt** is a theatre and media historian as well as a writer. Her scholarly activities are characterized by a strong interdisciplinary approach and focus on global theatre, media and popular cultures at the turn of the twentieth century as well as on contemporary visual and urban cultures and Digital Humanities. She was visiting professor for Inter Artes at the University of Cologne in 2015 and 2016, and has been the associate director of the Centre for Global Theatre History in Munich. Her book publications include *Piktoral-Dramaturgie. Visuelle Kultur und Theater im 19. Jahrhundert* (2007), and *Durch Blicke im Bild. Stereoskopie im 19. und 20. Jahrhundert* (2016). She is also co-editor of the online *Journal of Global Theatre History*. Her current research focuses on transatlantic theatrical entrepreneurship at the turn of the twentieth century.

**Peter W. Marx** holds the chair in Media and Theatre Studies at the University of Cologne. He is also director of the Theaterwissenschaftliche Sammlung [Theatre Collection] Cologne. His publications include *Theatre and Cultural Memory* (German, 2003), *Max Reinhardt* (German, 2006, currently in translation, forthcoming 2017), *A Theatrical Age* (German, 2008). He edited a handbook on Drama (German, 2012) and one on *Hamlet* (German, 2014). He is currently writing a book on *Hamlet's Voyage to Germany*.

**Derek Miller** is an Assistant Professor of English at Harvard University where he teaches courses about theatre history and dramatic literature. His research on copyright, music-as-performance, and applying digital humanities methods to Broadway history has appeared in *Theatre Journal*, *Contemporary Theatre Review* and *Studies in Musical Theatre*. He is currently completing a monograph on the nineteenth-century development of performance rights laws.

**Sophie Nield** is a Senior Lecturer at the Department of Drama, Theatre and Dance, Royal Holloway, University of London. She works on aspects of nineteenth-century performance and cultural histories, and on questions of space, theatricality and representation in political life and the law. Recent publications have appeared in *Contemporary Theatre Review, Social History* and *About Performance,* focusing on the figure of the refugee, the theatricality of protest and the political viability of the riot from the nineteenth century to the present day.

**Laurence Senelick** is Fletcher Professor of Drama and Oratory at Tufts University, a Fellow of the American Academy of Arts and Sciences, and a Distinguished Scholar of the American Society for Theatre Research. He is the author of some 25 books and over 100 articles, including *Gordon Craig's Moscow Hamlet* (1982); *The Age and Stage of George L. Fox* (1988); *The Chekhov Theatre* (1997); *The Changing Room: Sex, Drag and Theatre* (2000); and *Soviet Theatre: A Documentary History* (2014). He is editor of the Library of America volume on the American stage and has just completed a work on the international culture influence of Jacques Offenbach.

**Stanca Scholz-Cionca** is Professor Emerita of Japanese Studies at the University of Trier. She has widely published in English, French, German, Japanese and Romanian. Her publications include *Entstehung und Morphologie des klassischen Kyōgen im 17. Jahrhundert* (1998); *Nô Theatre Transversal* (co-ed. with C. Balme, 2008); *Japanische Dramen der Jahrtausendwende* (2008); and *Japanese Theatre Transcultural* (co-ed. with A. Regelsberger, 2011). Her research focuses on Japanese theatre and its international and transcultural reception. She has just completed a study on Loïe Fuller as an impresaria for Japanese troupes touring Europe.

# SERIES PREFACE

*A Cultural History of Theatre* is a six-volume series examining a cultural practice that emerged in antiquity and today encompasses practically the whole globe. Theatre is generally acknowledged to be the most social of artistic practices, requiring collectives to both produce and consume it. Theatrical performance's ability to organize and cohere markers of cultural belonging, difference, and dissonance are the hallmarks of social life. Its production and reception have, however, altered significantly over the past two-and-a-half thousand years. Despite these changes the same chapter headings structure all six volumes: institutional frameworks, social functions, sexuality and gender, environment, circulation, interpretations, communities of production, repertoire and genres, technologies of performance and knowledge transmission. These headings represent significant cultural approaches as opposed to purely regional, national, aesthetic, or generic categories. This allows for comparative readings of key *cultural* questions affecting theatre both diachronically and synchronically. The six volumes divide the history of theatre as follows:

Volume 1: A Cultural History of Theatre in Antiquity (500 BC–1000 AD)
Volume 2: A Cultural History of Theatre in the Middle Ages (1000–1400)
Volume 3: A Cultural History of Theatre in the Early Modern Age
     (1400–1650)
Volume 4: A Cultural History of Theatre in the Age of Enlightenment
     (1650–1800)
Volume 5: A Cultural History of Theatre in the Age of Empire (1800–1920)
Volume 6: A Cultural History of Theatre in the Modern Age (1920–2000+)

*Christopher B. Balme and Tracy C. Davis, General Editors*

# EDITOR'S ACKNOWLEDGEMENTS

I wish to thank the general editors of this series, Christopher B. Balme and Tracy C. Davis, for including me in this project. In this project, Chris and Tracy have set out to really change the discourse of theatre historiography. I am grateful for their confidence and for their patience. They have had an open ear throughout and have helped to form both this volume's argument as well as its shape. I really appreciate their help.

I also would like to thank the contributors to this volume. It has been a pleasure and an honour to work with you and to benefit from your expertise and your generous willingness to share thoughts and arguments and to respond to various requests.

My editor at Bloomsbury, Mark Dudgeon, has been a responsive and equally generous partner in this process. With great admiration and appreciation, I observed the way in which he juggles various mega-projects at the same time, dealing with authors and editors from all corners of the world. As a non-native-speaker, I particularly appreciated his guidance.

Conducting such a project is not possible without the help of various people who assisted with the revision of the manuscript. I would like to name in particular, Elena Weber who assisted me in the process and made herself an indispensable resource on all practical matters. Dr Jenny Sager was a wonderful and patient help in finding my way through the linguistic transitions. I also would like to mention Dr Hedwig Müller and Nora Probst at the Theatre Collection of the University of Cologne, as well as Laurence Senelick who did the lion's share to make sure that the 'Age of Empire' would also become visually present in the following pages.

# Introduction

## Cartographing the Long Nineteenth Century

### PETER W. MARX

The period comprised in this volume is genuinely a 'performing century'[1] or even a 'theatrical age'.[2] This diagnosis is not only true with respect to the multifaceted and fast growing theatrical landscape and its diverse networks but also given that theatre and performance (in the broadest sense of the words) became a ubiquitous figure of thought. When – at the beginning of this period – Goethe, in his notorious *Regeln für Schauspieler* [*Rules for Actors*, *c*.1803] admonishes that actors should behave in every moment of their lives, on- and off-stage, as if they were at any moment watched by spectators he invokes a panoptic regime of observation and attention that is symptomatic for this period. 'Appearing in public' becomes a discursive motif as well as a cultural technique. Goethe's statement can also be turned towards the spectators themselves: they should also be aware that they appear on a public stage and are equally spectators as well as actors. Theatre in this period is an art form that represents but also provides a social scene that catalyses and transmits concepts of social behaviour, political ideas, consumption habits and new technologies: indeed, it becomes a cultural technique that is well adapted to be participant and agent during this turbulent period.

The historical profile of the nineteenth century is difficult to grasp. Sometimes dubbed the 'long nineteenth century', some historians have argued that this period comprises the French Revolution (1789) as well as the end of the Great War (1918); others have subdivided this period in smaller portions and steps, such as the Napoleonic Era (1799–1815), a period of restoration (*c*.1815–1830)

FIGURE 0.1: The audience of the Berlin Kurfürstendamm Theatre at the beginning of the twentieth century. The gathering is equally a community of spectators as well as of actors for each other, *c.*1920. Photography by Zander and Labisch, FTBN398. Theaterwissenschaftliche Sammlung, University of Cologne.

and more or less successful revolutions (1848/49 and 1917), and the rise of the nation-state or the beginning of the globalized era. Others have focused on economic and technological developments that had a lasting effect on the organization and structure of Western societies, incorporating industrialization, the emergence of the consumer society and the rise of the labour movement, forming in a nutshell many of the conflicts persisting into the twentieth century.

Despite the diversity of the theatrical landscape, theatre historians have traditionally described the period as a kind of backdrop for the rise of *modernism*[3] in the twentieth century: they largely followed a *grand récit* provided by the historic avant-garde and some of its spearhead representatives such as the Italian Futurists and their rants against tradition and the canon. In the light of this radical plea for the *new* as a value in itself, the nineteenth century appeared as a period of epigones, commercialization and a sclerotic cultural structure supporting a political and social elite that needed to be swept away by the future. It is no coincidence that many political thinkers dreamed of radical social, cultural and political changes that would usher in the *new* in all dimensions of human life.

But such a teleological perspective can hardly provide a satisfying framework for a cultural history of this decisive and formative period for the Western world: one cannot dispute that the period between 1800 and 1920 (the time frame comprised by this volume) was a period of sustainable change and transformation, starting in Western societies and reaching out to other areas of the globe rapidly. But, and this makes the period so interesting and so difficult at the same time, it was as formative as it was contradictory in its developments: we equally see the rise of the nation-state as the quintessential political entity *and* the 'first-phase globalization'[4] with the emergence of transnational networks. We see a confusing plethora of social and cultural movements, partly shared by single individuals at the same time. While we might consider these as symptomatic cases of *cultural dissonance*, that is adhering to contradictory convictions and systems of belief at the same time, Walter Benjamin's diagnosis of the devaluation of the individual experience is striking when he states that a comprehensive and encompassing experience no longer allows for a unifying understanding of the world: this causes the schizoid simultaneity of univocal triumph and euphoria and a deeply shattered confidence at the same time. Walter Benjamin gives an impressive image for this situation – looking at the individual at the end of the First World War:

> A generation that had gone to school in a horse-drawn streetcar now stood under the open sky in a countryside in which nothing remained unchanged but the clouds, and beneath these clouds, in a field of force of destructive torrents and explosions, was the tiny, fragile human body.[5]

Acceleration, technification in all fields of everyday life, the thorough capitalization of all social relations and the rise of new political subjects and systems – these are just keywords that circumscribe a deeply affecting process of modernization that came to full fruit in the twentieth century but clearly started in the nineteenth. Thus, to think about the profile of this period calls for an approach that requires thinking in dialectical contradictions – without a unifying synthesis. In general, these contradictions cannot be reduced to a logic of development and residues – rather on the contrary, conflicting developments occurred simultaneously and needed to be acted out publicly. Thus, from the end of the *ancien régime* to the emergence of a new political order after the First World War, the nineteenth century is a period of radical transformation while at the same time working in conceptual frames and political metaphors that try to eclipse especially this transformation. When Peter Gay noted that the legendary Weimar Culture of Germany in the 1920s was widely present in the Wilhelmine era,[6] he also gave an analysis for most Western states at the end of the nineteenth century: while the avant-garde celebrated novelty as the antidote to tradition and canon, the splendid rhetoric hides the complex process of negotiation that underlies the allegedly purely nostalgic forms of Historicism.[7] Thus, to grasp the historical profile calls for tracing the various threads that constitute the 'long' nineteenth century.

## AN AGE OF EMPIRE?

As far as the political order is concerned, we face two key and overlapping concepts: nation and empire.

The notion of *empire* that figures so prominently in the title of this volume, directs attention to a specific perspective: focusing on the emergence of global structures that establish and provide a supranational scope of action, partly by economic strength, partly by force, partly by an overabundance of goods, cultural products and technological innovations. Here, the British Empire figures as the iconic example of such an economic and political system. But, as the historian Jürgen Osterhammel has argued in his seminal study *The Transformation of the World* (2014), imperial structures should be seen as complementary to national structures that came into being at the Congress of Vienna (1814/15).

Osterhammel clearly distinguishes two different types of comprehensive political structures by differentiating conceptually between nation-state and empire. Whereas in the French and German discourse the concept of empire is fuelled by historical associations to the *imperium romanum* and its medieval successor, the British perspective is rather pragmatic. Osterhammel points out some of the criteria that mark the difference between the two models such as territorial integrity (nation-state) versus a vague border of influence (empire), legitimizing power 'from below' (nation-state) versus a political elite, citizenship (nation-state) versus a modified catalogue of entitlements. Two aspects are of particular interest for the following argument:

a) the *question of homogeneity*. In the context of the nation-state
   participation was defined through national, usually ethnic, belonging.
   Osterhammel states: 'A nation-state, congruent in the ideal case with a
   single nation, proclaims its own homogeneity and indivisibility. An
   empire emphasizes all manner of heterogeneity and difference, seeking
   cultural integration only at the level of the top imperial elite.'[8] Thus, the
   'sensation of rootedness'[9] becomes a key element in analysing the
   cultural structures of states in the nineteenth century: they either rely on
   the idea of autochthony or on the concept of circulation and a visible
   system of hierarchical entitlements. The effect was immediately evident
   in cultural institutions, such as universities, which while remaining the
   domain of the cultural elite, also allowed for a certain amount of social

mobility. Integration and social mobility can also be seen in the field of public theatre. Other institutions rather represent the failure to allow for these dynamics: in German court theatres, for example, even after 1871 when a general liberty was granted, theatre practitioners were not appointed on the basis of their expertise or skills but rather on the basis of their social standing within the aristocracy. This tendency untethered these institutions from theatrical aesthetic discourse and essentially doomed their artistic endeavours to insignificance. This leads to the second point,

b) the *question of cultural ownership*. Osterhammel writes: 'Cultural affinities – language, religion, everyday practices – tend to be shared by the whole population of a nation-state. In an empire they are limited to the imperial elite in the core and its colonial offshoots. [. . .] By virtue of its supposedly higher civilization, the central elite of an empire feels that it has a kind of mission to create an educated social stratum at the periphery. The extremes of complete assimilation (France, at least in theory) and extermination (the Nazi Empire in Eastern Europe) are rarely encountered.'[10] Here, Osterhammel indicates the political and social consequences of the two different models: the idea of the nation-state as a homogenous, territorially defined entity establishes a clear system of belonging and cultural ownership. When in the nineteenth century, a discrepancy between civil rights and 'genuine belonging' appeared, as in the case of Jewish people living in Germany, for example, an essentialist order of differences was proclaimed: the rise of anti-Semitism as an ideology based on allegedly 'neutral', biological facts, was a direct response to the conflicting claims of cultural ownership and belonging.[11] Whereas the juridical system afforded equal civil rights to all citizens, the intensifying anti-Semitism created an invisible order based on alleged biological markers that were not subject to change such as categories like citizenship or even religion. The very fact that actors of Jewish descent were more or less forced to 'hide' their Jewishness behind 'neutral' pseudonyms – such as in the case of Otto Brahm (née Abrahamson), Fritz Kortner (née Kohn) or Max Reinhardt (née Goldmann) – highlights the hypocritical tension between a liberal legislation and a discriminatory politics.

Yet it would be naïve to consider empires as inclusive structures: although they provided some kind of social mobility, they still were built to reserve key positions for the old elites and to secure the continuity of administrative, military, economic and cultural asymmetries.

The nation-state of the nineteenth century is bound up with the amalgamation of people and territory in light of the idea of an autochthony 'which claims roots deeper than history itself'.[12] The empire, by contrast, includes a feature Lynn Hunt has identified as a key element of globalization: *deterritorialization*, where 'transactions no longer occur in a particular place'.[13] According to Hunt, globalization is neither merely a recent phenomenon nor simply fuelled by the explorations of non-Western territories by Western forces but by a process of increasing interconnection and interdependence. The historical mark she sets is the moment when 'Europe and the Americas became dependent on each other'.[14] But Hunt also points out that globalization – and the concept of empire – is not simply a Western strategy:

> The West did not globalize the world on its own; adventurous and enterprising people across the world brought their various locales into greater interconnection and interdependence with each other. Since globalization is not therefore a uniquely Western creation, the globalization paradigm must be modified to take account of these multiple origins and processes.[15]

Globalization is not merely a relation of cause and effect with a clear-cut division of centre and periphery – as it is indicated in the colonial imagery: globalization rather creates a field of action that is certainly dominated by hegemonic forces that claim supremacy (in economic, political or military respect) – yet it is also open for groups and individuals who use the rules and dynamics of this field to gain visibility for themselves or for their political cause. Katie Gough in her contribution to this volume traces the development of the *Abbey style* in early twentieth-century Ireland as a strategy for the Irish community to gain international visibility by using modern media technology and the international appreciation for 'realistic' styles of acting, whereas Zoltán Imre in his corresponding piece describes the almost subterranean presence and influence of Hungarian entrepreneurs in the second half of the nineteenth century: engaging in developing and propagating the genre of the operetta, through which they created a virtual Hungarian presence on the Western stage thwarting the political appropriation of Hungary by the Habsburg Empire. The distinct style of operetta, widely recognized as 'Hungarian' as well as the comic character of the operetta-Hungarian created a visibility of the Hungarian people – under the condition of a political system and cultural mainstream that did not allow for autonomous political self-representation.

But the global scene of the nineteenth century is rather incomplete if we eclipse the non-Western empires that were partners and sometimes competitors or even adversaries in the global arena:

- The *Ottoman Empire* has been the iconic counterpart of the West, beginning in the fourteenth century and lasting into the better part of modern period. Encompassing territories from the Levant, to the

Balkans and eastward to Persia, this huge empire represented the 'Other' in the European imagery. As Osterhammel has pointed out, it is one of the significant weaknesses of the post-Vienna order that the Ottoman Empire was absent from the negotiations,[16] yet since the Napoleonic invasion of Egypt (1798–1801) a multifaceted process of modernization was instigated within its territories.[17]

- The *Chinese Empire*, established about 200 BC, reaching the form of a centralist state in the 1760s, had developed an order of its own – which guaranteed its independence for a long period. In the second half of the nineteenth century, the Chinese Empire was attacked several times and became the object of colonial desires. Although China never officially lost its political autonomy, it was forced to open up for Western enterprises.[18]

- The case of the *Japanese Empire* is an extremely interesting one: Japan, which had employed a radical policy of closure (with the exception of China), was compelled by the military force of the US navy to open the country in 1854. Subsequently, the Japanese elite started a rapid process of modernization, known in Japanese history as the Meiji period, in which a centralist political order headed by the *tenno*, the Japanese emperor, was installed. This modernization – which also comprised the importation of Western drama and theatre – was the foundation of Japan's predominance. Japan became a colonial power controlling Korea and Taiwan after the Sino-Japanese War (1894/95).[19]

- In addition to these traditional states one could also count the United States as one of the rising empires although it never defined itself as a colonial power in the traditional sense. But following the *Monroe doctrine* of 1823[20] the US made the claim that the American hemisphere must be kept out of the European hegemonic sphere. The Spanish-American War of 1898 marks how this claim was buttressed by the readiness to use military power in the pursuit of hemispheric interests.

In addition to these rather stable political systems, sustained by diplomatic relations, bureaucracies, and more or less clearly defined administrations, the global politics in the nineteenth century was determined by the rise of hegemonic and colonial relations of various kinds and structures: Africa, especially, was subject to Western hegemonic aspirations which led to a division of the continent – without any consideration of existing ethnic, tribal, political or historical units. Imposing the Western concept of statehood on almost every region in the world, ignoring traditional structures of loyalty and adherence, created a political geography whose contradictions and aporia are still present in the twenty-first century.

For theatre people, this newly established global arena gave rise to new kinds of profitable activity. Tracing the activities of the actor-entrepreneur Maurice

Bandmann (1872–1922) who was active in a spatial arena that reached from the Mediterranean through India up to Japan and the Philippines, Christopher Balme has sketched the prototypical structure of a theatrical network that followed the path of European colonial power – fuelled by global capitalism and the claim of bringing Western civilization to the world.[21] Yet the increase of touring troupes is not to be reduced to a single-road perspective of Western artists and entrepreneurs flooding the world with their artistic fare, we also see the rising significance of international troupes touring not only regionally but also in the West. Of course, these are partly included in the colonial framework – for example the ethnic troupes appearing at the World Exhibitions – but others appear as self-confident representatives of their culture, claiming a cultural exchange on an equal footing.

The history of many of these troupes is still largely unwritten – eclipsed by a historiographic framework that still favours the nation as its point of reference. Figure 0.2 shows one of these examples: the troupe of Burhanettin Tepsi of Constantinople – here shown at their visit in Berlin in the early twentieth century – presents itself as an 'Oriental' troupe although they were considered (and sometimes faced political repression) as modernizers in the Ottoman Empire.

FIGURE 0.2: The troupe of Burhanettin Tepsi during their Berlin tour in the 1910s. P8144. Theaterwissenschaftliche Sammlung, University of Cologne.

In her contribution to this volume Stanca Scholz-Cionca discusses at length the example of the Japanese actress Sadayakko, who toured with great success through Europe and the US managed by Loïe Fuller, the famed skirt dancer. Even this prominent performer consciously walked the line between the stereotypical expectations of Western audiences and her own self-concept as artist. In a broader perspective, not all non-Western artists were granted individual appreciation: while Sadayakko became famous in her own right, other performers were unnamed and considered 'specimens' of their ethnic culture, largely forgotten by (theatre) history.

## THE IDEA OF THE NATION

The concept of empire cannot be understood without its dialectical counter-part: the *nation*. One key transition in the political system from the *ancien régime* to the post-Napoleonic structure is the rise of the idea of nationhood as a formative political category. The French Revolution – in this matter symptomatically different from the earlier American Revolution that created a different concept of 'the people' – centred on the idea of the people as the central political subject. Therefore, when Napoleon crowned himself as *Empereur des Français* [Emperor of the French], the legitimizing reference was the French as people not a hereditary line.[22] The Napoleonic Wars stirred the national sentiment in all European regions, mostly to be contained afterwards and disappointed by the Congress of Vienna that aimed at restoring some sort of aristocratic order. But the Congress of Vienna did not simply return to the 'old' aristocratic order that was organized by dynasties but started to define political entities by their territorial core.

This new-old aristocratic order created political entities in Europe that were vaguely based on traditional dominions – such as the kingdom of Bavaria – that aimed at amalgamating territories and dynasties.[23] Yet, many of the national claims were rejected by this process – partly in order to avoid the predominance of a single party in Europe – thus neither Italy nor Germany became a nation-state before the second half of the nineteenth century, with the creation of the Kingdom of Italy in 1861 and the German 'unification', creating the German Kaiser, in 1871. Other entities such as Poland or Hungary disappeared from the stage of nation-states and became parts of larger supranational empires. The strategy to create a 'European equilibrium'[24] provided a stable order in Europe of some sorts, but also created the aporia and tensions that led to various revolutionary movements but also to the First World War in 1914.

But 'old' nations and those that emerged from the Congress of Vienna order alike depended on a process that Benedict Anderson has famously described as imagining communities.[25] His notion describes a complex process of construction using mass media and mass communication. Theatrical events as well as institutions had their share in this process as well – often providing an immediate experience of an otherwise rather abstract community. According to Anderson, the nation must not be understood as an a priori given entity, unfolding through the course of time, but as the product of a process that has to be concealed to be socially and culturally effective.

But these requirements of public representation did not only affect the 'people'. As Johannes Paulmann has pointed out, at the end of the nineteenth century the restored 'national' monarchies were desperately in need of public visibility. Therefore, they relied on various forms of media representation such as staging royal encounters, or selling photographs of them. Paulmann goes as far as to state that the representation of the national community was built on a community of consumers who bought these modern icons.[26] A caricature in the German journal *Simplicissimus* captures this very moment very pointedly: six small boxes represent the 'most photographed Europeans' divided in two groups: 'Real and theatrical heroes.'

As Anderson and Hobsbawm/Ranger[27] have shown, 'nation-building' requires not only a complex cultural mediation of partly conflicting interests but also the imagination of a common denominator that constitutes the nation as a political subject. Here, all forms of arts were called to duty but theatre – due to its specific semiotic mode of gathering an audience in a place – was considered to be particularly apt for making a contribution to the creation of a nation. The Comédie Française (founded in 1680) served as the model for a theatre that rightly could claim to define the nation's cultural centre. Thus, we see in various countries the foundation of 'national theatres' claiming ownership and authority to represent the cultural heart of the nation that is about to come into being. The contribution on 'Interpretation' in this volume discusses the impact of the concept of nation and ethnification to the understanding of theatre.

Theatre thereby became – even in the field of 'mere entertainment' – a contested battleground for self-representation and gaining visibility. The emergence of Yiddish theatre after 1862 in Eastern Europe started as part of an inner-Jewish process of Enlightenment but it soon created a sense of national identity among the Jewish communities. The Yiddish theatre is an interesting case in point because it soon spread throughout the Jewish diaspora and took hold in all metropolises such as London, Vienna, New York, as well as in Buenos Aires.[28] After the formation of Zionism as a political movement, the idea of a Hebrew theatre emerged – using a language that was not commonly in use by then. The formation of the HaBima (today Israel's State Theatre) in 1918 under the auspices of Konstantin Stanislavsky and Yevgeny Vakhtangov in Moscow can be seen as an act of 'imagining a community' with theatrical means[29] – long before any territorial identity could be claimed. As the case makes clear, theatre was not only politically effective as a social institution but also – as Arjun

FIGURE 0.3: 'The most photographed Europeans: Real and stage heroes'; Olaf Gulbransson caricature in the German magazine *Simplicissimus* 12, no. 34, 1907. VG-Bildkunst.

Appadurai has argued so convincingly – as an institution to imagine possible future realities:

> The imagination [. . .] has a projective sense about it, has a sense of being a prelude to some sort of expression, whether aesthetic or otherwise. [. . .] It is the imagination in its collective forms, that creates ideas of neighborhood and nationhood, of moral economies and unjust rule, of higher wages and foreign labor prospects. The imagination is today a staging ground for action, and not only for escape.[30]

## COSMOPOLITANISM

In contrast to the nationalistic discourse and its emphasis on genuine national and autochthonous traditions and forms of art, the nineteenth century also sees the emergence of an international and increasingly internationally connected sphere of theatre.

This phenomenon of course is rooted in the processes of global migration that span the globe: partly through the transatlantic and trans-Pacific trade routes, partly through the movement to the colonial settlements, people migrated around the globe. In this period of increased mobility, most societies were much less linguistically monolithic as we tend to imagine them from today's perspective. German, for example, was the second most common language in the US until the US entered the First World War in 1916. Thus, German actors and ensembles could perform in their mother-tongue, able to rely on a community of expatriates who were grateful to hear the sound of their 'home'. But these guest performances – in German and in many other languages – did not just attract expatriate communities: foreign-language performances were in principle much more common.[31] At the same time we see an intensive exchange of plays: as with many other prestigious goods of consumption and luxury, Paris would also be the leading exporter of dramatic commodities.[32] Nic Leonhardt points out in her contribution on 'Circulation' that this new sphere was fostered and fuelled by a new type of agent, cultural go-betweens who secured a constant flow and exchange of performers, plays, sceneries and costumes in order to keep the cycle of novelties running.

These international exchanges also constituted a specific cultural profile: the long-standing director of the Viennese Burgtheater, Heinrich Laube, for example, developed a repertoire that he defined as *Welttheater* (World Theatre) referring to a concept of World Literature as defined by Goethe in the eighteenth century.[33] Laube's concept of *Welttheater* was based on the idea of gathering essential, canonical works from all historical periods that would encompass an entirety of 'human knowledge' less on the idea of creating an actual intercultural exchange.

In contrast to Goethe/Laube's ideal of a global canon, the exchange was also tied into the politics and conflicts of political autonomy – played out as controversies over cultural ownership. The New York Astor Place Riots of 1849 can be read as a paradigmatic event: 22 people were killed by the city militia that fought against protesters who formally protested the pricing and dress code policy of the Astor Place Opera House that marketed itself as an elitist venue for 'High Culture'. The trigger for the events was a guest performance by the English actor William Macready. Underlying the outbreak of violence was the question of cultural ownership over Shakespeare, as Macready had been engaged in a long-standing competition with the American actor Edwin Forrest who was considered the proto-American star, claiming cultural autonomy against the former colonial power.[34]

Under the rubric of 'Repertoire and Genre' Christopher Balme discusses the development of the dramatic canon. It is significant that on the one hand the idea of classics took hold of the theatrical landscape – first and foremost Shakespeare – but also how new genres emerged – in accordance with the audience's demand for novelties and sensations.

The cult of the virtuosi started at latest in the eighteenth century, probably in the field of opera where famous singers emerged and created an aura of artistic excellence, erotic desirability and undisputable success. In the field of drama, one could probably call David Garrick the first global star: his performances not only impressed and won over his local audience in London but was translated into other media and soon his style of acting became an internationally recognized and visible brand.[35] The new technologies of transportation and the structures of an increasingly globalized economy (also in the field of entertainment) fostered the professionalization in this field. Artists like Sarah Bernhardt (1844–1923), Eleonore Duse (1858–1924) and Jenny Lind (1820–1887) as well as their male counterparts Tommaso Salvini (1829–1915), Charles Kean (1811–1868) and Enrico Caruso (1873–1921) were no longer tied to a single country but rather turned themselves into global icons. Though still recognized as being connected to a specific national origin (being English, French, Italian or Swedish), these artists developed a global persona that allowed them to be present in various contexts. At the same time, these global presences cannot be understood without acknowledging the influence of new forms of commodification and marketing: to a remarkable degree, Sarah Bernhardt's iconic presence is due to her prominence in advertising fashionable goods such as liqueurs or biscuits. Already in their day, critics discussed these close interconnections with the production of luxury goods. It was a well-established fact that the major Parisian fashion houses had actresses under contract to provide their costumes. With respect to the popularity of contemporary and domestic settings in many plays, one can easily see that many of these productions were fashion shows as much as theatrical performances. The German word *Toilettenkünstlerin* (artist of fashion, specifically women)[36] emphasizes this connection – partly to criticize it. The effect of these global virtuosi was built on the creation of a cultural icon that transcended the single performance, connected it to the world of commodities, but also on the availability of dramatic goods that allowed these artists to gain the required prestige. Shakespeare, of course, was always a safe option when it comes to this kind of cultural capital, but we also see artists appropriating specific characters and turning them into their signature role, such as Sarah Bernhardt as Marguerite Gautier from *La Dame aux camélias* by Alexandre Dumas *fils*.

The increasing number of touring virtuosi – actors as well as musicians – also catered to scattered communities of expatriates. Joseph Roach has described this effect *en detail* for the Irish-American community in the nineteenth century: he also discusses to what extent this effect was fuelled by P. T. Barnum who developed a strategy to specifically address these communities.[37] Thus, these expatriate communities, some of whom defined themselves as only temporarily absent from 'home' (emigrés) and others who recognized that their situation would be permanent (immigrants), were an intrinsic part of the global entertainment industry. Some of them allied with hegemonic structures of colonialism – as can be seen from touring English troupes in the colonies who were poised to secure the cultural and emotional ties to the motherland – whereas others created independent structures.

Again, the Yiddish theatre and entertainment industry is a paradigmatic example: centres in Warsaw, Vienna, London, Odessa, New York and Moscow marked the routes of migration and exchange rather than political or national structures. Richard Butsch describes how, in New York at the turn of the century, the Italian and the Yiddish stage were two symptomatic cases of immigrant theatre.[38] He defines them both as primarily working-class entertainments, attracting families, catering to the specific experiences and problems of their respective constituency:

> It constituted an autonomous, working-class public sphere, a place where the audience could formulate and rehearse a common understanding of their experience and common identity. [. . .] [T]heir effect most likely was to cement community solidarity among these working-class immigrants in facing the world outside.[39]

Actors, plays and playwrights usually circulated globally along the routes of immigration and diasporic communities, allowing for a comparable theatrical experience in the various centres of the diaspora. This holds particularly true for the Yiddish-speaking community. Interestingly the availability of film in the early twentieth century gave rise to a short period of flourishing Yiddish films, especially since they were able to address an audience around the globe and translated versions were easily produced. As in comparable cases, the introduction of sound

SARAH-BERNHARDT (LA DAME AUX CAMÉLIAS.)

FIGURE 0.4: Lithograph of Sarah Bernhardt, 1897. Alphonse Mucha, *La Samaritaine*. Courtesy Los Angeles County Museum of Art, Kurt J. Wagner, M. D. and C. Kathleen Wagner Collection.

movies was the end to this kind of immigrants' cinematic culture.[40] Sabine Haenni, in addition to Butsch's argument, has pointed out that these theatres did not only cater to the nostalgic needs of their constituencies but rather also helped them in arriving in their new home through offering 'testing grounds where people could experiment with new forms of collective and individual identity'.[41]

A different type of international theatrical development emerges in the last third of the nineteenth century: influenced by scholarly discussions, such as the rise of Positivism, and scientific developments in the aftermath of Darwinian biology and its doctrine of evolutionary developments, new styles of aesthetic representation spread all over the West (and soon globally): *naturalism* and *realism*. Starting out in France and in Scandinavia, this new provocative mode of representation does not simply promise an unabashed gaze on the new social reality but also a totally revolutionary new mode of representation. It was the Norwegian author Henrik Ibsen (1828–1906) who became the figurehead of this development. His play *Ghosts*, a signature play of naturalism, premiered in 1881 in Chicago, followed by numerous productions throughout Europe. All performances were highly controversial because Ibsen addressed the issue of venereal disease in a very direct way, deliberately breaking the code of bourgeois decorum. But Ibsen and his fame was the starting point for a new wave that included further dramatists such as Gerhart Hauptmann, August Strindberg and Emile Zola and many others as well as the founding of new ensembles that focused on performing these new plays that called for a new aesthetics. Most famous is the Théâtre Libre, founded by André Antoine in 1887 in Paris, and the Freie Bühne, founded by Otto Brahm in 1889 in Berlin.

A third pillar in the formation of a new kind of cosmopolitan, international theatrical experiences was the rise of touring troupes. At the beginning of this development stand the Meininger, the ensemble of the Court Theatre of the small German duchy of Saxe-Meiningen. In 1869, the reigning prince Georg II (1826–1914), together with his wife, the former actress Helene Baroness of Heldburg (née Ellen Franz), took over the directorship of his court theatre. Georg not only studied literature at university, he also used various opportunities to attend the theatre and to see the top performances of his day. Therefore, his two trips to London in 1846 and 1857 provided him with the chance to get to know the Shakespeare performances of Charles Kean. Georg wrote in a letter about the latter's Richard II:

> The scenery is of an extraordinary splendor, the costumes extremely authentic, but the acting leaves a great deal to be desired; the only exception is Kean, son of the famous Kean, who performs very well as Richard II.[42]

When Georg eventually took over the directorship of his court theatre, he was poised to create a totally new style of theatre whose governing principle was historical accuracy. As he had praised Kean for the authenticity of costumes and scenery, Georg made the question of decoration and costume a signature element of his style of theatre. He even corresponded with leading historians and archaeologists to get the costumes as correct as possible. But he also addressed the issue of acting in an ensemble: it was a governing principle of the Meininger that every actor had to play the role assigned to him or her, even if it was a minor part. Thus, Georg abolished the star system that had become so common with the touring virtuosi. The effect on the audience was stunning: reviewers travelling from Berlin to Meiningen praised the new style of theatre and called for it to come to Berlin, which eventually became the instigation for almost two decades of touring through Europe.

The extensive touring activities of the Meininger was also due to economic considerations: How should a comparatively small town like Meiningen with its 9,000 inhabitants (in 1870) sustain such a comparatively costly enterprise? In 1874, the Meininger started touring, performing in more than 38 cities all over in Europe, staging over 2,500 performances until 1890.[43] The Meininger's reach stretched from the west (London, Amsterdam, Antwerp) to the north (Copenhagen, Stockholm), the east (St Petersburg, Moscow, Kiev and Odessa) to the south (Trieste). Within a brief period, the Meininger had become a brand that constantly attracted large audiences and received praise for the style of performance. Thus, Georg II is often called 'the father of modern directing' because he had introduced a new principle in organizing a performance. From today's perspective, one is inclined to see the novelty of the Meininger not so much in the aspect of historical accuracy – a concept that is problematic anyway – but rather in the emphasis on the unifying perspective of the director who arranges scenery, costumes and actors as parts of the whole – thereby reducing the single, outstanding star to being a part of the ensemble.

As John Osborne has shown, the tours proved to be a profitable enterprise, not only covering expenditures but also granting a small surplus in most years.[44] But what is even more important, the Meininger had a lasting impact on the European theatrical landscape – the impression of their style can be equally found in Berlin, London and Moscow: Stanislavsky, for example, described attending a Meininger performance as a genuinely revelatory experience. It is a common irony in theatre history, that success feeds on its inventors: the Meiningen style soon became so popular that it was often copied and adapted (decried as 'Meiningerei') so that by 1890 they had lost their unique appeal and gave up touring.

Nevertheless, the principle of the touring ensemble (in contrast to the virtuoso) became a fixture in the modern theatrical landscape. The grand tours of the Moscow Art Theatre, Max Reinhardt's productions, or the much acclaimed stagings by Vakhtangov, Meyerhold, etc. devolve from the practice established by the Meininger, contributing to the emergence of a genuinely international theatrical style, establishing an aesthetic language that was considered to define the 'state of the art'.

This phenomenon must not be considered as isolated or confined to the field of 'high art'. Rather on the contrary, the end of the nineteenth century saw the emergence of massive touring entertainment enterprises: after the American Civil War (1861–1865), popular culture in the United States increasingly grew into an industry in its own right, requiring logistically as well as economically quasi-industrial means.[45] With the formation of Barnum & Bailey, according to their own advertisement the 'Greatest Show on Earth', the iconic American circus appeared on stage. With its highly mobile structure, the circus became the epitome of travelling popular culture and its influence went beyond the USA.[46]

How deep this emerging international popular culture reached in the visited countries can be well observed with the tours of *Buffalo Bill's Wild West Show*: William Cody (aka Buffalo Bill) designed a major outdoor show, including horse-riding, staged fights and shootings, 'celebrating' the frontier and the achievements of the American civilization. While these shows certainly prove the social mechanism described by Hobsbawm and Ranger as the 'invention of tradition', the export of this show had a different appeal on their European audiences.

> The intention of Buffalo Bill's staging was certainly to make the story of the American West merge with the story of European expansion at a time when European colonization reached the far frontiers of its own empires. [. . .] The American West had already been appropriated and made to serve as a projection screen for European fantasies, for of White-Indian male bonding in a setting reminiscent of German dreams of pristine nature.[47]

Buffalo Bill's appearance on the European scene (starting in 1887) spawned a wave of imitators,[48] yet is at the core of an 'Americanized', truly international, Western popular culture that reached its peak in the twentieth century. Theatre, circus, pageantry – these were just the forerunners of what would then become 'modern' popular culture that spread vastly through the new media of film, radio and television.

## MODERNIZATION

This picture of nineteenth-century 'global performance culture'[49] would be incomplete without acknowledging the deep-reaching impact of the technological and economic changes during this period. The nineteenth century saw the invention and mass-distribution of a plethora of new technologies that had an immediate impact on the *Lebenswelt* [the world as experienced] of individuals all over the globe. Apart from the mass-production of consumer goods that allowed for an availability and affordability of goods on a new scale (and a new cycle of acquisition, consumption and waste) – it is probably the transport of people, goods and messages that led to the significant 'compression of time and space'.[50]

It is in particular the railway system (following the opening of the first commercial line in England in 1825) and the use of steamships that changed the tempo-spatial dimension of the globe: a trip from Paris to Lille (219 km) lasted 34 hours in 1814 whereas the same journey took only 4 hours and 50 minutes by train in 1854.[51] Transatlantic passages also shrank at a similar rate: the first ocean liner from Liverpool to New York City (already a major improvement in comparison to sailing clippers) took 15 days in 1838, whereas in 1900 the time was already reduced to about 6 days.

Whereas these innovations might be regarded as extensions of familiar forms of transporting physical objects from place to place, the invention of the telegraph created a categorically new phenomenon: the installation of the telegraph, starting in 1849 in the US, allowed for a fast and reliable transmission around the globe, shrinking the spatial distances almost into a relation of simultaneity. The installation of the first transatlantic telegraph cable in 1858 brought the US and Europe almost within earshot. Thus, it is no coincidence that the technological

FIGURE 0.5: Costume sketch for the *Ballet of Ranks*. The sketch presents three fairy-like beings, allegorical representations of major technological achievements: transport/telegraphy on the left; electricity on the right; and taking the central position a figure representing transport by holding a golden railway engine and donning a miniature clipper on her head, *c*.1900. Basil Crage, Atelier Hugo Baruch, G986952Hz. Theaterwissenschaftliche Sammlung, University of Cologne.

development was concomitant with the creation of news agencies that provided, augmented and partly controlled the flow of information, literally creating an international scene that was the precondition of media coverage in our sense.[52] Thus, the advent of radio, television and Internet in the twentieth century might be seen as an offspring of a technological and institutional structure that was created already in the nineteenth century.[53]

It was not only the infrastructural frame that changed the culture and practice of media representation. As Vanessa R. Schwartz and Jeannene M. Przyblynski point out, the sheer number of pictures printed between 1800 and 1901 was larger than the total number of pictures printed before.[54] Thus, we can define the nineteenth century as a period of an unmatched ubiquity of images and their availability. This of course is not meant as to argue that images were rare in the periods before but they were less accessible and probably less invasive. Schwartz and Przyblynski identify a shift of the epistemological framework caused by this profusion of visual culture:

> In short, the explosion of image-making made visual experience and visual literacy important elements in the rubric of modernity. In the largest sense, one might claim that the transformations associated with modernity, both at the formal and at the social historical level, can be generalized as having been waged along a central axis between investment in the positivist certainty of visual facts and ambivalence regarding the illusiveness of mere appearance.[55]

Notwithstanding the importance of new technologies of printing and image reproduction that fostered this new 'scopic regime'[56] it is the spread of photography (available since 1840[57]) that epitomizes this new form of visual culture: photography (allegedly providing an image without immediate human, i.e. intentional, influence[58]) not only allowed for the mass-production of images but also fostered the rise of realism as the new norm of representation. When cinema started to take its place in the media landscape after 1895 its mode of representation seemed to fall into the same pattern.[59]

In her chapter on 'Technologies of Performance', Sophie Nield demonstrates to what extent theatre was closely linked with these technological innovations (optic, mechanical and electric inventions) and to what extent it was not only a passive recipient of these but also an active propagator – in putting these technologies to the test and creating social acceptance for them.

## LOCATING THE NINETEENTH CENTURY: THE CITY

If one tried to locate these multi-vocal developments in the nineteenth century, the city would be the locale where they coincided as a social reality. Cities were no longer dependent on the importance of a residing aristocrat. Rather on the contrary, the modern metropolis gained its importance and cultural aura from its logistical and economic power – one might think of New York, San Francisco or Calcutta as emblematic of this new metropolis.

A brief glance at the development of cities in Europe highlights the formative dimension of this process that is only vaguely covered by the buzzword urbanization (see Table 1). While it is no surprise that England had the highest rate of urbanization through the entire nineteenth century (and significantly above the European average), it is symptomatic to see that a massive urbanization in France and Germany happened between 1850 and 1910. The city was not only the physical place where the majority of the population lived, probably even more important, it became the quintessential point of reference of the modernized *Lebenswelt* – thus expanding the influence of urbanization beyond the physical confines of actual cities.

The general growth of urbanization is partly due to an increased life expectancy and the reduction of infant mortality but it is largely the product of infra-European migration. The social consequences of this development can barely be overstated. According to a German statistic from 1907, less than 50 per cent of all city dwellers lived in the city where they were born.[60] What the sheer numerical information obscures is the fact that this means an erosion of traditional social bonds and milieux. When Ferdinand Tönnies, the 'father of German sociology', published his legendary book *Gemeinschaft und Gesellschaft* (1887), the opposition of his two key concepts *Gemeinschaft* [community] – modelled after the ideal of the family and an intimate community that is based on shared values and a joint historical experience – versus *Gesellschaft* [society] reflects this development: society, a synonym for the modern metropolis, is based on a social contract to pacify an imminent war – the society is at best a permanent ceasefire,[61] granting liberty to its members but lacking any sort of inner cohesion. Tönnies' nostalgic, sometimes anti-modern diagnosis of the modern state, describes modern society as being in a permanent state of loss. As Fritz Stern has noted so precisely, the German society of the nineteenth century was a 'society in motion, and mobility was its essence and its trauma'.[62] Here it is important to recognize that mobility is not only meant in a metaphorical way but rather has a very direct and real physical presence: the architectural model

**TABLE 1: Percentage of the population living in cities with more than 5,000 inhabitants**[63]

| Year | England | France | Germany | Russia | Europe |
|------|---------|--------|---------|--------|--------|
| 1800 | 23 | 12 | 9 | 6 | 12 |
| 1850 | 45 | 19 | 15 | 7 | 19 |
| 1910 | 75 | 38 | 49 | 14 | 41 |

of the new city – the ideal of the modern metropolis – soon became a recognizable form, determined by broad boulevards and central squares. Starting with Parisian Haussmanization, through Vienna and Berlin – and then again copied by many smaller cities – the purlieus of modern cities created a social scene for the modern society.

As Hobsbawm and Ranger have shown so convincingly, the nineteenth century did not simply hail novelty as its leading principle. Rather on the contrary, most Western societies sought to respond to the multiple changes by emphasizing their rootedness in history through the 'invention of traditions'. The social meaning of these ties to the past was less in their authenticity than in providing points of orientation in a fast-changing world: 'Quite new, or old but dramatically transformed, social groups, environments and social contexts called for new devices to ensure or express social cohesion and identity and to structure social relations.'[64]

Despite making a claim on a 'traditional past' that had to respond to contemporary requirements, the metropolis's physical space exceeded the human scale – distances too far for walking, neighbourhoods too diverse and volatile to be known, the social entity of the metropolis depended on mediation to be experienceable. Peter Fritzsche has argued that these now conglomerates were as much built of words as of stone:

> More than anything else, the machinery and the social relations of industrial development reworked the look of cities to the point of unfamiliarity. They did not simply so by tearing down medieval walls or by adding immense factories and settling thousands of new laborers, although these were undeniably dramatic events, but by sustaining this busy activity over time. Neither industrial progress nor commercial activity were geared to preserve the physical character or the social makeup of urban space. As a result, the nineteenth-century city was less of a new creation and more of an incalculable, ongoing process.[65]

Fritzsche's argument about the cultural impact of the 'word city' should be complemented by adding the idea of the *stage city* or the *theatrical city* in the sense that theatrical activities and scenic displays equally added to the image of the new metropolis and turned the social landscape of the new metropolis into a palpable social scene.

Thus, we find a twofold, sometimes even contradictory development in the discourse of urban identity in the nineteenth century: on the one hand the invention of tradition, making broad claims about historical descent and continuity, on the other hand a discourse that celebrated innovation and novelty. A further distinctive hallmark of this discourse is – as Heinz Reif has noted – that the metropolises serve as laboratories of progress; not on their own but through mutual observation, the *transmetropolitan discourse*.[66] This is a key element in cultural negotiations and in the process of cultural circulation: from the language of advertising performances – measuring the importance of goods and performances by naming previous stations or the point of origin – to an intensive change of goods, ideas, stories, habits – the transmetropolitan discourse is the foundation for a fashionable lifestyle that defines itself by being a member of an international circle of urban dwellers – notwithstanding the actual living conditions.

## URBANIZATION OF THE THEATRE

Urbanization not only changed the environment of theatres but also deeply affected the theatrical trade itself: during the eighteenth century, theatres were mostly part of court life, however the emergence of purpose-built theatres saw playhouses become central to the urban social and civic life. In *Places of Performance* (1989), Marvin Carlson defines two different types of theatre buildings that can be seen as symptomatic for the nineteenth-century metropolitan structure. On the one hand, there is the facade-theatre, a building that is fully integrated into the closed facades of the boulevards. Starting in 1759 but achieving its heyday in the nineteenth century, the Parisian Boulevard du Temple was the first modern entertainment district: its many theatres constituted an explicitly urban environment and led to the creation of a new type of drama and performance, the so-called *boulevard drama*.[67] Laurence Senelick, in his chapter on 'Sexuality and Gender' analyses at length the diversity of new forms of entertainment and theatrical forms that emerged in Paris and afterwards found their way to almost all other European metropolises.

Carlson also highlights theatres that were designed and built as free-standing prestigious, monumental edifices, often resembling temple-like architecture. Key examples include the *Opera Garnier* in Paris (1875), the Viennese *Burgtheater* (1888) or the *Schauspielhaus* in Berlin (1821). Evolving in the late eighteenth century, this architectural type soon became a key element in the portfolio of representative, urban buildings and often served as landmarks:

The facades of the great monumental theatres of the late eighteenth century employed standard classic motifs and were virtually indistinguishable from other major buildings of the period. Although this generally rather severe style remained popular through the nineteenth century for public structures aimed to project an image of stability, tradition, and civic respectability, such as banks and court houses, the monumental theatre developed a more elaborate and baroque visual vocabulary, the outstanding example of which is the facade of Charles Garnier's Paris Opéra, composed of an almost overwhelming accumulation of cultural references.[68]

Carlson refers to the impression of respectability, tradition and stability as core values to be expressed in the architectural style. Thereby, the monumental theatres served the rising bourgeois' desire for self-representation: positions previously held by princely palaces or churches and were transferred to civic, public buildings that represented the constitutional change that came with an increased creation of civic rights.[69] Theatres thus became iconic public spaces, equally aligned with art, education and entertainment. The monumental theatre – often preserved for the performances of operas – is symptomatic of this shift in function. The architectural type also reflects the process of social ennoblement of theatre since the eighteenth century: respectability and prestige came with its ascension to a central social institution – oscillating between the poles of (commercial) entertainment and *Bildung* [education]. Anselm Heinrich discusses this development in his chapter by comparing the respective developments in England and Germany – showing how deeply financial questions (especially subsidies) are rooted in the cultural profile of these institutions.

These buildings provided ample space for the bourgeois and urban self-representation, their splendid foyers and halls borrowing the glamour of princely palaces, even though combined with splendid restaurants and bars. As one can take it from advice books on running a theatre, the gastronomic structure was an integral element of the theatrical experience as well as of the economic structure of the enterprises. Therefore, it is merely consistent that many theatrical venues secured their existence by allying themselves with other forms of leisure. In his chapter, Tobias Becker gives an overview of how theatre interacted with other forms of urban entertainment, drawing a comparative picture of Paris, London and Berlin that shows how the theatrical landscape thrived in a cultural biotope.

Marvin Carlson has pointed out that already the ground plan of these buildings indicates this shift in social function:

> The great monumental theatres of the eighteenth and nineteenth centuries [. . .] became favored gathering places for the new monied classes [in part because] their public spaces became a kind of indoor parade ground not only for the gathering of fashionable society, but even more important, for its display. Audience support spaces proliferated – lobbies, galleries, vestibules, grand staircases, until they occupied, in the great opera houses of the late nineteenth century, more space than either the auditorium or the stage.[70]

Following Veblen's concept of *conspicuous consumption* as a key strategy of social (self-)identification,[71] one might argue that the elements of former aristocratic splendour – now provided and made available for 'the people' – can be equally seen as a kind of democratization and of a new politics of distinction rooted in commodification: being part of this new urban society was no longer based on privileges of birth or office but rather on consumer culture, i.e. the question of whether one could afford the literal ticket into this society.[72] In his contribution to this volume, Jim Davis discusses the formative dimension of the theatrical experience – not only as an aesthetic experience but also as a social practice. Davis also emphasizes how much this experience depended on the place: theatre-going in London was a substantially different experience than attending the theatre in colonial India or Australia.

The physical space of these new urban conglomerates exceeded the human scale in many respects, making public transportation a key requirement for urban life, creating new habits (taking a walk) and contact zones. In his seminal essay, *The Metropolis and Mental Life* (1904), the German philosopher Georg Simmel describes the metropolis as a 'highly complex organism' built by 'the aggregation of so many people with such differentiated interests'. This new organism totally depends on a synchronized definition of time:

> If all clocks and watches in Berlin would suddenly go wrong in different ways, even if only by one hour, all economic life and communication of the city would be disrupted for a long time, in addition an apparently mere external factor: long distances, would make all waiting and broken appointments result in an ill-afforded waste of time. Thus, the technique of metropolitan life is unimaginable without the most punctual integration of all activities and mutual relations into a stable and impersonal time schedule.[73]

Here, the semiotic constitution of theatre performances, the simultaneity of production and reception in the same space, attributes to this scheme of impersonal synchronization described by Simmel: the fixed starting time of a performance took part in forming the temporal profile of urban life. Dennis Kennedy has described this with respect to the curtain times in Paris: 'Curtain times grew later to accommodate working hours, advancing from 5.30 or 6.30 pm in 1840 to 8.00 or 9.00 in 1845, further persuaded by Hausmann's civic lighting scheme which made the streets safer for pedestrians'.[74]

As Tracy C. Davis has shown in her groundbreaking study *The Economics of the British Stage*, theatre was not an isolated art form – following its inner principles of aesthetic evolution – but deeply embedded in the complex economic relationships of nineteenth-century urban life. The urbanized theatres of the nineteenth century were at the same time highly visible public places, used for negotiation of pressing social and political issues and advertising new goods and fashions alike, commercial enterprises at the crossroads of new modes of (media) representation, technological innovation (for example electric light), and education. These new urban theatres epitomize the new division of work and leisure time as well as the pleasure and uncanniness of the new urban landscape. Derek Miller in his chapter on 'Knowledge Transmission' discusses the process of professionalization in the field by looking at the labour conditions as well as on the training practices in this period. He also highlights the juridical framework of this theatrical landscape, with an international agreement (Berne Convention, 1886) securing for the first time in history royalties for playwrights on an international scale and thus enhancing the international exchange of dramatic wares.

## THE EXHIBITIONARY COMPLEX AND SPECTATORSHIP AS A CULTURAL PRACTICE

The *scopic regime* of nineteenth-century Western visual culture encompassed rules and assumptions about the epistemological status of images – can pictures lie? Have they an intrinsic documentary quality? – as well as cultural institutions, practices and the economy of visual culture that secured the implementation of these images in the *Lebenswelt*. It is symptomatic that the nineteenth century saw the emergence of new types of public display that quickly became closely intertwined with theatre. It is equally symptomatic how these institutions emerge in different countries (see Table 2).

At the core of the scopic regime of the nineteenth century are institutions for displaying objects (and sometimes human beings), ranging from art objects, through scientific specimens (dead or alive) to commodities presented for future consumption (or at least acquisition). Museums and zoos underwent a process of epistemological ennoblement during which they were transformed from courtly entertainments (such as menageries or cabinets of curiosities) to more-or-less scientifically organized collections that also claimed to provide public education.[75] The department store as well as the world fairs, in contrast, did not exist prior to the nineteenth century; they depended on industrialization and its

TABLE 2: Scopic regime of the nineteenth century

| Institution | England | France | Germany | USA |
|---|---|---|---|---|
| **Museum** | British Museum (1857) | Louvre (1793/1801) | Städel in Frankfurt/ Main (1815) | Metropolitan Museum of Art (1872) |
| **Exhibition/Fair** | London (1851) | Great Exhibition Paris (1855) | Only national exhibitions | Philadelphia (1876) |
| **Department Store** | Harrods (1849) | Au bon marché (1838) | Wertheim (1896) | Marble Palace (1846) |
| **Zoo** | London (1828) | Ménagerie du Jardin des Plantes, Paris (1794) | Zoologischer Garten Berlin (1844) | Philadelphia Zoo (1859, opened 1874) |

system of selling pre-manufactured goods (and creating a new cycle of demand and supply), the accumulation of capital and the development of a consumer society in the modern sense of the word.

Although the differences between these institutions are evident, they are connected by a shared principle of staging and presenting objects to the gaze of the spectator – a technique that is complemented by the practice of a new kind of spectatorship that helped to form the modern subject. Thus, Tony Bennett has argued that they build a central social field of experience that he calls the *exhibitionary complex*.[76] Bennett defines three crucial moments for the emergence of this complex:

- 'the tendency for society itself [. . .] to be rendered as a spectacle'
- 'the increasing involvement of the state in the provision of such spectacles'
- 'The exhibitionary complex provided a context for the permanent display of power/knowledge.'[77]

All three conditions are fuelled by a fundamental reorganization of social, cultural and political values and structures. Peter Hoffenberg has argued with respect to the exhibitions in the British Empire that these actually created the public sphere:

> One might even suggest that participation in the exhibitions did not only generate public opinion, a topic on the minds of most politicians at the time, but, in fact, created what we might call the Victorian public itself.[78]

Notwithstanding a broad discourse that aimed at denouncing the spectacle as 'inauthentic', merely theatrical (in contrast to an implicitly assumed 'reality'), these politics of the spectacle were at the core of public representation. Whereas Habermas sees the public sphere as a rather abstract concept – truly realized only in the free discourse of the eighteenth century – recent scholarship has pointed to the spatial dimension of the public sphere, and its close connection to the visual culture of the nineteenth century.[79] Thus, it is the amalgamation of image technology, power, capital, institutions and social and cultural practices we have to ask for. Guy Debord's much quoted notion of the *society of spectacle*,[80] notwithstanding its historical inaccuracy, hints at the emergence of a new scopic regime that encompasses very different cultural institutions and connected them via the circulation of goods, practices and cultural and social values.

When the *Illustrated Weekly News* proclaimed the 'age of exhibitions'[81] in 1862 it stated the obvious: exhibitions had become a quintessential element of the international discourse, not only as arenas to present and advertise the latest inventions and products but also as spectacles of the meaning of these products:

Vast engines for showcasing material culture during the industrialist and imperialist age, they [i.e. The Great Exhibitions] are not interesting for scholars of visual culture primarily as a catalogue of that culture (and as a point of entry for discussions of the use-value of such objects as steam locomotives, silk purses, and machine guns), but as a particular site for transforming such disparate elements into spectacle (of exoticism, commodity fetishism, or technological wizardry, to name just a few examples).[82]

As early as 1908 the German economist and later dramatist Alfons Paquet argued that the economic category of 'value' should be expanded to include the *value of presentation* or *Schauwert* [sensation].[83] In fact, throughout the nineteenth century there was a discussion as to the extent that various exhibitions – world exhibitions were only the tip of the iceberg – actually cost more than they returned in revenue.[84] This deficit ratio can also be seen in the practice of creating landmarks that became iconic yet of little practical value. This is seen in the Crystal Palace of London's Great Exhibition (1851), and in the White City of Chicago's World's Columbian Exposition (1893), but the epitome is certainly Paris's Eiffel Tower from the Exposition Universelle (1889), an edifice described by Dennis Kennedy as having the 'meaning of pure display – a work of silent theatre.'[85]

It is hard to overestimate the effect of such exhibitions on the nineteenth-century perception of the world: it is not only that the exhibitions marked the site where they took place – the Eiffel Tower becoming the iconic representation of Paris – but they projected an image of the 'world' and its order:

> Exhibitions were at the heart of imperial and national social and commercial enterprises during the Victorian and Edwardian eras. They were spectacles of tangible fantasy, in which participants frothed nations and the Empire, both imaginary and material.[86]

These 'spectacles of tangible fantasy' attracted vast numbers of visitors, truly a world audience: Parisian exhibitions had 16 million visitors in 1878 and 25 million in 1889, at a moment when England and France each had populations of 38 million and Germany had 56 million. To grasp the influence of these events we should keep in mind that they brought about the rise of modern tourism with Thomas Cook organizing journeys to the World Exhibition in Paris in 1861 and that they received wide media coverage.

At the same time, comparable techniques of presentation were present in everyday life and were applied by various institutions of the exhibitionary complex. The most prominent among them for the urban life was the department store which created a new kind of pastime – *shopping*. Its economic profile not only depended on the availability of prefabricated commodities but on their theatrical display:

At the heart of the department store's representation lay a paradox: the goods offered to the aspirant consumer market were often mass-produced and aggressively priced, yet the culture to be sold with it was one of luxury, indulgence and good taste. It was less the products which created the sense of elegance and good living than the department store setting in which they were sold.[87]

Thus, the department store provided a scene for its goods, but also a public venue for the new bourgeois that also invited women to dawdle there without male accompany. By providing food and beverages in small cafés and restaurants, and by ostentatiously linking itself to other forms of urban life and entertainment such as theatres (through selling tickets), the department store epitomized the amalgamation of a social venue with consumer culture. Department stores presented products using theatrical techniques – think of the *period room* for example – which marks how decidedly theatricality was at the heart of nineteenth-century Western society. Timothy Mitchell even claims that the exhibition (and its derivatives) created a new kind of social epistemology:

The exhibition persuades people that the world is divided into two fundamental realms – the representation and the original, the exhibit and the external reality, the text and the world. Everything is organized as if this were the case. But *reality*, it turns out, means that which can be represented, that which presents itself as an exhibit before an observer. The so-called real world outside is something experienced and grasped only as a series of further representations, an extended exhibition.[88]

## THE FORMATION OF THE SPECTATOR AS A PUBLIC SUBJECT

What about the visitor or the spectator? Were spectators merely passive subjects to these superstructures of presentation? In his seminal study *The Birth of the Museum* Tony Bennett has looked at the impact of museums for the formation of the new, modernized subjectivity. While Foucault has focused on mechanisms of repression and punishment, Bennett argues that the institutions of the exhibitionary complex aimed at establishing a social order by transforming social problems into cultural ones and by 'winning hearts and minds as well as the disciplining and training of bodies'.[89]

From Bennett's point of view, the opening of the great museums in all major metropolises was an act of instigating a process of self-formation of the citizens – not only in the sense of self-education although in most cases this is the predominant feature in the official discourse but also in terms of the inner formation of behaviour and practices of perception.

To see and to be seen, to survey yet always be under surveillance, the object of an unknown but controlling look: in these ways, as micro-worlds rendered constantly visible to themselves, expositions realized some of the ideals of panopticism in transforming the crowd into a constantly surveyed, self-watching, self-regulating, and, as the historical record suggests, consistently orderly public – a society watching over itself. [. . .] The exhibitionary complex [. . .] perfected a self-monitoring system of looks in which the subject and object positions can be exchanged, in which the crowd comes to commune with and regulate itself through interiorizing the ideal and ordered view of itself as seen from the controlling vision of power – aside of sight accessible to all.[90]

The exhibitionary complex reveals itself as a catalyst for the formation of a new kind of subjectivity in amalgamating consumerism, technologies, new zones of contact and the sensation of novelty with the thrilling experience of being a part of an international, modernized culture. Like Goethe in his *Rules for Actors*, Bennett's museum visitor is formed in the interplay of looking at the objects (and other visitors) and the ubiquitous gaze of his/her fellow-visitors.

The exhibitionary complex is less a technique of surveillance than a performative practice. By dubbing the nineteenth century the 'performing century', Davis and Holland highlight an aspect of nineteenth-century societies that explicitly includes the spectator as an active part of the exhibitionary complex: his/her task was to produce a social identification through active participation, through imitating a habitus and thereby to obtain a recognizable social identity. Mass migration into the cities, industrialization and the emergence of a new system of commerce destabilized or superseded previous class structures. The new class of city dwellers – low to upper middle class – sought a social status they neither inherited nor gained through professional training and education alone. This process can be seen in the seemingly trivial rise in the production of commodities such as china, cutlery and home furnishings. Remotely imitating aristocratic manners, the new 'bourgeois' identity was acquired through performing newly-emergent bourgeois habits.

Thomas Richards concluded that this process of appropriating social habits and forms of conduct through spectatorship was based on the transformation of goods from the mere economic exchange into a way of making the world 'accessible' materially and intellectually. Thus, he sees the exhibition as the nucleus for a new kind of social identity: 'In a very real sense the exhibition (which featured modern manufactures) fashioned a phenomenology and a psychology for a new kind of being, the consumer, and new strain of ideology, consumerism.'[91]

In this light, we can also read Dennis Kennedy's argument that spectatorship cannot be seen as a simple act of physical presence but rather as a 'very distinct form of cultural capital'[92] that has to be learned in order to avoid social regulation. Thus, we can partly read the nineteenth-century definition of spectatorship (on all levels of the exhibitionary complex) as an act of social formation with respect to the requirements of the new public sphere.

At about the same time, the literary (and actual) figure of the sleepy, inattentive spectator appears in the lampoons of artists and advocates for a new art: the stereotype of the urban dweller who attends a performance only for reasons of being socially visible.[93] In contrast to other institutions of the exhibitionary complex, theatre had to address the spectator not as a single individual but as a social group in its own right. A new means of 'management of attention' was exerted when it became common practice to dim the auditorium, directing the audience's attention to the stage.[94] Jonathan Crary notes:

> In the late twentieth century as in the late nineteenth, the management of attention depends on the capacity of an observer to adjust to continual repatternings of the ways in which a sensory world can be consumed. Throughout changing modes of production, attention has continued to be a disciplinary immobilization as well as an accommodation of the subject to change and novelty – as long as the consumption of novelty is subsumed within repetitive forms.[95]

In this light, we might recognize theatre and its various offsprings as emblematic for the cultural strategy of coping with an accelerated, technicized, socially unstable environment – providing places of self-reflection, group consolidation, social experiments and consumerist reassurance.

## CONCLUSION

The long nineteenth century truly was a theatrical age fuelled and expedited by technological innovations, new forms of media and visual representation and an economy that capitalized on distribution, velocity and novelty. Coming out of the Age of Enlightenment's optimistic celebration of rationalism, the new orders of labour resulting from the Industrial Revolution contributed to what Max Weber described as the 'disenchantment of the world'. And yet the longing for wonder, amazement, play and illusion also contribute to the signature modes of the period. In the midst of all the changes described above, many Western cultures clearly sought comfort in nostalgic forms – often provided and embellished by the theatre and its various genres and styles. Underneath these reputed residual forms lie complex negotiations of the conflicting interests and developments. When the period came to an end in the horror of the trenches of the Great War, rationalization, velocity, technological innovation and the massive forces of capital and labour show themselves as potentially pernicious at a previously unknown scale. Modernization and nostalgia, mobility and perseverance are the legacy of the period that will echo well into the twentieth century, if not beyond.

# CHAPTER ONE

# Institutional Frameworks

## *Britain and Germany, 1800 to 1920*

ANSELM HEINRICH

During the long nineteenth century different concepts of managing, organizing and overseeing theatrical entertainments were being discussed across Europe: differences which became manifest in particular in varying ideas about funding the performing arts. Increasingly from the turn of the eighteenth century onwards commentators established a binary between theatre as trade versus theatre as art. The different institutional frameworks established across Europe related to the different concepts of what theatre's function in society was supposed to be. At the two ends of the spectrum were Britain, where theatre was largely seen as a commercial enterprise, and Germany, where theatre was increasingly regarded as an educational tool, which needed financial support from the taxpayer. These differences became more pronounced in the early twentieth century with more and more German theatres being in receipt of regular subsidies from the state as well as local authorities. The development from relatively similar to fundamentally different theatre systems, the seriousness of the debates, and the effect these debates had on their respective societies, make Germany and Britain particularly fascinating case studies in this context.

The foundation of the Comédie Française in Paris in 1680 established the national theatre as a royal institution as part of a programme of both centralization and control. While issues of governance were put into question after 1789 the principle of setting national standards and artistic principles remained important in French theatrical discourse throughout the nineteenth century – a basic agreement missing from German and British contexts where discussions around the frameworks of theatrical production appear to have been more fluid, pronounced and existential. Both British and German commentators frequently looked up to the French who already in the seventeenth century seemed to have created a confident, influential and well-equipped national theatre which successfully set national standards of productions and was generously funded by the French state. In many ways, the opposite may be said of the American theatre which throughout the nineteenth century borrowed from continental Europe in search for its identity. The fact that, as Don B. Wilmeth and Tice L. Miller claim, this process 'did not reach its full potential until after WW I' largely puts the American scene outside of the frame of the investigation here.[1]

Approaches to funding theatres in Britain only changed during the Second World War when subsidies were first paid linked to the country's war effort.[2] However, monies earmarked for a future national theatre in 1949 were slow in coming forward and a purpose-built playhouse only opened in 1976. Paying subsidies to theatres still seems alien, almost frivolous, to a large segment of the British public today, and they remain heavily scrutinized. Some commentators have claimed that this animosity may be explained by Britain's theatre history. After all, the country's 'national poet' seemed to operate successfully within a commercial framework. Indeed, Richard Foulkes suggests that Shakespeare's international fame was due to an economic theatre model capable of exporting his plays around the world – a success story which, according to Foulkes, could not have been accomplished by a subsidized theatre system.[3]

During the period under consideration theatre expanded significantly in both countries and in part due to legislation which stressed the theatre's economic role in society. By the early 1800s it had become apparent in Britain that the 1737 Licensing Act, which had tightened censorship and restricted theatrical performances to patent playhouses, was impractical and new legislation was needed to deal with the growing number of 'illegitimate' but often tolerated theatres. Both the British 1843 Theatres Regulation Act and the German 1869 *Gewerbefreiheit* Law regulated theatre as a trade and both led to a phenomenal increase of places of entertainment.

In the following I will look at the 1832 and 1866 British Select Committees, the 1843 Theatres Act, and the parliamentary debates around the 1913 National Theatre Bill. For Germany I will look at the 1869 *Gewerbefreiheit* bill, the 1919 Weimar Constitution, which put theatre and cinema under Reich jurisdiction, and, particularly, municipal frameworks of governing theatres. The focus on these legal frameworks will be embedded in a discussion of the wider socio-political context from which they originated.

## DISCOURSES

In Victorian and Edwardian Britain, and in a society focused on the primacy of individual economic success, and the individual in opposition to the collective, discussing theatre in an essay on 'institutional frameworks' would have seemed an odd undertaking. Theatres were largely seen as private affairs and not as necessarily contributing to the common good. Even worse, for Victorian Britain's Christian majority the theatre was often regarded as morally suspect. Many were intensely suspicious, saw play-going as a distraction from religion and as a promoter of frivolity, vanity and female forwardness. In a typical comment of the time Reverend William Adamson replied to the question whether it was 'possible to reform the theatre, and make it the centre of an elevating influence', that this 'has been tried again and again, without success [. . .] The reason being, the evil is essential, not accidental; and if this is the case, permanent reformation is impossible'.[4] John Bennett entitled his 1838 Dublin sermon – which was subsequently published – 'The Evil of Theatrical Amusements', and there were numerous similar publications.[5] Theatres were 'linked to prostitution, juvenile delinquency, idleness, drunkenness and frivolity' – in fact they were the 'antithesis of the Victorian world view which prized respectability, gentility, decency, education and uplift', as Jeffrey Richards has argued.[6] In many quarters and until at least the later decades of the nineteenth century, theatre was 'regarded as the lowliest of the arts, if one at all'.[7]

At the same time the various forms of theatrical entertainments became immensely popular. Simon Shepherd and Peter Womack have posited that in the Victorian period 'there were probably more performances in more theatres seen by more people than at any other period, including the present'.[8] It also helped that actor-managers like Henry Irving and Herbert Beerbohm Tree strove to make the theatre 'respectable', and worthy of middle-class patronage.[9] Irving's Lyceum Theatre was referred to as 'a national theatre [. . .] without a subsidy'.[10] Theatres underwent substantial renovation programmes creating richly decorated auditoria with comfortable seating, expensive carpets and curtains, and the latest stage technology. Acting professionalized and ticket prices were raised. To many commentators it appeared as if the theatre had attracted the middle class back into its confines, and Matthew Arnold saw 'our community turning to the theater with eagerness' again.[11] 'Virtuous' entertainment with Shakespeare and Molière as well as educational melodramas, Toga Plays and Pantomime represented a powerful tool to 'better' the lower middle and working classes. It is worth keeping in mind though that even when the influential actor-managers of late Victorian and Edwardian Britain referred to the theatre's important role in nation building (e.g. Wilson Barrett) they had a commercial model in mind, not a subsidized one. Charles Wyndham and Henry Irving cherished their independence and decidedly turned against the 'fostering of a State nurse'.[12] They claimed that theatre 'must be carried on as a business or it will fail as an art'.[13] *The Era* concurred and declared that 'free trade is good in the long run whatever people may say',[14] and John Hollingshead, manager and lessee of the Gaiety Theatre, spoke of 'the English suspicion of institutionalised bureaucracy in state-funded theatres'.[15] When Herbert Beerbohm Tree opened the new Her Majesty's in 1897 the undertaking was celebrated as a successful counter-model to subsidized continental theatres.[16] Instead of putting up a building which 'rivals the parliament house, or the cathedral as a public building [like] in some Continental cities' Tree had not only kept the costs down but had also built 'quite the handsomest theatre in London [which] must go altogether to the credit of Mr Tree's public spirit and artistic conscience'.[17]

By that time the German discourse had already internalized Friedrich Schiller's dictum of the theatre as a 'moral institution' and as contributing to a general cultural education (*Bildung*).[18] The theatre's role was not only to preserve the nation's cultural heritage it was also meant to contribute to establishing it in the first place.[19] In contrast to Britain, therefore, theatre in late eighteenth- and early nineteenth-century Germany was charged to help bring about the establishment of a truly German drama and – by doing so – to contribute to the establishment of a German nation-state – both in opposition to the overwhelming political and cultural influence of revolutionary France. Going to and supporting the theatre, therefore, went beyond a mundane need for entertainment. In 1831 the German politician and philosopher Paul Pfizer claimed that it was only when seeing an opera or a play that the citizen would be able to understand 'the way of the world and the laws of history' and become aware of his own 'moral principles and his own intellectual freedom'.[20] This

FIGURE 1.1:  Cover, 'Beerbohm Tree Souvenir', 1907. Collection Anselm Heinrich.

FIGURE 1.2: Sir Herbert Draper Beerbohm Tree as Malvolio in *Twelfth Night*, date unknown. Photography by Zander and Labisch. Theaterwissenschaftliche Sammlung, University of Cologne.

deep appreciation, veneration almost, of the theatre was soon seen as something typically German. Thomas Mann in his 1907 essay on 'The Theatre as Temple' claimed that

> a deep respect for theatre is something we Germans are being born with and receive an education for. No other nation is like this. What the rest of Europe sees as a social form of entertainment we see at least as a matter of cultural education (*Bildungsfaktor*).[21]

The emphasis on contributing to a cultural education as inherent to what theatres did, indeed what constituted their responsibility, became linked to issues of funding. Crucially, and in contrast to the discourse in Britain, German commentators called upon the state (as in the community of all citizens, not central government) to provide for their theatrical entertainment. When the city of Leipzig closed its *Operettentheater* in 1924 and opened its municipally funded *Kulturtheater* instead it justified its decision by remarking that operettas did not possess any 'aesthetic or educational qualities'.[22] However, had the new municipal theatre not lived up to the required educational mission it would soon have got into trouble both with the city authorities and its mostly bourgeois patrons.

In the course of the nineteenth century we see a growing consensus among German audiences and commentators that their vision of an arts theatre could only be provided in opposition to economically driven entertainment. In his fascinating study on modernism in Munich, Peter Jelavich explains that it was not only new forms of artistic expression the protagonists of this movement intended to put in place but that they saw their entire practice as being in fundamental opposition to the economic impetus of the entertainment industry. They 'deplored the fact that they were compelled to submit to market demands at all'.[23] In general German theatre practitioners were much more afraid of being constrained by market forces than by the potential problems associated with state interference through funding. In fact it was the state which seemed to provide the framework of free artistic expression in the first place, it was its raison d'être. In view of the system of municipal subsidies which were being introduced in the second half of the nineteenth century historian Frank Möller has asserted that it was 'these subsidies [. . .] which for the first time gave theatre directors the financial independence which was needed to achieve their higher artistic vision' – a claim hardly to be found in Anglo-American theatre historiography.[24] Claire Cochrane in her recent book on twentieth-century British theatre, for example, claims that subsidies compromised artistic freedom and 'radical principles'.[25] Instead throughout her book she specifically focuses on 'theatre as an industry' in order to 'demystify' and bring 'within the economic realm the working basis of even the most idealized artistic experiment'.[26]

Eminent historian of nineteenth-century British theatre Richard Foulkes celebrates the economic basis of the performing arts as, after all,

> Britain's monarchs did not erect grandiose court theatres, its governments did not aggrandise themselves with imposing state theatres and its municipalities did not minister to their citizens through the medium of subsidised theatres.[27]

Instead the history of British theatre had shown that a much more effective way to support the arts was the bestowal of peerages by the monarchy on actors and managers which did not only result in a social elevation but which also translated into profits at the box office.[28] This system of indirect subsidy had been a practice at German court theatres, too, but increasingly German commentators wanted not just financial support for its own sake but as linked to a particular repertoire.[29] Schiller had already argued in 1784 that a theatre which contributed to a general popular education had its 'position among the first institutions of the state assured'.[30]

Commentators in both countries were acutely aware of the differences. There has been frequent admiration but vilification, too. In the early twentieth century, British commentators were in awe of the official support German theatres were in receipt of and the repertoire they were offering. The English playwright and critic Ashley Dukes, for example, praised Munich's theatres for producing 'almost the entire list of controversial plays of the period' and added that all 'the works that our Stage Society had presented on experimental Sunday evenings were played here nightly as matter of course, before a regular and appreciative public'.[31] At the same time British commentators were amused by the seriousness with which the Germans took their theatre, and their 'odd' taste for monumental Schiller productions and the radical avant-garde.[32] German commentators on the other hand by and large vilified the commercial character of the British theatre (without appreciating that theatre in Germany had been largely organized along commercial lines as well until at least the early 1920s). In 1921 Eduard Engel commented that theatre in Britain was little more than an 'amusing place of entertainment in order to kill time between dinner and going to bed'.[33] Using a similar metaphor the Italian critic Mario Borsa claimed that British audiences went to the theatre 'not to be worried but amused, not to digest thought but their dinners'.[34]

## 'TYRANNY OF THE MAJORITY'

Supporters open to changes to the ideological, political and economic frameworks in which British theatre operated during the nineteenth century did not only face criticism from large sections of society who rejected the idea of theatres having an educational purpose and receiving government subsidies, but they were also challenged from within the theatre world. When Harley Granville-Barker (and others, like Edward Gordon Craig) introduced the idea of ensemble playing to British stages – influenced by Russian and German practitioners such as Stanislavsky, Max Reinhardt and the Meiningen company before them – some commentators criticized the very concept of an ensemble as undermining personal autonomy in favour of the group. In a society where discourses of individual liberty as the principal property in human existence had taken root since the first half of the nineteenth century, a theatre system dominated by individual stars and actor-managers seemed better suited to the British character. The influential philosopher John Stuart Mill argued in his study 'On Liberty' in 1859 against the 'illegitimate interference with the rightful liberty of the individual'. He labelled this 'interference of the public' the 'tyranny of the majority' as an 'evil[s] against which society requires to be on its guard'.[35] Concepts of tyranny seemed to be made even worse by the equally foreign concept of the director as leading an ensemble. Whereas in an ensemble according to Mill's 'tyranny of the majority' at least one group could see itself represented, a director did not need any regard for his ensemble members. He could exercise total power over a company of individuals who would see their individual freedom curtailed. Complaints of this nature were in fact widely publicized in relation to Harley Granville-Barker who was accused of authoritarianism in 1913.[36] Ahead of the First World War it equally did not help that some of the most important influences concerning a director's theatre came from Germany. Max Reinhardt's presence in London and his triumphal performances were seen as 'thoroughbred German art [. . .] asserting in a cousinly way its right to dominate the Nordic stage'.[37]

Still, towards the end of the nineteenth century, and linking to a rising interest by a small but significant minority of practitioners, the commercial theatre system in Britain was increasingly criticized. For directors such as Edward Gordon Craig this critique was linked to the established star system with theatre productions built around a charismatic actor-manager and a supporting cast which did just that: support the actor-manager's artistic vision without a significant role of their own which would distract from the main protagonist. The celebrated London visit of the Saxe-Meiningen company in the 1870s offered new ways of appreciating the ensemble as an important part of a performance in its own right. However, although influential, actor-managers such as Henry Irving or Herbert Beerbohm Tree were interested rather in well-trained casts creating perfectly synchronized mass movements than their potentially liberating effect on ensemble acting. For Craig on the other hand, the ensemble was the star – which of course did not mean that he would establish democratic structures. Craig repeatedly stipulated the need for a dominating patriarchal figure in the theatre which would control proceedings

FIGURE 1.3: The Meininger celebrating the 100th birthday of Georg II in 1926 – in costume of their legendary *Julius Caesar*, 1926. Photography by L. Otto Weber. Theaterwissenschaftliche Sammlung, University of Cologne.

and have absolute power.[38] Craig's 'Purcell Operatic Society' disbanded after only two years of operation in 1902, however, and Craig left the country for Germany. Frustrated, he noted:

> I am perhaps more miserable than ever before in my life because I realise the hopeless vanity and folly of [Britain's] stage, the utter stupidity of every one connected with the Arts in England, the death-like complacency with which London thinks it is active and intelligent about these matters, the idiocy of the Press which calls every courageous attempt to revive life and art 'eccentric' [. . .]. The English actors have no chance; their system of management is bad: they get no chance of study or experience, and dare not rebel or they would lose their bread and butter; so they laugh their life away as best they can, that is to say, grimly.[39]

## LEGISLATION

In nineteenth- and early twentieth-century Britain a comprehensive legal framework for the performing arts, a Royal Charter even, was not only missing but also unthinkable, even unwanted. Lord Melbourne's 1834 statement 'God help the minister that meddles with art' defined for decades a stance of non-intervention.[40] As Marjorie Garber has recently argued 'throughout the nineteenth and into the twentieth century, suspicion of the value of public funding of art and artists in Britain persisted in multiple arenas'.[41] Not surprisingly, therefore, the two most important instances of institutional frameworks for theatrical performances in Britain during the period under investigation were licensing laws and censorship. In 1800 the only two theatres licensed to perform the 'legitimate drama' in London were Drury Lane and Covent Garden although this duopoly was already breaking down and becoming untenable in London with rising urban populations and an increasing demand for entertainments. Many theatres were built in the 1830s and 1840s but they largely concentrated on farce, musical entertainments, and pantomime – as their status as 'illegitimate' theatres determined. The difference between the two categories, however, was much more than just a legal one, as Kate Newey has recently argued.[42] For the middle-class commentators dominating the discourse on the performing arts in Victorian Britain, 'illegitimate' was also a social and a moral judgement – 'illegitimate' was inferior, rough, working class, politically and morally suspect, if not outright dangerous to the status quo. When reviewing – only in passing of course – a number of productions at 'seven minor theatres' in 1843 the *Athenaeum* concluded that 'there is little chance for the Shakespearian drama in those quarters'.[43]

In the absence of subsidies, economic factors played an equally important role. The early music halls (taverns and inns) offered dramatic performances to increase alcohol sales. A drink doubled up as the ticket for performances taking place in the back room or upstairs (as was the case in Glasgow's Britannia Panopticon). As the performances themselves grew increasingly popular, music hall proprietors started to charge for admission towards the end of the nineteenth century. Drink was removed, prostitution banned, and the new music halls became well-appointed Variety Theatres offering wholesome entertainment for the whole family. Popular entertainment in Britain had become respectable – part of a general development to reform manners and turn the British public into 'polite and civil' citizens.[44] The driver for this development, however, was not an artistic one but was dictated by economic thought.

Throughout the period of investigation the business character of the British theatre was never put into question, linking more generally to the almost universally accepted 'great rule of free trade'.[45] In contrast to Germany the state in Victorian Britain remained 'elusive', as Theodore Hoppen has succinctly put it.[46] 'Government' was a much more tangible concept. The 'state' as a term was never properly theorized as a coherent entity in mid-Victorian Britain. If discussed at all it was mostly to defend individual liberties from outside (i.e. state/government/society) interference, a negative rather than a positive definition not of what the state was and the possibilities it could offer but rather of what the state should not do.

What allowed many to square the circle was the belief that state interference was permissible if designed to strengthen individual liberties by helping place all citizens in an initial condition of equality in the struggle of life.[47]

This struggle of life, or its eventual fulfilment, was the individual's achievement of maximum happiness and to 'allow the free market to work its miracles of growth'.[48] The fear of an interfering rather than a supporting state was certainly borne out by legislation concerning the theatre. The regulations around licensing and censorship did not suggest a 'caring' state but one that curtailed artistic activity.[49] Suggestions by Matthew Arnold to 'organise the theatre' on continental lines largely fell on deaf ears.[50]

On the contrary, it seems that around 1900 the concept of free trade in the theatre was stronger than ever, and epitomized by the famous, wealthy and independent actor-managers of the time. Theodore Hoppen almost proudly comments on the 'theatre's commercial imperatives, and the powers and profits these gave to managers' and then lists how much different managers were 'worth' on their retirement: 'In the 1870s and 1880s the Bancrofts retired with over £174,000 and George Conquest, W. H. Kendal, and J. L. Toole died worth, respectively, £64,000, £66,000, and £80,000'.[51] The 'commercial imperative' also meant that although actor-managers needed some understanding of theatrical processes and an eye for artistic quality, they could only hope of surviving in the profession if they had an acute business sense.[52] Free trade as the guiding principle for theatres (rather than institutional frameworks provided by the state) remained widely accepted throughout the period under investigation. Dissenting voices were few and far between. One of them was the critic Theodore Martin. Martin argued against the crippling effect of the long run in the commercial theatre as treating playwrights, plays and actors solely as commodities who needed to guarantee a financial success. Martin observed that 'free-trade has nothing to do with art, whether on the stage or elsewhere. [. . .] It never has developed, and never will develop art'.[53] Perhaps tellingly, however, his book was only printed for 'private circulation' and not publicly available.[54]

According to a utilitarian world view having a monopoly of patent playhouses hardly made sense in a growing market of competing theatrical performances. That, and a distinct educational agenda, was the driver for the 1832 House of Commons Select Committee Inquiry into the Laws Affecting Dramatic Literature. As part of the deliberations of the Select Committee, testimony was sought from managers, playwrights, actors, theatre proprietors and owners. Their testimony suggested that the lifting of the monopoly of the patent theatres was indeed advisable.[55] It took a few years, but in 1843 the Theatres Act finally abolished the duopoly of Drury Lane and Covent Garden and established the theatrical free trade, but at the same time confirmed the Lord Chamberlain's right to censor plays and performances – despite growing criticism.[56] Music

halls were outside the jurisdiction of the Lord Chamberlain as not performing
what was termed 'the legitimate spoken drama', but they were tightly regulated
by local councils with inspectors monitoring events and penalizing 'licentious'
behaviour on stage.[57] In London, for example, a committee of the London
County Council ruled over the music halls and did so not only concerning
'issues of safety, but also on matters pertaining to social morality'.[58] Still, the
Theatres Act led to a building boom, and between 1843 and 1866 thirty new
music halls opened in London alone. Although the 1866 Report from the Select
Committee on Theatrical Licences and Regulations did finally formally
recognize the music hall it did not acknowledge it as a new and vibrant art
form. Instead the emphasis continued to be on issues of regulation and licence
– and on separation both practically (the music halls continued to be allowed to
sell alcohol in the auditorium whereas the theatres were not) and ideologically
from the theatre proper. In 1913 Henry Arthur Jones still proposed a clear
distinction between 'popular amusement' and the 'art of drama'.[59]

Although the 1866 Select Committee claimed to be concerned with theatre
as a *national* institution it seemed more interested to safeguard established
theatres from allegedly undue competition and respect the business interests of
well-respected managers.[60] At the same time, however, recent research has
claimed that this may be a narrow interpretation of the 1866 Select Committee,
which does not take into account wider issues beyond economics. Richard
Schoch, for example, posits that the '1866 Select Committee points to something
beyond economics, beyond free trade' seeking 'perfection through culture'
(following Matthew Arnold).[61] He argues that the committee members were in
fact less patronizing and more progressive than they have been given credit for
and that their endeavour to get Shakespeare into the music hall was based on
their hope for a 'shared culture that would unite all segments of the population'.
Schoch suggests that instead of reading this moment in history as 'hegemonic
force [. . .] exercised over a marginalised community' the impetus may have
been a different one: the utopian non-elitist vision of a society unified through
culture.[62]

In Germany, the 1869 *Gewerbefreiheit* Law regulated theatre as a trade and
granted it equal status (and therefore recognition) to all other business ventures.
This led to a phenomenal increase of places of entertainment with so-called
*Spezialitätentheater*, *Varietés* and circuses shooting up like mushrooms all over
Berlin in the second half of the nineteenth century, 13 of them in 1869 alone.[63]
In 1897 Berlin had 15 major private theatres plus countless other privately
owned 'speciality' venues with 38,000 seats – over eight times the number of
the seats available at Berlin's court theatres.[64] The lavish productions of the
stationary Berlin *Zirkus Busch* epitomize the boom as well as the belief that
there was money to be made in theatre. Further, *Zirkus Busch*'s focus on variety
acts, comedy and mime, fairy-tale plots and expansive shows featuring gigantic

FIGURE 1.4: Apollo Theatre, Bochum, date unknown. Postcard, P. Caspar. Theaterwissenschaftliche Sammlung, University of Cologne.

casts, ballet performances, wild animals on stage and 'exotic natives', is reminiscent of both pantomime and music hall/variety in Britain.[65] As late as 1909 the dazzling opening night of the Apollo-Theater in Bochum featured a programme which resembled a British variety theatre bill almost perfectly.[66] The building boom following the 1869 bill not only resulted in many more playhouses but also much more elaborate ones. Berlin received palaces of entertainment such as the Apollo (1884) and the Metropol (1892).

Many contemporary commentators were unimpressed. Eduard Devrient, in a way not too dissimilar from Matthew Arnold, criticized a law which only related to theatre as a business and neglected referring to it as 'dramatic art' or discussing its importance for society. Devrient's criticism reflects the Schillerian discourse, and he finishes his theatre history with a reminder to his readers that

> only the independent state is able to properly support the ideal drama in its autonomous dignity; the industrial dependency on audiences pulls it down to a banality or a grotesque grimace.[67]

This and similar comments grew in confidence. Paul Schlenther has been quoted referring to the enormously popular shows on the Friedrichstrasse as 'theatrical deadwood'.[68] Although some amendments to the 1869 bill tightened the way licences were granted, and police control and censorship naturally remained in place, the overall theatrical landscape in Germany did not change radically until at least the turn of the twentieth century when municipal funding started to increase significantly.[69]

# SHAKESPEARE

In both countries, Shakespeare featured strongly in discussions about frameworks for theatrical production (as, for example, the discussions during the 1866 Select Committee as discussed above). As has already been shown, commentators such as Richard Foulkes refer to the business model of Shakespeare's own theatre and the fact that savvy entrepreneurs had managed to export Shakespeare's plays worldwide without the 'benefit' of subsidies as evidence of the superiority of Britain economic model for the arts. German commentators by contrast, pointed to the fact that only in the framework of a subsidized theatre had it been possible to produce Shakespeare more often than in any other country in the world and to a higher standard. Since that late eighteenth century, Shakespeare had been an integral part of German culture. The status of the Schlegel-Tieck translations was particularly significant and some commentators asserted that they rivalled the original work.[70] Shakespeare anniversaries received well-publicized events in Germany, where the *Deutsche Shakespeare Gesellschaft* [German Shakespeare Association] was founded in 1864. In the same year, and on the occasion of the tercentenary celebrations at Stratford, a sizeable German delegation travelled to England to stake their claim on the Bard.[71] In April 1914, two years before the tercentenary of Shakespeare's death, the Germans mounted a grand festival in Weimar to commemorate the Bard's 350th birthday. And in terms of Shakespearean productions coinciding with the tercentenary all over Europe, the theatre historian Huntly Carter in 1925 was quite overwhelmed when relating to Germany and simply stated 'it is impossible to give figures'.[72] The *Shakespeare-Jahrbuch*, the leading German language academic journal on Shakespeare scholarship, reviewed productions of Shakespearean drama in London, but not without stressing that his work was only truly understood and appreciated in Germany. After all, Ferdinand von Freiligrath had already declared in 1844 that 'Germany is Hamlet', and Edwina Booth, daughter of the famous American actor Edwin Booth, claimed in 1883 that Berlin audiences were positively 'Shakespearean' in their knowledge of and appreciation for the Bard.[73]

In Britain during the run up to the tercentenary of Shakespeare's death in 1916, the public discussions about the nation's poet and how he should be honoured had turned increasingly political. Initial ideas to erect a monument to commemorate the Bard turned into plans to build a substantial state-subsidized Shakespeare Memorial National Theatre.[74] In lively debates commentators looked abroad and compared theatre provision in Germany to Britain. The German theatre, William Archer had noted despairingly in 1902, 'treats Shakespeare far more intelligently than we do ourselves', and Henry Arthur Jones remarked a few years later that Britain needed a Shakespeare memorial theatre so that people had 'the privilege of seeing as many of his plays performed in the course of a year as if they were living in a second-rate German town'.[75] German commentators were quick to rub this point in. They claimed that given the high number of performances of Shakespearean drama on German stages the 'real' home of the Bard was in fact Germany. In 1909 the *Deutsches Shakespeare-Jahrbuch* celebrated him as 'Germany's great Renaissance poet'.[76] A year later Otto von Schleinitz claimed that 'Lessing and Goethe have laid the foundation of Shakespeare's global status as a literary figure at a time when he had been all but forgotten by his countrymen'.[77] During the war these debates became increasingly heated with both countries claiming to be the true keepers of Shakespeare's heritage. Gerhart Hauptmann, for example, claimed in 1915 that: 'there is no nation – not even England – which has acquired a similar claim to Shakespeare than Germany. Shakespeare's characters are part of our world, his soul has become one with ours: and although he was born and buried in England it is Germany where he truly lives.'[78]

## NATIONAL THEATRE

Despite Germany's federal structure, and the fact that it was not a unified nation-state with a capital until 1871, a number of national theatres were founded during the eighteenth and nineteenth centuries and in different parts of German-speaking Europe. Vienna, Hamburg, Mannheim, Weimar and Munich all featured national theatres, some of them only very briefly (Hamburg). Others, like the *Preußisches Schauspielhaus* in Berlin, fulfilled this role in all but name. Following on from Friedrich Schiller, the chief aim of these theatres was to present a repertoire, which was morally instructive, contributed to a broad cultural education and fostered Germanness in opposition to an over-bearing French influence.[79] In contrast to Schiller's vision for German theatre to help bring about an absent national unity, in Britain calls for a National Theatre were almost always linked to an imperial agenda.

At the turn of the twentieth century calls for a national theatre led to the establishment of the Shakespeare Memorial National Theatre committee. Corresponding to the general free trade approach, William Archer favoured the idea of a 'self-supporting' house, invested in by 'a body of art-lovers, who should be content with a moderate interest on this investment'[80] – a group of influential men with independent means providing an educational repertoire for Granville-Barker's 'leisured class' and Matthew Arnold's bourgeois theatre-goers.[81] However, there was also a growing number of people calling for the state to provide the necessary funds. This 'conception of the state as an enlightened and beneficent patron of the arts' was of course 'not entirely realistic' as Bridges-Adams concluded.[82] Still, the Liberal government showed an interest and seemed prepared to endow the undertaking if the building costs were met by public subscription – a model, incidentally, which was not too different from pre-First World War Germany where city councils were keen for bourgeois audiences to contribute to building costs.[83] The project failed, both because of the outbreak of the First World War and because of the fact that sufficient funds had not been donated. Interestingly, the project never seemed to have caught the public's imagination. Writing in the 1960s Bridges-Adams claimed that is was almost natural for this 'cautious, democratically administered and state-subsidized institution' to fail.[84]

This failure may be surprising given the fact that the impetus for a British national theatre had been an imperial one with the National becoming a 'guardian as well as the repository of the dramatic heritage of the nation'[85] and educating 'the world through our Shakespeare'.[86] The envisioned national house 'placed the cultural past as a refuge, or point of nostalgic purity, through which national identity could be preserved.'[87] A national theatre as a representative cultural asset and as both a vehicle for imperial propaganda and a teaching institution aimed at stabilizing social relations, did not only call for a repertoire which was conservative rather than avant-garde, elite rather than popular, but also suggested itself for state subsidy.[88] In April 1913, the British parliament debated and voted on a motion to establish a subsidized national playhouse in London. The motion asked for a theatre 'for the performance of plays by Shakespeare and other dramas of recognised merit', a focus the committee of the Shakespeare Memorial National Theatre had lobbied for since 1909.[89] Although a number of MPs emphatically argued that such a playhouse offered ways to make Shakespeare accessible to a broader segment of the population, at the heart of the parliamentary debate was the political issue of how to reclaim Shakespeare from the Germans. Halford Mackinder MP quoted performance figures of Shakespearean drama at German theatres and explained that 'we have nothing in this land of Shakespeare to show which is comparable in the least degree to the facts indicated by these figures'.[90] This, however, proved too much praise for imperial Germany for some. Arthur Lynch MP spoke for a large segment of the House when he warned against the desire to 'Prussianise our institutions'.[91] The motion was narrowly defeated.

By this time, and reflecting the country's federal structure, German cities had begun to subsidize professional theatres. Between the last years of the nineteenth century and into the early 1920s the German theatre landscape changed dramatically. It may even be argued that a network of publicly funded civic theatres all over Germany increasingly constituted the national theatre. Most of these theatres had initially been founded as private businesses by groups of influential citizens or through endowments of industrialists (see above). For example, in the Ruhrgebiet alone, Germany's industrial heartland, a string of theatres were founded in Duisburg, Essen, Bochum, Dortmund and Hagen between 1870 and 1920, and in the wider region Düsseldorf (1875), Münster (1895) and Cologne (1902) received new premises or were costly refurbished.[92] In Mönchengladbach, Friedrich Bühring's donation of 70,000 Marks was crucial for the erection of the *Tonhalle* in 1901, and in Düren, industrialists Hoesch gave almost 600,000 Marks towards the building of the local theatre (1905–1907).[93] As in Britain, it proved difficult, however, to run these theatres at a profit, and particularly with the classical fare the bourgeois citizens wanted to see represented. Interestingly, and in contrast to Britain, the playhouses were not left to their own devices, however, but they were gradually taken over by city councils to be run as municipal theatres after 1918.[94] Discourses around the educational function of theatre played an important part, but aspects of regional competition cannot be entirely discarded here either. Bochum tried hard to be recognized for its cultural credentials sandwiched as it was between the much larger cities of Essen and Dortmund, Duisburg wanted to compete with Düsseldorf and Cologne, and Hagen was eager to establish its role as the cultural hub of the southern Ruhr area. Although, therefore, the foundations of civic theatres had not been laid by city councils, towns and cities all over Germany soon realized the cultural capital they could gain from supporting these enterprises. They associated themselves with influential groups of local citizens and benefited from their engagement with the arts. In return city councils offered prime real estate for theatres to be erected, increasingly provided financial assistance, and – after 1918 – took over most of these theatres into public ownership.

## CONCLUSION

The failed German revolution of 1918/19 had significant repercussions in the cultural sector, including the theatre. The 1919 Weimar constitution established a notion of the German state defined as a cultural nation. As a result, the constitution clarified that theatre and cinema were to be regulated by law.[95] Court theatres, playhouses with a mixed business model (private and public), and the many commercial theatres were taken into public ownership, mostly on a local (by city council) and some on a regional and national level (regional touring companies and state theatres). In the new republic ideas of common good and democratization of access loomed large, and trade unions and working-class visitors' organizations wanted to break into the world of bourgeois leisure pursuits. Crucially, their interest was not to destroy the established theatre system but to open this up to their influence by using subsidies to provide tickets at reduced prices.[96] The result was a theatre system which by the mid-1920s had been almost entirely taken into public ownership, a process which was further strengthened during the Third Reich. Rehearsal periods lengthened, productions became more elaborate, systems institutionalized. Practitioners turned into civil servants and theatres into civic institutions.

The situation could not be further removed from the 1870s when, following the *Gewerbefreiheit* bill, the German theatre landscape had become very similar to the one in Britain. Apart from the fact that court theatres, which had no equivalent in Britain, continued to play an important part, both countries viewed theatre primarily as a trade in the second half of the nineteenth century. In contrast to Britain, however, where this business model remained in operation until the 1940s (and some would argue until today), the continuing belief that theatre served a role beyond economics and as providing a cultural education did not seem to fit well to the laissez-faire ideal put forward by the *Gewerbefreiheit* bill in Germany. From the late nineteenth century onwards subsidies were increasingly being paid to theatres in Germany, provided with a legal framework in the 1919 constitution, and further taken into public ownership after 1933 (a situation not changed after 1945). This development mirrored general discourses relating to the function of theatre in society, which in Germany moved away from the *Geschäftstheater* model towards an ideal of theatre as a *Kunstinstitut*.

In Britain the economic prerogative was regularly put into question by different significant minorities but never entirely overturned. In a typical statement from the 1930s, David Fairweather, editor of the *Theatre World* journal, argued that if the British nation really wanted a national theatre it would have subscribed the needed £1 million already. The fact that only half of that sum had been found was an indicator that the people did not want such a theatre. It is interesting to note that the idea of a state subsidy as a possible solution to the funding problem did not seem to occur to him.[97] As in Germany, legislative frameworks of performance reflected a general consensus of the theatre's role in British society. Here these frameworks remained restrictive whereas in Germany they grew increasingly prescriptive linking the receipt of subsidies to a particularly (preferably educational) repertoire and rewarding such a choice with generous funding.

# CHAPTER TWO

# Social Functions

## The Social Function of Theatre

### JIM DAVIS

A key social function of nineteenth-century theatre was to enable audiences to engage and negotiate with the uncertainties and crises arising from modernity. If we are to understand the social function of nineteenth-century European theatre, especially its outreach and its significance, locally and globally, we need to understand its relationship to modernity, even if modernity is not a term susceptible to easy definition. We also need to consider the extent to which it was democratizing or containing, promoting internationalism, social awareness and progress on the one hand, while on the other enacting imperial and colonial agendas, and endorsing rather than questioning the status quo. While theatre was invariably organized on a commercial basis, contemporary questions around its social function were often formulated in the late nineteenth century around discussions focused on its relationship with aesthetics, imaginative stimulus, morality and social status.[1] Throughout the century the social function of theatre expanded and changed, although issues of inclusion and exclusion because of class, race, income and accessibility of transport remained relevant. While such changes are clearly tied into national histories, we need to engage with notions of mobility, altered perception, emotional journeying, mediation and modernity if we are to place those histories, in relation to the social function of theatre, within a more international and/or global framework.

The nineteenth century has often been appropriated as the century in which modernity emerged with a vengeance, although the term is highly contested. Lynda Nead cites Marshall Berman's definition of modernity:

There is a mode of vital experience – experience of space and time, of the self and others, of life's possibilities and perils – that is shared by men and women all over the world today. I will call this body of experience 'modernity'. To be modern is to find ourselves in an environment that promises us adventure, power, joy, growth, transformation of ourselves and the world – and, at the same time, that threatens to destroy everything that we have, everything we know, everything we are.[2]

Nead herself sees modernity as not so much 'a rupture with the past, or as a fresh start, but as a set of processes and representations that were engaged in an urgent and inventive dialogue with their own historical conditions of existence'. Modernity, she suggests, 'can be imagined as pleated or crumpled time drawing together past, present and future into constant and unexpected relations and the product of a multiplicity of historical eras'.[3] Ben Singer, writing on melodrama, argues for more complex definitions. He locates modernity in the changes that have occurred over the last two hundred years, in modernization that encompassed everything from rapid urbanization and population growth to extensive migration and emigration, the proliferation of new technologies and transportation, the rise of the nation-state, and 'the explosion of mass communication and mass amusements as well as mass merchandizing and consumerism'.[4] Singer also sees rationalism, secularism and cultural discontinuity as outcomes of modernity, while mobility and circulation became very important, resulting in 'a prevalent conception of modernity as an epoch of ceaseless change, instability, fragmentation, complexity and chaos'.[5] Urban environments were central to modernity since they accentuated sensory and subjective perceptions, providing new stimuli to the way that individuals interacted with their surroundings. Singer concedes that the impact of modernity on spectator perception can only be discussed speculatively, for even melodrama, despite its ability to capture and perhaps assuage contemporary anxieties, veers from the utopian to the dystopian in its explanation of the contemporary world. It gives no clear answers to the problems of modernity.

Within the context of modernity, as outlined above, the social function of theatre changed considerably during the nineteenth century. The advent of the industrial revolution resulted in population shifts from rural to urban areas and an increasing need for new and more centres of entertainment. Those countries dependent on colonies and/or empire grew more prosperous and theatre both reflected and mediated imperial and colonial expansion (and their impact) to empire builders and colonizers as well as to their subjects. International trade routes and global networks were established by sea, while transport on land improved through the building of proper roadways, canal systems and the coming of the railways. Steam power and the invention of the telegraph enhanced communications and notions of space, distance and even time were challenged through migration, tourism, cultural tourism, networking and increased opportunities for circulation of both people and goods. New power structures were created and old ones altered or enhanced: the metropolis took precedence over the provincial and rural, national centres strengthened their hold over their empires and/or colonies. All these developments call for a rethinking of the social function of nineteenth-century theatre history from a more global perspective on the one hand, while changes in modes of perception and emotional engagement also require a rethinking of nineteenth-century theatre spectatorship on the other.

## VISCERAL AND EMOTIONAL REACTION

When the comic actor John Emery appeared for the first time in the west of England as Tyke, a villainous Yorkshire rustic in Thomas Morton's *The School of Reform*, the ladies of the genteel city of Bath, unaccustomed to Yorkshire rustics, were unprepared for 'the grotesquely terrible, the savage air' he assumed, when dragged on stage in the first scene 'and screamed as at the sight of a wild animal'.[6] Whether this account of the early nineteenth-century Bath ladies reveals their sensibility, a tendency to rhetorical excess or their relative inexperience of life beyond Bath, it certainly creates a picture of an audience capable of strong reaction. That Emery's performance had a visceral effect on spectators is confirmed by the old playgoer, William Robson, who recalls how

> I could not sit still upon my seat, my flesh crawled, my hair rose, my pulsations were suffocating, and tears streamed down my then young cheeks. I had [. . .] wept at the pity-stirring sorrows of the fair, the weak, the aged or the oppressed; but here was the frantic working of remorse in a rude, uncultivated nature [. . .] it was awful![7]

The critic Leigh Hunt, who saw the first night of this performance in 1805, described how it 'electrified' the audience,[8] while the *European Magazine* stated that, in the scene where he displayed his remorse 'there was hardly a dry eye to be seen among the spectators'.[9]

Anne Vincent-Buffault devotes a considerable amount of space to the history of tears in eighteenth- and early nineteenth-century French theatre. She demonstrates how the communal aspects of spectatorship bring people together, quoting Baron de Grimm's view that 'Men are all friends when leaving a play. They have hated vice, loved virtue, cried together, developed the good and just elements of the human heart side by side. They found themselves to be far better than they thought'.[10] Sensibility expressed through tears was a function of collective theatrical spectatorship in eighteenth-century France, although, some, like Rousseau, queried its value. For Rousseau spectators' emotions enabled them to escape into isolation rather than into a community of shared values and experiences. In the nineteenth century, after the Revolution, the French theatrical public expanded. In the mid-nineteenth century Flaubert wrote of a theatre visit in 1856: 'The beautiful weeping ladies of the boxes [. . .] did not omit to weep, and towards the end there was such a display of handkerchiefs that one might have supposed oneself to be in a laundry'.[11] Sensibility could be a demonstrably male as well as female trait, but accounts of sensibility expressed through tears increasingly emphasize it as a feminine response.

Melodrama provoked strong emotional responses in nineteenth-century France, so much so that William Makepeace Thackeray wrote: 'You see fat old men crying like babies, sucking enormous sticks of barley-sugar'.[12] *L'effet du mélodrame*,[13] painted by Louis Léopold Boilly in the 1820s, shows a woman who has fainted as a result of the performance she has been watching. Here the classical composition of the figures seems rather contrived, calling into question the genuineness of the emotion on display (apart from the genuine agitation of her child, who is a member of the party). Patricia Smyth refers to its choreographed quality and to the notion that fainting like this is a form of social ritual.[14] Thus the authenticity of the emotional response is compromised

FIGURE 2.1: *L'effet du mélodrame*, oil on canvas, *c.*1830, Léopold Boilly. Alamy Stock Photo.

by the constructedly picturesque nature of its representation. This questioning of the absolute sincerity of intense emotional response in the theatre had already emerged in Britain in the late eighteenth century, when caricaturists began to target such responses. In Thomas Rowlandson's *Tragedy in London*,[15] many of the spectators and even a member of the orchestra are in tears. In the eyes of Rowlandson and other contemporary caricaturists there is clearly something comical, even absurd, about the display of such blatant emotion by spectators. However genuine the tears that are shed, they are made to seem ridiculous. There is a suggestion, even assumption, of insincerity, as if emotional reactions are something to be performed rather than experienced. Responses such as weeping and fainting are mocked or questioned, inviting us both to doubt their sincerity and to see spectator response as a sort of performance. The artifice of theatrical performance is thus mirrored (in some instances) by the artifice of audience response. Sensibility becomes suspect, affect rhetorical.

Despite such critiques, spectators throughout the nineteenth century were arguably seeking experiences that drove them to tears or laughter, that thrilled and shocked them, that triggered physical sensations, as Tiffany Watt Smith suggests in her recent study *On Flinching*. One facet of spectatorship which she pursues is spectator response to sensation drama, popular from the 1860s onwards. These dramas usually featured 'one climactic scene of thrilling

FIGURE 2.2: *Tragedy in London* (1807), Thomas Rowlandson.

technological effects', designed to 'hold the spectator breathless, to harrow up his soul, to excite him [. . .] and make the flesh creep'.[16] The sensation scene was the moment when 'the interest of the spectator' was 'visibly concentrated'. Michael Diamond defines 'sensation' for the Victorians as a 'condition of excited feeling produced in a community by some occurrence'.[17] In Watt Smith's view theatre spectators 'simultaneously experienced emotions and monitored them too'. Their encounter with sensation and reaction to it was a knowing one: their consumption was not just of the sensation, in the full knowledge it was a theatrical illusion, but also of their own emotional and visceral responses to it.[18] Such responses to sensation drama were arguably common in European, Australasian and North American theatres: what changed was not necessarily emotional and visceral response to the event itself, but understanding of and attitudes towards contextual meaning. Whether the sharing of emotional and visceral reactions in a confined space created the sort of fellow feeling described by Baron de Grimm may be open to question, but the social function of the theatrical space as a place where normally private sensations could be publicly experienced must certainly be acknowledged.

## VISUAL PERCEPTION

The centrality of visual experience to so many forms of nineteenth-century entertainment was to some extent due to the centrality of new technologies in recreating and redefining the experience of the spectator in this period. The nineteenth century was a time when objects, cityscapes, landscapes, took on new meanings, whether through the ever-increasing speed of travelling or the changing perceptions of colour and locality wrought by gas and then electric lighting. A world framed, for instance, by railway carriage windows, mediating that world at ever increasing speeds, is a world that has to be perceived differently. Thus, once we discuss the increased networking and mobility made possible in the nineteenth century, we also need to ask how this impacted on perception and ways of looking, especially in relation to entertainment. We have plenty of records of what people saw, from paintings and prints to illustrations and photographs, but surely the more interesting question is how they looked at the world around them.

Christopher Balme reminds us of 'the historical contingency of spectatorship', adding that 'the question of what spectators "do" during a performance, how they act, react and make (non)sense of what they actually apprehend is obviously a central one for theatre and performance'.[19] Dennis Kennedy acknowledges just how complex spectatorship can be:

Assisting at the spectacle is not a stable condition but a process of negotiation among the self of the spectator, the other of performance, and a third order, the indistinct but powerful police force of the gathering. Perhaps Certeau's free cats and Foucault's caged dogs are more similar than first appears, and live together.[20]

And Bruce McConachie takes issue with the social historical approach to theatre audiences and argues for more of a focus on cognitive engagement.[21] If we are to understand the social function of theatre in the nineteenth century it is essential we not only engage with emotional and visceral response, but also with how audiences listened and, more particularly, with how they looked.

Jonathan Crary has had a profound but controversial effect on the way we consider perception during the nineteenth century, in particular arguing against an overemphasis on the changes wrought by photographic realism and modernist art. For Crary, shifts in representational practices are insufficient as a means of establishing ways in which vision changed historically. Instead he suggests we should focus on the observer.[22] Crary prefers 'observer' as a term to that of 'spectator' because, in his view, spectator in the nineteenth century carries the connotation of 'one who is a passive onlooker at a spectacle, as at an art gallery or theatre'.[23] The erasure of theatre from his discussion of the observer and the rather dismissive attitude towards the spectator's passivity is problematic and a recurrent problem in histories of perception and visualization in the nineteenth century. Chris Otter offers a more open approach and considers the arguments that panoptical spaces – such as exhibitions and theatres – encouraged self-regulation:

> In theatres, it was important that 'the audience should see each other, so as to allow all who wish it an opportunity for personal display, and for scrutinising the appearance of others.' The ideals of the panopticon are, in some sense, spatially secured here, in that conduct is visually regulated. But both means and forms are fundamentally different. One could, of course, always voluntarily leave the exposition and escape the gaze of fellow visitors.[24]

This approach also has limitations both in its Foucauldian assumption that the theatre auditorium is a panoptical space visually regulating conduct and that individual or collective agency can be expressed only through departure from that space.

Otter acknowledges that, in the nineteenth century, changes in illumination were responsible for changes in perception, something that is also emphasized by Lynda Nead. She suggests that gas lighting in the early nineteenth century turned London (and other) city streets into a stage, people into characters and clothes into costumes: 'lit by the gas, faces have a hectic, flushed appearance as though painted with stage make-up. Gas [. . .] made the lives that it illuminated seem staged and unreal'.[25] Equally, gas changed the nature of theatrical experience, creating 'a dream world which blurred, the uncertain boundaries between the real and the imagined and which was encapsulated in the space of the Victorian theatre [. . .] On stage, gaslight created the illusion that "the action was reality itself"'.[26] Nead hints at a paradox: gas illumination creates a 'fantasy' world, but one which is mistaken as reality. Thus, when W. B. Donne complains of the need of audiences to see the 'palpably real'[27] on stage or Percy Fitzgerald states that nineteenth-century audiences flocked to the theatre to witness familiar objects and environments,[28] such critiques need to be tempered by an appreciation of the way changes in stage lighting were changing perceptions of reality. Developments in stage lighting and stage machinery, in fact, may not have turned audiences into passive recipients of the familiar, but may have encouraged them to see anew as the world around them was defamiliarized by new technologies.

Perception changed again as electric lighting replaced gaslight in the late nineteenth century. Otter suggests that this was not always a welcome development, since 'most people were accustomed to seeing yellow. This is how normal night appeared: ocherous, cosy, peppery. The whiteness of electric illumination was often an unpleasant shock, registered chromatically as bluish.'[29] The white light of electricity was clearly relative, but it took time to accept new illuminations:

> New perceptual habits had to be slowly learned: instantaneous revolution in colour perception is perhaps, physiologically impossible since such perception is always relative and never absolute. And what was true of the eyes was true of the spaces in which they saw. Paint, wallpaper, carpeting, clothing, and cosmetics had often been designed to be seen by gas, oil and candle. The introduction of electric light generated numerous chromatic problems.[30]

This was particularly true for theatre, since the 'naked trashiness' of electricity, as Ellen Terry termed it, distorted scenery and make-up. Equally, art galleries, in adopting electric lighting, changed perceptions of paintings that had been composed by and painted to be seen by candlelight and other earlier forms of lighting and 'probably robbed them of their intended viewing conditions'.[31] Moreover, electricity impacted on ventilation in theatres, since 'sun burners and chandeliers were regularly used as much for ventilation as for illumination. Simply replacing gaslight with electric lighting could lead to rising temperatures.'[32] Thus the installation of electric lighting at the Savoy Theatre, the first London theatre to make the changeover, sometimes led to tropical temperatures, although gas lighting had sometimes had a similar effect in theatre galleries. Otter is particularly interested in patterns and networks of perception: his focus is on Britain in the nineteenth century, but his work helps to suggest the ways in which perception itself was changing globally within our period.

Despite her own comments on the limitations of Crary's approach, Kate Flint disappointingly all but ignores the theatre in her study of *The Victorians and the Visual Imagination*. The experience of the individual spectator and the individual reader are more central to her concerns:

Visualising in the mind's eye, observing the natural world, interpreting paintings – in all these and many other acts of spectatorship, the process of seeing incessantly moves between the subjective and the objective, blurring the distinction between the two. Throughout the period, Victorians were fascinated with the technology of vision [. . .] For them, however, problematizing vision meant a great deal more than a consideration of the conceptual and mechanical implications of these means of seeing. It involved acknowledging the individualism of consciously evoked social knowledge and experience, and of factors of memory and association which belonged to the increasingly investigated world of the unconscious.[33]

Flint's nineteenth-century spectator foreshadows the emancipated spectator of Rancière, demonstrating the ways in which advances in new technologies and their application to vision may have fragmented and even undermined collective spectator response.

Tiffany Watt Smith has valuably critiqued Crary's approach, drawing attention also to the critiques of Crary by Otter and Kate Flint. While acknowledging theatre is not a central aspect of Crary's discourse around the observer, Watt Smith draws attention to the limitations of his argument in her own book *On Flinching*, which

interrogates the equation between theatrical audiences and passivity by arguing that embodied and affective audience performances might be understood as a form of interactivity and participation in the live event [. . .] [T]he theatre auditorium was a space around which questions about looking – and particularly, about the collective, affective and visceral aspects of spectatorship – were raised and contested.[34]

Watt Smith emphasizes the importance of self-consciousness, self-awareness and performance as components of nineteenth-century theatre-going and of the auditorium as a space which prompted questions about how to look. She also draws analogies between scientific observers and nineteenth-century audiences, broadening the basis for discussion of nineteenth-century spectatorship.

An increasing emphasis on spectacle in nineteenth-century theatre created disparate worlds for spectators. For John Ruskin, mid-Victorian pantomime presented its spectators with the possibility of imagining a better and more ideal existence, away from 'the woeful interlude of the outside world'.[35] Conversely, many melodramas enabled spectators to marvel at the world around them. Thus, as the metropolis expanded internationally during the nineteenth century, so did its significance in theatrical representation. According to Michael Booth, discussing theatre spectacle in Victorian Britain:

> The elaboration of theatrical spectacle corresponded to the elaboration of urban architecture from the 1820s until after the end of the nineteenth century. The rapid growth of the metropolis and other cities, the concomitantly rising prosperity of the nation, and the spread of empire and mercantile imperialism means the construction of docks, warehouses, bridges, factories, gasworks, railway stations, hotels, banks, department stores, office blocks, government buildings, insurance offices and exhibition halls on a scale previously unimaginable: massive monuments in wealth, imperial glory, and commercial supremacy, self-important spectacle productions in real stone, brick, steel, iron, and glass. The fact that many of these same monuments appeared repeatedly on the canvas of scene painters is evidence that the new architectural environment was too significant and too much a source of pleasure to be left outside the theatre. Conditioned to mass, grandeur, and elaborate ornamentation in the buildings around them, it is not surprising that the public responded enthusiastically to the same sort of thing translated into the values of theatrical production.[36]

Such emphasis on the visually real raises significant questions around the social function of theatre in the nineteenth century. However hard it tries, theatre can never represent reality with total conviction, whether scenically or via the expressive techniques through which actors communicate with spectators in live performance. The theatrical experience is still illusionistic and dependent on the audience's acceptance of conventions of representation. Yet, through an emphasis on verisimilitude the nineteenth-century theatre certainly helped to prepare audiences for the eventual predominance of naturalism and realism not only on stage, but also in the new media of the twentieth century. Spectacle certainly undermined both imaginative and intellectual responses to performance, although it may also have encouraged more sophisticated modes of looking. While there is always a danger that what looks real may also be perceived as true, what is being mediated can still be questioned and critiqued. The mass consumption of spectacle by nineteenth-century audiences need not imply a loss of individual agency.

The darkening of the auditorium in the late nineteenth century wrought further changes in the social function of theatre in relation to spectator perception. There had been complaints about the lit auditorium, largely on aesthetic grounds, earlier in the century. Richard Wagner, Henry Irving and André Antoine were key proponents of the darkened auditorium and their innovations were to have widespread consequences. A major factor in the erasure of the spectator, according to Victor Emeljanow, may have been 'the increasing middle class determination to separate private and public spheres of activity'.[37] He cites Schivelbusch's *Disenchanted Night* which refers to 'the twilight world of bourgeois interiors' in which 'everything private [. . .] was shut off from a public which is thought to be more and more unpleasant' and 'is reflected in attempts to prevent light from the street from falling directly into rooms'.[38] The darkened auditorium not only turned the spectator, in Antoine's words, into 'a silent witness' rather than an active participant, but also reduced the socializing potential of theatre both between spectators and between actor and spectator. As long as the auditorium was lit the social function of theatre was arguably dialogic, although not intentionally so. Darkened auditoriums recreated the stage as an aesthetically lit and decorated space, drawing the solitary gaze of each spectator, but perhaps negating a sense of shared experience. The notion of the theatre as a shared social space was undermined and to some extent destroyed by this new development, made possible by technological progress and the use of electricity. While one of the social functions of nineteenth-century theatre was to negotiate and even mitigate the impact of modernity, modernity itself changed forever the social formations generated by theatre-going in Western theatre.

## PUBLIC SPHERE

Theatrical entertainment in the nineteenth century both operated within and constituted an aspect of the public sphere. Theatres were among the largest secular indoor meeting places in which the public could assemble and, while entertainment might be a primary objective of such gatherings, theatre auditoria also functioned as meeting places too. That theatre should be morally (and even politically) instructive was certainly a view shared by a number of late eighteenth- and early nineteenth-century commentators. Charles Nodier, in his introduction to the collected works of Pixérécourt, who developed the genre of melodrama in France, considered that Pixérécourt's plays 'take the place of the silent pulpit in providing serious and profitable lessons for the souls of his audiences, and always in a charming form'. In Nodier's view melodrama supplied religious and social education and 'provided a means of applying the fundamental principles of any civilization'.[39] According to Pixérécourt himself, in what appears to be an attempt to appease the Ministry of Police over theatre's impact on public opinion, '[Morality] needs rallying points, where men are drawn to come and hear its lessons. The theatres are there, so to speak, to present the distillation, the essence of the virtues, either political or personal, which every citizen must profess.'[40] Such a position was subsequently disputed, but the secular function of theatre as an alternative to the pulpit surfaces throughout the nineteenth century. In 1876, Henry Irving claimed for 'histrionic art affinity with much that is beneficent and elevating in religion. What forms the basis of almost very standard play, but some useful moral lesson forcibly impressed by the aid of fable?'[41] On a more superficial level genres such as farce might also influence behaviour, as suggested by the *New Monthly Magazine* in 1827, referring to 'the very great effect which even the farce of a season has upon manners – the colouring which it gives to conversation and habits of expression – and the way in which the stage modifies the ordinary language and ordinary ideas of the numerous class of persons who frequent the theatres'.[42]

The relationship between the theatre and the state is also an ongoing factor in any discussion of the theatre's function in the nineteenth century. In London in 1795, John Thewall gave two lectures 'On the Political Prostitution of our Public Theatres', suggesting that the monopoly enjoyed by the patent theatres, Covent Garden and Drury Lane, as well as the existence of theatrical censorship, enabled the state to determine the nature of sentiments to be uttered and factions to be supported by what was permitted to take place on their stages. As in earlier periods there was a danger that the theatre would be used not only as 'powerful engines to improve and instruct the people', but also 'as powerful engines to bring virtue into discredit. And to mislead and delude mankind; and thus to support that tyranny and oppression which nothing but delusion can perpetuate in any country'.[43] Jane Moody draws analogies between Thewall's concerns and the Old Price Riots at Covent Garden Theatre in 1809, when the drama itself became secondary to the confrontation and expressions of dissent enacted by the spectators. Towards the end of the nineteenth century the social function of theatre was linked to the commercial and ideological exploitation of spectators. In 1893, Georg Simmel attacked the Apollo and Ranacher Theatres in Berlin on the grounds their diet of variety and operetta was pandering to the needs of a population exhausted by work and the miseries of everyday life.[44] In effect a social function of theatre was to provide the opiate that maintained a compliant workforce for their capitalist masters.

If, as suggested above, spectators performed emotion in the theatre auditorium, they even more decidedly performed class. From the eighteenth through to the twentieth century theatre architecture designated specific areas of the theatre to specific social groups. Box, pit and gallery separated spectators socially, professionally and economically. Ironically, insofar as some theatre buildings brought together spectators from divergent social backgrounds into the same space, they then segregated them according to social hierarchy. This division is reflected in Cruikshank's satire 'Pit, Boxes and Gallery' (1836)[45] and in many of the illustrations of pantomime audiences, such as those by Hablot K. Browne in the *Illustrated London News* (8 January 1848)[46]. Class differences were reinforced by the separate entrances provided to different parts of the auditorium. While this reinforced a sense of social and economic hierarchy,

FIGURE 2.3: Detail from 'Pit, Boxes and Gallery' (1836), George Cruikshank.

FIGURE 2.4: 'The Pantomime', *Illustrated Times*, 1855. Hablot K. Browne (Phiz).

separation of audiences during the mid-nineteenth century was also driven by (often misguided) fears of contracting infectious diseases from the lower orders.[47] Ticket prices determined in which part of the auditorium audience members were accommodated or even excluded potential audiences altogether. In some neighbourhood and provincial theatres seat prices were lower, but social segregation still existed on a more miniature scale.

Wherever spectators were located, they still engaged in social interaction. Prints of audiences sometimes show members conversing, flirting or even gazing elsewhere during performances.[48] Audience behaviour was the subject of extensive commentary in newspapers and journals, especially when rowdy incidents occur, although an emphasis on specific occurrences should not be generalized into the norm. Sometimes audiences were generalized in order to push a social agenda, as in Dickens's accounts of popular theatre audience, whose right to amusement (and the moral instruction it may offer) he rigorously defends.[49] A good example of theatre operating as a social space is the Britannia Theatre in Hoxton, a working-class district of East London. The Britannia Saloon had come into being in the early 1840s and from 1843 had been licensed to perform plays. In 1858 the Britannia Saloon was demolished and the building that replaced it was henceforth known as the Britannia Theatre. Every year (at least from the 1850s) the season ended with the Britannia Festival: the green-baize curtain (known as the 'cabbage leaf') rose to reveal each actor seated in a semi-circle dressed for their most popular role of the year and subsequently gifts and floral tributes were showered upon the stage by the audience. A description of the 1866 Britannia Festival states that

> though tributes of admiration are occasionally flung on the stage in the form of wreaths and bouquets and bead head-dresses, the number of such offerings is far excelled by cardboard boxes, embossed packages tied with ribbon and seeming to contain French plums and sweetmeats, the while that more substantial are homely bound paper parcels that go whirling amongst the footlights and may be supposed to enclose anything from a leg of pork to a packet of homely sandwiches to a clean shirt and half a dozen collars.[50]

H. Chance Newton recalls 'pipes, tobacco pouches, umbrellas, walking sticks, a batch of neckties, pairs of boots, hats, comforters, pairs of socks, and even pairs of trousers' hurtling onto the stage for the male actors, while the actresses received 'rounds of beef, a fine parcel of sausages, a goose, pairs of ducks, legs of pork, and sundry articles of wearing apparel'. In addition some of the female patrons 'would hand over the footlights cheap (and often gaudy) clocks, glass cases of waxed fruits, and flowers', as well as home-made sprays of artificial flowers.[51] A real sense of a shared community was fostered between the theatre's actors and its local audiences, to some extent enhanced by the fact that many of

FIGURE 2.5: Royal Cobourg Theatre as first opened 11 May 1818. Schnebbelie, London 1829, engraved Stow.

the actors and stagehands were themselves also living in the local neighbourhood.[52] The theatre's repertoire also took heed of the local community: its dramatists possessed 'a complete knowledge of the audience they catered for. Everything that had once tickled and pleased a Britannia audience was more or less thinly disguised in every play that succeeded, they were all cast in the true Britannia mould'.[53] Repertoire also reflected the social concerns of its audiences, generally taking the side of the poor and oppressed and openly criticizing social injustice.[54]

The Britannia was a theatre where audiences not only watched plays, but also ate and drank. Describing the provision of refreshments in the newly built theatre the *Illustrated Times* (11 December 1858) commented:

> There are three distinct refreshment rooms upon the railway model, divided into first, second and third class – gallery, pit and boxes [. . .] [T]here is plenty of good wholesome beer and ale, joins of meat and loaves of bread, and sandwiches piled up like mahogany planks at a timber wharf. The spirits you get *are* spirits, the wine *is* wine. Bottled beer is confined to the first-class refreshment room, and draught beer to the second and third.

Theatre critic H. G. Hibbert recalled how 'men walked to and fro incessantly with trays groaning beneath the weight of pies in infinite variety, thick slices of bread plastered with jam, chunks of cheese, slabby sandwiches, fried fish, jellied eels'.[55] Draught beer was also available in the theatre itself, from servers who were constantly in motion around the auditorium. Some vendors even attached compartmentalized barrels of porter and ale to their waist by zinc belts, each provided with taps from which they drew off mugs of either liquid for patrons.

The Britannia Theatre[56] is a reminder that we cannot treat the social function of theatre generically. It varied from community to community, from neighbourhood to neighbourhood, from town to town and from country to country. The Britannia is unique in many ways, a theatre built for a working-class local audience. The rebuilt theatre of 1858 was praised for its provision of sightlines from all parts of the house, the quality of its ventilation and its emphasis on spectator comfort. It was very much a part of the local community, but also attracted visitors from further afield. It certainly retained the class divisions of box, pit and gallery, but prices of admission reflected the spending power of its local patrons. Theatres such as the Britannia were companionable places providing greater warmth and comfort than some of their patrons enjoyed at home, enabling the consumption of food and drink as well as entertainment on the premises. The repertoire they offered amused, but also instructed, a point Charles Dickens emphasized in accounts of his visits to

FIGURE 2.6: Interior of the Britannia Theatre, Hoxton, from the Auditorium, from *The Builder* 13 November 1858.

Victoria and Britannia Theatres. The *Builder* (25 September 1858) described the Britannia Theatre as 'a school for 500,000 to 600,000 persons annually, where instruction, evil or good is conveyed [. . .] and will most powerfully operate on the moral and social condition of society at large'.

The fact that until the 1880s the auditorium was normally lit, not only at the Britannia but in most nineteenth-century theatres, designated the interior of the theatre as a shared social environment, accommodating performers and spectators as mutual participants in a shared experience, even if spectators were largely separated by rank, income and compartmentalized spaces. Nevertheless, nineteenth-century theatre, lit or unlit, did not necessarily render its spectators passive. The enduring popularity of melodrama lay as much in its championing of the underdog as in its maintenance of the status quo. Social injustices were regularly addressed in melodrama – in part through the seminal influence of Kotzebue and Pixérécourt – and even when they were righted to ensure a happy ending, the injustices had been articulated, often to audiences who may have greeted happy endings with a strong sense of irony. In Britain by the 1830s melodrama often championed the poor and oppressed in such plays as *Black-Ey'd Susan*, *The Rent Day*, *Luke the Labourer* and *The Factory Lad*. In the late nineteenth century, the social critiques inherent in both naturalist and experimental forms of theatre sometimes suffered from censorship, but theatre as social critique continued to function through the plays of Ibsen, Strindberg, Shaw and Hauptmann, for example. Yet such critiques have shifted from plays with a broader popular appeal to plays aimed more at the more educated middle classes. In the late nineteenth and early twentieth century a minority audience emerges for plays that seriously debate contemporary issues, but for the majority the theatre continues to function on a more popular, if slightly less critical, level.

## THE TRANSNATIONAL CONTEXT

The social function of theatre in the nineteenth century was also one of mediating different places and different cultures both at home and abroad. Actors toured abroad and mediated their own culture and that of the countries they visited to spectators. A prime example in the early nineteenth century is Charles Mathews the elder. His 'At Homes' became a serious fixture in the British theatrical calendar from 1818 until the early 1830s. He not only created a whimsical world of British and Irish characters, highly individualized and carefully observed, for his fellow countrymen, but furthermore he taught them how to look at other nationalities, as in *A Trip to Paris* (1819) and *A Trip to America* (1824). He not only played a significant role in national identity formation, but also created French, German, Yankee and Afro-American stereotypes that impacted on the way the British looked at other nationalities.[57]

N.º124

Mʳ. MATHEWS, as JONATHAN.

FIGURE 2.7: Mr Mathews as Jonathan. This print shows Charles Mathews as Jonathan W. Doubikin, the Yankee character he first created for his one-man show, *A Trip to America*, 1824.

Touring actors and touring theatre companies became more and more prolific as the century progressed and changed the social function of theatre from a local to a global phenomenon. Many have discussed the phenomenon of global expansion and its relationship to theatre already. Marty Gould suggests that:

> Popular spectacles domesticated the empire for the home audience, mediating Britons' encounter with the rest of the world and encouraging public commitment to their nation's costly and ambitious project of global expansion. For in the nineteenth century the theatre served as a primary site for the imperial encounter, providing dynamic representations of Britain's ever-growing territorial claims and giving concrete form to those remote people and places that had 'absent-mindedly' got attached to Britain, but that were, for most Britons, alien and only vaguely imagined.[58]

There are many other invaluable studies that consider how the British theatre mediated the rest of the world to its own population or enabled negotiation with the anxieties created by imperialism, modernity and progress.[59] but there are limitations to these approaches. We can endlessly consider how play after play deals explicitly or implicitly with other places, other races, otherness per se. Yet, despite allowances made for the fact that such plays engage and even influence live audiences, the focus is on dramatic literature and its representations rather than on theatrical encounters and networks. This is not to discredit the engagement of most national theatres with national identity, national myth-making, community (imagined or otherwise) or a national drama. Nor do I seek to undermine the significance of dramatic texts as historical documents in their own right, especially if contextualized, as far as is possible, by their circumstances of performance. But there is surely a case, as global trade, global economies, global networks become more predominant, for a transnational theatre history that reassesses the social function of the theatre from a transnational perspective based on the mobility of performers, cultural exchange and global financial transaction.

## AUSTRALIA

In recent years, scholarship in Australian theatre has focused on what was specifically Australian in the dramatic entertainment on offer. Yet, as Richard Waterhouse has argued, 'in their search for the holy grail of a unique Australian character, theatre historians and indeed historians of our culture as a whole, have ignored other issues and questions that are equally significant and essential'. In consequence '[t]he failure to explore the role of imported stage entertainments has distorted our understanding of Australia's theatrical past'.[60]

The significance of British cultural capital in nineteenth-century Australia has also been discussed by Waterhouse:

> The authorities no doubt sought to establish a society based on patriarchy and deference as a means of guaranteeing order, hierarchy and their own authority. In subsequent years, as a class of wealthy free settlers emerged, they too espoused such values as a means of establishing their legitimacy as a new world gentry.[61]

By the second half of the nineteenth century the 'values associated with an increasingly commercialized and industrialized British culture continued to be transmitted to Australia',[62] while a growing American influence was also noticeable.

The social function of the theatre in nineteenth-century Australia, at least officially, was to uphold British values, particularly those associated with Shakespeare. In the early 1860s, William Hoskins, an English actor who spent his last thirty years in Australia, mounted a production of *The Tempest* at Ballarat and made a speech after the first performance extolling Shakespeare as a civilizing force around the globe, 'making his way through distant climes and foreign regions, vanquishing race after race, as our conquerors did of old . . .'. He exhorted his audience to guard Shakespeare's 'throne' in Australia, adding:

> To the youth of Australia I would say, think, soar, and speculate, and above all cultivate literature and art. From these twain, science shall spring, and master minds arise, taking the forms of artisans and poets, heroes and statesmen, whose works and deeds shall win renown, and place this young country on as proud a pedestal as the capitals of the olden world.[63]

In 1887 an Australian advertisement for a production of George Rignold's *Henry V* insisted that 'the boy from School will carry away with him the high thoughts and aspirations of the noble Henry's Christian fortitude, chivalrous daring and self-sacrificing courage, while all will have their minds carried beyond the ordinary thoughts of conventional life, and have a keener appreciation of the noble and the good'.[64] Touring actors were very much cultural ambassadors, upholding the values of the mother country. In 1901, the English actor-manager Wilson Barrett informed an Australian audience that, in the light of Federation:

> They were now a people, a nation, young and sturdy, not running fast at present, as in the plenitude of space, but beginning to walk with no uncertain step. (Cheers) [. . .] They must learn to make haste slowly. Rome was not built in a day. (Cheers) Their progress must in all things tend to England's greatness, to the greatness of the British Empire. (Cheers)[65]

Wilson Barrett is appealing to an ex-patriot nostalgia for and identification with the mother country. Yet Australian theatre audience were also comprised of second and third generation settlers who no longer felt such firm ties to empire.

Consequently, this does not tell us the whole story. Firstly, although visits by touring actors to Australia may have endorsed colonial ties and offered cultural capital, there was ambivalence in Australian reactions to such impositions, suggestive of a nationalistic desire not to be imposed upon by European culture, a perspective endlessly reiterated in the pro-republican *Bulletin*. Secondly, the commercial theatrical transactions between countries were not just one-way. An investigation of the Bland Holt archives in Australia not only indicates how desperate British theatrical managements were to sell their productions to overseas buyers, but also how entrepreneurs such as Holt took ownership of such products, often transforming them into something specifically Australian along the way.[66] Such productions were often sold to American buyers as well and both the British and Australians bought and adapted American productions.

FIGURE 2.8: Postcard of Bland Holt and a scene from Hall Caine's *The Bondman*, which Holt produced in Australia.

Holt staged many of the melodramas performed at Drury Lane and the Adelphi during the late nineteenth and early twentieth century.[67] He expended huge sums on purchasing the rights to these productions, which were often staged almost as they had been in London, but at other times were localized for home consumption. The plays were often partially adapted or rewritten by Henry Fletcher and Edward Dyson to ensure a good low comedy role for Holt, to improve on dramatic structure and to make them more accessible verbally to local audiences. A number of exceptionally talented scenic artists worked with Holt to realize these productions for Australian audiences. Holt discovered that localization was popular with audiences and maintained that, 'it has been a great pleasure to me to produce shows of marked Australian colour, and presenting forms of Australian life with undoubted truth. These Australian dramas have excited the warm approval of my audiences [. . .] and I am encouraged to continue their presentation [. . .] the success of the Australian series quite refutes the oft expressed idea that our playgoers here do not want local scenes and stories'.[68] Through localization Holt demonstrated that, even in an age of global communication, international productions could be appropriated and transformed into a valorization of the local.

# INDIA

The social function of theatre served imperial and colonial ends both at home and abroad, if not always successfully. In 1879 the German-born Shakespearean actor Daniel Bandmann commenced a tour of Australia and New Zealand, departing from San Francisco to Sydney, then proceeding to Ceylon, Madras, Calcutta, Bombay, Shanghai, Hong Kong, Canton, Singapore, Ceylon, Bombay, Madras, Rangoon and Moulmein, before returning back to Australia and then home via Hawaii. In his account of his travels, Bandmann's observations are tinged with an assumption of the superiority of European culture, as in his comments on India's reception of Shakespeare:

> In fact, the love of Shakespeare is inherent in the Hindu mind, or rather, it is an inevitable blossoming of inherent qualities and dispositions beneath the influence of European education, which all the higher classes in India now enjoy [. . .] The Hindu learns his English through the immortal Bard [. . .] he loves poetry, and Shakespeare's sublime ideas and magnificent diction touch him to the quick.[69]

For Bandmann it was 'a pleasure beyond description to see the natives of India enjoying a Shakespearean performance; the intelligence and enthusiasm they evince far succeeded that of any European audience with whom I am acquainted'.[70] In Bombay the Parsees, whom Bandmann considered 'the cleverest people in India', also showed themselves to be great lovers of Shakespeare, even volunteering to play with Bandmann's company on one occasion, doing wonders, said Bandmann, 'considering that they were alien to the language, and not even Europeans'.[71] In these accounts there is certainly a touch of the cultural missionary or even schoolmaster; Bandmann is almost infantilizing his Indian spectators in his approving account of their powers of reception and comprehension. He ignores the fact that by this time the Parsees had created a flourishing theatre culture of their own which included adaptations of Shakespeare. Of course, the background to Indian Shakespeare is enshrined in Macauley's notorious minute of 1835 on Indian Education:

> English is better worth knowing than Sanskrit or Arabic [. . .] We must at present do our best to form a class who may be interpreters between us and the millions whom we govern, a class of persons Indian in blood and colour, but English in taste, in opinions, in morals and intellect.[72]

This certainly complicates the ways in which we might write about Bandmann's comments on Shakespeare in India and his uncritical acceptance of the cultural imperialist agenda behind this phenomenon. Moreover, Bandmann's view of his reception in India may be rather idealized – he wasn't always so well received critically in primarily English-speaking countries, partly because his strong German accent sometimes rendered him incomprehensible.

Despite the linguistic imperialism implicit in Bandmann's comments, Shakespearean and other British dramas were often adapted to reflect Indian life: they were effectively localized and music and song were introduced. A history of Indian theatre written in 1934 states:

> On account of the national taste, the greatest emphasis was usually laid on the emotional side ('heart interest') in the altered versions. The sentimental affect of such scenes as those of 'Arthur and Hubert' [*King John*] and the 'Sentinel and Rolla' [*Pizarro*] were indeed extraordinary throughout India. Pathetic situations in Shakespeare and others appealed deeply to the emotional nature of the playgoers. Intellectuality was generally neglected.[73]

Despite generalization this indication of adaptation and localization chimes with the Australian rewriting of British and American melodramas by Bland Holt and his team of authors.

On one level the social function of European theatre in India was to uphold an implicitly colonial agenda. When it came to amateur performances by both soldiers and civilians, however, the motivation was determined by nostalgia and the need for recreation. Like many other amateur theatre actors, whether indulging in country house or garrison theatricals, amateur performers in India, such as those stationed in Simla, tended to enact popular farces and comedies. Derek Forbes suggests that:

> One of the results of this sheltered repertoire [of middle-brow English plays] [. . .] would surely have been to give nostalgic comfort for the certainties of the motherland [. . .] Easy-going plays which reminded participants and audiences of life in the old country were consoling, perhaps fortifying, to engage in or watch [. . .] the act of theatre could allow expatriates to imagine themselves back home.[74]

Yet in a country like India social functions could sometimes clash. When Colonel Moore-Lane – then a captain – arranged to take a company of amateurs on tour through all the big cities of India, playing *My Milliner's Bill*, *The Parvenu*, and *Creatures of Impulse*, – a tour eventually abandoned because of his wife's (who was leading lady) illness – he was persuaded to admit local children to a dress rehearsal at Poona:

> Colonel Moore-Lane, being a kindly soul, and also knowing what a splendid audience school children make, consented willingly. He was surprised, however, to find, instead of the hundreds of smiling white faces he expected to see, row upon row of grave little copper-coloured visages, the little Indian children from the missionary schools. The harder he and his company worked to raise a laugh, the graver and graver this audience grew. They had been brought up to regard every sahib with the greatest respect, and the more ridiculous the sahibs on the stage made themselves, the more cause the little brown scholars found for not being drawn into anything so disrespectful as a laugh.[75]

Given the repertoire they were playing, it is hardly surprising that the amateurs had little relevance to their spectators or that, given the nature of colonial power structures, they could not elicit a response.

## CONCLUSION

The social function of theatre in the period under review, at least as indicated in the examples discussed above, was multifaceted to say the least. Endless adaptability to changes in technology, communications and modes of perception was mediated via theatres, which became the conduits through which innovation was both demonstrated and critiqued. Theatres helped educate spectators to see anew, but also assuaged anxieties about the destabilizing effects of change. Paradoxically, the social function of theatre was also contradictory: endorsing social hierarchies in its architecture while sometimes criticizing the injustices arising from such hierarchies in what was performed; imposing imperial values abroad, culturally and linguistically, but sometimes facing resistance rather than endorsement in spectator reaction. Some argued that the theatre propagated moral values; others criticized it on the grounds that it fostered immorality. At the beginning of the period it brought people together in a lighted auditorium; by the end they were sitting in the dark, in a more controlled and less socialized space, and theatre's social function changed forever.

# CHAPTER THREE

# Sexuality and Gender

LAURENCE SENELICK

## 'THE DEVIL'S CHAPEL'

Acting, exhibiting one's body to the public, has been equated with prostitution from the earliest records of performance. The performer's physical availability may be hedged round with religious or ritual atavisms, but he and particularly she are subject to the desires and appetites of the spectator. From Republican Rome to Tokugawa Japan, from Tudor England to Ottoman Turkey, the actor's body has been a cynosure for sexual fantasies. Spectating can easily turn into voyeurism (see Figure 3.1).

Consequently, the professional theatre has attracted the opprobrium of society's agencies of control. For the godly, the playhouse was 'the devil's chapel', to be shunned at all costs, and players forbidden interment in holy ground. The integration of the actor into society and the acceptance of theatre as a cultural asset were resisted at every step. A latent suspicion that the emotions aroused by the theatre were dangerously subversive was never entirely dispelled.

The narrative of Western theatre in the nineteenth century may be read as its progress from disreputable diversion to agent of national identity and cultural enlightenment. Such a triumphalist account would point to the actors' own determination to lose the label of 'rogues and vagabonds' and to be absorbed into the bourgeois norm.[1] It might begin with the 1810 charter of the Stuttgart *Theaterbund* which excluded 'adventurers, dissolute students, etc., suchlike people of ambiguous calling and character'.[2] It would point out how Denmark's leading actress Johanna Pätges received royal permission to be billed as Fru (rather than Madame) Heiberg, and how actors of serf origin in the Russian Imperial troupes were allowed to have a 'Г.' for Gospodin or Gospozha (Mister and Mrs)

FIGURE 3.1: The spectator as voyeur. P. T. Barnum ogling the dancer Ernestine de Faiber, New York, *c*. 1861. Photography by Mathew Brady, published by E. and H. T. Anthony. Laurence Senelick Collection.

before their names in the playbill. And it would culminate on a high point with the Emperor Franz Joseph ennobling a Jewish tragedian, Adolf Sonnenthal, and Queen Victoria knighting Henry Irving, while statues were erected to Josef Kainz in Vienna and to Edwin Booth in New York. Sarah Bernhardt, who had begun her career as a vendible *figurante*, ended it as a national monument.

A counter-narrative is also possible, however. This would trace the persistence of the theatre's sexually subversive aspect, remaining a challenge to the *embourgeoisement* of the ambient society. Good repute, attained with difficulty, never reached to every corner of public opinion. Moreover, it entailed a loss of what had long constituted theatre's main attraction. As one eminently respectable Victorian actress, Madge Kendal, remarked to another, Eva Moore, in their old age, 'Think of all the things we have missed, people like you and me, through leading – er – shall we say "well-conducted lives"! And, make no mistake, we *have* missed them!'[3]

On the Continent, the various revolutions and uprisings of 1848 had profoundly shocked the middle class. As its closest financial interests were jeopardized by bankruptcies and stock fluctuations, it retrenched by policing public morals, especially in the arts. The managerial class henceforth protected with vigilance any threat to a controlled society and what sustains it: religion and respectability. This is the motivation for rescuing Shakespeare, a cultural totem, from pollution by 'bowdlerizing' his works.[4] This is what lies behind the trials for obscenity of the writings of Baudelaire, Flaubert and the Goncourts, along with the persecution of Ernest Renan for scepticism in sacred matters. Much nineteenth-century theatre was made to contribute to the age's great preoccupation, safeguarding established values.

Still, it is hazardous to generalize, since moral attitudes differ widely from nation to nation, from capital to provinces, from class to class. What is praised in Paris might appal London and Munich; the *dernier cri* in New York might be seen as *vieux jeu* in Vienna. Fashionable trends may win favour temporarily, but trend to be trumped by indigenous mores. French phenomena in particular cross international borders and enjoy success, but always with modifications and adjustments to the sensibilities of the native public.

## THE PROSTITUTE AS ACTRESS AND VICE-VERSA

At the Vienna Court Theatre, the word '*Hure*' (whore) in classic plays was replaced by '*Metze*' (strumpet).[5] Such cosmetic touches could not conceal the fact that prostitution flourished within and without playhouses. It was reported that there were between 40,000 and 60,000 prostitutes in London alone; on the Continent licensed brothels were sanctioned by the municipal authorities and a blind eye cast on the youth of the girls. The conspicuousness of what the French call '*filles publiques*' was not accompanied by an equivalent tolerance. The more blatant the prostitute in public places, the more euphemistic, decorous and in-denial the social discourse about her. The fathers of Communism were shocked to observe the prostitutional ethos percolating up through society. Marx and Engels in their Communist manifesto of 1848 accused the bourgeois of seeing 'in his wife a bare instrument of production . . . Our bourgeois, not content to make their wives and daughters available to the proletarian, not to speak of official prostitution, find a high pleasure in seducing their wives mutually.'[6]

The conflation of actress with prostitute was slow to be effaced and, in certain elevated or pietistic circles, never was. A copious bibliography of 1864 devoted to books about women and eroticism indiscriminately included hundreds of items about theatre and dance halls.[7] One of the most durable pornographic novels of the time, the German answer to *Fanny Hill*, took a reigning queen of opera as its protagonist.[8] The avoidance of playhouses because they were the haunts of harlots was often justified: theatres and brothels sometimes occupied the same urban precincts. The 'third tier' in American theatres[9] and the 'second tier' and various promenades in their European counterparts were common ground for cruising and assignations. Managers might collude with prostitutes by selling them cut-rate season tickets. Noblemen, plutocrats and fashionables regarded the green room and the ballet school as licensed game preserves (Manet's 1873 painting *Masked Ball at the Opera* records this sport). The most egregious example was the children's ballet, founded at the Theater an der Wien in 1816; four years later the police had to be called in to stop the paedophilic predations of Count Kaunitz-Redburg, who had commissioned paintings of his frolics with dancers aged twelve to fourteen.[10]

It was assumed that any actress would traditionally enhance her income and influence by being kept. The actress had the responsibility of providing her own costumes; with the growing popularity of drawing-room drama, this meant an elegant and up-to-date toilette. Arkadina in Chekhov's *The Seagull* (1896) complains that her wardrobe is ruining her. So an extra-mural source of funding was imperative. Actresses who tried to maintain their virtue were seen to be anomalies or hypocrites; marriage might be a safe camouflage or a notice of retirement. As late as 1927, one apologist felt obliged to spend 460 pages arguing that it is unfair to equate actresses with prostitutes because the former strive for artistic greatness whereas the latter are merely enjoying themselves.[11]

Victor Hugo set out to move boundary markers when he made a courtesan in love the protagonist of *Marion de Lorme* (1828); he intended it as a direct provocation to neoclassic tradition, to the strict separation of lines of business, and to the moral conventions of the time. Owing to its novelty, the play was accepted by the Porte-St-Martin and the Comédie Française, and was bid for by the Odéon. The Minister of the Interior forbade the opening, however, not because of the prominence of a courtesan, but because the portrayal of Louis XIII was seen to be too disrespectful. The *drame* was finally performed two years later at the Comédie, with the ending rewritten so that the heroic role is displaced to the dying lover who forgives Marion. The drama failed to make the stir Hugo intended, in part because it was set in the age of Richelieu and lacked immediacy.[12]

This was not the case with *La Dame aux camélias*, which the *doyen* of French critics, Francisque Sarcey, named one of the era's three groundbreaking theatre pieces.[13] Alexandre Dumas *fils* had based his novel of 1849 on his own love affair with the celebrity demi-rep Marie Duplessis and, in reworking it for the stage, intensified the elements of self-sacrifice. Marguerite Gautier is both heroine and victim, nobly surrendering her own happiness for that of her lover, and nobly forgiving him as she succumbs to consumption exacerbated by disappointment. The line 'A woman's virginity belongs to her first love, not her first lover' stands as the motto of redemption.[14]

This did not impress the censor, whose first report (28 August 1851) described it as 'a picture in which the choice of characters and the crudeness of the coloring go beyond the furthest limit of theatrical toleration'.[15] It was not until the *bon viveur*, Morny, was appointed Minister of the Interior that it was licensed to be performed the following year. The play's success then and afterwards was due in part to the fact that Marguerite dies repentant and hence the social order is not disturbed; but, as Jules Janin noted, 'Respectable women want to know how other women live and die.'[16] The relationship of the stage to its society was patent: when Mme Doche created the leading role, the nobleman who kept her was sitting in the front rows. Moreover, her acting and that of her Armand, Charles Fechter, eschewed the histrionic for the familiar. The English journalist Edmund Yates recalled, 'when, [not yet twenty-one], I first saw it I was more moved than I ever had been by a theatrical performance [. . .]; and, again, such realistic acting, as exhibited both by man and woman, I had never seen. I can see Doche standing before the fireplace, *achevant la toilette de ses ongles*, and listening with delight to Armand's narration of his visit of inquiry during her illness . . .'.[17] The enduring power of the play also emanates from Marguerite being the embodiment of an ideal, an updated version of the romantic Fated Man, whose 'unrecognized merit show[s] itself superior to external circumstance'.[18] It similarly draws on the theme of the great worth to be found in *les misérables*, the despised and rejected, here enhanced by the theme of remorse. Dumas may shock but also reassures, another cause of the play's longevity.

Without intending to, Dumas created a fashion for plays featuring the lives of kept women.[19] A snatch of dialogue from Émile Augier's *Le Mariage d'Olympe* (1855), intended as a counterblast to Dumas, is telling:

MONTRICHARD.   To show you how far these fine ladies have gone in obtaining civil rights in public morals, the theatre is able to put them on stage!

MARQUIS.   What? Right on the stage? Women who . . . And the high-priced seats put up with it?

MONTRICHARD.   Quite well. [. . .] The craze [*turlutaine*] of our time is the rehabilitation of the lost woman or fallen woman, as they're called.[20]

Such women flocked to the theatre to see themselves portrayed in so favourable a light, and, according to one source, modelled their behaviour on the dramatic heroines. After *Dame aux camélias*, sex-workers insisted on cultivating a sincere romantic interest; 'Camélias' became the nickname for those who professed to be obsessed by an exclusive love. After Théodore Barrère's *Les Filles de marbre* (1853), they exasperated their suitors with their coldness; after Octave Feuillet's *Dalila* (1857) they wanted an artist for a lover; after Dumas *fils' Un Père prodigue* (1859), they saved their money and kept accounts.[21]

# A DIONYSIAN INTERLUDE

Pleasure and its organization come to the fore with the consolidation of the Second Empire in France. As it extends its power, material prosperity increases; stock companies are founded whose chief interest is speculation. Bourgeois society, more venturesome in its money-making and more secure in its income, aspires to imitate the court. It grows avid for pleasure and is harder to shock.

> *Sans la toilette*
> *Et le Plaisir*
> *Faut en convenir*
> *La vie est bête.*[22]

> [Without fashionable clothes/
> And Pleasure/
> You have to agree/
> Life is stupid.]

It parades its specialist knowledge of the theatre, inquires after the private lives of actors, displays a preference for fairy-tale pantomimes and musical entertainments over tragedy and literary drama. Napoleon III sponsors great exhibitions and diplomatic conferences with the deliberate intention of making Paris the centre of the world. One of Dumas's characters remarks on the elements that are eroding parochial narrow-mindedness and traditional morality: 'the invasion of foreign women, the glorification of courtesans, the daily arrival of exotic customs on all the railway lines coming to precipitate local degeneracies'.[23] This is the point at which Paris gains its reputation as the Mecca for pleasure-seekers. Or to quote the Offenbach operetta that celebrated the confluence to the Exposition Universelle of 1867:

> *Du plaisir à perdre haleine*
> *Oui, voilà la vie parisienne!*[24]

> [To pant with pleasure/
> Yes, that's life in Paris.]

Offenbach sounds the leitmotif of sensuality. His *opéras bouffes* undermine the prevailing value system by exalting the sway of gaiety over earnestness, carnal love over sentiment. The heroines of *Orphée aux enfers* (1858), *La belle Hélène* (1864), *La Grande Duchesse de Gérolstein* (1867) and *La Périchole* (1868) exemplify this new hedonism: they are women who glory in their sexuality and are glorified for it. A year before *Hélène* appeared, Baudelaire had insisted that the modern woman has a responsibility to make herself desirable: 'she even fulfills a kind of duty by taking pains to appear enchanting and supernatural; it is necessary that she astonishes, that she bewitches; an idol, she must begild herself in order to be worshipped'.[25] Offenbach's music suffused a bacchanalian spirit that released the inhibitions of a society eager to plunge into self-gratification *jusque-là* (as a Swedish tourist puts it in *La Vie parisienne* [1866]).

Offenbach's message was not only a lure for international visitors to Paris, but served as a cultural export of great power. The first Western performances to be seen in Egypt and Japan were of Offenbach operettas. August Strindberg claimed that it was *La belle Hélène* that first revealed to him the potential of his libido.[26] Anton Chekhov used Offenbach to undercut earnestness in his stories and Nietzsche praised him as the anti-Wagner.[27] One of his tunes became the US Marine anthem and another a rallying-cry for the International Workers of the World. A claim has been made that the carnival of Rio de Janeiro was democratized owing to Offenbach. His music crossed cultural boundaries so influentially that, next to Shakespeare, his was the most global theatrical presence of the period.

Although Offenbach proved as popular in Anglophone countries as elsewhere, there the conservative press railed against the shameless displays of the cancan and the general tenor of immorality, to no avail (see Figure 3.2). *The Times*, in advising 'all fastidious persons' to leave *Orphée aux enfers* after the third tableau were

*'ötter–Cancan*                                                                          *Gustave Doré*

FIGURE 3.2: The bacchanalian galop that concludes Offenbach's *Orphée aux enfers*, 1858. Engraving by Gustave Doré. Laurence Senelick Collection.

'perfectly aware that by this very device we are only recommending a large majority of the audience to remain in the theatre till the final descent of the curtain.'[28]

There too, the private lives of the performers were under a more censorious scrutiny. In June 1868 Hortense Schneider presented her greatest role, *La Grande Duchesse de Gérolstein,* in London, with phenomenal success. Figuring that the large portion of the public ignorant of French would appreciate a cheaper English version, an adaptation was slapped together for Mrs Howard Paul to play the lead. She proved to be an excellent *ersatz,* even copying the dresses of the original; but it was telling that 'the embroidery on the white satin petticoat in the second dress is not to be compared with the elaborate luxury of the Parisian *artiste*'.[29] Mrs Paul was a respectable married lady, dependent on the short commons of a London minor theatre; Schneider not only enjoyed an exorbitant salary, but benefited from the perquisites of a kept woman, so courted by royalty that she was known as *Le Passage des Princes*. It was a telling distinction between the English and the French stages.

To the censorious, sexual spectacle was endemic everywhere, and the equation of the stage to the whorehouse was equally prevalent. The actor Eduard Devrient complained of the 'Bordellismus' that prevailed in German commercial managements.[30] *The Theatrical Journal*, while congratulating William Macready on purifying Covent Garden and Drury Lane, condemned the other London playhouses as 'great public brothels . . . the very hot-beds of vice . . . houses of ill fame on a large scale'.[31] The manager of the Délassements Comiques told the Goncourt brothers that his theatre was a brothel, his actresses whores and his actors 'all pimps and fairies'.[32] (See Figure 3.3.)

In Paris, minor theatres sprang up with the sole purpose of displaying feminine pulchritude in rapidly carpentered *pièces à femmes*. Nevertheless, connoisseurs could tell the difference between the talented actress who bestowed her favours on the chosen few and the loose woman blatantly advertising her availability from a stage.

> What distinguishes in effect the prostitute from the actress, the student of a great procurer from the student of the Conservatoire, is that the prostitute, who knows admirably how to undress in front of a rich gentleman of the best society, is absolutely ignorant of the art of dressing to appear before theatre buffs. Whether she is an odalisque, a Neapolitan fisher girl, a Norman peasant, a gypsy, a Louis XV soubrette, she will never be able to look like anything but a jeweller's show-window, and those stupid female buccaneers of filthy and venal debauch display on the boards their diamond sprays and necklaces, their bracelets and their rings . . .[33]

When the notorious courtesan Cora Pearl appeared as Cupidon in *Orphée aux enfers* in 1867 the house was filled with titles and brilliants, clubmen

PLEASURES OF THE MATINEE—FLIRTATION BEFORE THE SCENES.          PLEASURES OF THE MATINEE—FLIRTATION BEHIND THE SCENES.

FIGURE 3.3: A woodcut commenting on theatrical opportunism. *New York Clipper,*
*c.*1870. Laurence Senelick Collection.

and high society. But her inept performance failed to attract beyond three
performances.[34]

The only spectacle to advertise itself as explicitly pornographic was the
*Théâtre érotique de la rue de Santé*, the Rabelaisian creation of a group of
Parisian writers and actors (1862–63). It was performed by puppets to an
invited audience.[35] However, new technologies which served to advance
publicity and advertising contributed to the stage's reputation for licentiousness.
At the beginning of the century, Edmund Kean's affair with an alderman's wife
or Chancellor Cambacérès's taste for an actor's well-rounded buttocks could be
pilloried by caricatures and 'secret chronicles'. By mid-century, the cheap press
and the 'American' innovation of the interview could bring the public more
directly into the boudoirs and dressing-rooms of stage favourites.

Photography, which was now capable of printing images on paper and
proliferating them widely, abetted the general public's confusion of actresses
with love for sale. One of the earliest books to be illustrated with photographs
was Jules Janin's study of the tragedienne Rachel, but it was rapidly followed by
a ghost-written biography of the high-kicking dancer Rigolboche (see Figure 3.4).

'Rigolbochomanie' was another manifestation of the prurient interest in the
female habituées of dance halls and opera balls, easily accosted and escorted.[36]
Pornographic pictures were available as stereographic cards, providing a three-
dimensional frisson, while the collecting of photographic *cartes de visite*

FIGURE 3.4: Rigolboche (Marguerite Badel), Paris, date unknown. Photography by Pierre Petit. Laurence Senelick Collection.

enabled men, like Zola's Maxime in *La Curée* (1871–72), to imagine their pockets peopled with personal harems. The display of the photographs of 'pretty horse breakers' next to those of attractive stage stars in shop windows shocked puritanical passersby and sowed confusion in the family album. These forms often boasted a realism unattainable in earlier modes of representation. Meanwhile, lithographic posters emblazoned garish physiques on walls, fences and the newly-invented Morris columns.[37]

Reputable theatres banned actual kissing, so acting manuals had to explain how to simulate it. Charlotte Cushman could be praised as the most effective Romeo on the English-language stage because, as a woman, she was allowed more physical contact with her Juliet than any male actor might be. What the censorious condemned as nudity was also a simulacrum: a flesh-coloured body suit, low-cut décolletage and the display of nether limbs otherwise hidden under crinolines. Female legs were fetishized. 'Legmania', acrobatic dancing with high kicks and splits, became a fad (see Figure 3.5).

The French *féerie*, the British pantomime and burlesque, grand and comic opera, all provided plentiful opportunities for women to show off their legs *en*

FIGURE 3.5: Alice la Provençale doing the splits. Paris, date unknown. Photography by Pierre Petit. Laurence Senelick Collection.

*travesti* as princes and peasants. Ballet skirts grew increasingly abbreviated (in part to avoid contact with incendiary footlights) until they dwindled into the tutu; the leotard, named for the famous trapezist, allowed the musculature of circus artistes to be on display. The English diarist, Henry Munby, assiduously attended gymnastic performances to observe shapely female forms.[38] The so-called 'Naked Lady', Adah Isaacs Menken, replied to charges of obscenity by saying that her undraped poses were in good taste because they were based on sculpture, especially the works of Canova.[39] A similar justification was offered by the *tableaux vivants*, in which immobility and a coating of chalk could excuse more blatant nakedness. Largely female troupes, such as Lydia Thompson's British Blondes, in the new genre of burlesque, performed 'Amazon marches' in stockinette tights and a regimented exhibition of the body.[40]

## 'OH, WHAT A FALL WAS THERE!'

It was to combat these conventions – cross-dressing, female exhibitionism, racy innuendo and equivocal situations; in short, to provide a decorous alternative to Offenbach and burlesque – that the comic operas of Gilbert and Sullivan were devised. The immediate and immense popularity of the Savoy operas, as they came to be called, was a symptom of a rearguard action among the *bien-pensant*, troubled by the ubiquity of sex on stage. The Austro-Hungarian ambassador to the court of Napoleon III, Prince Richard von Metternich, wrote back home after escorting his wife to the opening night of *La belle Hélène*: 'We were wrong to attend the premiere. Our name will appear in all the newspapers, and it is not pleasant for a woman as it were officially to have been at such a play.'[41] The defeat of Napoleon III in the Franco-Prussian War produced a counterblast of moral rectitude; German thinkers, Wagner at the fore, attributed the debacle squarely to the Second Empire's alleged frivolity, corruption and decadence. Its art and music were condemned as emanations of its licentiousness. Even the historical paintings of Gérôme, such as *Phryne Before the Tribunal*, were attacked as pornographic lampoons, antiquity seen through the lens of Offenbach.[42] The theatre had to help redress the balance, and since the central concern of the stage was woman, her representation underwent a radical transformation.

At a time when respectable women preferred to attend the theatre in private boxes, *le haut du pavé* (the upper-crust of the streets) grew conspicuous throughout the audience, especially at premieres.[43] As the courtesan, euphemized as a 'soiled dove', emerges from the shadow of ignominy into the limelight of celebrity, the fear of contamination, both of class and of hygiene, grows. It is bad enough that she has colonized public spaces. What if she were to infiltrate the domestic hearth? Augier's *Le Mariage d'Olympe* puts just such a case, and the social order is set to rights only when her father-in-law, an elderly marquis, shoots the interloper. The double standard, which insists that a young man gain sexual experience before entering into marriage with an immaculate maiden, ran the danger of polluting the union with venereal disease. This common situation could barely be touched on in drama; hence the opprobrium visited on Ibsen's *Ghosts* (*Gengaengere*, 1881). Two decades later even so didactic a homily as Brieux's *Damaged Goods* (*Les Avariés*, 1901) had to be performed privately.[44]

The courtesan was a creature of the gutter; the only way she could go was up. The fallen woman, however, usually descended from a reputable position as a wife and mother or, worse yet, fiancée. The nineteenth-century dramatic obsession with adultery battens on this character and its variations. In late Romantic historic plays, the emphasis is on purity: when virgins are under attack, they either have to die to remain unsullied, as in Sheridan Knowles's *Virginius* (1820), or have an ecclesiastical ban invoked to protect them, as in Bulwer Lytton's *Richelieu* (1839). By the second half of the century, the commonplace is the young woman falsely accused, cursed, cast out, and eventually rehabilitated, as in Dion Boucicault's *Flying Scud* (1866), Steele Mackaye's *Hazel Kirke* (1880), or Lottie Blair Parker's '*Way Down East* (1897).[45]

The most recurrent avatar, however, is the errant wife and she appears most often in the *pièce à these* or problem play. Its leading themes are not only the porosity of social castes, with *louche* women defiling upright families, but also respectable women tempted to go astray. The prototype can be seen in Kotzebue's *Menschenhass und Reue* (1789), known on the English-speaking stage as *The Stranger*. Here both partners are at fault and the erring wife is offered a hearing and a second chance. There is something refreshingly adult about Kotzebue's awareness that there are two sides to infidelity.

In the *pièce à thèse*, however, even when husbands are shown to be tyrants and parents to be obtuse, there is no fundamental challenge to the social infrastructure and its code of morality. Just as unmarried girls are supposed to be ignorant of the facts of life, so a proper married woman is supposed to be devoid of sexual desire or sensation. In 1858, when Augier had presented a kept married woman in *Les Lionnes pauvres*, the censorship waxed indignant: 'This woman is *not even punished*. We think it would be indecorous for the dignity of marriage and the tranquility of hearth and home to strip this wound naked in this way before the public.'[46] A decade later, Augier and Dumas *fils*, pluming themselves as reformers, marched in step with this opinion. In their later plays and those of their contemporaries, women who committed a single fault for love (or were raped) had to make up for it by blind and self-sacrificial devotion to their children (even if illegitimate) and renunciation of personal happiness. The rare exception, to quote the Canadian novelist Robertson Davies, 'may be redeemed by a good man's love, rather as in our time a member of the Humane Society scrapes the heavy oil from the plumage of a seagull; of course, it remains a dirty bird, unless it has the good grace to die . . .'[47] Dumas *fils* may give the impression of being subversive but he isn't: when he attacks marital rights and upper-class morals in *Diane de Lys* (1856), the death of the lover restores social equilibrium. The trigger for an unhappy marriage and the subsequent adultery is often a traumatic wedding night, but that is no excuse: the 'little spasmodic act' is equated with prostitution. 'A man loves only a woman he can respect and he never respects a woman who can give herself to him only by sharing herself.'[48]

That melodramatic warhorse, *East Lynne*, dramatized innumerable times from Mrs Henry Wood's novel (1861), appears to be the *locus classicus* in English. Lady Isabel leaves her husband for a cad, owing to a misunderstanding; thought first to be outside the pale of society and then dead, she comes back disguised in a white wig and blue spectacles as governess to her dying son. She too expires, forgiven by her husband, and, in some productions, she and her child are enthroned on a golden cloud. More daring is *Froufrou* (1869) by Offenbach's librettists Meilhac and Halévy, in which a wife is treated as a plaything; when she perceives that her husband prefers her sister, she runs away with her lover. He proves disloyal, so she returns home repentant to die, forgiven. This is *La Dame aux camélias* transferred to the domestic sphere, and the leading role of Gabrielle attracted many of the same actresses who assumed Marguerite. As late as 1902, a critic could pronounce that it was 'even now among the living plays of the present century'.[49] The startling novelty of Ibsen's *A Doll House* can be fully understood only when seen against the popularity of *Froufrou*.

One further variation on the fallen woman was launched by Dumas *fils*: the woman with a past. *Le Demi-monde* (1855), which centres on a noblewoman revealed to be a former courtesan, invented a new word for a new phenomenon, 'the class of the déclassé'; this included young women who had made a misstep, women who lived in morganatic marriages, elegant foreigners of obscure background and women who supported their lovers (his 1873 play *Monsieur Alphonse* may be said to have introduced the gigolo as a type).

By the time he wrote the sententious prefaces to his collected plays in the 1870s, Dumas was in full cry: prostitution is universal, society women compete with whores, young men are turning to homosexuality, Jews are too influential – all reasons for France's defeat. In his later plays, the woman with a past is transformed into an adventuress; in *L'Affaire Clemenceau* (1866) Iza's 'immodesty, ingratitude, sensuality, demoralization' are said to be instinctual. Such *femmes fatales* are presented as monsters, 'savage natures' (*l'Étrangère*, 1873) and husbands are well within their rights to kill them, most conveniently with the newly-invented pocket pistol.

A revival of *La Dame aux camélias* in 1873 evoked the condemnation that 'The stain of mud on the brow of the courtesan is indelible, like the stain of blood on the key in the fairy tale.'[50] The first English staging of Verdi's operatic treatment *La Traviata* had to be set in 1700 to suit the censor. However, in this new climate, Marguerite Gautier lost a good deal of her professional identity and thus her shock value. As the play persisted in repertoires, its leading role too tempting for actresses to forgo, a good deal of its sensationalism was eradicated or toned down. In antebellum America, as *Camille, or The Fate of a Coquette* (1856), Matilda Heron made a career of the part by downplaying the source of her heroine's livelihood. This Marguerite is deeply remorseful, her profession not of her choosing. A numinous spell is woven, an aura of saintliness not to be dispelled by mercenary considerations. The lost lady transfigured by suffering supplants the whore with the heart of gold and lungs of tissue paper. The Lord Chamberlain's office finally granted a license to an English version of *La Dame* in 1875. The result, James Mortimer's *Heartsease*, its heroine now an actress, was so anodyne that the *Daily Telegraph* compared it to a patent stain remover that 'sacrific[es] the colour and texture of all material subjected to the treatment'.[51] When Sarah Bernhardt appeared as Marguerite before Queen Victoria in 1881, she was told 'You play the part with modesty, and no one can complain.'[52]

The same year that *Heartsease* diluted *La Dame* to the point of dramatic anaemia, Wilkie Collins sought to refresh the theme of the prostitute redeemed in *The New Magdalen*; kind-hearted Mercy Merrick, street-walker turned nurse, strives for respectability but is constantly thwarted. After stealing an identity, attempting to marry an upright young man and letting his former fiancée be committed to a madhouse, she makes a full confession. As reward, a broad-minded clergyman proclaims her 'the noblest of Heaven's creatures' and offers her marriage and a fresh start in the new world.[53] This was too much for the conservative press which excoriated Collins's 'special pleading' and found it 'opposed to all one's sense of justice and moral right'. The English stage could still not square its moral righteousness with what seemed to be an over-generous dose of forgiveness.[54]

By 1890, Jules Janin stated that the boundary between *le monde* (good society) and *le demi-monde* had been effaced.[55] This did not, however, prevent the types of the adventuress, the woman with a past and the *femme fatale* from proliferating, since they provided ambitious actresses with juicy roles and dramatists with a convenient plot device. Although Oscar Wilde's Mrs Erlynne (*Lady Windermere's Fan*, 1892) or Pinero's *Second Mrs Tanqueray* (1893) may come to mind, the most significant instance is Hermann Sudermann's Magda in *Heimat* (1893), 'played in almost all the languages of modern Europe'.[56] Here the tables are turned: the erring and outcast daughter returns home as a famous opera singer, refuses a marriage offer from the man who 'ruined her' because he will not acknowledge their bastard son, and confronts her pistol-wielding father, who dies of apoplexy when he hears she may have had more than one lover. The role of Magda was irresistible to the usual suspects: Bernhardt, Duse, Modjeska and the other divas of the drama, and no wonder. The fallen woman has risen by her own efforts and rejects the social norms that rejected her. She has become a type of the New Woman.[57]

## SOCIAL CLIMBING

In the latter half of the nineteenth century the so-called legitimate theatre raised admission prices and imposed rigid dress codes on the audience. A certain levelling could be seen in the architecture of new theatres: private boxes were reduced in number and the gallery removed. The intention was to provide entertainment for a growing and prosperous middle class and eliminate those elements which might put it off. Staid husband-and-wife teams began to run some theatres in England, and managers insisted on proper behaviour in their companies. In some cases, actresses' salaries were raised from £5 to £10 to £60 a week, often with payment for their dresses.[58] Under those conditions, they no longer needed to be kept (although underpaid chorines and ballet girls might be, and stars found it advantageous publicity to have liaisons with prominent men). As the acting profession was made more attractive to middle-class aspirants, *Punch* ran cartoons about scions of the nobility elbowing out veteran stagers. In actuality, they were more likely to marry well-bred stars of variety and musical comedy.

The managerial measures to ensure respectability tended to exclude the working class from the legitimate theatre. Eating, drinking, smoking and the presence of women soliciting clients were still allowed in the preferred plebeian forms of variety entertainment, based on song and specialty acts. While the problem play was exploring such burning issues as the double standard, divorce and female emancipation in an increasingly serious fashion, popular amusements revelled in saucy jokes, bawdy byplay and gender switching. In their earliest European guises, their stages presented a semicircle of attractive women sitting along the back, *la corbeille* or flower-basket; their only function was to be decorative wallpaper, on display as if in a brothel showroom. In provincial small towns throughout Europe, young women who accepted contracts to appear in music halls found that they were obliged to drink and sleep with the clientele, and their salaries were withheld to prevent their escape. This became known as *la traite des chanteuses* or white slavery of singers.[59]

The pioneering German sexologist, Iwan Bloch, reported the appeal of such salacious amusements to the modern *homme moyen sensuel*:

> What he wants is the satisfaction of his desire for sensations by the appearance of more or less décolleté singers, dancers, acrobats, male and female, by the representation of tableaux vivants, in which the parts are played by beautiful women, by the kinematography, or by pantomime, by spicy songs, by the performance of clever jugglers by wrestling and boxing matches between men and women, and all kinds of spectacles, etc.

Bloch attributed the public's attraction to such places to 'the monotony, the emptiness of their life'.[60] The grey routine of the urban everyday required the gaudy contrast of carnal spectacle.

The performing arts have always been a haven for sexual minorities. Within the theatrical profession, a large number of performers, designers and stage managers were reputed to be unorthodox in their proclivities. Havelock Ellis noted that the 'passionate friendships among girls [. . .] are extremely common in theater, both among actresses and, ever more, among chorus – and ballet – girls'.[61] (See Figure 3.6.)

While the rumours of lesbian relations that assailed Rachel and Bernhardt were meant to be defamatory, some female stars, among them Charlotte Cushman, Clara Ziegler and Felicita von Vestali, made no effort to conceal their intimacy with other women. Certain operations, such as Berlin's Nationaltheater and Viktoriatheater and the illustrious troupe of the Duke of

FIGURE 3.6: Blanche Williams and Lizzie Kelsey, dancers in the extravaganza *The Black Crook*, *c*.1872. Photography by London Stereoscopic and Photographic Co. Laurence Senelick Collection.

Saxe-Meiningen, were known to be staffed by 'same-sexualists' and, as such, attracted like-minded patrons and audiences.[62] In London, 'Margeries' and 'Pooffs' were reported to haunt the gallery of the Empire Theatre of Varieties, the Pavilion Theatre, and the bar of the St James Theatre. Indignant managers occasionally felt obliged to expel the more blatant 'sodomites'.

Variety's new genre of 'impersonation' allowed members of homosexual subcultures to indulge in glamorous cross-dressing with impunity. The American male impersonator Annie Hindle, performing as a fast man about town, received more fan mail than the matinee idol Harry Montague. When two male tarts, Ernest Boulton and Frederick Park, were tried for sexual solicitation in 'drag' (another neologism) in London arcades and theatres, they were acquitted, having pled to being merely amateur actors advertising their prowess.[63] Cross-dressing was the rule in scholastic, military and salon dramatic societies, and therefore considered innocuous within the proper context.[64]

However, as they grew increasingly commercialized, industrialized and even internationalized, these popular entertainments were also bowdlerized. A changing nomenclature reveals the evolution: in France, the down-market *beuglant* is upgraded to the *café chantant* which moves indoors as the *café concert* and is next glamorized with an English loan-word as *le music-hall*. In the United Kingdom, song-and-supper rooms and the tavern concert become music halls which in turn become Palaces of Variety. In Germany, the brothel-like *Tingel-Tangel* evolves into the circus-like *Variété*; in the United States, concert saloons and variety shows are repackaged as vaudeville, even 'polite or refined vaudeville'. Managements aspire to 'family friendly' status: in New York, Tony Pastor instituted matinees for housewives at which he gave away bags of flour. Contracts contained clauses and house managers posted notices backstage to the effect that 'a high plane of respectability and moral cleanliness' was to be maintained. 'Your act must be free from all vulgarity and suggestiveness in words, action, and costume . . .' (see Figure 3.7). One lady told a journalist, 'They [the vaudeville theatres] are the only theatres in New York where I should feel absolutely safe in taking a young girl without making preliminary inquiries. Though they may offend the taste, they never offend one's sense of decency.'[65]

In England, county councils withheld licenses from music halls against which complaints of indecency had been lodged, and in 1895 a purity campaign forced management, if not to ban high-class prostitutes from the Empire promenade, then to put up screens to hide them from the general view.[66] More broad-minded critics regarded such moves as insidious by making the overt covert. 'The broad Smollett jest has shrivelled to the sideways leer', one commentator lamented. 'Innuendoes – there will always be innuendoes as long as man is man – are indecently veiled. You no longer shriek at them. You snigger.'[67]

THE BALLET OF THE BAGS
We Hope this Suggestion will Mollify the Clerical Opponents of the National Opera Company's Ballet

FIGURE 3.7: The Ballet of the Bags. 'We Hope this Suggestion will Mollify the Clerical Opponents of the National Opera Company's Ballet'. Caricature by A. B. Shults, *Puck*, New York, 15 December 1886. Courtesy Laurence Senelick Collection.

The same theatre histories that promote the progressive picture of the nineteenth-century stage choose to portray the *fin de siècle* as a period of breakthroughs in the dramatic treatment of sex: the Théâtre Libre offers candid glimpses at the squalid lives of street-walkers and pimps; Strindberg introduces the first stage lesbian in *Comrades (Kamraterna*, 1888) and the first allusions to menstruation and off-stage coition in *Miss Julie (Fröken Julie,* 1888); Shaw discusses the economics of white slavery in *Mrs Warren's Profession* (1893, produced 1902); Wedekind constructs tragedies out of confused puberty and sexual obsession. These are, nevertheless, the exceptions, often resisted or suppressed.[68] For every forward-looking drama that champions the New Woman and universal suffrage there is a decadent or sensational one that reprograms the *femme fatale* as man-eating vampire. Sex in the theatre remains largely a matter of voyeurism and hint-hint-nudge-nudge. Antoine reneges on producing Gabriel Mourey's drama of Sapphic passion *Lawn-tennis* (1891)[69] at a time when Colette and her lover, the Marquise de Belboeuf, in male drag are playing a suggestive sketch on the cabaret stage. As the century turns the most popular revue act is a striptease 'The Bride Goes to Bed'; the most popular gender-bending takes place in the anodyne comedy *Charley's Aunt*; the most popular box-office hits are bedroom farces in which adultery is skirted but seldom achieved. It will take the Great War to eradicate many of the persistent moral attitudes of the previous generation and allow more open treatment of hitherto taboo subjects. Even then, most of the familiar tropes and types of the nineteenth-century stage will be transferred to the cinema unchanged, as if the sensibility of the spectator had been arrested in 1852 when Marguerite Gautier expired in an odour of sanctity.

# CHAPTER FOUR

# The Environment of Theatre

TOBIAS BECKER

That space is an essential component of theatre seems obvious. As early as 1931, Max Herrmann, the founding father of Theatre Studies, declared that 'theatrical art' is a 'spatial art'.[1] Over time this has become a truism. As Marvin Carlson observes in *Places of Performance*: 'The way an audience experiences and interprets a play, we now recognize, is by no means governed solely by what happens on the stage. The entire theatre, its audience arrangements, its other public spaces, its physical appearance, even its location within a city, are all important elements of the process by which an audience makes meaning of its experience.'[2] Jen Harvie, too, insists: 'Where a theatre is located directly affects what it means.'[3]

However, the location of a theatre – whether in a capital or a provincial city, in the city centre or on its fringe – does not only affect the meaning of its performances but every aspect of its work: the composition of its audiences; the quality of its ensemble; the plays it performs; and how it performs them. Of course, the relationship between theatre and space is at its most interesting where there are many theatres and conflicting spaces. In the nineteenth century only major cities like London, Paris, Vienna, Berlin and New York had a large enough theatre-going public to sustain a diverse landscape of playhouses. All of these cities witnessed a rapid expansion of their populations during the course of the nineteenth century. London, then as now the biggest European city, already had a million inhabitants in 1800, and its population grew to 2.6 million in 1850 and 6.5 million by 1900. The population of Paris increased from half a million in 1800 to a million in 1850 and 2.7 million in 1900. In the same span of time, Vienna grew from a quarter of a million inhabitants in 1800 to nearly half a million in 1850 and 1.6 million in 1900. However, the fastest growing European city was without a doubt Berlin. From 172,000 in 1800 it grew to 419,000 in 1850 and 1.8 million in 1900.[4]

All of these cities were imperial cities if imperial city means 'a political command center, a collection point for information, an economically parasitic beneficiary of asymmetrical relations with its various peripheries, and a showplace for emblems of the dominant ideology'.[5] Not all of them ruled over vast colonial territories as London did as seat of the British government, financial hub and port city. However, all of them claimed to be imperial cities in the sense that they were capitals of empires: Paris of the French Empire, after Napoleon crowned himself Emperor of the French in 1804, Vienna of the Austro-Hungarian Empire and Berlin of the German Empire after 1871.

The imperial character of these cities was also visible in cityscapes and architecture – if least so in London. Though it was the first city 'to embark on a comprehensive program of reconstruction and embellishment', city planning soon ground to a halt.[6] The 'center of the only world empire of the age [. . .] remained the ugly duckling of Europe's metropolises, always looking poorer than it really was'.[7] Large-scale projects like the construction of railways and termini or the Thames embankment were driven by practical reasons – economy,

FIGURE 4.1: Façade of the Opéra Garnier, Paris, *c.*1880. TWS G 00/335/1DR. Theaterwissenschaftliche Sammlung, University of Cologne.

transport, hygiene and so on – rather than political or aesthetic ones. The transformation of an entire city required a despot with almost unlimited power and this was exactly what happened in Paris in the 1850s under Napoleon III, when large parts of the medieval city were demolished. With its magnificent boulevards and grandiose architecture, Paris became the model all other cities aspired to. Following its example, Vienna demolished the city walls around its old city centre in the second half of the nineteenth century and replaced them with the Ringstraße, a circular road on which the parliament, the town hall, the university and other important institutions were located.[8] In Berlin, a city famously characterized by industry and long stretches of tenement blocks (*Mietskasernen*), town planning was largely confined to laying out long, straight avenues. But even Berlin had a representative boulevard in Unter den Linden, which stretched from the Brandenburg Gate to Alexanderplatz and along which two palaces, a number of military buildings, the university, the Royal Theatre and the Royal Opera House were located.

New York was not an imperial city in any sense of the word; it was not even a capital. However, in 1898 its five boroughs were consolidated into a single city, making New York the second most populous city in the world (after London). As a major port city it was connected to every part of the globe. In terms of theatre, it was during the latter part of the period that New York began to free itself from Europe's cultural influence. It continued to welcome actors, ensembles and plays from Europe, but the cultural transfer across the Atlantic ceased to be a one-way street and the theatre in New York underwent much the same changes as in Europe.

Therefore, I will mainly focus on London, Paris, Berlin, Vienna and New York, and ask where theatres were located, how they were shaped by their environment and how they in turn shaped their environment. I will be starting off by looking at the theatres in their relation to one another and then examine other entertainment venues and businesses in their vicinity before examining how spatial proximity fostered contacts. Far from being isolated islands, theatres were connected with surrounding institutions and industries, all together constituting the entertainment district, perhaps one of the most diverse and hardest to pin down of all urban spaces.

## THEATRE DISTRICTS

As a rule, theatres are usually located in the city centre so that they are easily accessible from all parts of the city. In the eighteenth century, playhouses often fulfilled an official function. They were either court theatres and as such funded by the monarch, catering primarily to the court and aristocratic society – as in Paris, Vienna and Berlin – or they were at least dependent on a royal patent, as in London. They were either to be found in a central location like Drury Lane and Covent Garden in London or close to the royal palace like the Comédie Française in Paris (which was housed in the Tuileries Palace till 1799, when it was moved to the Palais Royal), the Burgtheater in Vienna and the Royal Theatre and the Royal Opera in Berlin at the Gendarmenmarkt.

Especially during the first half of the nineteenth century, authorities everywhere were reluctant to allow new theatres to open, partly because they wanted to protect the monopoly of the court theatres, but also because the theatre was seen as a potential threat to social and political stability. If new playhouses were built during this time, it was often outside the immediate town centre, in the suburbs. Indeed it was in such locations that a bourgeois, middle-class theatre tradition was born.

In addition to its suburban theatres, Paris also had a number of theatres along the Boulevard du Temple, which ran from the Place de la République to the Place Pasdeloup. This location gave the genre its name: 'boulevard theatre'. In 1807 Napoleon reduced the number of theatres in Paris to eight, divided into four *Grands théâtres* (Théâtre Français, Théâtre de l'Impératrice, Théâtre de l'Opéra, Théâtre de l'Opéra-Comique), which performed tragedies, comedies and opera, and four *Théâtres secondaires* (Théâtre du Vaudeville, Théâtre des Variétés, Théâtre de la Porte Saint-Martin and Théâtre de la Gaîté), which performed more lowbrow fare.[9]

In London, the Licensing Act of 1737 had been intended to suppress all theatrical performance outside of Drury Lane and Covent Garden. However,

FIGURE 4.2: Théâtre du Vaudeville, Paris, second building (1840–69). Postcard. Theaterwissenschaftliche Sammlung, University of Cologne.

magistrates increasingly licensed venues for music and dancing (encompassed by new genres such as burletta and melodrama) after 1800. So popular was this fare that the 'minor theatres' soon challenged the supremacy of the patent theatres. When the patentees' monopoly was finally abolished by the Theatres Act in 1843, there were about two dozen minor theatres in London, many of them outside the city's centre.[10]

Vienna enjoyed the most liberal theatre laws thanks to a 1776 edict by Joseph II, following which three suburban theatres – modelled on the example of the Parisian boulevard theatres – were built: the Theater in der Leopoldstadt in 1781; the Wiedner Theater 1787 (renamed Theater an der Wien in 1801); and the Theater in der Josefstadt in 1788. These theatres primarily catered to local neighbourhoods, but also attracted playgoers from across town.[11]

In Berlin, the first bourgeois theatre, the Königsstädtisches Theater, was located on Alexanderplatz, in the eastern part of the city. But even it owed its existence largely to Frederick William III, who had developed a liking for the Parisian boulevard theatre, the model for the new venue. From the 1840s onwards, beer gardens outside the city tried to attract visitors by offering theatrical performances on makeshift wooden stages. Some of these summer theatres, as they were called, were later supplanted by purpose-built playhouses. As the city grew and the former suburbs became part of central Berlin, the theatres suddenly occupied a central location.[12]

The success of the suburban theatre proves that there was a wider audience eager for theatrical entertainment, as well as entrepreneurs willing to enter the business. However, the authorities kept the growth of the theatre business in check and prevented it from spreading to the centre. When the overall political climate became more liberal in the second half of the nineteenth century, official attitudes towards the theatre changed. Throughout Europe, the authorities increasingly abandoned the old, restrictive system in favour of a more lenient one. In 1843 the Theatres Act abolished the monopoly of Drury Lane and Covent Garden, in 1864 Napoleon III lifted the last restrictions on the theatre and in 1869 Prussia introduced a new, liberal industrial code under which the theatre was included.[13] Opening and running a theatre still required a licence, but it could now be obtained much more easily. What remained – other than in France – in most countries was the censorship of plays, the severity of which differed from country to country, and sometimes even from city to city.[14] In general, however, the development of the theatre depended far more on economic factors as opposed to the goodwill of the authorities. With the former restrictions gone, theatre became primarily a business.

Though the theatre sector grew everywhere, nowhere did it grow as quickly as in London, Berlin and New York. The theatres now being built were no longer located in the suburbs but in the city centre. This led to the development of entire streets and districts devoted to theatrical entertainment. One of the first proper theatre districts, the Boulevard du Temple in Paris, was home to seven theatres in the first half of the nineteenth century. Though the boulevard theatres attracted a heterogeneous public, audiences became more and more working class as one moved from west to east. During the redevelopment of Paris under Napoleon III, all buildings along the boulevard were pulled down. After that Paris did not have a theatre district in the strict sense. However, most of the city's theatres were located in its centre, along the ring of boulevards between the ninth and tenth arrondissement in the north and the second arrondissement in the south.[15]

In the last quarter of the nineteenth century, the West End emerged as London's central theatre district, or 'Theatre-Land', as it now began to be called.[16] Up to that point, there had been roughly as many theatres in the eastern as in the western part of the city. Now the balance tipped in favour of the West End. While hardly a single new theatre was built in the east of London, twenty-five playhouses were erected in the area around Leicester Square, along Shaftesbury Avenue, Charing Cross Road and the Strand.[17] At the same time, many theatres in the East End were either converted into music halls or pulled down. In 1907, the brothers Walter and Frederick Melville, whose melodramas had been extremely popular with working-class audiences in east London, sold their theatre to a music hall trust and relocated their business to the West End, where they took over the Lyceum Theatre.[18]

In Berlin, the liberalization of the theatre law was followed by a building boom in theatres, most of which were located along Friedrichstraße, one of Berlin's major thoroughfares which led from the southernmost part of the city to its far north. Close to where Friedrichstraße crossed Leipziger Straße, famous for its sumptuous department store, stood the Metropol-Theater, one of Berlin's most beautiful theatres at the time. It was also one of the most successful theatres, staging spectacular revues and operettas. A particular centre of theatrical life was the district immediately north of the Weidendammer Bridge, where Friedrichstraße crosses the river Spree. Here the Komische Oper, the Circus Renz – later converted by Max Reinhardt into a massive theatre seating an audience of 5,000 – the Deutsches Theater and four other theatres were to be found. The exact number of theatres changed from year to year as directors successively declared bankruptcy and playhouses were demolished, renovated or turned into music halls (or the other way round). However, in 1900 there were about a dozen playhouses located on Friedrichstraße and its surrounding streets, not counting variety theatres and cabarets. And although a new theatre district arose in Berlin's fashionable western half, in the vicinity of Kurfürstendamm and Tautenzienstraße, Friedrichstraße would remain Berlin's foremost theatre district well into the Second World War.[19]

The rise of New York's Broadway took place almost simultaneously with that of the West End and Friedrichstraße in the second half of the nineteenth century. When the American Theatre was built on Eighth Avenue and 41st Street in 1893, Broadway was largely a residential district and Times Square was still known as Longacre Square. The theatres were spread along twenty-five blocks of streets north of Union Square. During the next quarter century, however, theatres were built at a staggering rate. In the 1890s Broadway was established as New York's theatrical thoroughfare with more than twenty-five theatres added to the existing ones in less than twenty-five years.[20]

The growth of the theatre industry in nineteenth century cities was driven by the growth of the urban population. As London, Berlin and New York grew faster than Paris and Vienna, it was little wonder that the number of theatres did as well. More people meant larger potential audiences. The centralization of new theatres in specific streets and districts was partly due to increasing land prices. As a result, the residential population as well as industries that required a lot of space moved to the outskirts. What remained in the city centre were the service industries – banks, insurance companies, department stores and the entertainment industry. As it was not uncommon for a street to be dominated by one industry – finance, retail, fashion and so on, the concentration of theatres along Shaftesbury Avenue and Charing Cross Road in London, Friedrichstraße in Berlin and Broadway in New York was hardly extraordinary, but rather part of a general process of spatial concentration that could be observed in many cities.

As a rule, theatres in the theatre districts catered to more diverse and heterogenous audiences, among them many visitors from the provinces and foreign countries. Suburban theatres – for example, the theatres in the east of London or Berlin – were primarily frequented by people living in the neighbourhood. Their audiences consequently tended to be more homogeneous. But there were exceptions, of course. In Berlin, social democratic theatre clubs rented the Metropol on Sundays to perform plays for working-class audiences and in Paris the music hall Moulin Rouge was frequented by many bourgeois men, who came here to cast off the shackles of bourgeois respectability.[21]

The repertoire also varied according to where a theatre was located. Provincial and suburban theatres necessarily needed to mobilize the same limited number of theatregoers over and over again and thus presented an extremely varied repertoire that included tragedies, comedies, classics, melodramas, musical plays and sometimes even variety. Centrally located theatres in big cities were highly specialized, often concentrating on a single genre and performing a play as often as possible. Once a theatre had had success with a certain fare it stuck with the winning formula. In this way the Savoy Theatre in London became associated with the comic operas of Gilbert and Sullivan, the Gaiety Theatre with musical comedy, the Folies-Bergère in Paris and the Metropol-Theater in Berlin with revue. Other theatres concentrated on opera, operetta or melodrama.

Theatre was an expensive and risky business. All theatres in the theatre district invested huge sums in their productions to attract audiences. To reap such investments, they had to keep a production in the repertoire for as long as possible. Therefore, it was not uncommon for a successful play to be performed over 600, 700 or sometimes even over 1,000 times prior to the First World War. The largest part of these costs were, of course, spent on personnel. Big theatres could employ a staff of over a hundred people, especially if they were performing musical plays, which required an orchestra and dancers. However, this was nothing compared to what they paid stars, who drew in huge audiences.

Given these expenditures, attracting large audiences was therefore imperative. It can come as no surprise, then, that theatres were built along busy thoroughfares such as Shaftesbury Avenue, Friedrichstraße and Broadway. This made them easily accessible and allowed them to attract passing customers. A good connection to means of transport was vital for the theatre industry. The West End, for instance, became London's theatre-land only after Charing Cross Station had opened in 1864. Theatre managers were well aware of the importance of public transport. As John Hollingshead noted in 1866, 'provincial people come up to town, and fresh audiences are created every night'.[22] Friedrichstraße was served by the Potsdamer and Anhalter station to the south, by the Stettiner and Hamburger stations to the north and, most importantly, by Friedrichstraße station, which opened in 1883 and which was the most centrally located train station in Berlin. Broadway profited from its vicinity to Grand Central Terminal and Pennsylvania Station and also by the introduction of streetcars.[23]

Equally important to the railway were improvements to urban public transport, especially the building of subway and tram lines, which allowed people living in the suburbs to come to town to see a show and return home after its end. As early as 1892, George Edwardes, manager of the Gaiety Theatre in London, counted the 'suburban ladies' among his most reliable and important customers.[24] The Melvilles' decision to relocate to the West End was most likely facilitated by the hope to find new audiences while their former customers could follow them to the West End using the Underground. The London Underground indirectly promoted the theatre on posters with advertising slogans like 'Where it is never dull', 'To Central London for shops and theatres', or 'By tram in comfort to the theatres'.[25] A central location may have promised large audiences, but what it guaranteed was astronomical rents, which made it – again – all the more necessary to play to full houses for as long as possible. Though potentially extremely profitable, managing a theatre in the theatre district was extremely risky as the many bankruptcies and often rapidly changing managements testify.

FIGURE 4.3: Sketch of a theatre including a tram station, Berlin 1898. August Scherl. Theaterwissenschaftliche Sammlung, University of Cologne.

## ENTERTAINMENT DISTRICTS

Of course theatre districts were never only about theatre. Rather, theatres were built in the hope that they would benefit from the service industries already located in the neighbourhood. Most theatre districts, for instance, were also hotel districts. Having arrived by train, travellers from the provinces and abroad were well-served by an abundance of hotels, ranging from cheap boarding houses to famous grand hotels. Among many others, London boasted the Savoy Hotel at the Strand, Britain's first luxury hotel; New York the Clarendon Hotel on Union Square, favoured by the British aristocracy, and, later, the Astor Hotel on Times Square; and Berlin the Adlon on Unter den Linden.[26]

Theatres and hotels were often neighbours and sometimes even directly connected. Both the Gaiety Theatre in London and the Metropol-Theater in Berlin were attached to hotels next door, and the Savoy Theatre in London was part of the same building complex as the Savoy Hotel: one premiered Gilbert and Sullivan's new comic operas, the other electric lighting, lifts and en-suite bathrooms.[27] An important urban space in its own right, the hotel – especially when it deemed itself 'grand' – was more than just a place to sleep; it was a meeting point and a turnstile, guiding its customers to the nearby spaces of entertainment and, finally, a stage on which urban life was performed. Unsurprisingly, the hotel was a favourite setting for many novels and plays in the 1900s.

From hotels people moved on to nearby restaurants, with which entertainment districts were amply supplied. As a contemporary source stated, 'each evening some thousands of dinners are laid on West-end restaurant tables'.[28] A French traveller in Berlin estimated that in 250 buildings along Friedrichstraße there were more than 250 eating places, restaurants, inns and delicatessen shops.[29] A

similar assessment can be made for Broadway.[30] Many theatres, like the Gaiety
Theatre in London, the Casino Theatre in New York or the Metropol-Theater
in Berlin, had their own restaurants, and the latter even featured tables in the
auditorium, allowing theatregoers to drink, eat and smoke while watching a
show.[31] This made it look more like a music hall than a theatre where food and
drink were usually prohibited.

More surprising than theatre's links to hotels and restaurants might be those
to department stores. The department store, which offered a wide range of
products from clothes to furniture and services, was an invention of the
nineteenth century. One of the first was the famous Le Bon Marché in Paris,
whose iron frame and glass-covered roof was engineered by Gustave Eiffel and
which served as the protagonist of Émile Zola's novel *Au Bonheur des Dames*.
Soon every major city had its cathedrals of consumption: London had Harrods
and Selfridges, Berlin Wertheim, Tietz and the Kaufhaus des Westens, New York
Macy's and Bloomingdale's. Though theatres and department stores were
seldom direct neighbours, they were often no more than a short walk away
from one another. The West End was London's 'shopping and entertainment
center', and Broadway served the same purpose in New York.[32] Berlin's main
shopping street was Leipziger Straße, and two of the city's biggest department
stores were close to where it intersected with Friedrichstraße.

Such spatial proximities – in themselves not particularly remarkable –
resulted in cross-industry ties. In Berlin, for instance, Adolf Jandorf, a
department store owner on a level with Gordon Selfridge, sat on the board of
directors of an operetta theatre.[33] By investing in theatre companies' stocks,
department stores made sure that these theatres would buy what they needed
from them rather than from their competitors. At the same time, department
stores made quite a profit selling theatre tickets – Wertheim, for instance, to the
tune of 1.5 million marks in 1907.[34] In return, employees of department stores
often got a discount.[35]

When it came to staging their merchandise, department stores naturally
looked to the theatre for inspiration. The shop windows in particularly were
designed to look like miniature stages, with curtains, theatrical lighting and
props. Occasionally they would even engage 'living models' to attract the
attention of passersby.[36] Some department stores were also equipped with halls
in which they would stage little theatre shows or concerts.[37] Macy's and
Gimble's, for instance, 'spent thousands of dollars staging elaborate spectacles
that rivalled anything seen in Broadway's first class theaters', and the same
could be said for department stores in Paris, London and Berlin.[38]

In the age before glossy catalogues and radio and television commercials, the
theatre was one of the most important means of advertisement. Beginning with
the *Shop Girl* in 1894, London saw a throng of musical comedies set in
department stores, which embraced the new consumerism and sometimes even

particular stores. The 1909 show *Our Miss Gibbs* was set in a department store called, transparently enough, Garrods. It celebrated the splendours of the department store, the abundance of goods and the pleasure of shopping via both its texts and its sumptuous decoration and costumes.[39] Selfridge took up the gauntlet, and in the following year the Savoy Theatre produced a one act play entitled *Selfrich's Annual Sale*.[40] So popular were these department store musical comedies that many of them transferred to New York.[41] The annual revues staged at the Metropol-Theater in Berlin in the first decade of the twentieth century often included references to Berlin's major department stores, too.[42]

However, theatre's closest links were perhaps with the fashion industry. As many contemporaries observed, genres like the drawing-room comedy, the musical comedy and the society play were as much fashion shows as plays. Nowhere was the relationship between the theatre and the fashion industry closer than in Paris, the capital of fashion. The Paris Opéra was famous as 'one of the temples of fashion', as the French writer Jules Janin noted in his book *An American in Paris* published in 1844, referring to both the audience and the stage.[43] It was not uncommon for fashion to take precedence over the play, as the Vicomtesse de Renneville, a fashion reporter, noted in 1882: 'In most cases the theatre can be certain of big crowds when sumptuous dresses can be seen on stage. [. . .] Hardly has the rumour gone round that in a certain play new toilettes will be shown, than a considerable part of the population is in a frenzy of excitement – dressmakers, modists, makers of lingerie and designers.'[44]

Theatre managers were well aware of the attraction for fashion on the audience and actively sought out cooperation with popular designers of the day. The Broadway producer Charles Frohman paid his leading actresses to order their dresses from the leading fashion houses in New York, London and Paris.[45] In London, George Edwardes went one step further. He took his star Lily Elsie to Lucy Duff-Gordon's exclusive fashion house, Maison Lucile, on Hanover Square, to get her outfitted for her lead role in *The Merry Widow*. Duff-Gordon was ideally suited to the task. Whether or not she invented the fashion show, as she claims in her memoir, she certainly had a talent for *mise en scène* and performance. The dress parades she began holding in her atelier shortly after 1900 were directly inspired by the theatre. They were performed on a stage with curtains and were supposed to be 'as entertaining to watch as a play'.[46] When Edwardes asked her to design the dresses for his production, she immediately seized the opportunity. It was a marriage made in heaven. Edwardes' show became an immediate hit, playing for 778 performances in the West End, while Duff-Gordon's Merry Widow hat became the accessory no fashion-conscious lady could do without.[47] While Duff-Gordon's designs added more than a little to the appeal of Edwardes' production, the show itself was the best advertisement she could have wished for. Edwardes' example was much copied, especially in New York, where *The Merry Widow* and the hat of the same name were also very successful.

On the wings of her success with *The Merry Widow*, Duff-Gordon opened a branch of her business in Paris in 1911. At the same time, the French fashion designer Paul Poiret, perhaps inspired by her example, began to stage fashion shows similar to those she had pioneered in London. Poiret also made use of the theatre as a promotional tool. He designed dresses for the stage, allowed his mannequins to wear his creations to the theatre, and at one time even appeared on the stage himself.[48] One of the leading fashion designers of the world, Poiret was an international celebrity. The Metropol-Theater's annual revue of 1911 devoted an entire act to the fashion show he had brought to Berlin that year.[49] As the theatre critics reiterated time after time, the Metropol was one of Berlin's most important places to be seen – preferably in a new and expensive gown. Meanwhile, fashion was a major if not a dominant topic onstage.[50] The revue lent itself better than any other genre to fashion displays. It can come as no surprise therefore that the Broadway impresario Florenz Ziegfeld introduced the fashion show into his Follies of 1912.[51]

Theatre was not the only entertainment available in the entertainment district; music hall was just as important. Having evolved from simple pub entertainments, by the 1850s variety was big business, by the 1900s it was an industry. Most urban neighbourhoods were served by music halls of varied size and quality. The most upscale houses were to be found in the centre of town: the Empire and Alhambra on Leicester Square in London; the Folies-Bergère in the rue Richer in the ninth arrondissement in Paris; the Wintergarten close to Friedrichstraße station in Berlin; and Koster and Bial's Music Hall on Broadway and 34th Street in New York. On the surface, theatres and music halls often appeared to compete with one another for audiences. In reality, however, many people frequented both and the two were interconnected on various levels. Some managers, like George Edwardes, even simultaneously managed theatres and music halls.[52]

Music halls were one of the first places where the urban population came into contact with a completely new form of entertainment: the motion picture. In December 1895, Auguste and Louis Lumière first exhibited their films to a paying audience at the Salon Indien du Grand Café. Only four months later they already featured in the bill of the Empire Theatre in London.[53] Although the Lumières are now generally credited as the first filmmakers, another pair of brothers, Max and Emil Skladanowsky, had shown a number of shorts films at the Wintergarten in Berlin one month before the Lumières.[54] And in April 1896, Thomas Edison premiered his projection device at Koster and Bial's Music Hall in New York.[55] Subsequently moving pictures became an integral part of the music hall bill, eventually securing for themselves a fixed spot at the

FIGURE 4.4: The Wintergarten, Berlin, date unknown. Postcard. FAN 05849.
Theaterwissenschaftliche Sammlung, University of Cologne.

end of a show. Yet, what began as a part of variety theatre soon came to
overshadow it and in the end would supersede it.

In 1913, 497 places in London, 300 to 400 in Berlin and more than 500 in
New York were showing films.[56] The biggest and most important cinemas were
located in the entertainment district. In London, 'the "key" cinemas, which
premiered new films before they were released in the suburbs and provinces',
were to be found around Leicester Square.[57] Berlin's key cinemas were on
Kurfürstendamm. New films played here first, and their success or failure
decided whether they were shown in other cinemas, too.[58] Still, Friedrichstraße
also has a place in the history of film in Germany. In the pioneer period before
filmmakers needed huge outdoor lots, Friedrichstraße was 'the centre of
German film business'.[59] Similarly, the British film industry made its first home
in the heart of the theatre-land, in Charing Cross Road and especially in Cecil
Court, known as 'Flicker Alley'.[60] And although Thomas Alva Edison's studio
was located in New Jersey, his biggest competitor, the American Mutoscope
and Biograph Company, opened its first studio on the roof of 841 Broadway at
13th Street in Manhattan, close to Union Square.[61]

For filmmakers it made sense to set up shop near theatres. At that time the
film industry relied heavily on theatrical talent, both in front of and behind the
camera.[62] Film producers and theatre managers sometimes even worked hand

in hand. Oskar Meester, for instance, a Berlin film pioneer with a studio on Friedrichstraße, filmed (and simultaneously recorded) the actors of the Metropol singing their hit songs. He would then show these films in his own cinema, also located on Friedrichstraße. At the same time, he filmed scenes that were incorporated into the Metropol's revues.[63] His French colleague, George Méliès, also made short films with the actors of the Folies-Bergère, which were shown as part of the revues.[64] Additionally, throughout the silent era operettas were being filmed by the dozen.[65]

In general it was the cinema that looked to the theatre in this period. For one, cinemas – especially those that appealed to the middle classes – were located in the theatre districts and were made to look like theatres, even going so far as to adopt superfluous customs like the curtain. More importantly perhaps, the films shown were highly influenced by the theatre. Of the American film output between 1894 and 1912, 'over one third [. . .] were either derived from stage plays [. . .] or at least in some way simulated the illusion of a theatrical presentation', and the same applies to Europe.[66] Film companies also adopted the star system and emulated the distribution practices of the theatre.[67]

Finally, it should not be forgotten that entertainment districts were areas of commercialized sex. Prostitutes were omnipresent in the streets around Covent Garden in the eighteenth and early nineteenth century. 'It is often difficult to keep off these repulsive beings, especially when they are drunk, which is not seldom the case', the German Prince Pückler-Muskau complained in 1826 after visiting Drury Lane.[68] In the changed moral climate of the Victorian Age, theatre managers, anxious to achieve respectability, succeeded in driving the streetwalkers out of the theatre (and with them large parts of the working-class audience). However, the prostitutes soon found a new home in the increasingly popular variety theatre. The Empire Music Hall on Leicester Square, the Folies-Bergère in Paris and the Metropol in Berlin were well-known prowling grounds of a better class of prostitute on the lookout for upper- and middle-class customers. As long as they blended in with the audience, they were often accommodated by the music hall managers.[69]

For many observers this was only consistent with the entertainment provided by these venues. In London the social reformer and feminist Laura Ormiston Chant, equally appalled by the short skirts of the performers and by the young women in the audience, 'most of them very much painted, all of them more or less gaudily dressed', almost succeeded in getting the Empire closed down by the London County Council.[70] The Folies-Bergère, where prostitutes plied their trade even more openly, never faced such threats.[71] In Berlin, the journalist and ethnographer Hans Ostwald refrained from moralizing, but he, too, linked the 'highly-paid cocottes in the promenade, dressed in the latest fashion, with expensive, not always elegant hats and silken petticoats' to the 'teeming of naked arms, bare shoulders and legs dressed in tights' on the stage of the Metropol.[72] In New York, too, prostitution in the theatre was an open secret.[73]

# CONCLUSION

Although the theatre always had a close relationship with the surrounding city this relationship was perhaps never more pronounced than in the nineteenth century. It was perhaps the true age of theatre-going in the sense that people, unlike today, had to go somewhere for their entertainment and that this entertainment to a very large degree consisted of theatre and other kinds of live entertainment. It is impossible to imagine the West End or Broadway around 1900 without the theatres, with which these districts became synonymous. The growth of cities and their populations produced a demand for entertainment that led to the establishment of theatre districts, where a large number of playhouses competed for audiences. Once confined to the periphery of the city, the theatre achieved a permanent position in its very heart. With its conspicuous architecture, its advertisement posters and its generous use of external lighting, it came to define how the big city looked and how it was imagined. By turning what would otherwise have been simple thoroughfares into bustling beehives, the theatre influenced its environment.

Conversely, the theatre was influenced by its environment. Where a theatre was situated determined the make-up of its audience. Theatre in the suburbs and in working-class neighbourhoods appealed primarily – but not exclusively – to the people living in the vicinity.[74] Centrally located theatres, on the other hand, attracted more diverse, heterogenous but largely better-off audiences because of good access to public transport and higher ticket prices. As theatres catered to specific audiences, location also influenced which kind of genres and plays they performed.

The theatre was part of the larger urban economy. It did not simply share the same space with other industries; it benefited from the proximity of railway stations, hotels and restaurants. It maintained close relationships with other industries, for example, by cooperating with fashion designers or department stores. Sometimes such collaborations were hidden from the public, more often they were obvious to everyone. Theatres not only named the firms supplying dresses, shoes and hats on the playbills, they advertised hotels, bars and various products. By using well-known department stores, hotels and restaurants as settings they pioneered product-placement. They also cooperated with other entertainment industries such as the music hall or the film industry. While these relationships did not depend on physical proximity, they were often triggered and certainly simplified by it.

However, setting plays in hotels or department stores did not necessarily have to do with advertising. The theatre revelled in bringing the city alive on the stage. While the melodrama was obsessed with the darker aspects of urbanization like crime, poverty, prostitution and alcoholism, society plays and musical comedies preferred the playgrounds of the upper ten thousands: grand hotels, fashionable restaurants, luxury stores, racing courses or casinos. Given this obsession for urban life and the close relationship with their environment, it was only natural for these genres to be named after the places of their origin: the *Boulevard* theatre (named after the Boulevard du Temple), *Viennese* and *Berlin* operetta, the *West End* musical comedy and the *Broadway* musical. These genres lived up to their names by celebrating the cities of their origin. This does not, however, mean that they did not travel. Rather the opposite was the case: successful plays were quickly adapted in other cities. Translators only had to change allusions to local places or events. As cities like Paris, London, Berlin and New York had much in common with one another, plays could be local and cosmopolitan at the same time.

Even when for many of the audience going to the theatre may have been a special occasion it was not an isolated event but part of the experience of the city, preceded perhaps by a day in town, visiting museums, shopping at department stores or going to a restaurant. As Erika Rappaport has shown for London's West End, '[s]hopping and theatergoing were [. . .] integrated forms of consumption'.[75] Accordingly, the theatre needs to be understood not detached from its surroundings but as part of a larger urban environment and as interconnected with other spaces and industries. And though the theatre changed and though its environment changed, we can still observe this relationship today, especially in theatre districts like the West End or Broadway that came into existence during the nineteenth century.

# CHAPTER FIVE

# Circulation

## *Theatrical Mobility and its Professionalization in the Nineteenth Century*

### NIC LEONHARDT AND STANCA SCHOLZ-CIONCA

The nineteenth century has been termed the century on the move. It saw the invention of railway technology, steamships, bicycles, motor cars and, if we include the first decade of the twentieth, the aeroplane. It is also the period that witnessed the largest intercontinental mass migration in history which saw an estimated 67 million people leave their homes. Technological advancements, particularly in printing and telegraphy, enabled the circulation of information at a speed hitherto unimagined. At the same time, the world was gradually reordered into a number of imperial spheres that both blurred and subsequently enabled national and ethnic differences. It is above all the period in which liberalist capitalism unleashed its transformative forces, an economic system whose market was, as Eric Hobsbawm noted, 'at its limits, global'.[1]

The combination of technological advancements and the growing networks of colonial trading posts and administrative centres, as well as the exponential expansion of the press, created the prerequisites for globalization in the sense we understand it today. Although these developments begin in the first half of the century and sometimes earlier, they only really gain significant traction and distribution in the second half. For this reason, many historians regard the period between 1850 and 1914 as a 'first phase' of globalization in as much as it evinces many parallels with current uses of the term. As Frederic Miskin notes from an economic perspective:

The current Age of Globalization is the second great wave of globalization of international trade and capital flows. The first occurred from 1870 to 1914, when international trade grew at 4 per cent annually, rising from 10 per cent of global output [. . .] in 1870 to over 20 per cent in 1914, while international flows of capital grew annually at 4.8 per cent and increased from 7 per cent of GDP in 1870 to close to 20 per cent in 1914. [. . .] This first wave of globalization was accompanied by unprecedented prosperity.[2]

Theatre participated in this period of unprecedented prosperity. We know from research into shipping routes, submarine telegraph trajectories and telephone cables that very specific lines of communication were established and maintained primarily to service either the lines themselves or the colonial towns and cities they connected. These were also used by the burgeoning entertainment industry. The latter provided in turn a kind of cultural superstructure to enhance living conditions in what were often initially entirely commercial, administrative and military centres. From the mid-nineteenth century on, theatrical circulation expands exponentially throughout Europe and the USA, and, in the wake of colonial expansion, into most other parts of the then known world. As the colonies expanded, and the settler populations grew, so too did the demand for theatrical entertainment of many kinds.

This chapter examines the activities of touring troupes, itinerant performers, theatrical brokers and managers in the context of early globalization. A study of the transnational circulation of theatre in the nineteenth century must address in particular the infrastructures of transregional or even global mobility, the inter-connectedness, and the professionalization of the international theatre industry. Each of these paths – mobility, interconnectedness and professionalization – are characterized by tensions typical for the nineteenth century: political nation-building versus international expansion, local homogeneity and stability versus cultural intermingling, the cementation of geographical borders and territories and the transgression of the same by new means of communication and transport; on the aesthetic level, a growing separation of arts and genres as well as nationally-specific aesthetics on the one hand, and a 'delight' in encountering transcultural forms on the other. The latter aspect will be the focus of the second section of the chapter, which explores how Japanese performers made use of the new transportation and economic infrastructure to embark on influential tours that had a significant impact on Euro-American theatre. The tours of the self-made, eccentric performer and troupe leader, Kawakami Otojirō, starring his wife, Sadayakko, and those of the former geisha Hanako, managed by the American dancer and theatre impresaria Loïe Fuller, exposed Western audiences to Japanese performance culture. This exposure stands in turn *pars pro toto* for a much larger amount of theatrical activity that saw intercultural exchange and traffic that moved in the wake of the waves of migration.

# MOBILITY MATTERS

After the mid-nineteenth century, cultural mobility grows in intensity, a development which is doubtless closely tied to and caused by the aforementioned innovations and improvements in the infrastructures of travel (trains and steamships) and communication – the (illustrated) press, cablegram and postal services. People and regions become better connected than ever before and new means of transportation facilitate the worldwide diffusion of commodities, ideas and ideologies on a scale hitherto unimaginable. Geographical distances shrink both perceptually and in real time while knowledge of the world's regions and cultures increases, as demonstrated by the world exhibitions beginning in 1851 but also by the newspapers that inform readers about topical events both local and global. Important newspapers have local correspondents to report on the latest news, be it from Europe, Africa, Asia or the Americas. Daily and weekly newspapers as well as trade papers of the time not only reported on local events, political affairs and shows, but also informed their readers about the metropolitan cultures of theatre capitals and the cultural life of cities all over the globe. Nineteenth-century readers were well informed about the amusements and theatrical gossip in town, but could also familiarize themselves with novelties, productions as well as cultural and political events abroad. Going to the theatre, vaudeville or opera was a crucial leisure activity in the nineteenth century, regardless of social class. In tandem, the theatre and entertainment sector became an important business.

In the 1840s the first telegraph cables were laid, and this, as Bern Dibner notes 'was the first important and large-scale practical application of the new electrical force. It shrunk distances across continents to almost nothing, for it took no longer to transmit a message across a continent than it did across a street.'[3] In 1858, the first transatlantic cable was spliced over a distance of 1,950 miles. No less a figure than the American showman and impresario P. T. Barnum identified the public reach and the advertising potential of this historic event: as Irving Wallace remarks in *The Fabulous Showman*, Barnum offered $5,000 'for the privilege of sending the first twenty-word message from London to his Museum in New York by this cable.'[4] His request was denied, yet, as he affirmed afterwards, it was meant seriously: 'There would have been no especial value in the message itself, but if I had secured the notoriety of sending the first words through the cable, instead of five thousand dollars the message might have been worth a million to me.'[5]

In his *Cultural Mobility: A Manifesto*, Stephen Greenblatt enlists keys for describing and coming to terms with the mobility of cultures. Mobility needs to be taken in a truly literal sense: 'the physical, infrastructural, and institutional conditions of movements, the available routes, the maps, the vehicles' should be taken into consideration; light needs to be shed on hidden as well as conspicuous 'movements of peoples, objects, images, texts, and ideas'; and last, but not least, 'contact zones' have to be identified and analysed, where cultures intermingle, and 'cultural goods are exchanged'.[6] Theatre and popular entertainment are fruitful fields of study for tracking transnational exchanges and forms of dynamic intermingling. Theatre, it could be argued, can be regarded as a contact zone *sui generis* in that it gathers together people from various cultural backgrounds, and serves as a port of call and springboard for performers, directors, choreographers, composers, and stage and costume designers from different parts of the world.

## THEATRESCAPES: GLOBAL SPREAD OF ARTS AND ENTERTAINMENT

Debates about contemporary globalization have also raised awareness of its historical dimensions. Within the larger scholarly framework of 'global' or 'transnational' or 'transcultural' history that has emerged during the last two decades, the study of connections, exchanges, networks or entanglements, to mention the most prevalent perspectives, have taken centre stage in historical research. Magisterial studies by Jürgen Osterhammel or Christopher Bayly,[7] to name only two representatives of the field of global history, have made it obvious that by the nineteenth century we can speak of dense international networks and global exchanges of cultural goods, ideas, political systems and commodities. If contemporary globalization, as Arjun Appadurai has pointed out, is characterized by the formation of interrelated *scapes* of media, economy, images and technologies, could not historical networks in theatre be described in similar terms? Given the density of theatrical networks, the shifting centres of theatrical business and the transnational flow of theatre aesthetics, forms and formats, one could perhaps speak of 'theatrescapes.'[8]

Recent approaches to global theatre history support this understanding of the period's history as a connected rather than a (nationally) divided one: the nineteenth century is a century of circulations encompassing the circulation of forms (opera, musical comedy, dances, costumes, plays and fashions) as well as forms of circulation (print media such as scripts and images, advertising and later standardized design and recorded media, etc.). Plays, theatrical genres, aesthetics concepts and performers migrated on a large scale between North and South America, Europe and Asia. This was facilitated by parallel craft industries. The company of Hugo Baruch (1848–1905; the company existed between 1887 and 1927), for example, produced and distributed stock costumes and stage designs and employed marketing and distribution strategies characteristic of international companies and department stores. Costume and fashion designer Lucile Ltd. (i.e. Lady Duff-Gordon [1863–1935]) designed theatre costumes for the big stages in London, New York and Paris and opened branches of her fashion stores in New York, Paris and Chicago by the 1910s

(Lucile's business started in 1893 and closed in 1924). International theatrical and artistic touring, which had always been part and parcel of the entertainment business, peaked in the late nineteenth and early twentieth centuries. Performers of this period became 'celebrities' and 'stars' not only because of their respective talents, but also due to their clever usage of new media in the context of their international mobility. As Le Roux and Garnier observe in *Acrobats and Mountebanks*:

> Dispersed throughout the four quarters of the world, the *banquistes* [meaning 'all persons showing or performing on a fair ground, circus, or variety entertainment'] have placed themselves in perpetual communication with, first, managers and impresarios, and then with their comrades, by means of a certain number of agencies and newspapers belonging to their corporation.[9]

The French actress Sarah Bernhardt is by far the most famous example here, but also Russian dancer Anna Pavlova, Italian opera singer Enrico Caruso or the American showman and impresario P. T. Barnum represent this international mobility of showmanship. From a transnational historical perspective, neither theatre as an art form nor as a business can work without the patronage of professional mediators. When Sarah Bernhardt toured Europe, North and South America in the late nineteenth and early twentieth centuries, she could not have done so without professional agents and managers. They were responsible and compensated for arranging her contracts, negotiating her royalties; they organized the logistics of travel, (ship passages, rail travel, accommodation, customs), arranged her itinerary, the transport of her costumes and publicity.

## PROFESSIONALIZING THEATRICAL CIRCULATION: BROKERS AND AGENTS

The theatrical brokers and agents who initiated and fostered these exchanges – and who tried to make a fortune through the mediation of acts and plays, of performers and troupes on an international scale – have seldom been studied, yet their contribution to the circulation of theatre was crucial.

The photograph in Figure 5.1 shows a tiny room entirely decorated with large posters depicting vaudeville acts and performers. A barely recognizable desk in front of the wall, packed with folders and files, reveals that this room is supposed to be an office. On a chair in the middle of the room, the body turned towards the beholder, the head turned away, sits a man in a business suit; his hands rest on his legs, both his gaze and posture seem to be open and expecting, and 'on the go'. The picture, which is used on the letterhead of the New York-based 'Global Amusement Explorer', depicts the agent Richard Pitrot. It was taken by the Byron Company of New York, which specialized in theatre photography. It seems to encapsulate the title of a seminal study from 1910, Robert Grau's *The Businessman in the Amusement World*, devoted to America's theatrical managers and artistic brokers (both male and female) who kept the local and international entertainment business of the late nineteenth and early twentieth century going. By means of public relations photography and the iconographic repertoire and conventions of presenting art dealers, Richard Pitrot, it seems, presents himself as such a 'Businessman in the Amusement World'. Surrounded by posters and advertisements of international acts – the 'artworks' he deals with – he positions himself as the all-round man at his office on 47 West 28th Street, New York, reaching out into the world.

Richard Pitrot can be regarded a 'cross-over' artist in multiple ways: biographically, professionally, in terms of the genres he represented, and the overlapping use of contemporary media that he harnessed for self-presentation as both artist and agent as well as for promoting his clients. Born in Vienna in 1852, Pitrot started his career as an impersonator; he moved to the United States when still young, was head of a Globe Trotting Circus that toured South America and South Africa, he acted for the famous Orpheum (later Keith's) Circuit, a chain of vaudeville theatres along the West Coast of the US that was initially founded by vaudeville impresario Gustav Walter (in the late 1880s), wrote for *The New York Clipper*, was busy as a broker for vaudeville and circus artists (among them Harry Houdini), built 'Midget City' on Coney Island (a city inhabited by people of short stature), and functioned as the 'exclusive American representative' of the Cinoplasticon – to name only a few of his

FIGURE 5.1: Richard Pitrot. Letterhead detail from a letter dated 19 December 1911, New York. The Shubert Archive.

countless activities. Contemporary newspapers and magazines of the time call Richard Pitrot 'the globe trotting agent', or an 'impresario by occupation and "globe-trotter" by choice.'[10] 'He has been called "The Globe Trotter"', writes Robert Grau, 'and the title is justified if his many voyages all over the world would give that designation. Pitrot's influence is very great and in Europe no man connected with the variety stage is more respected.'[11] His business card reads 'Richard Pitrot. International Amusement Explorer Representing the Entire Amusement World'; and his stationery indexes the global spread of his business in that he lists his branch offices and places of business located in the Americas, Europe, China, India, South Africa and Australia.

Richard Pitrot personalizes and quite literally incorporates the transnational connectedness and circulation of theatrical entertainment during the nineteenth and the early twentieth century: he is both a product and promoter of the amusement world, who cleverly employs new media and marketing strategies, makes use of a dense network of artists and their brokers and contributes to the institutionalization, internationalization and professionalization of a business field – theatre, circus and variety – which is highly volatile and mobile. The marketing picture he uses for his stationery crystalizes these mechanisms and is therefore a valuable source for approaching the cultural history of theatre.

In 1923, American play broker and producer Elizabeth Marbury recalled in her reminiscences *My Crystal Ball* an 'international' life:

> My life for many years seemed a constant journey between New York, Paris and London. Each incident of it was international, so it is impossible to reduce my experiences and impressions to any sequence or dates. I never kept a diary and never had a notebook. It is all haphazard in my mind, it is a living cinema, unravelling the story, introducing the actors, and presenting the close-ups![12]

Her 'constant journey' is typical for theatrical performers and agents of the time. It goes without saying that the global migration of artists and the spread of diverse theatrical and entertainment formats would not have been possible without major advances in transportation and communication infrastructures as well as in innovative technologies such as telegraphy, or later, the telephone. As Marlis Schweitzer describes in *When Broadway was the Runway*:

> Beginning in the 1890s, theater managers and booking agents in vaudeville and the 'legitimate' theater moved to consolidate their business interests, extending many of the same processes of rationalization and standardization that characterized modern manufacturing to streamline touring practices and establish greater control over the production, distribution, and consumption of theatrical commodities.[13]

Who were these theatrical brokers? What role did they play in the international theatre business? Performers, impresarios and agents of this period had cosmopolitan biographies, they travelled frequently, they were experienced in various professions, and had transnational 'workspaces' and global reputations. Some of them achieved worldwide outreach and influence. Alexander Pantages (1867–1936), for example, maintained a theatre circuit in the United States, the so called Pantages Circuit; Arthur Hirsch, based in Berlin, brokered acts for the German and American stages; Sol Hurok (1888–1974) managed numerous artists and actors, among them Mikhail Fokine, Anna Pavlova and Isaac Stern; British manager and impresario Maurice Bandmann (1872–1922) began his business in England and made use of the infrastructure of the British Empire to expand in India and throughout the Far East.[14] But there were also female agents who equalled their male colleagues in the business of promoting theatrical entertainment. Alice Kauser (1872–1945), born in Budapest, acted as a play broker and managed the rights and international dissemination of playwrights such as Henrik Ibsen, Herman Sudermann and Maurice Maeterlinck; New York-based agent and producer Elisabeth Marbury (1856–1933) promoted French and American playwrights, produced the *Little Lord Fauntleroy*, and made the dancing couple Vernon and Irene Castle famous in the early twentieth century. Helen Lenoir, later Helen D'Oyly Carte (1852–1913) played a prominent role in the organization and management of the D'Oyly Carte Company, before and after the death of her partner Richard after whom the company was named. Robert Grau calls her Richard's 'most trusted aid':

> In the heyday of the Gilbert and Sullivan opera, when the late R. Doyle [*sic*] Carte was wont to pursue the pirate vigorously, it was a woman who rendered him the most efficient service. Helen Lenoir was the name of the English impresario's most trusted aid, and well is she remembered in America for her business qualities, as well as for her amazing energy.[15]

What these agents and brokers have in common are their cosmopolitan biographies, and that they commuted regularly between the United States, Europe and Asia. With few exceptions (who only focused on plays and playwrights), theatrical agents of the time brokered diverse theatrical formats, including musical comedy, circus or vaudeville acts (and later on, film). Yet despite their importance, very few agents of the period have been documented at all,[16] and those who have were primarily based in North America (e.g. the Shubert brothers, Charles and Daniel Frohman, Helen and Richard D'Oyly Carte, Martin Beck).[17] Besides these there are many more, both male and female, who were highly influential on both a local and international market, but whose professional careers we have only begun to retrieve.

Like the artists and acts they represented, theatrical agents more often than not have transnational biographies, are polyglot and widely educated. They are early 'global players', have quasi 'cross-cultural competency', and might be regarded as cultural mediators or cultural brokers *avant la lettre*. Agent H. B. Marinelli, who originally started as a contortionist and became an agent for artists in the late nineteenth century, names his business 'The World's Agency', or 'The World's Theatrical Exchange': he maintained branch offices in Paris, London, Berlin and New York and presented himself as the expert for promoting artists from and to Europe, the United States, South America, Africa and Australia and promised guaranteed bookings of a duration up three or four years. Among his clients were (allegedly) stars such as Vesta Tilley, Sarah Bernhardt, Harry Lauder, Marie Lloyd, Lillie Langtry and Vesta Victoria.[18]

The period 1860–1920 can be defined as the heyday of the profession of agents, impresarios and managers in the performing arts. The emergence of agencies for promoting and brokering theatrical artists, acts and plays goes hand in hand with the rise of an international theatre industry and its professionalization. The agencies follow more or less the establishment of newspaper and picture agencies[19] and function as crucial hubs for local and international theatrical exchange and circulation: agents select, trade with and disseminate news, images, cultural artefacts and practices, goods, knowledge – and performative arts. By so doing they created influential professional and social networks and interconnections and functioned as cultural mediators. Theatrical brokers in the nineteenth century fostered cultural circulation and promoted transnational connectedness between artists and managers, venues and media. Their areas of activity had a truly transnational dimension: an agent in Vienna could book acts for a circus in India, an American impresario might organize a tour of performers in South Africa, a German agent could become the representative for German playwrights in France, and so on. The same holds true for the management and organization of national, transnational or global tours of other, less popular actresses, actors and performers of all kinds. Their activities were embedded into and benefited from technological innovations such as newspapers, professional photography, media of communication and transport networks. Consequently, source material that help us to understand the profession of brokers is characterized by a variety of media and formats: letters on stationery, cablegrams, photographs, juridical papers, business cards, picture postcards, contracts, theatrical programmes, newspapers, books, journals, (auto-)biographies, passenger lists, passport applications, census files and directories. Trade papers inform their readers about the latest news of agencies, but also display the addresses and scope of agencies in all parts of the world. The latter applies particularly to the publications for the circus and variety business, such as *The Artist: The International Organ of the Vaudeville Profession*, which was established in 1882 and published in New York and Düsseldorf, or *The Era* (London) or *Das Organ* (Düsseldorf). Some of these papers were published in three different languages (mostly English, French and German) in order to cater to their internationally diverse readership. These papers provided subscribers not only with news about the novelties in the field, but also with information on international touring, living costs, local currencies and customs, size, equipment and facilities of local venues, travel guides and recommendations for routes and contact persons. Occasionally, performers or impresarios published reports of their foreign travel in these magazines.

Successful agents could make a fortune by brokering theatre acts and performers. This profession was not without financial risk, however, as Elisabeth Marbury notes: 'The perils of Wall Street are nothing as compared to the pitfalls of Upper Broadway', and indicates the strategic challenges of dealing with the theatre trade: 'In this connection let me state that one of the peculiarities of this business is that when a manager makes six productions, four of which are successes and two of which are failures, the two failures more than consume the profits of the four successes.'[20]

Yet theatre could be a lucrative business, especially in the last third of the nineteenth century, and hence the profession of agent was considered promising, too. Around the turn of the twentieth century the number of agencies grew significantly. 'The vaudeville agent – ever a factor,' writes Robert Grau in 1909, 'is to-day everywhere to be found; there are probably two hundred in New York alone. Twenty-five years ago they could be counted on one hand.'[21] Hugues Le Roux and Jules Garnier observed that all capitals in the world hosted agencies for theatrical entertainment:

> Between the artist who seeks for an engagement and the manager always on the look out for an extraordinary 'novelty,' a third person necessarily intervenes, the middle-man, who arises everywhere between buyer and seller. And, in fact, at the present time all the principal cities of the world have their agents for performing artists of every kind. These personages are very important.[22]

The 'cultural capital' of theatrical agents, regardless if they acted on a national or international level, required optimal connection, metaphorically and literally, by means of the latest communication media and technology. For demonstrating their connectedness, many managers – and Pitrot whom I began this chapter with, was a master in this field – ostentatiously mark their use of media technology by adding illustrations of media such as telephone or telegraph on their business cards, adverts or stationery, or by presenting themselves on public relations images using these media.

In an exceptional manner, performers both make use of these innovations and contribute to their proliferation. The global spread of diverse theatrical forms and formats in the nineteenth century as well as the global migration of artists are inextricably tied to steamship routes, railway timetables and telegraphic cable connections. If one seeks to track the movement of performers and the trade routes of their managers, it is necessary to study the products or by-products of these innovations: to examine cablegrams and correspondence, passenger lists, passport applications, as well as newspapers and trade magazines and journals.

Although agents and impresarios were already active in the eighteenth century – particularly in the field of music and opera – it is only after 1850 that the professionalization of cultural brokers and the establishment of agencies began to emerge on an almost global scale. Paradoxically though, their ubiquity is not reflected in significant research.[23] The work of agents and agencies have remained in the background of scholarly attention, yet their very strategies of selecting, curating, distributing news, images and knowledge were extremely powerful and influential in terms of creating transnational imaginaries and public spheres as well as developing global markets.[24] One of these markets for the performing arts was Japan, which became both an importer and exporter of theatrical entertainment in the second half of the nineteenth century.

## JAPAN IN INTERNATIONAL THEATRE TRAFFIC 1866–1920

In the globalizing entertainment traffic, the case of Japan is both typical and eccentric, with a distinct shift from colonial patterns to a self-assertive thrust on the world market. The start was tumultuous and chaotic, although performers and their shows were among the first export hits, promoted by a high demand on the international market as well as by the desperate economic condition of native street artists in the mid-nineteenth century. Thus, although the first passports ever granted to commoners by the Tokugawa shogunate (1603–1868) were issued for a troupe of mountebanks recruited for a world tour scheduled to start in San Francisco in December 1866, even so, they were outdone by rival compatriots, who had passed the border clandestinely to perform in the city a couple of weeks ahead of their arrival.[25] Such was the momentum of the market a few years after the 'unequal treaties' with Western powers (1858) which forced Japan to open its ports to foreign trade, triggering radical socio-political shifts and a fierce race towards modernization, out of which the country would emerge within decades as a new imperial world power.

Moving abroad was an option for street performers and geisha dancers coming from the fringe of the rich and sophisticated theatre culture of the country. Established genres – the elegant *nō*, monopolized by the warrior elites and absorbed by courtly ceremonial, but also kabuki and the puppet art, the licensed theatre of commoners – eschewed international traffic, being hampered by rigid institutional structures and embedded in specialized interpretive communities of connoisseurs. It is significant, that the first kabuki tour abroad took place in 1928, while nō was not seen in Europe before 1954, to say nothing of the elaborate puppet theatre bunraku, which took even longer to move. Meanwhile, international circulation was left to hosts of lowbrow entertainers and subsequently to fringe actors, who inevitably transported a tainted image of Japanese theatrical culture abroad.

## COLONIAL FRAMEWORKS AND WESTERN THEATRE IMPORTS

From the very start, theatre traffic, as part and parcel of international trade, was premised on the expansion of colonial power structures and their technologies of transport and communication. Foreigners' concessions in Japanese port cities (Nagasaki, Kobe, Yokohama) developed the microstructure of colonial centres – with churches and cemeteries, hospitals, horserace and cricket grounds, and last but not least, venues for theatrical entertainment. Already in the mid-1860s, the Royal Olympic Amphitheatre in Yokohama hosted entertainment shows from other parts of the world, followed in 1870 by the Gaiety Theatre, which around 1900 would become a nodal point in the Eastern Circuit, part of a world-encompassing system of theatre touring that disseminated high-quality European theatricals from the centre to the periphery of the empire.[26]

Along with ten eponymous venues in East Asia, all products of colonial expansion, two successive halls called The Yokohama Gaiety (accommodating, after refurbishments, up to 500 spectators) hosted a broad gamut of Western shows: concerts – from military music to virtuoso European classics; spoken drama reaching from burlesques, farces and melodrama to highbrow modern plays; popular entertainment comprising circus, magicians and prestidigitators; folklore dances and ballet; puppet theatre (marionettes) and pantomimes; musicals and British-style musical comedies and operetta; and, eventually, the new medium of cinema. Spoken drama at the Gaiety included Shakespeare, Sheridan, Goldsmith and Molière, but also modern classics like Oscar Wilde, George Bernard Shaw, along with popular authors like Edward Bulwer-Lytton and Arthur Conan Doyle. Musical genres were represented by the trendy Gilbert and Sullivan (despite the Japanese ban of *The Mikado*), Offenbach, Donizetti, Gounod, Bizet and other famous European composers of the day. Along with small family troupes (for instance, G. C. Miln, who brought the first Shakespeare performances to Japan), Yokohama was visited after the turn of the century by large ensembles specialized in international touring, such as the Hughes Musical Comedy Company, Ferris Hartmann Company, Teal Musical Comedy Company and Allen Wilkie Company, to say nothing of the various troupes circulated by Maurice Bandmann, which came at regular intervals to

Japan between 1906 and 1921 and ultimately conquered broad native audiences at the Tokyo Imperial Theatre (opened in 1911).

For half a century (1870–1923), the Yokohama Gaiety catered to the *Heimweh* of foreign residents, while also offering natives a unique portal to Western theatre culture and direct contact with settlers of various nationalities. Occasionally frequented by kabuki actors, writers, intellectuals and diplomats, the venue played a seminal role in implanting Western theatricalities on Japanese soil. Thus, the Gaiety: mediated the first appearance of European operetta singers on a kabuki stage;[27] provided the prominent theatre reformer Tsubouchi Shōyō with his first experience of 'authentic Shakespeare'; and offered the theatre reformer and 'father of *shingeki*', Osanai Kaoru, opportunity to consolidate his knowledge of Western stage practices, to mention but a few decisive encounters. All in all, the foreigners' venue in Yokohama functioned as a hub in transnational theatre exchange, although, soon after its collapse during the Great Kantō Earthquake of 1923, the Gaiety faded from collective memory – becoming a forgotten chapter of theatre history, that still waits for reassessment by the scholars' community.[28]

## WESTERN MANAGERS AND JAPANESE PERFORMERS ABROAD

In contrast to the regular and systematic import of entertainment to Japan, exports remained for decades sporadic and chaotic. The structural imbalance typical of colonial traffic favoured Western agency in the circulation in either direction and encouraged international brokers to try their fortune in Japan. From the 1860s onward, international entrepreneurs rushed to Yokohama to recruit performers for international tours. Of course, none of them considered to move troupes from the theatre establishment, but traded instead exotic bodies and skills for ethnic shows in cities of the 'civilized world'. Responding to the demand of the entertainment market, they hired acrobats and jugglers, dancers and musicians, geisha, tea-serving girls, wrestlers, sword-fighters, storytellers, lion-dance performers and their likes for special venues: zoological gardens, circuses, variety theatres, beer gardens, and especially huge World Fairs held in metropolitan centres at ever shorter intervals to celebrate technological progress and colonial expansion.[29] Those performers, the last inheritors of a pullulating and highly competitive world of street entertainment of Edo Japan, which was to be doomed by the modernization efforts,[30] baffled European and American audiences with stupendous acrobatic dexterity and accomplished performative skills, underpinning in the West the myth of an exquisitely aesthetic, exotic Far East. Their shows reinforced the craze for things Japanese spearheaded by art and handicraft products and prompted the vogue of *japonisme*, a hallmark of the decadent *belle époque*.

Some of those entrepreneurs have recently received scholarly attention, for instance the famous circus artist and director, 'Professor Risley', who sent the passport-holder acrobats mentioned above around the world, helping to establish a long-lasting Japanese dominance in international circus business.[31] However, other influential brokers remain mysterious figures, such as the versatile Dutch impresario, Tannaker Buhicrosan, who recruited and managed a great number of performers and artisans for the hugely successful Japanese Village at the London World Fair of 1885.

Western agency was not less decisive in the international circulation of genuine theatre. Typically, one of the two geishas who became star actresses on Western stages, Ōta Hisa (1868–1945) – better known by her stage name Hanako[32] – left Japan in 1902 with a large group of acrobats, sword-fighters and wrestlers recruited by a Danish impresario for the Copenhagen zoo, thence passing from ethnic exhibition to petty stage business. Still, she owed her international career in the theatre to the dancer-impresaria, Loïe Fuller. Even the versatile showman, Kawakami Otojirō, the first (self-made) actor to lead a full-fledged theatre troupe from Japan through the US and hence to London and Paris in 1899–1900, had to rely heavily on Western agents.[33] Although his first expedition abroad claimed national representation and started under Japanese management – being invited to San Francisco by the energetic and experienced cultural broker, Kushibiki Yumito[34] – in the subsequent evolution of the tour Japanese agents played a marginal role, remaining pale intermediaries rather than full-fledged impresarios.[35]

The decisive role of the impresario in international touring is best illustrated by the Kawakami evolution in Europe. The American part of the tour was a risky enterprise, blatantly underplanned and shaky, mostly depending on local brokers contracted on the spot – among them, the picturesque Colonel James Hutton, who saved the troupe from starvation in Chicago, Alexander Comstock, who moved the Japanese along the Eastern Coast, or the fashionable Mrs Robert Osborne, whom Otojirō naively called 'the queen of high society ladies', who arranged their performances at the Bijou Theatre in New York. Subject to haphazard managerial shifts, the Japanese shows remained heavily dependent on imponderable circumstances, tribulations of the theatre market, diverse and capricious audiences and changing fashions and trends in the unstable theatre scene. In the US, triumph alternated with disaster, high box office earnings were followed by fiasco, high critical praise was mixed with poor reviews.

The situation changed radically in Europe due to an impresaria, who heavily refashioned the shows according to Parisian taste and her own artistic vision: the dancer Loïe Fuller (1862–1928), who became for almost one decade the exclusive manager of Japanese theatricals in Europe, leading the Kawakamis between 1900 and 1902, and subsequently Hanako between 1905 and 1908.[36] Fuller grounded her meteoric Parisian career on a speciality, which she patented, defended and commodified on a broad scale: the serpentine dance – an abstract form, in which bodily movement was amplified by swirling textiles and dazzling light effects, a slippery product that echoed the *Zeitgeist* and reverberated in music and the arts, sparking synergy effects and attracting to her entourage leading artists and writers of the time. Her alliance with the Kawakamis (Fuller travelled to London to hire them for the shows at the Exposition Universelle of 1900) was a serendipitous act, which not only brought the Japanese into the focus of public attention in Paris – and by extension, in Europe, but also imposed new frames of reception for her protégés. For the first time, Japanese performances came to be regarded as representative for a refined theatre culture comparable to the peaks of theatre art in Europe.

Hosted in Fuller's own theatre, built in extravagant *art nouveau* style imbued with *japonisme,* at the very centre of what Henry Adams aptly called a 'cultural powerhouse' (the Exposition was visited by some 50 million people), the Japanese were an overnight sensation while their star, Kawakami's wife, the former geisha Sadayakko (1871–1946), became an international diva whom critics compared to Sarah Bernhardt.[37] Their 369 shows (an average of three per day until the Exposition closed in October) reflected like a magnifying glass the ubiquitous *japonisme,* but also echoed, by contrast and similarities, Fuller's own dances. Paradoxically, the Japanese reinforced their manager's role as emblematic figure of the Fair: a mediator between the arts (with a strong impact on painters and composers), between highbrow and lowbrow culture, the arts and science (she experimented with radium dances), dance and technology (Fuller was dubbed the *fée éléctricité*), past and present (she pretended to resuscitate dances from ancient Greece), and as an inspired mediator between Orient and Occident.

For the ample European tour of the Kawakamis (1901–1902), Fuller assumed all financial risks, signing responsible for the planning, ticketing, advertisement and publicity, and logistics. Moreover, she streamlined the Japanese shows, expanding the number of actresses, stipulating the frequency of gory death and suicide scenes, providing innovative lighting effects, interfering with costumes and backdrops. Through aggressive advertising and international networking, using her own stardom for publicity, Fuller guaranteed her Japanese actors excellent visibility all along the way, and full recognition as ambassadors of a sophisticated theatre culture.

Fuller continued her role as cultural mobilizer and mediator after parting with the Kawakamis (on less than friendly terms), when she started promoting a tiny geisha discovered in curtain-raisers in the London Savoy Theatre: Ôta Hisa, whom she gave the stage name Hanako. For her new protégée, who lacked Sadayakko's glamour, the dancer-impresaria authored herself a formulaic repertoire – short schematic plays with conventional plots and characters of archetypal simplicity, focused on female victimhood and heart-rending suicide

FIGURE 5.2: Sadayakko and her husband, Otojirō Kawakami, accompanied by their adopted son and Loïe Fuller, Berlin 1901. Photography by Zander and Labisch. Theaterwissenschaftliche Sammlung, University of Cologne.

scenes. Her scheme worked, and during two European tours through twenty-three countries (in 1905–1906 and 1907–1908) under Fuller's management, the modest Japanese dancer emerged as a new international star. Even after separating from her manager, Hanako continued to tour this stock repertoire for several years through Europe and America. All in all, Fuller not only moved Japanese theatricals on well-organized circuits through dozens of countries, along trade routes that linked all important urban centres on the continent, from London and Paris to Moscow, from Finland to Rome, but she also put her stamp on the circulated product, reformatting the shows into what can be termed a product of international trade value – a Japanesque theatre that became a recognizable brand worldwide.[38]

## WESTERN AUDIENCES AND HAZY COMMUNICATION

All along their tours, the Japanese actors played to heterogeneous audiences dispersed across a vast geocultural space, whose members only shared their inability to decipher Japanese stage codes. Paradoxically, the hampered cross-cultural communication enhanced the aura of mystery and strangeness, triggering an effect essential to theatre experience: enchantment. Parts of the public indulged in the charms of exoticism, whereas discerning spectators – journalists and critics, artists, intellectuals and theatre experts – discovered refreshing alternatives to European stage practices. They were struck by the compelling formal coherence of the shows, by elaborate visual and rhythmic patterns that seemed to echo avant-garde positions, by the use of the actor's body as an abstract sign.

The spectrum of reactions to the Japanese performances also reflects fluid changes within the quickly globalizing artistic and intellectual climate in the countries visited. Critics on both sides of the Atlantic produced oxymoronic descriptions, creating confusion: the Japanese shows appeared both primitive and refined; naïve (even of infantile simplicity) and ritualistic; realistic and abstract; revelling in visual excess, but also practising austere simplicity and reduction. Occasionally, national proclivities steered the contrasting reactions: where French authors acknowledged realism ('frightening realism', 'crude realism', 'sophisticated realism'), British or German commentators diagnosed stylization or grotesque excess. Strongly diverging frames of perception are discernible between America and Europe (an extreme example is Hanako's impact on avant-garde directors in Russia – especially Evreinov and Meyerhold – compared to her mitigated success in America, where it was mainly her dwarfish figure that caused exotic thrills).[39] In that effervescent moment of European cultural life that produced a broad spectrum of avant-garde currents competing to disrupt aesthetic certainties (such as symbolism, imagism, expressionism, constructivism), the Japanese intrusion sparked within artistic and intellectual elites broad debates on basic aesthetic issues, which extended far beyond the theatrical public sphere.[40]

Nevertheless, beyond all discrepancies in perception, the experience of Japanese theatre fuelled discussion on basic theatrical issues and ultimately contributed to catalyse the emergence of globally coherent discourses on theatre. Moreover, by capturing the interest of elites across artistic boundaries, the Japanese intrusion underpinned the assessment of theatre as leading cultural medium in the age of empire.

## CONCLUSION: THE IMPACT OF CIRCULATION

In a period marked by massive theatre traffic and globalization, the Japanese tours display a high transformative potential – with effects upon all the 'actants' (*Greimas*) implied in the process: on actors, audiences as well as on the circulated shows. The very process of circulation reshaped the composition of the troupes, their repertoire and their acting styles. Moving at considerable speed between metropolitan centres, countries and continents affected the performers – prompting the emergence of a Japanesque international diva, who assimilated Western mannerisms (Sadayakko), and also an exquisite actress acclaimed by avant-garde directors (Hanako). The circuit also transformed an innovative dancer – Loïe Fuller – into an astute international impresaria: to say nothing of the versatile showman and troupe leader, Kawakami Otojirō, who acquired on the road the capacity and authority required to implement theatre reforms at home. Touring also reconfigured the shows in dramatic ways, producing a Japanesque style that may be safely called a *product of circulation* – a brand product for Euro-American markets. None of the programmes that enthralled Western spectators could ever have been performed before a Japanese audience.

However, despite their exceptional visibility and echo in the public sphere of all countries traversed, the Japanese shows remained a short-lived fashion. Although for a moment they had been a *must see* in all metropolitan centres, broadly acknowledged and intensely discussed, the shows and their stars soon slipped into oblivion. In 1908, the return of the Kawakami couple to Paris passed almost unobserved. Hanako, who continued to tour both Europe and the US with her miniature repertoire of archetypal pantomimes in cities as distant from each other as Lisbon, Moscow and Baku, ended her career as a restaurant owner in London. In Japan, she is remembered today mainly as Auguste Rodin's favourite model (the artist left at least sixty-nine portraits of her).

When Japan emerged as a new imperial power after the victory over Russia in 1905, the cliché of frail and vulnerable femininity, so cherished during the *fin de siècle* (in fact, a colonial cliché) was superseded by masculine images of 'Japan' – as propagated in bestsellers like *Bushidō* (1902) and *The Book of Tea* and later on in global theatre hits like *The Typhoon*. Those were self-assertive images of a strong modern nation – a new empire of the East. The excitement over the Japanesque performances faded along with the *japonisme* and the art nouveau, their inspiring potential exhausted. Thereafter, Japanese theatre exports were practically discontinued – with two exceptions[41] – until well after the Second World War, whereas the interest of Western audiences shifted from bodily experience (which had proved opaque and unreliable) to a fascination with the dramatic literature of Japan. During the following decades, Western reception focused on nō, however eschewing (deliberately in some cases, as Claudel) the stage in favour of the literary text. Thus, drama translations and scholarly studies became favoured strategies to access Japanese theatre. Nevertheless, distant echoes of those early tours are traceable in later European avant-garde theories, in stage practice and theatre perception (Brecht's theory of *Verfremdung* being just one of their indirect effects).

FIGURE 5.3: Postcard of Sadayakko in traditional Japanese performance attire, date unknown. Photography by P. Nadar. Theaterwissenschaftliche Sammlung, University of Cologne.

In Japan, the echoes of the tours produced a deep impact, enabling the Kawakami couple to promote Western drama in a series of adaptations in hybrid *shinpa* style, acknowledged by theatre historians as a decisive step towards a modern Japanese theatre. Their work was crowned by the inauguration

FIGURE 5.4:  Hanako in costume, Vienna, date unknown. Postcard, F. Kaiser.
Theaterwissenschaftliche Sammlung, University of Cologne.

of a big Western-style theatre hall in Osaka – The Imperial (1910) – and finally,
the foundation of Japan's first school of actresses, led by Sadayakko.

   In the theatre traffic with Japan, the imbalance between imports and exports
grew after the turn of the century. On the one hand, imported Western
entertainment conquered broad Japanese audiences – Bandmann's touring
troupes celebrated smashing triumphs in Tokyo, becoming a ferment in the
emergence of a modern entertainment culture that flourished during the whole
century. One of its offspring – the all-female musical theatre, Takarazuka,

opened in 1914 – even ascended, after a century of constant popularity, to the distinction of a classical genre. On the other hand, with the two exceptions mentioned, Japanese theatre exports were interrupted until the 1950s (if we put aside *nō* tours to colonised Korea). Thus, in the midst of an accelerated theatre traffic around the globe, Japan became again, after the short intermission of the Kawakamis and Hanako, a distant island.

# CHAPTER SIX

# Interpretations

## The Interpretation of Theatre

### PETER W. MARX

The nineteenth century was undoubtedly an important age for theatre and yet it was also a period that was perplexed by the meaning and social function of the art form. The preceding century had been a formative period of Western theatre that saw the rise of purpose-built theatres and permanent ensembles. Eighteenth-century theatre was characterized aesthetically by bourgeois drama and its corresponding style of acting. Theatre in the eighteenth century was a quintessential part of urban life and entertainment, affirming Schiller's claim that the stage functioned as a 'moral institution'. It is from this point of departure that nineteenth-century theatre came to reflect the major social, economic and cultural changes that came with modernization. The nineteenth century was shaped by the process of globalization, which was the formative force in creating the modernized, bourgeois society. While the eighteenth century was a period of consolidation of theatre, nineteenth-century theatre became a mirror and a catalyst for the various, and sometimes even contradictory, social, cultural, economic and intellectual developments of the era.

This central cultural position also multiplied the discourses and contexts in which theatre was seen and discussed. In the eighteenth century, there seems to have been a general consensus of what theatre (as an art form) was, allowing dramatists and commentators to focus on more specific questions, such as the morality or immorality of theatre, the styles of acting and play-writing. But in the nineteenth century, the ubiquity and growth of theatre-going and the diversification of its forms dissolved this former self-assurance. While the eighteenth century had a rather unified understanding of theatre, the nineteenth century understood theatre as a multifaceted discourse. While other chapters in this volume have traced the development of theatre through its organizational and legal structures (see Chapter 10), or with respect to its technological developments (see Chapter 9), this chapter aims to trace the various discourses that claimed to give a fundamental definition of theatre.

In this light, we can perceive a rather ambivalent process at a work. On the one hand, theatre is undergoing a deliberate and profound process of bourgeoisification and professionalization. Its, as yet, undisputed status of being an art form is being questioned. On the other hand, the theatre also reflects the epistemological shifts and crises of the nineteenth century. While the Age of Enlightenment was fuelled by the concept of rationality and the self-empowerment of human beings, the nineteenth century transferred the economic principle of the division of labour to the arts and sciences. The polymath was replaced by the scientist; the universal genius was replaced by the specialist. Hence, in the field of theatre, we see the emergence of the director, the professionally trained actor, the set designer and the technician, roles that in earlier periods would have been amalgamated and mostly gone unacknowledged.

But this process of the division of labour does not only concern the logistics of work; the consequences are actually far more wide-reaching, rooted as they are in the multiple trepidations that shook Western societies in this period. When Freud famously quipped about the three 'severe blows from the research of sciences', he sketched a panorama of the intellectual landscape that was the foundation (and the traumatic backdrop) for the process of modernization. Copernicus had ousted humanity from the middle of the universe, Darwin had expelled mankind from a supreme position in creation and psychoanalysis's description of the libidinal forces made it clear that the Ego was no longer even the master of its own household.[1] But Freud's observations eclipsed two further seismic shifts that also contributed to this intellectual horizon – Marx's interpretation of economic cycles, the call for a revolutionary change of social relations, on the one hand, and the growing acknowledgement of cultural contingencies provoked by the experiences of colonialism and globalization, on the other. Theatre, as an art form and a mass-medium of entertainment, was equally challenged and responded to these calls in different ways and on different levels. Sometimes by putting them at the fore, other times by refusing to acknowledge them at all. One thing was clear, theatre could no longer merely rely on an unquestioned concept of performance. In order to shed more light on the shifting nature of the performance in this period, this chapter will explore the professionalization of the stage, the relationship between the theatre and the public sphere, the link between nation-building and the national theatre movement and the quest to discover the hidden foundations of performance and ritual in the nineteenth century.

# PROFESSIONALIZING THE STAGE

The task of turning theatre into an institution of the bourgeois society (and thus making honourable people of actors) required the reorganization of the process of recruitment and training of theatrical professionals. As Jacky Bratton has pointed out, for the stage to be defined as 'a profession' in the nineteenth century, the theatres were required to do far more than merely pay their employees a wage:

> The induction of new people to an occupation is one of the ways in which its status is marked as being 'a profession', and the nineteenth-century stage had a great difficulty in meeting the requirements, not least because it included women practitioners who could never be said to be gentlemen, and were often admitted from anywhere in society, being qualified only by their good looks.[2]

Thus, artistic careers were very often determined by chance and accidental encounters; there were hardly any systematic procedures of preparing practitioners other than through private lessons or apprenticeships. Indeed, the 'training' of actors was rather unmethodical, focusing on declamation and vague instructions of how to behave on a stage. Goethe's legendary *Regeln für Schauspieler* [Rules for Actors] (*c.*1803) shed a light on the necessity of regulating the on- and off-stage behaviour of actors. This informal way of co-opting people into the trade derives ultimately from the pre-modern tradition of touring troupes. In a similar way to the commedia dell'arte and the English touring troupes of the early modern period, nineteenth-century theatre companies were structured around family ties that in many cases spawned dynasties of actors. This social practice reflects equally on the cohesiveness of the groups as well as on their precarious social status that did not 'invite' outsiders to join the profession. The tradition of actors (and other theatre practitioners) identifying and promoting themselves via their dynastic lineage continued well on into the twentieth century but this discourse had already begun to decline by the nineteenth century.[3] In England, there were a number of acting dynasties, including Edmund and Charles Kean and the Terry family (including among others Benjamin Terry, Sarah Ballard, Ellen Terry, her son Edward Gordon Craig and John Gielgud).[4] In the German-speaking sphere, the Devrient family was made up of actors, playwrights and directors and the Quaglio family were legendary set designers.[5] But these dynastic lines lost their importance in the nineteenth century, as the expansion of the theatrical trade called for a constant influx of new workers, which was partly organized by agents who secured the ongoing recruitment of new forces.[6] This system of agents, however, soon came in for harsh criticism for its abuse of power and for the use of exclusive contracts. Indeed, this arbitrary system of recruitment turned the agents into constant targets for criticism.[7]

While this system of agents was representative of the increasingly commercial nature of the theatre, the 'internal' workings of the theatrical profession was also changing. The nineteenth century saw a shift away from the previous system of actor training, which had a rather perfunctory understanding of the required qualifications and skills. There was also an emergence of a vibrant scene of theatre-lovers and amateurs, who were closely engaged with theatre. Konstantin Stanislavsky, probably one of the most influential theatre practitioners of the late nineteenth and early twentieth century, gives a paradigmatic account of his artistic biography in *My Life in Art* (1924). Starting out as an amateur who – by attending a performance of the Meininger – was motivated to pursue a superior form of theatre, he sought a method by which to improve his and his companions' style of acting. Although he had a remarkable semi-professional record of performing plays, to become a professional actor marked an important transition that seemed to him not achievable through the existing system of private lessons. He longed for a method that would allow him to (re)produce emotions and feelings in a precise way so as to make them an essential part of his performance. Stanislavsky continued to develop his acting technique, opening his theatre school at the Moscow Art Theatre in 1897.[8] Stanislavsky's theories were circling around the idea of an emotional memory that could be activated by actors. Therefore, he drew on the scientific discourses of his time, in particular psychology; his concept of theatrical training has ever since underscored the Western understanding of acting as a psychological act. Physical skills that had been central to the actors' trade well into the eighteenth century now became secondary to techniques of activating psychological reservoirs. Stanislavsky's training system and aesthetic was particularly successful in the context of the US, where the opening of the Actor's Studio in 1947 marked the institutionalization of Stanislavsky's model. It soon also became the prevailing training and aesthetic mode used in film acting.

Following this reform process, which implemented a style of acting rooted in the psychological constitution of the individual actor that performed a role and an aesthetic which demanded a precise and authentic representation of period setting, theatre was turned into a process based on the division of labour that required highly-trained specialists. At the end of the nineteenth century, set and costume design, acting, directing – in some cases even technical services such as lighting – had turned into highly specialized fields that required extensive training. The increasing complexity of the theatrical apparatus and the need for specialists corresponds with a general social and economic trend that Harold Perkin has described as the emergence of the *professional society*:

> The professional ideal, based on trained expertise and selection by merit, differed [. . .] in emphasizing human capital rather than passive or active property, highly skilled and differentiated labour rather than the simple labour theory of value, and selection by merit defined as trained and certified expertise.[9]

Perkin's criteria – a focus on human capital, highly skilled and differentiated labour and certified expertise – maps effectively onto the process of professionalization in the field of theatre and also emphasizes the extent to which a *professional society* was seen as a sign of social and economic progress.

To get a fuller picture, we should also acknowledge that this professionalization expands into the field of reception. The nineteenth century saw the rise of the professional theatre reviewer, who might even have had academic training in literary studies or a similar field. Peter Fritzsche's assertion that the modern metropolis was quintessentially a 'word city' sheds some light on the rise of daily newspapers but also documents the increasing importance of theatre reviews.[10] Theatres constantly provided material for press footage. Throughout the nineteenth century, there is a very clear link between the commercial activities of the stage and newspapers.

The peak of this process of social and cultural integration is the recognition of theatre as a subject worthy of scholarly reflection. In contrast to the public discourse about theatre, a scholarly discourse does not emerge before the mid-nineteenth century. In 1919, the German critic Adolfs Winds wrote that 'theatre history has become an academic discipline, taught from the lectern, renowned scholars research its area. The scoria of dilettantism drops down and it appears in priestly vestments.'[11] Up to this point, theatre history was told in the form of anecdotes and autobiographies and was a discourse of aficionados rather than of scholars. John Genest's *Some Account of the English Stage, from the Restoration in 1660 to 1830* (1832)[12] and Eduard Devrient's *Geschichte der deutschen Schauspielkunst* (*History of the German Art of Acting*) (1848–1874) as well as Max Martersteig's *Das Deutsche Theater im neunzehnten Jahrhundert* (*The German Theatre in the Nineteenth Century*) (1904) mark a shift in this process, as they aim to write theatre history in a more systematic way.[13] Collecting data, periodizing theatre as a cultural institution from within the context of economic, social and historical developments and systematizing one's own methodology are all hallmarks of this process. At the turn of the century, further scholarly discourses started to emerge, such as the foundation of the German academic society Gesellschaft für Theatergeschichte (Society for Theatre History) in 1902, which published a periodical of scholarly articles.[14] Subsequently study programmes for theatre and drama can be found that institutionalize and sanction theatre as a 'proper' art form.

## THE THEATRE AND THE PUBLIC SPHERE

As a moral institution – programmatically secular and independent from the institutions of power – theatre was an essential part of the emerging bourgeois public sphere. Thus, theatre was considered to be a key element in the public discourse on moral values, codes of behaviour and social questions.[15]

From within the context of the political restoration of the first half of the nineteenth century, European theatres show a continuity with the aesthetic forms and traditions of the late eighteenth century, a period often bemoaned as a 'stagnation'. But this lament, fuelled by an implemented concept of evolutionary progress, favouring innovation over continuity, eclipses the fact that theatre played a central role in forming new structures of public discourse. While the drama of this time is often described as being largely derivative in terms of imitating or preserving classical forms, it is rather through theatrical practice that the theatre contributed to the formation of a different kind of public discourse. Here, throughout Europe, the 'small' and less-reputed forms of drama, which might superficially seem rather nostalgic or conservative on the surface, are frequently more dynamic. Meike Wagner has argued that the alleged stagnation is actually just a problem of discursive concepts, rather than one of cultural practice. As she shows in her expanded study of Berlin, Munich and Vienna, theatre was undergoing a 'productive crisis', forming – together with the emerging press and the censorship authorities – a triangular stage on which key conflicts regarding the public sphere as a forum for the free exchange of ideas could be acted out.[16] According to Wagner, during this period the stage was genuinely a 'theatre of a social crisis'.[17] Following her argument, it is no coincidence that the most frequently performed drama in the German-speaking world of this period is set in the milieu of journalism: Gustav Freytag's 1852 *Die Journalisten* (*The Journalists*).

If one turns to common textbooks on nineteenth-century theatre, one finds the consensus that the second half of the nineteenth century is determined by a general trend towards historical accuracy, with realism forming an almost obligatory aesthetic code. Brockett et al., for example, describe this as the lasting influence of Comte's sociology and Darwin's biology, whose central thesis of causal effects, 'heredity and environment', allowed for a new dramaturgical and aesthetic concept of the stage that turned the *mise en scène* into a unit of observation.[18] Complementing this argument from the perspective of the history of ideas, Zarrilli et al. have argued that it was the invention and introduction of photography as a mass medium, providing a categorically new availability of images, that steered the stage towards realism and naturalism. Here, the existing mode of the 'box set' – a closed room with an 'open' fourth wall towards the audience – gained new meaning:

> Although the 'box set', which offered the illusion of three walls with realist doors and windows, was introduced on the London stage in the 1830s, it, together with real furniture, was not in regular use until the 1890s. [. . .] Further, electric illumination heightened the differences between black-and-white photographs, the new measure of the 'real', and the convention of painted scenery, which now looked quaintly superficial and immaterially flimsy by comparison.[19]

According to Zarrilli et al., photography not only provided a new standard of technological precision but also promised to document reality, in a way that exceeded conventional modes of representation.[20] Correspondingly, the German playwright Arno Holz developed a formula to describe the naturalistic aesthetic: Art = Nature − X, with the variable X being be as small as possible. Holz's formula claimed a scientific status for dramaturgical representation, which sought to legitimize its aesthetic. Despite an apparent concern that many of these plays lacked compassion, Holz's formula provides a useful method for defining the aesthetic purpose of these plays.

To understand the social position of these plays and productions, one has to acknowledge that the new paradigm of realism coincided with the rise of specific social movements and an increasing awareness of the problems and shortcomings of modernization. Thus, it is a small wonder that the number of playwrights that can be included in this group is as international as modernization itself. Famous representatives include the Norwegian author Henrik Ibsen (*A Doll's House*, 1879; *An Enemy of the People* and *Ghosts*, 1882; and *Hedda Gabler*, 1891), the Russian playwrights Anton Chekhov (*Uncle Vanya*, 1899; *Three Sisters*, 1901; and *The Seagull*, 1896) and Aleksandr Ostrovsky (*The

FIGURE 6.1: Sketch for a production of Hauptmann's *Friedensfest*, Berlin 1896. Sketch by Emil Orlik. INV1666. Theaterwissenschaftliche Sammlung, University of Cologne.

*Thunderstorm*, 1860; *The Forrest* 1870; and *Talents and Admirers*, 1881), and the German Gerhart Hauptmann (*Before Sunrise*, 1889; and *The Weavers*, 1892). In France, Émile Zola (*Thérèse Raquin*, 1873; and *Jacques Damour*, stage adaptation by Léon Hennique, 1887) was instrumental, and similarly many of the works of the Swedish playwright August Strindberg (*The Father*, 1887; and *Miss Julie*, 1888) also belong to this group. One of the hallmarks of all of these plays is that they circulated quickly throughout Western theatre; this was a genuinely international art wave.

Thematically, these plays tend to explore issues of social change but also phenomena that were considered the symptoms and causes of social distress. Thus, they turned to subjects and topics that violated the decorum of bourgeois theatre, such as venereal disease, alcoholism, mental illness and ennui, the lack of social mobility, unequal marriage and bankruptcy. The shock that these topics provoked in the audiences is very prominently illustrated in a caricature from the *Kladderadatsch* in 1890 (see Figure 6.2) that shows the 'new theatre' of naturalism. On top of the pediment of the main entrance, we see the allegorical figure of naturalism chewing the sole of his shoe to indicate that the subject matter of these artworks is unpalatable. In the tympanum, we see the muse of naturalism digging in the trash for items she could put in her basket, inscribed as the 'Repertoire'. On the left, we see a cigar-smoking woman with a bowler hat, nudging a man suggestively, dubbed 'the free woman', whereas on the other side, we can see a man holding a child by its hand, both drinking (presumably) alcohol from bottles, figures inscribed as 'Heredity'. The bourgeois in the foreground of the image is hastening away from this venue, holding his nose against the smell while another one stumbles out of the building, visibly sickened by what he has just experienced.

The caricature captures many contemporary responses to realism/naturalism, with its supposed fascination with the 'dark' side of modernization. The official response followed suit. Due to their subject matter, which was considered inappropriate for public display (and discussion), many naturalistic plays were more or less banned from public performance in many Western countries. Hence, we find the paradoxical situation of a literary movement that is often heard (and controversially discussed) but virtually never seen on stage, or if it was seen, then heavily censored. According to the rules of censorship in most European countries, only public performances were subject to investigation, closed or private performances were exempt. Thus, we observe the founding of the Théâtre Libre by André Antoine in Paris in 1887, the Freie Bühne in Berlin in 1889 and the Independent Theatre Society in London in 1891, where the system of membership and subscription was an effective way to circumvent censorship. Despite gaining public attention through extensive press coverage, these performances were very controversial and provoked much public anxiety and discussion.

FIGURE 6.2: Caricature depicting the Freie Bühne. *Kladderadatsch* 43, no. 17, 1890.
Cartoon by Ernst Retemeyer. University of Heidelberg.

The 1890s saw a wave of public performances of naturalistic plays on stage, attracting rather large audiences. For example, the Lessing-Theater in Berlin, a rather exclusive venue for contemporary plays but usually preferring rather lighter fare, staged a series of plays by Hermann Sudermann with remarkable success. His play *Honour* premiered at the Lessing-Theater during the 1889/90 season and was a surprising box-office hit with ninety-eight performances. But critics were puzzled by the success. Karl Frenzel moaned that the rich audiences of the Lessing-Theater were fickle and constantly required innovation and variety of subject matter, concluding that:

> Out of certain proclivity for contrasts it learns between pity and awe of the hunger of poor and pays a visit to their tenements (*Hinterhaus*) with a full stomach. Only one mustn't assume that this proclivity will become habit. Soon enough it will be drawn back from the dark to the light, from gloom to pleasure.[21]

According to the critic Leopold Schönhoff, it was merely 'social curiosity' – not compassion or any moral sentiment – that drove the audiences to these plays.[22] Paying a visit to the dark, mysterious and gloomy *Hinterhaus* had a curiosity and exoticism all of its own. As Barbara Kirshenblatt-Gimblett has pointed out, the development of the large metropolises at the end of the nineteenth century fostered a quasi-ethnographic interest amongst the middle classes towards migrants and labouring classes. Their *Lebenswelt*, their customs and their social life, was described and analysed as that of a mysterious tribe, a discourse which empowered the higher social strata in much the same way as colonialism had empowered the colonizers over the colonized subject:

> While respectability has the power to control access to sight, to conceal, poverty, madness, children, animals and the 'lower' orders of humankind reveal by exposing themselves fully to view. Historically, ethnography has constituted its subjects at the margins of geography, history, and society. Not surprisingly, then, in a convergence of moral adventure, social exploration, and sensation seeking, the inner city is constructed as a socially distant but physically proximate exotic – and erotic – territory.[23]

Thus, the *Hinterhaus* provided an exciting opportunity to learn more about the exotic natives of the new urban territories but it failed to incite social improvement and reform.[24] Although at first glance this might seem to be counterintuitive. After all, naturalism/realism frequently did not seek to hold up a mirror to the self-satisfied bourgeois middle class or emphasize the consequences and shortcoming of society's modernization.

To assess this problem more clearly, two issues need to be considered. On a formal level, the strict postulate of merely documenting 'reality' – avoiding any alterations in the course of time and space, having the characters speak in a realistic voice, sometimes using dialects even at the expense of comprehensibility – pays tribute to the ideal of precision in representation. On a dramaturgical and political level, this emphasis on social problems and marginalized groups must not be interpreted as a sign of drama adopting a liberal political attitude. On the contrary, it demonstrates that theatre was inspired by the idea of imposing Darwinian biology on social processes, with plays highlighting the unavoidability of fate, as opposed to advocating ideas of emancipation and liberation. At the centre of many of these plays, we find not an autonomous character but an externally determined subject. In Gerhart Hauptmann's naturalistic play *Before Sunrise*, the protagonist Loth rejects the love of Helene because he considers her as doomed because of the prevalence of alcoholism in her family. Although Helene does not drink herself, Loth regards the risk of a hereditary addiction as too high to pursue a relationship with her. Not even her suicide changes his attitude. Rather than being structured around individual actions and decisions, the play follows the logic of pre-determinism in regard to given situations. The autonomous individual – the centrepiece of the Enlightenment – is replaced by the mechanics of genetic and social determination. Rather than calling for political action, these plays not only accept the status quo but even seem to question the possibility of political change in the first place. Thus, a certain fatalism is wired into these plays, building a deeply conservative undertone.[25]

Notwithstanding the diverse political agendas of the different authors, bringing these, often repressed, topics to the fore turned theatre into an intrinsic part of the public sphere and fulfilled a central function for political debate. It is significant that writers such as Émile Zola also published widely in newspapers and magazines and that the Freie Bühne even published a journal of the same title, indicating that theatre was considered to be a forum for cultural and political discourse.

## NATION-BUILDING AND NATIONAL THEATRES

In the process of nation-building, theatre was a much-invoked institution; more often than not with commentators lamenting the absence of a 'proper' national theatre in their respective nations. The concept of national theatres was closely linked to the political rise of the nation-state and its prime model was the Comédie Française (established in 1680). Functioning as a forum to showcase the national production of plays, the idea of the national theatre was always part of wider language politics. Thus, the foundation of the Schouwburg in Amsterdam in 1638 was as important for the Dutch language, as was the opening of royal theatres in Denmark (1772) and Sweden (1773) for the respective Scandinavian languages. In the German-speaking sphere, the title 'national theatre' was common and sometimes used in a projective sense, to promote social progress (as in the case of Mannheim in 1777, where the term 'national' had more of the status of a manifesto than a basis in reality).[26] Still, in 1882, eleven years after the German unification, the Hart Brothers invoked the French-German War of 1870/71 and its most iconic battle, the Battle of Sedan (1870), when German troops took the French emperor Napoleon III as prisoner. Recalling the victory, they argued that the 'Sedan of iron arms' should be followed by a 'Sedan of the spirit', which would spawn a national theatre, whilst wistfully lamenting that so far no theatrical production had been able to express the latest developments of national history.[27]

Equating an iconic battle with the founding of a national theatre is symptomatic of this period of theatre history. Theatre was idealized as a national gathering site to celebrate and reaffirm shared values, with plays depicting the history, tradition, language and imagery of a patriotic nation. The concept of national theatre was also usually closely associated with literary drama and the vernacular, especially since language had been identified as a central hallmark of national communities.[28] The concept also became instrumental for communities who were still fighting for political independence and autonomy. For this reason, there were national theatre movements in Poland (especially since the 1830s), Hungary (with the foundation of the Magyar Theatre in Pest in 1837, which was recognized as a national theatre in 1840), Norway (with the opening of the first Norwegian state theatre in 1827 by Johan Peter Strømberg) and Ireland (1904). In contrast to the internationalization of theatrical repertoires and forms of production, the concept of national theatre sought to highlight the national peculiarities and specialties, sometimes by using folk-elements (such as dance, motif or specific tales), by developing a specific iconography, or a specific style of acting.[29]

While in some cases, the concept of a national theatre required public subsidies to enable the institution not to cater to the taste of the masses; allowing them to devote themselves exclusively to their assumed cultural mission. In most cases, however, the theatres were not subsidized or only to a minor extent. Sometimes, court theatres were supposed to fulfil the task of a national theatre, whereas in other cases privately run theatres turned into de facto national theatres – by the attendance of the general public. The Deutsches Theater in Berlin could be considered such a case.[30] While the official court theatre was considered old-fashioned, catering only to the taste and demands of the Hohenzollern court, the privately organized Deutsches Theater soon became the central meeting point of Berlin's new bourgeois middle-class.

## RICHARD WAGNER AND THE NATIONAL PILGRIMAGE

Wagner's enterprise of the Bayreuth festival needs to be understood from within the context of this public discourse on theatre as a nation-building institution. When Richard Wagner opened the festival of Bayreuth in 1876 with the premiere of *The Ring of the Nibelung*, a new concept of theatre had taken shape. The settings as well as motifs of Wagner's operas were remarkable, demonstrating his declared goal to create a new aesthetic experience programmatically aligned to the formation of a great nation-state.

Bayreuth, a Bavarian provincial town, was a rather unlikely setting for establishing such an ambitious enterprise. Although nineteenth-century opera is frequently categorized as an urban art form, Wagner deliberately opted for the contrary.[31] He did not want to go to one of the major cities but instead romanticized Bayreuth as being in the heart of Germany, surrounded by the 'immense Hercynian Forest into which the Romans never penetrated'.[32] At the core of his new festival was the desire to create an authentically German art form; an ideal which was rooted in his belief that Germany was all too easily prone to imitate foreign cultures, especially French art:

It is the opinion of many intelligent men that the recent enormous successes of German statesmanship have done nothing whatever toward doing away

with our stupid habit of imitating foreigners, or toward a desire for conforming
our existing institutions to the requirements of a peculiarly German culture.
[. . .] If a Parisian courtesan takes it into her head to give some strange shape
to her bonnet, all the women in Germany must adopt the new fashion.[33]

In this way, Wagner explicitly condemned the prevailing contemporary culture of
his day as being commercialized, superficial and overly influenced by foreign
elements that thwarted the nation's genuine expression of its identity. Wagner's
political position was closely linked to anti-modernism and thus also to anti-
Semitism. In his notorious *Das Judentum in der Musik* (*Jewry/Judaism in Music*)
of 1869, he argued that the Jewish people were unable to produce genuine art.[34]
Symptomatic of Wagner's style of argument is the invocation of quasi-historical
tradition, such as conjuring of the forest of Franconia to provide a natural
barrier against the Romans, in an oblique allusion to the French. Wagner's
concept of German culture was rather paradoxical; it was autochthonous and
bound to nature but was also simultaneously besieged and beleaguered. Thus,
turning his back on the densely-populated urban centres was a conscious act of
defining his project as a counter-movement. During the ceremony in which the
foundation stone was laid to the new Festspielhaus, Wagner envisioned himself as
a national prophet in his opening address: 'You believe in my vocation to found
for Germans a theatre of their own, and you place in my hands the means of
erecting this theatre in actual, material form before your eyes'.[35] In Wagner's
reading, Bayreuth was not just another theatrical venue; it was a sacred site for
the nation, the destiny of a pilgrimage. Wagner himself envisioned the 'Green
Hill' as a sanctuary:

> True, for the present, this structure will be but provisional – but so for centuries
> was the whole outer form of German life. But it is a characteristic of German
> life that it builds from within; the everlasting God lives within it long before
> He raises from it the temple of His glory. And this temple will be in just so far
> a manifestation of the spirit within, as it is consistent with it in its originality.[36]

What is striking about Wagner's *Festspiele* is that it amalgamates nationalistic
and anti-modern elements with explicitly modern and innovative ideas. The
Festspielhaus, the theatre built for the performance of Wagner's operas, was a
genuinely modern building, realizing many advanced aesthetic ideas. The
darkening of the auditorium and sinking of the orchestra pit, out of the sight of
the spectators, was designed to perfect the picture presented to the audience by
'freeing the vision from the observation of any intervening sense of reality' and
were genuinely innovative measures.[37] He also abolished the old system of
boxes and organized the audience into rows; a kind of democratic structure
that was in line with his idea of a national sanctuary.

FIGURE 6.3: The interior of the Festspielhaus, showing the set of *Parsifal, the Grailtemple, c.*1880. Note the simple, 'democratic' rows of seats. Photography by Rammes. Theaterwissenschaftliche Sammlung, University of Cologne.

By contrast, the plot and motifs of his operas were drawn from German and Scandinavian myths and folk-tales as well as from the medieval *Nibelungenlied*. Wagner strategically set out to create a quasi-mythological foundation for his cult of the nation. While his plots used traditional elements, they could also be read as an allegorical fable about the modernizing of society and the erosion of traditional structures. His plots idealized German/Germanic heroism and re-introduced mythological figures into the German landscape, such as the Rhine. Deliberately playing on contemporary misnomers regarding German prehistory, this evocative imagery helped to create an almost brand-like theatrical vocabulary. Another of Wagner's core innovations was the musical structure that he created for his operas. He created a new musical form that transcended the Italian as well as the German model, by abolishing the structure of arias and recitativo and replacing it with the use of leitmotifs as musical markers.

Wagner's initiative is unique not only in its amalgamation of aesthetic and political goals but also in the way in which it mobilized supporters and fans. This public support led to the formal foundation of *Wagner-Verband* (Wagner-Societies) in various cities and regions.[38] Initiated to support Wagner's plans for Bayreuth, the idea soon spread all over Germany, forming into international branches. This phenomenon is not just of anecdotal interest but rather demonstrates the extent to which Wagner was able to develop his idea of the

FIGURE 6.4: The driveway to the Festspielhaus in Bayreuth which is decorated with the national flag of the German Reich. The pilgrimage has turned into a procession of costly coaches, lining up and directed by the policeman in the centre of the image. A symptomatic depiction of the political reality of Bayreuth, being a rather elitist venue in close liaison with the state authorities, c 1870. Postcard, Carl Giessel. Theaterwissenschaftliche Sammlung, University of Cologne.

*Festspiel*, as a kind of secular ritual, into a structure that was firmly incorporated into the cultural and social life of its 'followers'.

## PERFORMANCE AS RITUAL

In 1872, Friedrich Nietzsche published his book *Die Geburt der Tragödie aus dem Geist der Musik* (*The Birth of Tragedy from the Spirit of Music*). His reading of classical tradition offered a radically new interpretation of the European tradition of drama and performance. In contrast to the conventional reading of the classics, Nietzsche argued that Greek theatrical culture was determined by the categorical opposition of the Apollonian and the Dionysian deities. In Nietzsche's reading, the two deities represented two divergent aspects of performance. The Apollonian stood for plasticity, clarity and beauty, whereas Dionysius epitomized the dark forces of transgression and (usually) repressed energy. His account of ritual is intrinsically connected to the interplay between these two principles:

The Dionysian arousal is capable of communicating to a whole mass of people this artistic constitution which allows one to see oneself surrounded by such a crowd of ghosts, with which one knows oneself to be intimately at one. This process of the tragic chorus is the original dramatic phenomenon: to see oneself transformed before one's very eyes and now to act as if one had really entered into another body and another character. This process stands at the beginning of the development of the drama. Here there is something different from the rhapsode who does not fuse with his images, but like the painter sees them outside himself with an observing eye; here there is already a surrender of the individual through an entering into an unfamiliar nature. And indeed this phenomenon emerged in epidemic proportions; a whole crowd felt itself enchanted in this way. The dithyramb is therefore essentially different from any other chorus song. The virgins who ceremonially approach the temple of Apollo bearing laurel branches and singing a procession song remain who they are and retain their names as citizens: the dithyrambic chorus is a chorus of people who have been transformed, who have completely forgotten their past as citizens, their social position: they have become the timeless servants of their god, living outside all spheres of society. All the other choral lyric poetry of the Hellenes is only a great intensification of the individual Apollonian singer; while in the dithyramb a community of unconscious actors stands before us who even among themselves regard themselves as transformed. Such enchantment is the precondition of all dramatic art. Under the influence of its spell, the Dionysian enthusiast sees himself as satyr, and as satyr he in turn beholds the god, that is, transformed in this way he sees a new vision outside himself, as the Apollonian completion of his state. With this vision, the drama is complete.[39]

For Nietzsche, the Dionysian element is rooted in music because it transgresses the field of language and semantics and creates an experience that transcends the ontological and social categories of identity and transforms its followers. While the Apollonian virgins preserve their good names and social identities, the Dionysian worshippers turn into satyrs, leaving their everyday identity behind them. Nietzsche's choice of words is revealing here; the effect of Dionysius is described as the spreading of a disease, with 'epidemic proportions', that not only spreads through 'a whole mass of people' but which also evades all control. While the eighteenth century had established an understanding of theatre that focused on intellectual recognition and moral judgement, Nietzsche's re-reading of Attic tragedy prioritizes the role of enchantment, vision and transformation. The opposition between Apollo and Dionysius is readily mapped onto the juxtaposition between the rational intellect and the irrational subconscious.

Nietzsche's reinterpretation of ancient tragedy was a blunt provocation for traditional philology and the bourgeois understanding of drama and theatre. In colourful terms, Nietzsche rejected the focus on narrative and moral doctrine that had fuelled drama in the bourgeois understanding and instead emphasized the 'dark', pre- or anti-rational elements of intoxication and transgression. Ever since French classicists had formulated the *doctrine classique*, Aristotle's allegedly clear-cut catalogue of what a proper tragedy should look like had been used to privilege, not only word over spectacle, but also intellectual and effective response, over celebration and captivating intoxication. Nietzsche claimed not only to have redefined the true origin of tragedy but to have also rediscovered a subterranean cultural tradition that had been eclipsed and banned by the moral forces of Christianity.

As Julie Stone Peters has argued, this process of the 'refiguring of Greek drama' that took place in the 1890s was concomitant with a general ethnographic interest.[40] As in the case of non-European cultures, the ancient Greeks were now perceived as 'primitive'. Classical theatre was not merely claimed to be a cherished, inherited cultural tradition but the plays were now interpreted as cultural practices based on the immediate, corporeal experience of ritualistic practices. Traditionally perceived as the pinnacle of the Western tradition of drama, tragedy was now understood as stemming from performative representations of hunting or harvesting, which recapitulated and anticipated existential experiences:

> The story of how these animal dances turned into Greek drama, in its most reduced form, went thus: Back in archaic prehistory, it was natural for people, in the intensity of emotion, to reenact exciting events such as the hunt; indeed, their gestural language was better developed than ours because their verbal language was more limited. Mimetic reenactment turned easily into preenactment: an attempt to produce certain outcomes by rehearsing or magically invoking them.[41]

Whereas Nietzsche had imagined the Dionysian practices in the light of his criticism of the Christianized culture, scholars such as the Cambridge Ritualists linked these ideas to archaeological evidence, contributing to a broader, ethnologically more informed understanding of Western antiquity.[42]

In the Germanophone tradition, scholars argued that there was a specific drive or desire to perform, the *Mimus*, which fuelled all theatrical and performative activities. Hermann Reich in his massive study *Der Mimus* (1903) attempted to trace the barely documented Roman tradition, which defined performance as an innate drive of human beings. Other scholars, such as Artur Kutscher and Carl Niessen, followed his argument. This thesis valorizes theatre and performance as primal forms of art. Although this line of thought is almost entirely overlooked today, this was a widespread idea in the nineteenth century that can be found within the work of theoreticians of various disciplines.[43]

The American scholar Brander Matthews equates the ontological and the phylogenetic evolution in these terms:

> In the childhood of a race or an individual, we discover that the lyric, the dramatic, and the narrative are only imperfectly differentiated from one another; and we can gain some insight into primitive conditions of drama by going back to our own childhood, since youth is the special season of make-believe, strong as that instinct is in all the seven ages of man.[44]

This equation of individual and cultural development is symptomatic of nineteenth-century attitudes towards the diversity of cultures. In his 1840 *Vorlesungen über die Philosophie der Geschichte* (*Lectures on the Philosophy of History*), Hegel divided the world into various spheres in relation to the age of man. In accordance with the imperialist logic of the time, the argument valorizes the idea of Western supremacy but the comparison nevertheless reveals some 'uncanny' parallels and similarities:

> As the Greeks began to look more like 'Red Indians' or 'Australian aborigines,' and their tragedy more like primitive animal dances, the wall that stadial aesthetic theory had painstakingly constructed between primitive artifact and civilized art began to crumble.[45]

Stone Peters has demonstrated the ways in which this perspective had a lasting impact on the theoretical understanding of drama and performance. It became evident that it was not just a 'clean' genre of literature but rather a cultural practice that involved a substantial transformation of the individual:

> The overall transformation in the identity and definition of drama – incorporating, as it now did, pantomime, dance, ritual, indeed any performance or 'representation by action' – challenged the sovereign place that the concept of mimesis had held in dramatic theory at least since Aristotle. Mimesis was, of course, still strongly present in primitive dramatic aesthetics as an originating principle (the reenactment of recent events in the heat of emotion), a utilitarian pursuit (one imitated the emu to call it to the hunt), and a magical practice (one imitated the totem to invoke its aid). But these acts seemed, in their ritual guises, to transcend mimesis. For primitive imitation contained an element of real embodiment: one did not merely imitate the god; one became the god.[46]

While this transformative quality can be also found in the later conceptualization of Performance Studies, for the historical context of the late nineteenth century, it is much more important to realize that this paradigm had a substantial influence on theoretical as well as on artistic discourse.[47] To fully understand this paradigm, it is important to keep in mind that the commonplace notion of 'primitive societies' was not only developed through printed visual and textual material but also through the exhibitionary culture of the period. At the world exhibitions, ethnographic spectacles displayed 'primitive cultures' to Western audiences, confronting them by their immediate, physical presence.[48] Notwithstanding the artificial, and in many cases commercial, character of these exhibitions, we know of many intellectuals who in one way or another were deeply touched by these encounters. In this context, it is also important to keep in mind that the end of the century saw an increasing number of touring companies, especially from China, Japan and occasionally from Indonesia, who presented their theatrical traditions to Western audiences. It is widely acknowledged that these performances had a substantial impact on the aesthetic of modernity, such as the presentation of the Indonesian Wayang on composers such as Debussy and Satie, later Balinese dancers on Artaud, or Chinese theatre on Brecht.

In a more abstract sense, discussions regarding ritual encouraged the development of different concepts of performance. Erika Fischer-Lichte has argued that Max Reinhardt's production of *Oedipus Rex* (1910) marks a shift in the theatrical mode of production. Reinhardt not only sought new performance spaces, like exhibition halls or circus buildings that were not purpose-built for theatre, but his productions also created an aesthetic experience that Fischer-Lichte describes as transformative. According to her reading, Reinhardt created a *theatrical community*:

> Since the sense of community did not arise through a common symbolism which explicitly referred to the beliefs, ideologies etc. shared by all spectators [. . .] but to very special physical effects brought about by the presence of the masses in the space and by the frequently changing atmosphere, it cannot be regarded as a political, national, religious or ideological community. It came into being mainly, if not exclusively, through performative means developed and refined by Reinhardt in his theatre since the turn of the century. Therefore, I shall call it a theatrical community. A theatrical community is not only a temporary community, as transitory and ephemeral as any performance. It exists, at best, throughout the whole course of the performance and dissolves, at its latest, at the very end.[49]

While the theatrical community pushed the concept of the *Festspiel*, in the Wagnerian tradition, even further towards the idea of a ritual, the intellectual effect of this 'discovered' line of tradition can be traced in two different directions. We can observe conservative thinkers, particularly in the *völkisch* discourse that emerged at the end of the nineteenth century, engaging in a rhetoric of self-ethnification.[50] Scholars of drama and performance paid increasing interest to

FIGURE 6.5: Paul Wegener as Oedipus confronting the masses in Max Reinhardt's production, 1910. Photography by Zander and Labisch. Theaterwissenschaftliche Sammlung, University of Cologne.

pre-enlightened practices and traditions that could be read in the light of the conceptual framework of transformative ritual. In *The Medieval Stage* (1903), E. K. Chambers discussed the significance of folk practices such as the *Sword-Dance*. According to Chambers, the practice of the Sword-Dance is mentioned in Tacitus' *Germania* (*c*. AD 98), although the oldest evidence he can provide of an actual performance is from Nuremberg in 1350. The dance apparently included a martial fight with swords, as well as a ritualistic dance, where the dancers were accompanied by grotesque figures and wore bells.[51] Chambers makes the argument that this kind of dance can be found not only in Germany, where it is best documented, but also in France, Italy, England and Eastern Europe. According to his understanding, the dance reflects the essential rhythm of rural society:

> Its essentially agricultural character seems to be shown by the grotesques traditionally associated with it, the man in woman's clothes, the skin or tail-wearing clown and the hobby-horse, all of which seem to find their natural explanation in the facts of agricultural worship. Again, the dance makes its appearance, not like heroic poetry in general as part of the minstrel repertory, but as a purely popular thing at the agricultural festivals.[52]

Chambers' insistence on the agricultural nature of the dance is central to his comparison of it with the rites of spring and the re-awakening from Frazer's

*Golden Bough* (1890/1906–15).[53] The reference to Frazer is symptomatic of the historical discourse as it emphasizes that Chambers conceived of theatre as being more closely linked to ritual and custom, as opposed to literature. Frazer's eminent comparative study of myth and religion across cultures was the model for a new form of studies that was partly fuelled by the desire to question the notion of Christianity as the dominant religious culture.[54] In his 1936 study *Kultspiele der Germanen* (*Rituals and Games of the Germans*), Robert Stumpfl argues that the Shrovetide plays are essentially of a pagan nature that pre-dates any liturgical or even literary tradition. Providing evidence to support his thesis, Stumpfl describes a series of material objects, such as masks and costumes. Although his ideas are rightly questioned today, Stumpfl's thesis is interesting because it demonstrates his desire to (re)construct a Germanic culture that pre-dates Christianization and which residually survives into his contemporary times. Here, *völkisch* ideology and the political framework of national socialism amalgamate into an inseparable unity, propelling the nation back in time to argue for a homogenous, ethnic identity.

While this self-ethnification played into the strategy for claiming a homogenous ethnic identity, a side-effect of this line of thought was cultural relativism, which was rooted in the practice of cultural comparison. For example, while Brander Matthews emphasized cultural difference – and maybe even a cultural superiority – by introducing the 'primitive' examples of 'childhood of a race or an individual', reducing non-Western ethnicities to the status of ontologically inferior beings. At the same time, he acknowledged the cultural equality of 'primitive play' by stating that it was 'a dramatic action, complete in itself, and yet extremely simple'.[55] The mere process of comparison challenged the concept of an undisputed Western superiority. In his six-volume *A History of Theatrical Art* (1903), the Danish actor and theatre scholar Karl Mantzius noted that:

> It is interesting to notice that the Greek drama so poetical and perfect in form does not differ essentially from the religious festivals of the Indians of the North-West, or that the masques and farces which are still performed in civilised Europe find analogies, for instance, among the Melanesian peoples, inhabitants of the South Sea Islands. We have set ourselves the task of first of all pointing out some fundamental features in the earliest stage of dramatic art, during which all nations may be treated nearly alike, and of subsequently giving an account of the forms of acting in use among some nations of more advanced civilisation.[56]

Although Mantzius structures his argument along a line of evolutionary development, leading up to Western drama, his cultural relativism is still recognizable.

Mantzius was not alone in voicing a paradoxical attitude to this matter. The German scholar Carl Niessen, who started teaching Theatre Studies in Cologne in 1919, came to a similar conclusion when he summarized his work in his *opus summum*, the unfinished *Handbuch der Theaterwissenschaft* (Handbook of Theatre Studies; 1949–58). Here, Niessen offered – through the prism of Mimus – a wide, sometimes rather associative, range of cultural phenomena which he understood as universal human practices.[57]

Niessen is an interesting case for two reasons. On the one hand, Niessen returned from the First World War as a conservative, *völkisch* intellectual, voicing rather anti-modern sentiments and regarding culture as the expression of the essence of a community. Yet his method of research contradicted this conviction, in so far as he departed from the idea of a general comparability, thus thwarting any idea of superiority. This inner conflict probably led to the idiosyncratic and fragmentary character of his *Handbuch*, which juxtaposes phenomena and examples but does not really integrate them in a broader comprehensive argument.

Niessen's methodology drew him to the material dimension of theatre and performance. He not only included a theatre in his newly established department – a step unprecedented at German universities at the time – but he also re-staged plays with his students, which he had found in archives, creating assemblages of historical texts and contemporary visual language. He often used his own

FIGURE 6.6: Carl Niessen and his students in his collection – note the different masks hanging on the wall behind him, *c.*1930. Photography by Hermann Beissel. Theaterwissenschaftliche Sammlung, University of Cologne.

archival findings, such as a 1590 version of *Everyman* performed in Cologne and written by Jaspar von Gennep, and 'investigated' them through the students' performance; an early version of practice as research, one might claim. But he also started to collect all sorts of material to document theatre and performance history. The collection that today forms the foundation of the Theatre Collection of the University of Cologne comprises puppets, shadow-puppets, masks, play-texts, reviews, set-models, sketches and photographs. Interestingly, the gathering of the material objects mirrors his associative method in the *Handbuch*: 'high' and popular culture, Western and non-Western objects can be equally found. Although unique in the omnivoric scope of its collecting policy, the foundation of archival collections of theatre material is also symptomatic for the broadened understanding of theatre in this period. Similarly, the Klara-Ziegler-Stiftung in Munich (founded in 1910), the Harvard Theatre Collection (founded in 1901) and the Theatre Collection at the University of Bristol (founded in 1951) were also established to gather material traces of theatre history.

The 'discovery' of performance as an academic field marks an important intellectual turning point that fuels scholarly discussion well into the twentieth century. By acknowledging the distinction between drama and performance, a light was shone on Performance Studies, a field that had been previously marginalized or even regarded as inferior. At the same time, the study of the materiality of theatre (the material artefacts that would substantiate the significance of the historical dimension of drama) helped to integrate theatre into the canon of cultural phenomena and to demonstrate its independence from the field of literature. Attracting scholarly interest from different perspectives such as literary studies, art history and ethnography, theatre found its way into the academic canon and thereby completed its embourgeoisement.

# CONCLUSION

The necessity to interpret theatre, to make sense of this art form and social venue, gained a strong momentum during the course of the nineteenth century. While the process of bourgeoisification that had started in the Age of Enlightenment carried on and determined the intellectual horizon of this quest, it was not an end or a satisfying explanation in itself. The omnipresence of theatre and theatrical practices in the modernized societies called for a more diversified foundation. The claim to be a 'moral institution' did not suffice and no longer truly resonated with the audience's experience. It was from within the net of multi-vocal discourses regarding professionalization, national identity, the quest to discover the hidden foundations of human beings and their society, that the purpose and function of theatre was overhauled and completely redefined in the nineteenth century.

# CHAPTER SEVEN

# Communities of Production

## *Introduction*

PETER W. MARX

While the concept of the *nation* is quintessential to the political discourse of this era, the concept itself is much more complicated in its cultural consequences than it appears at first sight: especially during the Napoleonic wars, the nation was increasingly defined as an ethnic community existing in its own autonomous territory. Thus, the order installed by the Congress of Vienna disappointed many nationalists as it partly restored an old, aristocratic order but paid little attention to the concept of nation and the many groups that sought to define themselves as nations. Germany and Italy each unified in 1871; other nations, such as Poland, Hungary and Ireland each identified internally as an ethnos but were absent from the political map, appropriated by larger states.

The term 'nation' gained its political impact partly from a nostalgic, partly anti-modern attitude that associated the nation with the concept of community. Ferdinand Tönnies, often praised as one of the founding fathers of German sociology, developed a central conceptual opposition in his 1887 *Gemeinschaft und Gesellschaft* (*Community and Society*, translated into English in 1957). While Tönnies describes the community as the expansion of what previously had been the familial group, society is described as a Hobbesian nightmare of a precarious ceasefire. The rising nationalism in the nineteenth century increasingly borrowed biological terms in order to naturalize and essentialize its political claims leaning on this fantasy of the community as the genuine nucleus of all social relations and political unities.

While this became a rather effective social catalyst in those states that claimed congruence of territory, a homogenous population, and a cooperative the political order, other communities found themselves in opposition to the political system, fighting for territorial autonomy and political independence. In these cases, artistic representation, in painting, music, literature and theatre became a central tool to make their claim.

This chapter comprises two different cases that are aligned in the same cause, creating a visible presence of their community on the international stage, but work on totally different schemes and with almost opposite means: Kathleen Gough discusses the emergence of what later became the Abbey Theatre style, a form of acting that was almost completely void of traditional theatrical means. This provocative style, praised as being the utmost in realism – even to the point of being not art at all – was rooted in the claim of authenticity, the product of a search for genuine Irish body language, in relation to modern technology such as the photograph and gramophone. It transformed traditional storytelling into an aesthetic form that would resonate as Modernist aesthetics while evoking traditional folkways.

Zoltán Imre, in contrast, traces the rise and transformation of Hungarian operetta. This popular music form is still largely ignored by scholars because it is considered as mere entertainment, a lesser form than the opera proper. But Imre shows how Hungarian operetta composers managed to create international visibility for a Hungarian identity on the international stage. The price was reducing the Hungarian to a stereotypical image that oscillated between the Eastern European Other and a variant of an unknown and unspecifiable continental culture. It was exactly the commercial and modifiable character of the operetta – its mouldability – that enhanced global circulation while also restricting national self-representation to a stereotypical stock character.

Both cases – independent from each other, yet in line with the question of propagating a national, ethnic identity even while facing the lack of any political foundation – reflect the fact that the nineteenth century was haunted by the idea of an ideal community, longed for yet absent from the everyday-life experience.

# The Techno-Primitive Routes of the Abbey Style: Acting and Not-Acting in the Irish National Theatre Society[1]

## KATHLEEN M. GOUGH

The Abbey style of acting has not been the subject of much critical attention in the cultural history of the Irish National Theatre Movement. While this is partly due to available materials, Anthony Roche rightly suggests that the critical attention paid to the literary side of the movement over examinations of theatricality have to do with the politics of an Irish cultural nationalism that did not want to admit to outside influences of any kind.[2] While critics and scholars have written about the Abbey Theatre as the cultural wing to Irish nationalism, attention to the Abbey style of acting demonstrates that the communities that helped to produce the Irish National Theatre were multiple and diffuse. Moving away from a literary teleology where 'authorial talent is paramount',[3] and, instead, focusing on the acting style reveals a web of interrelated communities of production of which the playwright is only one member.

Taking seriously W. G. Fay's claim that 'the Abbey Theatre was first and foremost a theatrical not a literary movement',[4] a cultural history of the Abbey style brings into focus the ways that playwrights, actors, critics, directors, storytellers and the concurrent appearance of new audio-visual technologies at the *fin de siècle* helped to produce this mode of 'realistic' acting. On the one hand, there was the European international theatre community that established a naturalistic style that supported amateur, non-commercial theatre that can be traced to Ibsen's dramaturgy in Norway (and productions of his plays in London), to Andre Antoine's direction at the Théâtre Libre in Paris, and Stanislavsky's theories of acting in Russia.[5] All of these influences – but particularly Antoine – informed the acting methods developed by the Fay brothers for the Abbey productions. This acting method then directly helped to establish a model for 'over six hundred little theatres all over the United States' that emerged following the Abbey's first 1911 tour to the US.[6]

There are also two communities of *indirect* influence that appear to be of completely different orders, but form a natural pairing at the *fin de siècle* and can be thought of as a kind of 'techno-primitivism'.[7] For the purposes of this chapter, 'techno-primitivism' is the manner in which the Abbey style of acting was informed by the simultaneous influence of the storytelling communities in the west of Ireland, and the audio-visual technologies invented in the late nineteenth century that radically changed human perception of time and space in the Euro–North American world. The acts of listening and seeing are central animating devices in folkloric descriptions of the ostensibly 'primitive' storytelling communities that were conceived of as spatially remote and temporally distant from the modern in the late nineteenth century. The technological corollaries to these 'human' acts of listening and seeing are manifest in the invention of the phonograph (later called the gramophone), the camera, and the nascent silent film device, called the kinetoscope – all of which were popular in Ireland in the 1890s.[8] While early electronic technologies were not used in the productions of the Irish plays of the *fin de siècle*, from the mid-nineteenth century 'the history of live performance [has been] bound up with the history of recorded media'.[9] The Abbey style was, in this respect, a mode of realistic acting that oscillated between the immediacy of traditional storytelling and the hypermediacy of new recorded media while attempting to efface these mediums; thus, it is best understood as a mode of 'techno-primitivism'.

As Anthony Roche reminds us, 'Irish drama arguably had its origins as much in the communal art of *seanchai*, the act of oral storytelling, as in a more formal written script performed on a proscenium stage in an urban centre'.[10] This is a good way of explaining the dramaturgical influences of the Abbey playwrights who borrowed from the immediacy of oral storytelling communities in the west of Ireland. However, the manner in which the Abbey style of acting borrowed from technological media indicates less direct intent; nevertheless, this media is part of the web of communities of production. The 'company's art of acting by doing nothing', writes Malcolm Kelsall, 'seems to have appeared a little weird, even stilted'.[11] Maurice Bourgeois further explains how the 'Irish players were taught to obliterate themselves as much as possible in order to concentrate the onlookers' attention on the speakers'.[12] The players' lack of movement, which simultaneously focuses attention on a single speaker, functions as the human equivalent to a zoom focus on a camera lens. In this way, if the critics had considered how the acting was itself unwittingly mirroring or reproducing the act of photography, then 'the art of acting by doing nothing' – which may have simply been read as 'not-acting' – might appear less 'weird'.

Even more telling is the manner in which, in the decades following the codification of this style, Hollywood drew as heavily on Abbey actors as the New York or London stages. This demonstrates how, for the Irish community, the 'Abbey style' was a means of gaining visibility both internally and in international contexts that encompassed live and recorded (film) media.[13] The 'peasant plays' of the Abbey repertoire highlight how the idiosyncratic theatrical style of the Abbey players was produced and refined by many communities: European non-commercial theatres; European and Irish directors; Irish playwrights; Irish amateur actors; the storytellers in the Irish-speaking communities of the west of Ireland where Synge and Gregory collected folklore for their plays; the critics who sought to articulate the idiosyncrasies of this new acting style; and the late nineteenth-century technological inventions in both sound and image that swiftly and subtly became the framing machinery by which the Euro–North American world understood what it meant to be 'realistic', or even 'real'.

Proto-routes of the Irish National Theatre Movement are illustrated in Augusta Gregory and J. M. Synge's collecting and recording of folklore and ethnography in the west of Ireland and the Aran islands in the 1890s.[14] What these collections unwittingly reveal is that the 'primitive' was always modern. In fact, the 'peasant culture' in the west of Ireland was at the apex of modernity:

FIGURES 7.1 and 7.2: Irish actress Kathleen Drago, *c.*1907. These photographs from the early Abbey period are indicative of the gestures and costumes used by actresses in Synge's peasant plays. Courtesy NUI Galway.

these spaces and the people residing in them were no more spatially remote and temporally distant than the technologies of the phonograph, the photograph and the kinetoscope that were beginning to be used to record their folkloric 'primitivity'. Bodies, stories and technologies all webbed their way back and forth across the Atlantic, to and from America, Europe, Ireland and the rest of the British Isles, and it was the culmination of all of these communities of production that was manifest on the Abbey stage.[15]

J. M. Synge's *Riders to the Sea* is one exemplary instance where we can recognize the narrow focus on authorial talent and literary teleology to reveal the diffuse communities responsible for producing the quintessential Abbey style of acting. The initial productions of this play illuminate the multiple modes of remediation happening on the stage. This is no 'simple repurposing, but perhaps of a more complex kind of borrowing in which one medium is itself incorporated or represented in another medium'.[16] This diffuse 'techno-primitive' community effort would then impact the directors, actors, and critics – all of whom worked intentionally and diligently to bring to life this new mode of realism.

## TECHNO-PRIMITIVE ROUTE 1: STORYTELLERS, THE CAMERA AND THE ABBEY STYLE

Synge's *The Aran Islands* recounts a moment when he returned to the islands for the second summer. Greeting his host family and local companions from his previous trip, he describes a scene that might best be understood as a kind of gendered techno-primitivism that eventually influences Synge's dramaturgy, and has an indirect influence on the work of the actresses in *Riders to the Sea*:

> I had some photographs to show them that I took here last year, and while I was sitting on a little stool near the door of the kitchen, showing them to the family, a beautiful young woman I had spoken to a few times last year slipped in, and after a wonderfully simple and cordial speech of welcome, she sat down on the floor beside me to look on also.
>
> The complete absence of shyness or self-consciousness in most of these people gives them a peculiar charm, and when this young and beautiful woman leaned across my knees to look nearer at some photograph that pleased her, I felt more than ever the strange simplicity of the island life.[17]

The woman's delight in gazing at the unnamed photographs is transformed into Synge's erotic delight as he converts the young woman's movements into a moving image of island life. Somewhere between text and image, the description begins to seem more like an early cinematic scene for a single viewer looking at moving images in a kinetoscope that first appeared in Dublin in 1895.[18]

In the late nineteenth century, the use of women's bodies to illustrate how the 'primitive', domestic and organic shape-shift into the innovative, scientific and inorganic is pervasive.[19] It serves as an important index for how naturalistic acting oscillated between the immediacy of everyday life and the hypermediacy of recorded media in the time-space of the theatrical performances (and where questions of naturalism and the 'woman question' were often mutually reinforcing).[20]

Immediately following this scene Synge writes, 'this year I see a darker side of life in the islands'.[21] He discusses the cold and grey weather, the reliance on fishing as a source of livelihood by the men – young and old – on the islands, and the loss of young men through death and migration. He also recounts a letter from America written by a son of the host family: 'All evening afterwards', he writes, 'the old woman sat on her stool at the corner of the fire with her shawl over her head, keening piteously to herself'. Reflecting on the harsh reality of island life, he continues this thought: 'The maternal feeling is so powerful on these islands that it gives a life of torment to the women. Their sons grow up to be banished as soon as they are of age, or live here in continual danger of the sea.'[22]

These brief lines, along with the description that precedes, encapsulates the entire *mise en scène* of *Riders to the Sea* – both its form and content. Take, for instance, the following scene in which Maurya, the Irish matriarch in *Riders to the Sea* who has just had a premonition that she has lost her sixth and final son to the sea, is then confirmed in her fear, which is also a kind of resignation. Maurya's monologue and the action that follows is a subtle mixture of realism and ritual that simultaneously coheres to the frame of the photograph on its way to becoming the kinetoscope:

I've had a husband, and a husband's father, and six sons in this house – six fine men, though it was a hard birth I had with every one of them and they coming to the world – and some of them were found, but they're gone now the lot of them [. . .] There was Stephen, and Shawn, were lost in the great wind [. . .] There was Patch after was drowned out of a curagh that turned over. I was sitting here with Bartley, and he a baby, lying on my two knees, and I seen two women, and three women, and four women coming in, and they crossing themselves, and not saying a word. I looked out then, and there were men coming after them, and they holding a thing in the half of a red sail, and water dripping out of it – it was a dry, dry day, Nora – and leaving a track to the door.

[*She pauses again with her hand stretched out towards the door. It opens softly and old women begin to come in, crossing themselves on the threshold, and kneeling down in front of the stage with red petticoats over their heads.*][23]

The red sail carrying a body, 'water dripping out of it' on a 'dry, dry day', evokes a montage of chilling images, all of which are imbued with both photo-realism and religious ritual: everything from water dripping from Christ's bloody body on a desert mount, to the power of the sea to act as nature's capricious provider and destroyer, and, of course, the dead body of her son. The image was so chilling that the critic for the *Irish Times*, in a review from 1904, said that the play was 'unfit for presentation', and that 'the long exposure of the dead body before an audience may be realistic, but it is certainly not artistic' (mirroring debates about the artistic merit of photography at this time).[24] Even the petticoat, an everyday object worn around a woman's body, becomes a metaphoric bloody womb, and a mourning veil as it stands in place of what has been violently expunged. This scene indicates that the 'spiritual austerity' of the Abbey style, as C. E. Montague describes it, has to do with a performance form that seems to owe to the intersection of ritual, theatre and photography.[25]

In a chapter entitled 'Good Acting' in Montague's *Dramatic Values* he discusses the 1906 production of *Riders to the Sea* that he first reviewed for the *Manchester Guardian,* and highlights aspects of the Abbey players such as 'composure', 'gesture', and 'haunting expressiveness' before making an analogy to how these attributes are akin to 'the painting of some masters':

> The Irishmen keep still and white, and tragic consequences enfolds them; set on that ground of grave and simple composure, the slightest gesture carries you far in divination of what prompts it; whole scenes put on a comely vesture of delicacy and containment and a haunting expressiveness, as, in the painting of some masters.[26]

Synge said that he wished to write 'like a monochromatic painting, all in shades of one colour'[27] which is a description more suggestive of the craft of early photography than painting. That is, the 'weird' quality that critics note of the Abbey style at this time stems from an ontological question: what is mirroring what? Are the actors behaving like the camera, or is the camera capturing their image? The relationship between humans and technology is in constant dialogue.

## TECHNO-PRIMITIVE ROUTE 2: STORYTELLERS, THE VOICE AND THE ABBEY STYLE

Notwithstanding the power of 'gesture' and 'composure' of the women in *Riders to the Sea* to help illustrate the Abbey style of acting, the musicality of language is vital to evoking those aspects of 'realism' that cannot be seen. In *Visions and Beliefs in the West of Ireland*, the collection of folklore Augusta Gregory gathered over two decades in both the Aran islands and in the west of

Ireland beginning in the 1890s, Gregory announces, 'even when I began to gather these stories, I cared less for evidence given in them than for the beautiful rhythmic sentences in which they were told', because they 'provide a clue, a thread, leading through the maze to that mountain top where things visible and invisible meet'.[28] She imagines her collection not so much as a textual equivalent to a photograph that offers a transparent window on social reality, but a sonic, rhythmic rendering of such a photograph. In other words, the collection operates like a phonograph recording.

In 1893, the same year that the phonograph appeared, the Gaelic League, founded by Douglas Hyde, began printing Irish-language material.[29] The phonograph made the commodification of Irish culture – particularly traditional music – possible to a greater degree. As a contributor to the 1893 magazine, *Phonogram*, wrote: 'transient speech has now been rendered not merely material and permanent, but capable of being transported through geographical space, like any other product of nature or art'.[30] Nevertheless, this did not make the 'Irishness' it recorded any less 'phantasmic'. As a way of describing the unreal, illusory or spectral, Christopher Morash's description of this 'phantasmic Irishness' as it relates to oral culture and the sound of the phonograph is also manifest on the Irish stage in plays such as *Riders to the Sea*. On the one hand, there is the question of how the voices of the actors are described as musical instruments – disembodied, like sound coming from a phonograph. This is evident in W. G. Fay's description of how he desired the actors to 'keep a music' in their speaking 'by having all of the voices harmonized'.[31] Gregory's makes an equivalent statement about the 'rhythmic sentences' of the oral storytellers, and Fay further describes how his brother Frank (who concentrated on the actors' speech in the rehearsal process) 'was convinced that the basis of all good acting was good speaking, and good speaking depended on good voice production'. In this way, Frank was determined to 'produce a speaking voice in himself, as the great Italian masters produce the singing voice in their opera pupils'.[32]

On the other hand, 'phantasmic Irishness' describes the extraordinary phenomena recounted in oral stories. Like all of Gregory's *Visions and Beliefs in the West of Ireland*, a testament to reality of the unseen. Sections of the collection take us through such territory as 'Seers and Healers', 'Away', 'The Unquiet Dead', 'Banshees and Warning' and 'Appearances'. And while all record experiences of pain, of loss, sickness, death and migration, the manner in which these experiences are expressed by Gregory's informant transports readers/listeners into the world of the phantasmic.

The figure of Biddy Early, for instance, a wise woman and healer who lived in County Clare, is the most prominent 'character' in the folklore collection. She is both reviled by the Catholic clergy and sought by the community for her powers to heal. As a bridge to the past (she has been dead twenty years when

Gregory goes to search for her), the stories told about her tell history in another way. We will never find Biddy Early in an archive (aside from the one Gregory now creates); she is known only through the voices of others. Take, for instance, the following story:

> There was a woman, Mrs. Leary, had something wrong with her, and she went to Biddy Early. And nothing would do her but to bring my son along with her, and I was vexed. What call had she to bring him with her? And when Biddy Early saw him she said, 'You'll travel far, but wherever you go you'll not escape them.' The woman he went up with died about six months after, but he went to America, and he wasn't long there when what was said came true, and he died. They followed him as far as he went.
>
> And one day since then I was on the road to Gort, and Madden said to me, 'Your son's on the road before you.' And I said, 'How can that be, and he dead?' But still I hurried on. And at Coole gate I met a little boy and I asked did he see any one and he said, 'You know well who I saw.' But I got no sight of him myfelf.[33]

This oral narrative of a young son returned as a ghost, appearing as a vision to those along the road in Gort, has an equivalent in *Riders to the Sea*. In the scene directly preceding Maurya's monologue recounting the death of her husband and six sons, she tells her daughters of the scene she just witnessed along the road, bringing home the news of death that blankets the play. It not only indicates the manner in which visions are considered everyday occurrences (as they are in the story of Biddy Early and Mrs Leary), but also indicates the importance of the cadence of the voice as it speaks slowly, softly, whispers, keens and remains silent. These are small rhythms and sounds less attuned to live theatrical performance than to either a fireside storytelling session, or a phonograph where one would need to listen at close distance:

> MAURYA.  (*speaking very slowly*). I've seen the fearfulest thing any person has seen, since the day Bride Dara seen the dead man with the child in his arms.
> CATHLEEN and NORA.  Uah. [*they crouch down in front of the old woman at the fire*]
> [. . .]
> MAURYA.  I've seen Michael himself.
> CATHLEEN (*speaking softly*).  You did not, mother; it wasn't Michael you seen, for his body is after being found in the far north, and he's got a clean burial by the grace of God.
> MAURYA (*a little defiantly*).  I'm after seeing him this day, and he riding and galloping. Bartley came first on the red mare; and I tried to say

'God speed you,' but something choked the words in my throat. He
went by quickly; and 'the blessing of God on you,' says he, and I could
say nothing. I looked up then, and I crying, at the gray pony, and there
was Michael upon it – with fine clothes on him, and new shoes on his
feet.

CATHLEEN (*begins to keen*).   It's destroyed we are from this day. It's
destroyed surely.[34]

Between 'speaking very slowly', 'speaking softly', speaking 'defiantly' and the
keening, the conversation is entirely preoccupied with what is 'seen'. Just like
the little boy in the story of Biddy Early's visionary powers who declares, 'you
know well who I saw', what cannot be seen is 'documented' by the voice.

In a complementary manner, what cannot be heard is documented by the
way the director attempts to 'write' the story with light, like still photographic
images. When *Riders to the Sea* was realized in its first performance in 1904,
theatre critics who were both laudatory and critical pointed to the affectless
style, or the affect of 'not-acting'. Joseph Holloway, the drama critic for *The
Leader*, praised, in particular, Sara Allgood's performance as Cathleen by saying
that she 'acted with a simplicity that resembled nature so closely it ceased to be
acting'.[35] The question remains: did it cease to be acting in the way that the
critic for the *Irish Times* said (of the same production) that the exposure of the
dead body on stage 'may be realistic, but it certainly is not artistic'?[36] The Abbey
style of acting demonstrates the sweeping changes in the ways that humans and
technology were co-evolving at the *fin de siècle*, and the multiple, diffuse
communities that were responsible for its emergence. It further underscores a
certain kind of radical theatre making no longer associated with naturalism – a
theatre making that made porous the boundaries between the hypermediacy of
artistry and the ostensible immediacy of realism. In a proto-postmodern reversal
of fortune, those qualities considered 'weird' on stage, and potentially even
more-than-human, were those that would soon become the benchmark for
'realism': the still image of the camera, the intricate sound captured on the
phonograph and the moving bodies of the kinetoscope.

# Representing a Nation through Popular Theatre: The Viennese-Budapest Operetta

ZOLTÁN IMRE

The Viennese-Budapest operetta, emerging in the vibrant theatrical landscape of the late nineteenth century, represents a popular genre that is genuinely an international, metropolitan phenomenon yet one that has political implications. Based on the popularity of Hungarian-born operetta composers like Imre Kálmán, Ferenc Lehár, Jenő Huszka, Albert Szírmai, Viktor Jacobi and others, we can declare that there was an interplay between various members of a national group, working in an international context, creating a visibility for a community that had lost its visibility in terms of statehood. As Benedict Anderson has shown, nations have to be imagined in particular and selective styles which achieve tangible and symbolic forms in the traditions, museums, galleries, monuments, ceremonies and other practices by which the images of their communion are constructed.

For the creation, maintenance and self-definition of such a community, it needs to manifest links between the physically separated individuals by representing their common elements and their difference from other peoples and communities. Hence, the representation of a nation as an imagined virtual community is theatrical both onstage – in the (national) theatre (especially) – and offstage, in the various performative manoeuvres of everyday life (parliamentary debate, strikes, receptions, dinners, opening ceremonies and so on).

Eric J. Hobsbawm argued that the formation of a nation-state in nineteenth-century Europe was, in practice, connected to a historically accepted and/or territorially independent country, administrative institutions, an aggressive political practice, an entrenched cultural elite, a national literature and an administrative language.[37] Without an independent state and administrative institutions, people were supposed to supply their legitimization through cultural practices and cultural institutions with symbolic power like the National Theatre, the Academy of Sciences, the National Museum and others. In the Hungarian context of the late nineteenth century, these cultural practices and symbolic institutions were extremely important, since Hungary was part of the Austro-Hungarian Monarchy. Though the Hungarian Kingdom was independent internally with its own parliament and administrative institutions, the financial issues, the army and the external affairs of the Monarchy belonged solely to the emperor, Franz Joseph I. In order to emphasize its power, wealth and possible independence for the future as a separate nation-state, and to defend itself from the emerging new nations (Serbs, Slovaks, Croats, Romanians, etc.) and their territorial claims within and outside the territory of Hungary, Hungary had to make itself visible in Europe and beyond through cultural practices, including popular theatre, and even operetta.

## OPERETTA AND ITS (CHANGING) PERCEPTION

Operetta or 'little opera' as 'the emblem of the emerging middle-class bourgeois society'[38] was developed in the middle of the nineteenth century in France by the composers Jacques Offenbach and Hervé. Carlotta Sorba has summarized its historical development, indicating that operetta was 'a new post-romantic genre of musical theatre, dedicated to fun and laughter'.[39] Within a few years, operetta established a reputation for offering captivating narrative, humour and light music. It gave rise to its own theatrical institutions, a varied and devoted audience, and rapidly expanding repertoire despite its decidedly ephemeral character. Soon, three main styles with distinct national characteristics developed: the French, the English and the Austro-Hungarian versions.[40]

Operetta is an inter- or cross-cultural genre in the sense that it references elite and popular contexts and borrows from various local and international traditions.[41] Though it is based on vaudeville, farce, dance, canzone, persiflage, ballad singing and other popular entertainment traditions, operetta has its own distinct elements. It devotes a central role to dance and music, fashioning new dances (waltz, mazurka, cancan, galop, later foxtrot, shimmy and others) that also garnered a life outside the theatre. It has a tendency to 'parody, drawing on popular and carnival traditions',[42] while telling stories representing ideals, desires and folk wisdom. Its staging is spectacular, involving lavish sets, rich costumes and vast ensembles, while it indulges in 'licentiousness, especially in the seduction of the female character'.[43] Apart from these features, the genre has also had a strong influence on popular culture through its themes, songs and humour, which most often refer to issues outside the theatre, and 'a strong cosmopolitan and transnational character, addressing an international public'.[44]

Though 'mere entertainment', operettas – like other commodities – had their trade routes, important nodal points and their stock exchanges (Vienna: Theater an der Wien, Johann Strauss Theater, Carltheater; London: Gaiety Theatre; Berlin; New York: New Amsterdam Theatre; Moscow and later Budapest: Király Színház), as well as with their sales managers (Wilhelm von Karczag, Karl Wallner, George Edwardes, Henry S. Savage, Marc Klam, Abraham L. Erlanger, László Beőthy and others). The network connected nearly the entire globe. As a result, operettas responded to the demands of the market economy: they were designed to satisfy their customers by producing profit to make the entire enterprise viable.

Though always extremely popular, operetta has tended to be neglected by theatre and cultural history.[45] The profitability of operetta might be one of the reasons why it has barely found its way into textbooks of theatre history, which tend to prefer highbrow artistic achievements over financial success.[46] The other reason might be that operetta composers, with the exception of Offenbach's works like *Tales of Hoffmann* for instance, produced texts that could be canonized. The genre itself has always been seen as second rate in comparison with (highbrow) genres of spoken theatre. Furthermore, as a musical genre, it has always been regarded as inferior to (highbrow) opera and classical music.

Despite these characterizations, operetta was a complex discursive phenomenon. Operettas usually addressed political issues and social problems, using contemporary political and social references, and often attempted to give social and political criticism. The most popular operettas defined and shaped the illusions, desires and expectations of millions and millions of spectators, despite living far away from one another in different cities, countries and continents.

Operettas circulated rapidly among the metropolises: Lehár's *Die lustige Witwe* (*The Merry Widow*), for instance, which premiered in Vienna in 1905 with enormous success, was also staged in Budapest, Hamburg, Leipzig, Berlin, Cologne, London, Madrid, Paris, Brussels, Stockholm and other cities during the following year and then in the United States (New York, Chicago). In 1907, it played in five theatres in five different languages in Buenos Aires, and 'Tripoli's new theatre was also opened with it in 1913'.[47] In Vienna, it was presented 400 times to full houses and in London it had 'an eight-hundred performance run seen by more than one million people'.[48] By the 1970s, its worldwide performances had exceeded 500,000 and 'the sale of piano scores, sheet music, and arrangements for small orchestras, [ran] to between twenty-five and thirty million, the sale of gramophone records [to] between forty and fifty million'.[49] Apart from its musical and theatrical success, the American production generated a new brand name outside the theatre, in a similar way to today's internationally successful musicals: 'Merry Widow hats, corsets, trains, lunches, cigarettes, cocktails, and so on swept the country'.[50]

FIGURE 7.3: Portrait of Lily Elsie in the title role of Sonia in *The Merry Widow*, London, 1908. Photography by Foulsham and Banfield. Theaterwissenschaftliche Sammlung, University of Cologne.

Apart from the individual impact of entrepreneurs and theatre managers, the international appearance of operetta was connected to the complex transformation of European theatre during the last decades of the nineteenth century. In the 1870s, an intense clamouring for spectacles and entertainments increased the number of custom-built venues, from the boulevard theatres in France to the music halls in England and the *Volkstheater* in Germany, Austria, Russia and Hungary. A new generation of commercial theatrical managers took advantage of the developing international commercial and public transport systems and the growing urban populations to offer light entertainment within major cities beyond Europe for people living in the outskirts and new neighbourhoods.[51]

In spite of their popularity and their influence inside and outside Europe, the internationally acclaimed operettas have not been studied and researched systematically, either in economic terms or from ideological, political and cultural points of view. Recently, however, a new trend has emerged in the work of Christopher Balme,[52] Camille Crittenden,[53] Moritz Csáky,[54] Gyöngyi Heltai,[55] Sorba,[56] Marlis Schweitzer[57] and others, which addresses operetta within the economic, political and ideological context of popular culture, and analyses in detail its contemporary interpretations, critical reception, and political, social and cultural references.

Though operetta circulated internationally it was also adapted to satisfy local needs. The entrepreneur-translator's aim of exploiting the operetta's commercial potential thus went through a process of re-contextualization and often renationalization. Though the title of Lehár's most famous operetta, for instance, was literally translated into English as *The Merry Widow*, for its London premiere (8 June 1907), Basil Hood (book) and Adrian Ross (lyrics) handled its content with considerable freedom. They 'turned Pontevedro into Marsovia, Hanna Glawari into Sonia, and Baron Mirko Zeta into Popoff, and let George Graves (in the latter part) interpolate much of his extraneous comic business into the play'.[58]

Kálmán's *Die Csárdásfürstin* was also staged with considerable alteration of character names, locations and narrative. It appeared in Budapest as *Csárdáskirályné* (1916), in Moscow as *Сильва* (1917), in New York as *The Riviera Girl* (1917) and in London as *The Gipsy Princess* (1921). Purchasing the exclusive rights for its performance gave the manager the freedom to translate and adapt the libretto to align it more appropriately with Hungarian, Russian, American or British sensibilities. The staging of Kálmán's *Die Csárdásfürstin* in Vienna, Budapest and London demonstrates that the ideas of national representation (especially how Hungarian characters or themes appeared and changed within an explicitly international phenomenon) are imposed by the community of production.

## *DIE CSÁRDÁSFÜRSTIN* (1915) IN VIENNA

Kálmán's operetta was premiered at the Johann Strauss Theater in 1915. Like other 'Silver Age' Viennese-Budapest operettas, *Die Csárdásfürstin* was set in the contemporary milieu of Budapest and Vienna. Like romantic comedies and other operettas, the main plot of *Die Csárdásfürstin* centred on love winning over social differences, national borders and social prejudices. The Austrian Prince Edwin von Lippert-Weilersheim falls in love with the star of the Budapest

Orpheum, the Czardas-Princess Sylva Varescu, and wants to marry her. His family, however, does not favour the misalliance and arranges another match with his cousin, Countess Stazi. Through various actions, matters are happily resolved when it turns out that the Prince's mother, Anhilte, had once also been an Orpheum singer.

Apart from the negative representation of the Monarchy's elite, the operetta satirically paraphrased one of the basic consensuses of the Monarchy: the 1867 Compromise, the compact that established the Austro-Hungarian dual monarchy. The title of the operetta referred to a dance and folksong, the *czardas*, which the audience could associate with Hungary and the Hungarians. Sylva was staged as a Hungarian operetta princess, and her lover Edwin as an Austrian prince. The happy ending – the scenario between the prince and the Orpheum girl – could thus be seen as a representation of the unification between Hungarians and Austrians under Austrian (male) hegemony. It was especially ironic as it was staged at a time of growing national, political and social tensions.

Kálmán's operetta paraphrased one of the central political issues of the day: the so-called 'supremacy' within the Kingdom of Hungary. Entering the stage of the Orpheum, Sylva was dressed in 'ungarisch-siebenbürgischen Nationalkostüm' ('Hungarian-Transylvanian national costume')[59], and in her entry song, a passionate *czardas*, she openly declared that 'in den Bergen ist mein Heimatland' ('In the mountain my Homeland is').[60] Her Hungarian costume, her passionate Hungarian dance and her reference to Transylvania, an area considered one of the most treasured territories of the nationalistic Hungarian imagination, would make her appear to be *the* perfect representation of Hungary and the Hungarian dream-girl. Her leading status among other nationalities in the Budapest Orpheum could also be meant to show that the Hungarians assumed supremacy over other nationalities. The fact that these nationalities represented by the Orpheum-girls appeared in such a doubtful institution, in the brothel-like Orpheum in Budapest, also satirized these nations and the entire eastern part of the empire.

The satirical effect of the perfect representation of Hungary comes from her name: Sylva Varescu. Her family name sounded Romanian for contemporary audiences in Vienna, and her Christian name referred to Carmen Sylva, the then widely known literary name of Pauline Elisabeth Ottilie Luise zu Wied (1843–1916), the Queen Consort of Romania. Thus, ironically, a Romanian represented the operetta's perfect Hungarian. It also indicated to audiences the conflictual relationship between Hungarians and Romanians, their territorial claims over Transylvania and the problem of national representation as such. The scandal was so huge that Kálmán had to write an apologetic letter to the Hungarian public, published in one of the newspapers.

The Viennese version of Kálmán's operetta successfully represented the ideas, desires and values of contemporary Viennese audiences from an Austrian, imperial point of view, though it also paraphrased the acute social, political, cultural and economic problems of the Monarchy. At the same time, most of the operettas – and among them *Die Csárdásfürstin* – in their times 'fulfilled socio-critical functions, confronted audiences with reality and the miseries of the social and political situation; and though entertaining and playful, they held a mirror up to the Monarchy'.[61] While offering escape, they also criticized bureaucracy and social hierarchy, commented on political, social issues and reflected the multinational and multicultural society of the Monarchy and the changing contemporary world.

## THE *CSÁRDÁSKIRÁLYNÉ* (1916) IN BUDAPEST

The *Csárdáskirályné* opened at Budapest's famous operetta theatre, the Király Színház [King Theatre] in 1916. The adaptation, made by the Hungarian writer and poet Andor Gábor, nationalized the libretto, situating it within the Hungarian literary and cultural tradition, and utilized it as a mnemonic site for the Hungarian cultural and political imagination – still offering allusions, sexual desires and escape from the harsh realities of the day.

Though the plot and the names of the characters were the same as in the Viennese version, the dialogue and the song lyrics, as the Hungarian literary historian Zoltán Hermann pointed out, 'were built on familiar fragments [of the Hungarian national canon] learned by heart at the Hungarian schools, and popular folklore proverbs, jokes, and maxims of the Budapest slang unconsciously built on the audience's understanding and their sense of humour'.[62] The Hungarian public could thus watch a Hungarian operetta, set in contemporary circumstances of the dualist Monarchy, and listen to the music of 'the real ancient Hungarian temperament',[63] while the contemporary jokes and maxims handled their cultural heritage with irony.

The process of nationalization can best be seen in the way Gábor changed the title from *Die Csárdásfürstin* into *Csárdáskirályné*. On one hand, the change elevated the main female character's status from princess (*Fürstin*) to queen consort (*királyné*). On the other, in Gábor's version, the slight difference between princess and queen consort referred to the notion that Hungarians imagined themselves not as weak females but rather as strong and even masculine subjects. As a result, the title focused on Hungary and the Hungarians as males, referring to the main female character only in the role of wife. In addition, the title also ironically suggested that it was she who would commit a misalliance beneath her rank: she was a queen consort and her lover was just a prince. The Hungarian adaptation thus attempted to offer a Hungarian counter-reading to the Viennese version.

Apart from the slight change in her social rank, the queen consort's name was changed radically from Silva Varescu into Szilvia Vereczky. Szilvia was a popular Hungarian second name at that time, and her surname referred to the Verecke Pass, one of the passes of the Inner Eastern Carpathian Mountains, where the ancient Hungarian tribes entered the Carpathian Basin in AD 896 and occupied the land of the future Kingdom of Hungary. Moreover, the letter 'y' at the end of her family name referred (symbolically and ironically) to her (real or assumed) aristocratic ancestors, as ancient Hungarian aristocratic family names often end with that letter (Esterhazy, Podmaniczky, etc.). As a result, the (offensive) suggestion of the Viennese version that the main female character is Romanian was eliminated, and when singing her entry song referring to Transylvania in Hungarian national costume, the queen consort of czardas was represented as an (aristocratic) Hungarian girl from Transylvania.

The ironic undertone of this seemingly perfect representation was that later, when she speaks about herself, she declares that 'I was born in Tiszadada, near Tiszalök'.[64] On one hand, Tiszadada was, and still is, a Hungarian village on the eastern part of Hungary. On the other, it was a compound word and sounded witty to Hungarian (especially urban) audiences. Its first part referred to the second longest river of Hungary, the Tisza, while its second part referred to a nanny (*dada*). Then she mentioned 'Tiszalök', another Hungarian village by the Tisza, near Tiszadada, which conveyed strong sexual undertones. Its second part (*lök*) literarily meant 'to push' or 'to toss', but it also referred to sexual intercourse in Budapest slang. Taking into consideration that her words were used at the Orpheum where sexual service was a usual part of the bargain, it conjured up in the audience's imagination the suspicion that she is not the innocent girl that she pretends to be. Though the libretto created a truly Hungarian character out of Szilvia, it handled her nationality, her origin and her profession with a great deal of irony. The Budapest version of Kálmán's operetta also proved to be a great success, and was performed 300 times, generating an income of one and a half million coronas.

## *THE GYPSY PRINCESS* (1921) IN LONDON

After its premiere in Vienna and Budapest, Kálmán's operetta became an international success, and appeared in Moscow as Сильва (1917), in New York as *The Riviera Girl* (1917) and in London as *The Gipsy Princess* (1921).[65] From the point of view of national representation, its London premiere is especially interesting. On 26 May 1921, the operetta, now entitled *The Gipsy Princess*, was premiered in the West End at the Prince of Wales Theatre. Arthur Miller and Arthur Stanley adopted the libretto to English sensibilities.[66] The operetta was relocated into the Princedom of Coezenach, as a far away or, as the Lord Chamberlain's Office remarked, 'imaginary princedom',[67] a land somewhere in the East.

Coezenach was an imaginary territory that belonged to the tradition established by Johann Strauss II's *Der Zigeunerbaron* (*The Gypsy Baron*) (1885) and Anthony Hope's *The Prisoner of Zenda* (1894), followed by Lehár's *Die lustige Witwe* (*The Merry Widow*), then used in the various novels by Hilda Gregg (aka Sydney C. Geier) and Albert Szírmai's *Mágnás Miska* (*Magnate Miska*) (1916) and Jenő Huszka's *Lili bárónő* (*Baroness Lili*) (1919). As Vesna Goldsworthy pointed out in her *Inventing Ruritania*, 'in the first decade of the [twentieth century] the fiction inspired by Balkan (and East European) royalty and politics was, in fact, reaching its zenith'.[68] These representations depicted Eastern Europe as imaginary landscapes 'particularly suitable for their kind of escapism, however far away and exotic the fictions, lands are portrayed as being, they still represent a recognizably European part of the world'.[69]

Another even more significant alteration in Kálmán's operetta was that the libretto changed the main female character's ethnic origin. In London, Sylva was characterized as the Eastern Gipsy. Apart from the dubious status of her institution, the Purple Kitten Cabaret, her 'Gipsy' entry song 'with Hungarian rhythms'[70] made explicit where she was from and described her characteristics of sensual and eternal pleasure, love, joy and wild delight.

At the time, the 'Gypsy' was one of the most popular representations in (children's) literature,[71] painting,[72] film and theatre. Gypsy characters also appeared in popular operettas like Strauss II's *Der Zigeunerbaron* (*The Gypsy Baron*) (1885), Kálmán's *Der Zigeunerprimas* (*The Gypsy Band Leader/Sari/The Gypsy Virtuoso*) (1910) and Lehár's *Zigeunerliebe* (1910) (*Gypsy Love*) (1911). Their popularity was due to the fact that, at that time, the highly-mythologized Romani travellers were thought to have immigrated into Western Europe from Bohemia and Hungary. The Romani, as Janet Lyon has pointed out, were associated 'by dominant European cultures with itinerant freedom, voluntary poverty, mysticism, extraordinary musicianship, and a refusal of sedentary culture; they were construed as a kind of European noble savage living beyond interpellation by the institutional dictates of modern nation states'.[73]

The Roma were thus conceptualized as the permanent non-European European, described 'as a refuser of state, law, and labour', that 'remained – magically, as it were – outside of history, outside of modernity'.[74] The 'Gypsy' epitomized the culturally alien and exotic Other. In *The Gipsy Princess*, Sylva is depicted as a passionate, free, sexually attractive female, who can seduce the white (Eastern and Western) European males. In Act III, for instance, when the lovers finally meet and are united, the script describes her as 'wearing Eastern costume with veil'.[75] As her costume was not really specified regionally, culturally and socially here, or anywhere in the directions, she was staged as the generalized representation of the Eastern Gipsy, as Other.

Casting the Hungarian actress Sári Petráss for the part of Sylva increased the calculated exoticism. Her appearance in London was a well-organized publicity campaign: capitalizing on details of her private life, the campaign highlighted similarities between Patráss and Sylva's story. Born in Budapest as an aristocrat, she became an actress, made her name in Budapest as an operetta star and then married an English nobleman. During the First World War, there were even rumours that she was executed in March 1916 as a spy.[76] In the 1910s and 1920s, she played leading soprano parts in Budapest, Vienna, London and New York, among them the role of Ilona in Lehár's *Gipsy Love* at London's Daly's Theatre. Before the 1921 premiere, she was so popular that even *The New York Times,* reporting about the theatrical premieres in London, wrote that 'the leading role will be sung in London by Sári Petráss, also familiar in these parts'.[77] The elements of her rather hectic private life, her previous roles and her Hungarian origin were thus built into the London character of Sylva.

At the time, the Hungarian national stereotype was associated with *czardas*, gipsy music, exotic foods and strange costumes. Petráss's Sylva was thus seen by contemporary London audiences as the representation of the definitive (East European) Other. The representation of the Other was even more complicated as Prince Ronald was played by a Serbian actor. Calling them 'Continental artists',[78] the casting also emphasized the fictional Eastern European characters that 'share the ambiguous narrative roles of princes and princesses in a fairy tale'.[79] Whereas, as the Viennese and Budapest versions allowed for references to the political system of the Habsburg monarchy, the London production eclipsed all these overtones.

Sylva in London was just the tamed, desirable and sexually attractive female beauty with an Eastern Gipsy flavour, but still a rather European-civilized woman. She was presented as the exotic stranger, stirring up strange illusions, and offering an escape from the everyday burdens of 'civilized European' life – providing a pleasant escape from the hardships of the day. In short, the grand rhetoric of a 'Land fit for heroes', which accompanied the 1918 election failed,[80] and as *The Times* put it: '*The Gipsy Princess*, as an attempt to make London brighter in these gloomy hours, deserves full houses'.[81]

In spite of these efforts, the London production of *The Gipsy Princess* was not an enormous success, though it still played over 200 performances in London, and then toured in England, Scotland and Wales. The relative failure was partly due to the fact that the operetta dealt with the gipsy theme in a very conventional way. The operetta was neither involved in British, English or even London affairs nor did it evoke a social, political or ideological context.

## CONCLUSION

The different stagings of Kálmán's operetta draw attention to the fact that operettas and other popular genres travel beyond national borders but not without consequences. Operetta and other popular genres also lead us to see how the Other has been represented. The representation of the West, for instance, has always needed to create a 'threatening, dangerous, powerful, and dangerous Other': either the Oriental outsider or the East European, or the Gipsy or the Turk inside Europe. From this point of view, Kálmán's operettas staged the Other as the Budapest Orpheum world and Sylva as the Gipsy Princess. As a result, mainly (West) European (cultural) hegemony and Eastern subordination before, during and after the First World War set a frame within which the West and the East could meet and interact and which leave marks which historians can identify as forms of (il)legibility. Despite fragmentations, divisions and exclusions there have always been connections and interchanges within these territories and cultures. We can treat these operettas and other popular genres, to use Edward W. Said's formulation, as 'overlapping territories with interdependent histories'[82]; and we can regard them and their receptions as 'overlapping areas of experience'[83] within and outside of Europe.

As a result, I have to reconsider my earlier suggestion that 'a national group was working for an entire community's visibility'. I would rather propose that only certain individuals worked this way, and while meeting the demands of the chosen genre and the local audiences' expectations, used the already available Western-projections about Hungarians for their own needs. It can be seen as a conscious effort on behalf of an entire nation; however, it also reflects how individuals put together and utilized the fragments of that projection.

# CHAPTER EIGHT

# Repertoire and Genres

CHRISTOPHER BALME

The long nineteenth century – roughly the period between the French Revolution and the outbreak of the First World War – sees a revolution in the content of theatre linked to shifts from the tightly regulated and licensed 'patent' theatres of London and their equivalents in France and Germany to progressive deregulation in the course of the century. Rapid urbanization had a far-reaching impact on theatre as cities became larger and more diverse and hence audiences more heterogeneous, which is reflected in turn in their tastes and proclivities. Theatre reacted to this social differentiation by initially providing evenings of 'mixed' entertainment and later, as the century progressed, by creating specialized venues devoted to particular genres. The nineteenth century is the century of 'popular' theatre, a highly-loaded term that requires careful parsing. Theatrical repertoire and the many genres that constituted it are an accurate indicator of the changing demographics of cities, the institutions and even the legal status of theatre when a distinction between 'legitimate' and 'illegitimate' drama is formulated, politically debated and legally codified. While the long nineteenth century can boast a repertoire consisting of Goethe's *Faust II*, Victor Hugo's *Hernani* and Oscar Wilde's *The Importance of Being Earnest*, and also covers romanticism, realism, naturalism and modernism with appropriate canonized works including Ibsen and Chekhov, it is also the century in which theatre finally and perhaps for the last time achieved the status of a mass medium which relied on a repertoire of recognizable but not always stable genres. The study of genre and repertoire within the framework of a cultural history of theatre must therefore include popular entertainment, 'high culture' forms such as ballet and opera as well as canonized authors, the most prominent being William Shakespeare whose theatrical presentation could in turn range from Charles Kean's 'authentic' revivals to rough burlesque in blackface.

Genre and repertoire are key terms for understanding theatre as a mass medium. During the course of the century the French term *répertoire* finds its way into most European languages but undergoes a shift in meaning from the early Victorian period, when it meant merely an actor's stock of roles. According to Tracy C. Davis, by the end of the century 'it came to denote something beyond an individual's proprietorship, as in the repertoire of a theatre company or even a repertoire company.'[1] Davis argues that repertoire contributes not only to the formation of often mutually exclusive publics but also acts as a key factor in enabling 'intertheatrical' intelligibility. This term, coined by Jacky Bratton, refers to audiences' ability to establish interconnections between theatrical texts.[2] A key component in such intelligibility was genre because it determines on the level of production assumed patterns of taste; as a receptive category genres are cognitive short-cuts that enable spectators to process the information-rich plethora of signs that any theatrical performance generates. Writers and producers, particularly in a commercially-oriented theatrical culture (and that was most of them in the long nineteenth century) utilized generic conventions to cater to assumed tastes and thereby minimize financial risk. The emergence and disappearance of specific genres can be seen as a way to study the shifting cultural horizons of expectation. The key concept to be explored in this chapter is cultural differentiation. If we see the nineteenth century as a period in which different 'cultures' emerge – working class, lower, middle and upper, as well as different ethnic and religious come into increased contact – then it is logical that this differentiation becomes reflected in the types of theatrical entertainment on offer. Generic variety was catered for in different ways: in smaller centres it is reflected in the mixed bill including dance numbers, melodrama and farce whereas in larger metropolitan centres specialized venues began to cater for particular genres whose audiences, however, often cut across class distinctions.

The chapter is framed by a discussion of institutional changes wrought by new legislation which, across Europe, moved to progressively deregulate theatre, which thereby enabled theatres to respond to the processes of cultural and class differentiation. This led in turn to the 'variety principle', meaning on the one hand that most evenings in the theatre consisted of a potpourri of different genres, and on the other the emergence of specialized theatres such as music hall and vaudeville that created a veritable industry. From amongst a bewildering number of genres the chapter will focus on the three that perhaps most clearly characterize nineteenth-century theatre: vaudeville, melodrama and pantomime. A connecting thread between many different genres is the principle of 'pictorial dramaturgy', whereby new visual technologies were harnessed to create new forms of storytelling predicated on visual rather than verbal means. A final section will look at the central importance of Shakespeare as a canonical author who became an essential part of the theatrical repertoire across genres, languages and cultures.

## GENRE AND INSTITUTIONAL CHANGE

The nineteenth century is the period of genre proliferation in the theatre. If at the beginning of the century genres were limited to a handful of familiar designations: tragedy, comedy, drama, tragicomedy and increasingly melodrama, by the end of the century this number had multiplied tenfold. In Germany, one study counted around forty-five different genres for spoken theatre alone that were current in the 1890s and most of which are today no longer current. Allardyce Nicoll's *History of English Drama* lists over sixty 'designations' for the second half of the nineteenth century compared to around twenty for the second half of the previous century.[3] This proliferation can only be understood against the background of fundamental institutional changes that transformed theatre throughout Europe from a small number of tightly regulated houses limited to specific genres – drama, opera, ballet, etc. – to a commercially-oriented theatre that needed to find a balance between familiarity and innovation for a highly differentiated public, particularly in the larger metropolitan centres, which a combination of mass migration and a population explosion had led to. The population of London for example grew sevenfold between the beginning and the end of the century; Paris and New York experienced similar growth.

These institutional changes had a direct effect on repertoire. In France before the French Revolution the Comédie Française and the Comédie Italienne, in London Covent Garden and Drury Lane, in Germany usually one court or municipal theatre, had monopolies on spoken drama. There was a clear policy on the part of the state to control the spoken word which was deemed potentially subversive in comparison to singing or dance. Already in the late eighteenth century this highly regulated system had led to the emergence of 'mixed' genres of music, dance and pantomime, which thus eschewed being defined as drama. The creation of new mixed genres was both a response to tastes not catered for by the mainstream dramatic genres and also a means to circumvent licensing restrictions.

In England, the licensing laws of the mid-eighteenth century remained in force until the Theatre Regulation Act of 1843 that significantly liberalized the conditions under which theatres could be established and managed and also the types of entertainment permitted to be performed in them. The legislation had been preceded by an intensive public debate over what was seen as the declining standard of theatrical entertainment despite (or because of) the monopoly system in place. Legally, only the patent theatres were permitted to perform so-called 'legitimate drama', a term that became increasingly contested and in the 1832 Parliamentary report from the Select Committee on Dramatic Literature a dichotomy became evident between works where 'the interest of the piece is mental' and an increasing number of genres, known inversely as 'illegitimate drama' (i.e. those works that were not 'legitimate dramas') where physicality or spectacularity dominated: genres such as harlequinades, pantomimes, burlesques and the new hybrid and immensely popular genre of melodrama eventually made the distinction on an institutional level untenable.[4] The report recommended the abolition of the patent system and with it the dichotomy of 'legitimate' and 'illegitimate drama'. Two irreconcilable principles needed to be synthesized: the civilizing notion of a drama as part of national literature, represented by Shakespeare and a canon of mainly Elizabethan worthies, and the equally sacred economic principles of free trade and competition: the latter won.

In France a similar dichotomy pertained. One of the immediate effects of the French Revolution was the temporary abolition of this regulatory system with the effect that many more theatres and performance venues sprang up but also new genres were invented, the most prominent being the revolutionary spectacles staged by the painter Jacques Louis David. This liberalization was retracted in stages until by 1807 Napoleon decreed the reintroduction of a licensing system which limited the number of theatres in Paris to four official and state-subsidized theatres (Théâtre-Français, Opéra, Opéra-Comique and the Opéra-Buffa) and four 'secondary' or commercial theatres (the Théâtre de la Gaîté, Théâtre Ambigu-Comique, Théâtre du Vaudeville and the Théâtre des Variétés). The regulation created three subdivisions that organized theatres according to the categories 'official', 'secondary' and 'fairground/curiosity' thereby taking into account a wider understanding of theatre in terms of theatricality or spectacle. Each venue was limited to performing its specific repertoire.[5]

In the German-speaking countries, theatre remained tightly controlled by similar systems of restrictive licensing with many regional variations determined by the multiplicity of mini-states and principalities.[6] The Prussian Trade Regulation Act of 1869 (*Gewerbefreiheit*), which was extended to the whole of the newly-founded German Reich in 1871, abolished restrictions on the founding of new theatres and established the basis for open market competition. This led indeed to a boom in theatre-building and a proliferation of theatrical venues, especially in the larger cities such as Berlin. After 1871 we see the emergence of numerous and highly-specialized genres that catered more to the eye than the ear. The harnessing of new visual technologies such as the diorama, panorama, projection technologies lead to specialized forms that narrated in visual as much as verbal terms.

From an institutional and legislative point of view genre and repertoire included opera and ballet with their own architectural and institutional frameworks. Although opera and ballet were both institutionally speaking largely court genres in the eighteenth century, this changes in the nineteenth as opera shifts 'from a courtly to a commercial, middle-class audience' so that the same processes of differentiation pertain as in dramatic theatre.[7] While the opera in the eighteenth century oscillated between a binary of 'serious' (*opera seria* or *tragédie lyrique*) and comic (*opera buffa* and *opéra comique*), this dichotomy was extended considerably with several national variations to include composer-specific genres such as the Wagnerian *Musikdrama*, to name only the most conspicuous. Genre could also be institutionally grounded, as in the French grand opera which was linked to the main Paris opera house and a number of prominent composers and librettists such as Giacomo Meyerbeer (1791–1864) and Eugène Scribe (1791–1861). A grand opera was also a genre in its own right distinguished by set of compositional, dramaturgical and scenic conventions that could only be deviated from at great risk. These included a five-act structure, an extended ballet interlude, spectacular crowd scenes, particularly processional scenes and a dramatis personae of elevated birth. The satirical and often parodic counter-model to this exercise in studied opulent grandeur and *gravitas* was the *Offenbachiade*, the brilliant exercises in grotesque satire, and risqué situations set in the demi-monde, synonymous not just with the eponymous composer Jacques Offenbach but also with the Théâtre des Bouffes-Parisiens.

We find analogous developments in Great Britain with the operettas of Gilbert and Sullivan which in their unique combination of fantastical plots, witty lyrics and topical subject matter became a genre *sui generis* and as closely linked institutionally to the Savoy Theatre in London as Offenbach was to the Bouffes-Parisiens. A more genuinely broad-based genre was the musical comedy associated with the Gaiety Theatre in London but by no means restricted to it. A form of musical entertainment that emerged in London's West End during the early 1890s, musical comedy remained popular until the early years of the First World War. This period is conventionally labelled as the age of Edwardian musical comedy, borrowing its name from King Edward VII and the eponymous era of British history (1901–1910). It therefore links the last comic operas of Gilbert and Sullivan with the Broadway musicals of the 1920s and 1930s. The figure who is unequivocally credited with having invented musical comedy is theatre manager and producer George Edwardes (1855–1915). Over a career spanning almost exactly thirty years, the tycoon established an entertainment empire in London's West End, where he owned and ran multiple theatres, including the Gaiety.[8]

For a long time this genre had been considered an obscure part of musical theatre history and thus demoted to the sidelines of musicology and theatre studies. It is now being critically re-assessed for the importance it played in the globalization of theatre during the first fifteen years of the twentieth century:

musical comedy became a medium of extraordinary mobility, transmitted via the transnational travel and communication networks that had been put into place during the nineteenth century. Its shows, which originated in London, were dispersed to all four corners of the earth by itinerant theatrical troupes, which utilized the enhanced travel infrastructures to travel from one urban centre to the next (see Chapter 5).

In the domain of theatrical dance we find analogous processes of differentiation and specialization in response to changing demographics. On the one hand, theatrical dance gains in professionalization and specialization, on the other it develops its own artistic language predicated on an 'exclusive reliance on non-verbal language.'[9] By the end of the eighteenth century, ballet begins to emancipate itself from its primary function as operatic *cour de ballet*. This emancipatory narrative leads finally to specific genres and repertoire, the dominant one being romantic ballet, an era as well as a genre that evolves mainly in France (but also in London) in the early part of the nineteenth century. Although located institutionally within the opera (at the Paris Opera and Her Majesty's Theatre respectively), where the companies continued to provide the necessary entr'actes and interludes required by grand opera, romantic ballet begins to be perceived as an autonomous theatrical form. Romantic ballet is roughly framed by *La Sylphide* (1827) which marked both the debut of Marie Taglioni dancing *en pointe* (i.e. in soft pumps on the tips of her toes), and the cult of the prima ballerina, and *Coppélia* (1870). The generic features of romantic ballet include a basic three-act structure, an eponymous female title figure, a story suffused with supernatural and spiritual elements represented by the now generic tutu, an early form of which Taglioni introduced, and aided technologically by the subtlety of gas lighting to create ethereal and supernatural effects. The classical romantic ballet often begins in a bucolic setting (countryside, market place) but moves in its second act to the oneiric realm, to the *ballet blanc*, where supernatural figures reign supreme. The third act marks a return to the 'empirical' world. In the latter half of the nineteenth century, ballet began to move in new directions and the gravitational centre shifted to Russia where, under the choreographic leadership of Marius Petipa and in collaboration with Tchaikovsky, the Imperial ballet in St Petersburg, with the now familiar 'classical' repertoire of major works such as *Swan Lake* (1877), *Sleeping Beauty* (1890) and *The Nutcracker* (1892) was created.

## THE VARIETY PRINCIPLE

Theatrical dance was not, however, limited to the institutional megaliths of the Paris Opera or the Russian imperial ballet. It flourished as well within the quotidian world of metropolitan and provincial theatre where solo dancers plied their trade as part of variegated evenings of theatrical entertainment, the norm of theatre-going throughout most of the century. The term 'variety' can be seen as both an aesthetic principle and as a template for a whole 'variety' of related genres. These variety genres are on the one hand specific to individual cultures, such as minstrel shows from the USA, music hall from England, or cabaret in France, but they also achieved global impact as the variety show as a format was adopted around the world albeit under different names.

A glance at an early nineteenth-century playbill (see Figure 8.1) from Glasgow shows a 'comic medley dance' on offer as well as several humorous songs. If we look closer at the offerings then it becomes evident that an evening at the theatre consisted of quite literally a variety of genres that evolve eventually in the course of the century into a genre of that name, variety theatre. Although the main offering is a 'Melo-Drama', *Mutineers: or, the Devil and the Dice*, the most popular genre of the century (which will be discussed below), spectators were also treated to a 'laughable Burletta' and a closing domestic Mele-Drama, *Love's Frailities: or, a Rustic's Revenge*. The next evening is also advertised, promising 'a variety of Entertainments'. This quite typical Friday evening at the theatre indexes how genre and repertoire were integrated into wider aesthetic, cultural and media-dependent principles predicated mainly on repetition and similarity. The structure of the evening alternating between 'serious' melodrama, musical interludes, comic short plays and a closing 'afterpiece' remained largely fixed. The variation can be found in the content of the plays. Apart from alternation between serious and comic, high and low, spoken word, song and dance also belonged to the fundamental generic categories of theatrical entertainment. In the light of this basic structure of heterogeneous entertainment forms arranged together, it is only logical that the variety principle, which has its roots in early modern courtly festivities, evolved into its own genre.

One of the most popular and widespread variety genres was the minstrel show which originated in the USA in the early part of the nineteenth century. The term 'minstrelsy' referred to popular ballads of any cultural provenance, although usually associated with a notion of folk tradition. The actual genre initially consisted of such songs with additional short sketches featuring the stock figure of the black southern slave in two main variations: the plantation worker Jim Crow and an urban dandy, to whom were added banjo players and solo dancers. In their aggregation these disparate elements finally solidified into a minstrel show performed by white performers in blackface whose comedic effect focused on replicating demeaning stereotypes of a black stock character. As a genre minstrel shows had a three-part structure consisting of songs and gags (fantasia), sketches and dances (olio) and a short burlesque play (burlesque) finished by a concluding 'walk around' featuring all performers (see Figure 8.2).

By mid-century minstrel shows had become an 'autonomous genre of entertainment with established conventions, a specific style of performance' with their own theatrical venues.[10] They also began to tour with troupes

FIGURE 8.1: Playbill of the Caledonian Theatre, Glasgow, 1828. Glasgow University Library.

# PROGRAMME.

## PART FIRST.

| | |
|---|---|
| Overture, Hero's Quick Step, | Full Band |
| Opening Chorus.—the spot we was born on, | Company |
| Rose of Alabama, | Raymond. |
| Sugar Cane Green, | Mr. White |
| Carry me back to old Virginia, | Company |
| Don't you hear the bells a ringing, | Mr. West |
| Luke of Tennessee, | Raymond |
| Stop that Knocking, | Raymond |

## PART SECOND.

| | |
|---|---|
| Overture, | Full Band |
| O bless that Lovely Yellow Girl, | Bryan |
| Fire down below, | Raymond |
| Lovely Fan, | West |
| The Old Jaw Bone, | White |
| Old Joe, | Bryan |
| Corn Husking, and Grand Festival Dance, | West and Bryan |

## PART THIRD.

| | |
|---|---|
| Rail Road Overture, | Full Band |
| Boatman dance, | White |
| Rise old Napper, | Raymond |
| Ca Chuca, | Mr Bryan |
| Whistling Solo, | West |
| Fare you well, Ladies, | Mestayer, Barry, White and Raymond |
| Miss LUCY LONG, in character, | Bryan |
| BURLESQUE POLKA, | West and Bryan |

TO CONCLUDE WITH AND THE

## DOORS OPEN AT 7.   Concert to commence at 8 precisely.

Cards of Admission 25

FIGURE 8.2: Minstrel show playbill advertising the Bryant Company and its programme, *c.*1860. Laurence Senelick Collection.

performing as far afield as India, South Africa and Australia. In England, Christy's Minstrels, an offshoot of a popular US troupe, crossed the Atlantic in 1857 and established the minstrel show as a hugely popular entertainment form featuring not just the usual singing and dancing but elaborate burlesques of circus and Italian opera alike. The use of blackface and comic stereotypes produced a curious and sometimes complex potential to refract European mores and art through the glass of racial inversion.[11] Their propensity to perform Tyrolean folk-dancing and singing in blackface found its logical and perhaps ultimate variation when a genuine African-American minstrel troupe toured Bavaria in the 1890s, performing Bavarian folk dances in *Lederhosen*.[12]

Perhaps the best-known variety genre in the English-speaking world and the quintessential Victorian popular entertainment form is the music hall, in the words of Barry Faulk, 'Britain's first indigenous and fully capitalized mass culture form'.[13] Originating in informal entertainment in public houses, taverns and penny gaffs, its spread has been seen as an unconscious reaction to the freedoms and restrictions provided by the Licensing Act of 1843: smoking, eating and drinking were banned in the auditoria of 'legitimate theatres' but permitted where singing and dancing were on offer. By 1860 music halls were established institutions, mentioned in parliamentary debates and journalism (usually pejoratively) and prominently featured in advertising as a kind of entertainment. Aimed at working- and lower middle-class audiences, they were also frequented by members of higher classes, particularly men. In the early iterations, music halls were a predominantly masculine form, replete with risqué songs and comedic turns. Their special feature was the provision and consumption of food and drink during the performance (see Figure 8.3). A programme consisted of short plays, particular farces of a domestic subject matter; topical songs in which anything of current interest could be thematized (they can be compared to couplets in popular theatre and vaudeville in France and Germany); also acrobatics, magicians and animal performances could and were integrated into the music hall format. By the 1870s music halls had obtained purpose-built venues, some exceptionally lavish that accommodated the performative and gastronomic requirements of the genre. By this time music hall and variety begin to merge. Because of the 'number' principle, by which single acts seldom exceeded fifteen minutes in length, in larger cities popular performers could appear in several venues in the course of an evening. At their heyday in the 1890s music halls could be found in most neighbourhoods and became differentiated between aristocratic and working-class forms.

In the Anglosphere variety gradually superseded the music hall as the dominant theatrical genre based on the variety principle (in the USA it was known as vaudeville). The principal difference between the two was the elimination of food and drink. Audiences at variety theatres sat in seats and boxes and there was little encouragement of the audience participation that

AN "ANTI-IDIOTIC ENTERTAINMENT COMPANY."

FIGURE 8.3: Music hall performance with spectators seated at tables. Caricature by Alfred Conanen, plate from James Greenwood, *The Wilds of London*, London: Chatto and Windus, 1876. Laurence Senelick Collection.

characterized music halls. Variety theatres spring up in the 1890s and become integrated into a global economy of peripatetic artists and 'variety acts'. This movement of artists (see Chapter 5 on circulation) literally spanned the globe, involving thousands of artists (and some animals). As many acts were largely non-verbal they could appear in Germany or France just as well as Australia. A variety show could include acrobats and ventriloquists but also high-class performers such as Sarah Bernhardt or even Diaghilev's Ballets Russes. Essentially any kind of theatrical entertainment, including early cinema, could be integrated into the variety theatre as long as it conformed to the temporal requirements. Sarah Bernhardt famously refused to perform between animal acts when invited to London ('no tigers') but the financial enticements were considerable. It was not unusual for erstwhile virtuosic actors to revisit their star turns within a variety show performance. In England, specialized and extremely large variety theatres were built after 1900, such as the Coliseum and the Hippodrome designed by Frank Matcham, to accommodate the growing demand.

On the continent and in the USA the same variety principle pertained but under different names: variety was known as vaudeville in the US, and as *variété* in France and Germany. In both Germany and France the variety principle in its cabaret version underwent a transformation from a form of mass popular theatre to a model for theatre reform and aesthetic innovation. In Germany, the Paris cabaret was refashioned into artistically ambitious intimate theatres in Berlin (Max Reinhardt's *Schall und Rauch*), in Munich (*Überbrettl* and Frank Wedekind's *Elf Scharfrichter*) and in Vienna (*Fledermaus*). All these smaller theatres followed the variety principle but attempted to integrate artistically ambitious material with mixed success. Such theatres did however provide a forum for experimental forms such as the free dance of Isadora Duncan, Ruth St Denis and Loïe Fuller, or the touring Japanese theatre of Kawakami and Sadayakko. They also provided a venue for the experimental genre of the one-act play, a form favoured by modernist dramatists such as Émile Zola, Anton Chekhov and August Strindberg.

## POPULAR GENRES: VAUDEVILLE, MELODRAMA AND PANTOMIME

The variety principle is often associated with the French vaudeville which has its origins in the eighteenth century where it arose in response to the strict licensing system and the monopoly of the two state theatres on spoken drama. Although it later became a synonym for variety theatre, for the first part of the nineteenth century, a vaudeville referred to a specific genre rather than a format for different acts. A highly unstable term even in France, a vaudeville was both a genre originating in the 'secondary' commercial theatre combining song, dance, and a short sketches, and the name for the theatres performing them. In the Napoleonic decree of 1807, the vaudeville was defined as 'small plays containing couplets to familiar melodies'. In the nineteenth century, the one-act sketch with songs developed into five-act, full-length plays, 'retaining a few songs and build around a single idea'.[14] The vaudeville developed many sub-genres usually indicated by a hyphen: *vaudeville-farce*, *vaudeville-anecdotique*, or *comédie-vaudeville*, each having a slightly different emphasis. Leading authors of this form were the hugely prolific dramatists Eugène Scribe und Eugène Marin Labiche. It is Scribe who combines vaudeville and comedy (but including songs as an essential component) into a dramatic form defined as a 'light piece with topical reference'.[15] The *vaudeville de mouvement* with its rapid concatenation of scenes and *coups de théâtre* received its literary form mid-century in the works of Labiche. Writing vaudevilles was not a fundamentally deleterious activity for reputation as both authors were inducted into the Academie Française. Judging by the number of written works, the vaudeville was by far the most popular genre on the nineteenth-century French stage, where it became not only synonymous with popular theatre in its country of origin but diffused throughout Europe in countless translations and local adaptations. In this sense the vaudeville can be regarded as the popular theatrical

FIGURE 8.4: *L'Auberge du Tohu-Bohu* by Maurice Ordonneau (libretto) and Victor Roger (music), a 'Vaudeville-Opcretta', was performed as *Hotel Topsy-Turvey* in London and New York, 1897. Hand-coloured etching by E. Buval. Laurence Senelick Collection.

genre par excellence distinguished by its flexibility rather than generic stability, (see Figure 8.4)

Generic instability also characterizes the term melodrama, perhaps the most famous and influential theatrical genre of the nineteenth century. Therefore it is necessary to distinguish between the word and the genre because they are by no means coterminous. The word, meaning quite literally the combination of music and drama, probably originates in a programmatic sense with Rousseau's famous experimental monodrama using pantomime and musical accompaniment, *Pygmalion* (1762). The theatrical genre originates around 1800 and is associated with two main authors: René-Charles Guilbert de Pixérécourt and August von Kotzebue. Their works, although not necessarily using the actual designation, created the special mixture of an emotionally comprehensible and 'manichean'[16] world populated by heroes, heroines and evil-doers where the distinction between good and evil, right and wrong is clearly graspable. Although originating in the theatre, the 'melodramatic mode of excess'[17] permeated into literature and art and continues to this day in cinema and television.

If a point of origin can be identified at all, then it is most probably René-Charles Guilbert de Pixérécourt's 'drama in three acts in prose and great spectacle', *Cœlina, ou L'enfant du mystère* (1800). Set in a pre-Revolution rural village, the title figure, impecunious but kind-hearted, loves Stéphany the son of her uncle and guardian, Monsieur Dufour. Another uncle, the calculating Truguelin knows that she is in fact a wealthy heiress whom he desires for his own son. To conceal the information he cut out the tongue of the poor beggar Francisque who was privy to the secret. During the engagement celebration of Coelina and Stéphany, Truguelin informs the family that she is in fact the daughter of the beggar and hence ineligible for marriage. She is banished from the house but in the meantime, thanks to a wondrous *deus ex machina*, a doctor has repaired Francisque's tongue who now reveals the truth about Truguelin. After a spectacular chase, the latter is arrested and the truth revealed: the beggar was in fact married to Coelina's mother. Emotional, familial and financial order are restored. Hugely successful and influential, the French version alone was performed over 2,000 times at the Théâtre de l'Ambigu-Comique where it established the basic model of the new genre: clear emotional and psychological dualisms representable in visual and musical terms, picturesque settings, and sudden revelations. In Thomas Holcroft's English adaptation and two-act redaction as *A Tale of Mystery* (1802) the generic designation 'melo-drame' was introduced which caught on and became the general designation for the formula. In the same year, a correspondent from Paris reported that at 'the theatre (Le Port St. Martin), an entirely novel species of entertainment is performed; called melodrama – mixing, as the name implies (*mêler drame*) the drama, and *ballêt* of action.'[18]

According to Peter Brooks total exteriority is the distinguishing characteristic of the genre which manifests itself in both psychological and theatrical terms.

> The desire to express all seems a fundamental characteristic of the melodramatic mode. Nothing is spared because nothing is left unsaid; the characters stand on stage and utter the unspeakable, give voice to their deepest feelings, dramatize through their heightened and polarized words and gestures the whole lesson of their relationship.[19]

Of course, this formula underwent numerous variations and refinements as the century progressed and writing responded to current fashions and concerns. The first phase, of which *Cœlina* is an example, (lasting until around 1830) has been termed 'providential melodrama' and usually features 'a single villain, alienated from the social institutions that provide order in this society of hard-working peasants and small shopkeepers'. The prerequisite happy ending is ensured by the fact that 'God watches over innocent goodness and His power will ensure a happy ending'.[20] Romantic melodrama, on the other hand, reveals a fascination with 'fantastic, exotic and supernatural situations.'[21] From mid-century onwards, social issues are also absorbed and processed according to the generic rules. Exemplary of this variation, which Bruce McConachie terms 'materialist melodrama', is Dion Boucicault's *The Poor of New York* (1857). The latter was performed in different versions in different cities and adapted to the local conditions. Instead of divine intervention, human institutions such as the law and the courts are invoked to punish the villain and restore order. The vicissitudes of the stock market and the banking system assume a new and more 'material' function in the scheme of things. In the second half the century, the villain too assumed more complex motivation and by 1870 we even find examples of a 'divided villain-hero'.[22]

Despite these many variations and developments, melodrama remained remarkably resilient in its basic structure throughout the century so that in 1914 a practitioner of the genre, Owen Davis, could still provide a satirical summation of his own practice:

> TITLE (at least fifty per cent of success)
> PLOT Brief story of the play.
> CAST Leading Man, very (even painfully) virtuous.
> Leading Woman, in love with him
> Comedy Man, always faithful friend of Hero.
> Soubrette, very worthy person (poor but honest) and always in love with Comedian.
> Heavy Man, a villain, not for any special reason, but [. . .] 'born bad'.[. . .]
> Father (or Mother) to provide sentiment.
> Fill in as desired with character parts.
> ACT I. – Start the trouble.
> ACT II. – Here things look bad. The lady (having left home) is quite at the mercy of the Villain.
> ACT III. – The lady is saved by the help of the stage carpenter. (The big scenic and mechanical effects were always in ACT III.)
> ACT IV. – The lovers are united and the villains are punished.[23]

If the melodrama dominated the serious category, its rival for the more light-hearted genre was the pantomime. It too was an unstable category with origins in the eighteenth century and replete with local variations. It is therefore perhaps one of the strange ironies of late eighteenth- and early nineteenth-century English theatre that momentous events of great topicality and public interest were presented within the generic coordinates of the pantomime. As a genre pantomime was largely non-verbal, heavily musical and predicated on logical absurdities. The pantomime on both sides of the channel is primarily musical in orientation but included substantial amounts of danced, physically enacted representation. For all its linguistic limitations and dramaturgical absurdities, the pantomime was the genre where 'history' and actuality were often enacted. In the pantomime, the new authenticity discourse of the Enlightenment found its theatrical expression, and not in conventional drama. Authenticity manifests itself, however, in the realm of scenography, not of dramaturgy or characterization.

By the late eighteenth century the English pantomime was a unique theatrical genre with no real equivalent in other European theatre cultures. It combined, 'a felicitous mixture of song, dialogue, accompanied recitative, dancing, farcical stage business, and elaborate scenic spectacle' with 'plots extracted from nursery fables, popular literature, chapbooks and broadsides'.[24] It required a large production team including a writer, a composer and scene designer.

The eclectic nature of the genre has already been noted. It was essentially a hybrid form of musical theatre that evolved parallel to the development of opera. In fact, pantomimes and operas were often created by the same composers. Pantomime music was continuous and made use of the same vocal elements such as arias, recitatives and choruses. It always underscored the mimed movement driving the action, a technique that, according to Roger Fiske, had an influence on the development of the *ballet d'action*.[25] The main motors of the mimed action were the commedia dell'arte figures: Harlequin, Columbine, Pantaloon and his Clown. Their fairly predictable adventures were superimposed onto the variable theme. In the early years, this was often mythological or macabre in nature, or both. By the end of the eighteenth century, however, the genre began to accommodate topical themes, and especially exotic locales. Apart from guaranteeing comedy the harlequinade invariably made extensive use of magic and other fantastical tricks. Harlequin disappeared in full view or transformed himself or other figures into animals or statues. It was also not unusual for Harlequin to venture as far afield as the moon or to travel to China or to appear as an American Indian to satirize modern life.

Pantomime theatres relied on the most up-to-date theatrical technology to facilitate spectacle that the genre required. In late eighteenth-century pantomime, such as *Omai, or A trip round the world* (1785) staged by Phillipe Jacques de Loutherbourg, autochthonous performance forms (songs, dances, costumes) culminating in a spectacular procession of newly-discovered Pacific peoples are replicated on stage in a quasi-ethnographic manner within the unlikely dramaturgical framework of a harlequinade. A late nineteenth-century example, the adaptation of *Alice in Wonderland* (1886) by Joseph Addison, still retains clear parallels with its predecessor. Its use of commedia dell'arte characters, transformation scenes and business plus improbable plot twists established a loose relationship with historical reference and events in the first example and a literary model in the second. Both – historical events and literary source – are, however, little more than points of departure for the generic exigencies of evoking wonder and mirth. In the late nineteenth-century development in England, the so-called Christmas pantomime, or 'panto' for short, introduced the cross-dressing convention of the Dame, meaning that the often evil, central female character was played by a man as a virtuosic comical role, whereas the male lead was played by a young and attractive woman (see Figure 8.5), a convention the pantomime shared with its raunchier cousin, the

FIGURE 8.5: Lydia Thompson as Robinson Crusoe and Willie Edouin as Man Friday in the *Burlesque Robinson Crusoe*, New York *c.*1876. Photography by Mora. Laurence Senelick Collection.

burlesque (see below). In the Christmas form, the pantomime demonstrated a remarkable resilience and continues to this day to enjoy great popularity in the English-speaking world.

## PICTORIAL DRAMATURGY

Although both the melodrama and pantomime invariably included spectacular scenes and were predicated on a visual dominant, this element was further developed in the nineteenth century to include specialized genres that derived from the technology used: panoramas, dioramas, magic lantern shows, *vues optiques*, etc., were all technologies that could and were adapted for presentation in theatres. Of these the most important were the panorama and diorama. The former were autonomous venues that enabled spectators to enjoy 360-degree, hyperrealistic representations of landscapes, cityscapes or battles. A special form was the moving panorama, which shared the name if not the actual technology with the permanent panorama. The moving variety consisted of paintings arranged on spools that were scrolled past the audience as if being seen from a moving train or coach. They were 'performed' both as autonomous entertainments and employed in plays such as melodramas as a kind of special effect. Because of their transportability, they were quickly integrated into the repertoire of minstrel and variety shows where they constituted a separate 'act' involving a lecturer to explain the images, a mechanist and an accompanying musician. The diorama, patented by John Arrowsmith in 1824 (although the technology was in fact invented by Louis Jacques Daguerre in Paris) was a 'flat picture with an illusion of depth and, most important, capable of changes in lighting so dramatic as to alter its aspect'.[26] Its key technical innovation consisted in the projection of daylight through a translucent surface. It too required initially specialized circular venues but later became integrated into scenography where artificial light was employed.

Another 'minor' but immensely popular visual genre was the tableau vivant (and its related solo forms such as the 'attitude'). The practice of presenting a static visual image using live performers had its origins in medieval theatre, but it became a dramaturgical and scenic device particularly popular in melodrama 'to depict a climax of action in melodrama and was entirely pictorial in groupings, attitudes, and the sense that all motion was absent'.[27] For this reason one can speak of 'pictorial dramaturgy' to convey the importance of this dimension throughout the many genres of nineteenth-century theatrical culture.[28] Apart from its use within performances, tableaux vivants, living statues and attitudes were also practised as an autonomous form within variety shows or as independent presentations. Famous paintings or statues were re-presented live and in costume for the delectation of a connoisseur audience; the more 'popular' variety made use of a legal loophole which permitted the public display of the nude body so long as it did not move.

## SHAKESPEARE HIGH AND LOW

Beyond all regional and national variations, the theatrical repertoire in Europe and the New World relied on the name and works of Shakespeare which remarkably straddled the emerging divides between 'legitimate' and 'illegitimate', between highbrow and lowbrow. In England in the eighteenth century the Bard had already been reclaimed not only as a national poet but also as the object of a 'national religion'.[29] That this process of deification progressed and even intensified in England in the nineteenth century is perhaps not surprising in the light of the century's propensity for finding or if need be, inventing, national traditions. The remarkable aspect of Shakespeare's importance in the theatrical repertoire is that he crossed linguistic and cultural boundaries so that by the end of the century he had also become a 'German' dramatist ('one of ours'), was the object of adulation amongst Indian university students and gradually occupied a central role on the French stage and provided plots for Italian operas.

In England, 'bardolatry' (in George Bernard Shaw's coinage) meant that Shakespeare occupied a remarkably wide cultural spectrum. At one end, we find the Romantic sacralization of a Samuel Taylor Coleridge or Charles Lamb who argued against staging the plays on account of the deleterious effect on their transcendent poetic quality.[30] At the other end, we find countless burlesques and parodies, which assume however at least a passing familiarity with the texts. In between there is a continual tradition of staging the texts themselves and in particular a gradual return to 'original' versions compared to the bowdlerized adaptations typical of the eighteenth century. For example, Charles Kemble staged *King Lear* in 1823 with its original tragic ending restored after 150 years of Nahum Tate's adaptation with a happy ending. In 1838 Charles Macready finally staged the text more-or-less uncut. The Shakespearean canon itself changes too. Plays such as *King John* and *A Winter's Tale* were hugely popular, not the least because they offered potential for processional spectacle on the one hand, and magical *feerie* on the other. Throughout, the century's predilection for antiquarianism manifested itself in staging practices that emphasized the 'historical', whether Elizabethan, Roman or Anglo-Saxon.

Although before 1843 the 'legitimate' theatres at Drury Lane and Covent Garden were supposed to have a monopoly on the Bard, the 'minor' theatres had found ways to circumvent the licensing laws by mixing the spoken text with singing and dancing and employing a mixture of 'recitative and silent gesture'.[31] The minor theatres also took liberties that the patent theatres did or would not, such as murdering the children in *Richard III* in full view to musical accompaniment, as staged at the Coburg in 1819/20. The repeated attempts to perform Shakespeare, sometimes in the face of prosecution, were justified by the managers as a 'duty' to cater for a wider public who were not able to access the 'national treasure' at the two patent theatres. It is therefore certainly correct to emphasize, as Jane Moody does, 'Shakespeare's pivotal, symbolic role in the emergence and definition of illegitimate culture'.[32] But it also points to the wider processes of cultural differentiation that meant that the works of the Bard needed to be refashioned for a variety of tastes and generic expectations.

It has been argued that in the USA after the 1850s Shakespeare became increasingly divorced from the broader world of everyday American culture: Lawrence Levine has argued that he ceased to be regarded as a popular and was instead redefined as a sacred author.[33] In other words, Shakespeare begins to shift from low to high, or at least his special status as a national author is harnessed to advance arguments for the sacralization of dramatic literature with its institutional face in the national theatre movement. In Britain, calls for a subsidized national theatre are invariably buttressed by giving obeisance to the Bard as one of the central foundations of such cultural justifications. The actual theatrical record and the wider cultural discourse make this narrative difficult to sustain, however. We should see Shakespeare instead as present in different repertoires. His sacralization begins earlier than mid-century, and by no means precludes his continued enjoyment at 'deconsecrated' performance venues such as the variety stage, where, as mentioned above, Shakespearean soliloquies and other key scenes enjoyed great popularity especially when delivered by star actors, some of whom were well past their prime.

While the figure of Shakespeare became an index to 'one's social position among Americans, by marking one's relative education, culture, and class status', as Frances Teague claims (and it could be applied beyond the borders of the USA too), it was not just an index of snobbishness.[34] The popular Shakespearean burlesque, parodies of the tragic plays mostly, occupy a largely forgotten place in the cultural imaginary where they figure as a kind of 'other' of bardoltry and the growing taste for antiquarianism. The burlesque has, by definition, a highly ambiguous relationship to the original, at once both affirming and disavowing it. By the same token the spectator could delight in recognizing the 'difference' between original and travesty and thus receive confirmation of a certain kind of cultural knowledge. That Othello spoke in the vernacular of minstrelsy, his first entry was announced by a sneeze rather a trumpet, and the famous handkerchief was replaced by a large towel, were all confirmations of an implied familiarity with a canonized author and play.[35]

By the late nineteenth century, Shakespeare was well and truly a European author with translations of his works into all major and many minor European languages. Great Shakespearean actors such as the African-American Ira Aldridge (1807–1867) were especially popular in central and eastern Europe, especially Russia. The German-Jewish actor Daniel Bandmann (1837–1905) performed a Shakespearean repertoire in German, English and French (sometimes on the same evening) and the most feted 'American' Shakespearean actress of the late nineteenth century, Helena Modjeska (1840–1909), was Polish.

Shakespeare performed cultural work beyond Europe. The University of Calcutta made his works part of the syllabus as early as 1857, well before they achieved similar status at English universities.[36] While there is little doubt that the textual promulgation of Shakespeare had a significant role to play in the imperial project, his theatrical reception is a different and much more contradictory matter. In India, European audiences were often less receptive to performances than the Indian spectators whose enthusiasm for the Bard provided a crucial economic basis for the touring English troupes. By the end of the nineteenth century, we can already speak of global Shakespeare, an author who was not just being read and translated throughout the world but also was being performed in vernacular versions. Most importantly, the Shakespeare trade was not just confined to British actors. The latter arrived in fact in theatrical centres where Shakespeare performances were already common. In India, the Straits Settlements (Malaya and Singapore) and the Dutch East Indies, local troupes had already begun to stage Shakespeare in their own languages, the most prominent and successful being the versions of the Parsi theatre in India. The Parsi community in Bombay, India's famous merchant class, had already begun to stage Shakespeare and Indian mythological stories in the mid-nineteenth century using European staging techniques and technology.[37] This local theatrical appropriation followed commercial, as much as ideological imperatives, and had already effectively indigenized the Bard.

# CHAPTER NINE

# Technologies of Performance

SOPHIE NIELD

Were we required to characterize this age of ours by any single epithet, we should be tempted to call it, not an Heroical, Devotional, Philosophical or Moral Age, but, above all others, the Mechanical Age. It is the Age of Machinery, in every outward and inward sense of that word; the age which, with its whole undivided might, forwards, teaches and practices the great art of adapting means to ends [. . .] These things [. . .] are yet of deep import, and indicate a mighty change in our whole manner of existence. For the same habit regulates not our modes of action alone, but our modes of thought and feeling. Men are grown mechanical in head and heart, as well as in hand [. . .] Their whole efforts, attachments, opinions, turn on mechanism, and are of a mechanical character.

— Thomas Carlyle, 'Signs of the Times', 1829

The nineteenth century saw extraordinarily rapid technological innovation and invention, producing fundamental transformations in the industrialization of energy, the development of railways, engines, mechanical devices, optical illusions, the rationalization of labour and the expanding and exporting of regimes of knowledge. New technologies shrank the world, not only through the exporting of machines, engines, strategies of power and exploitation in the project of colonial expansion, but also through the reproduction as image of so much of the wider global culture in the centres of Western power. Nineteenth-century culture staged the beginnings of the technological annihilation of time and space described so vividly by Stephen Kern in his *The Culture of Time and Space*,[1] and which was to find its destination in the dissociations of modernist subjectivity experienced in the early twentieth-century metropolis, for with the coming of light came a narrative of enlightenment.

It is unsurprising that the trajectory of theatrical development through the century was oriented around similar concerns and imperatives. Drawing on a rich range of visual innovations and technological developments, theatres extended in size and complexity, responding to the rapid changes in audience demographic and taste, and competing in an increasingly congested and energized marketplace. Alongside architectural and legislative shifts, the central story of the nineteenth-century stage is of technologically-driven scenic spectacle, as the theatres responded to, adapted, adopted and imported mechanical and technical devices in their journey towards dramatic realism. The organization of visual culture extended itself into consumption, shopping and urban spectatorship; new forms of entertainment and education emerged, such as the public museum, scientific exhibitions, waxworks, domestic photography and the illustrated newspaper. The sociological gaze extended itself in darker directions: towards class and the colonial 'other'; into social surveillance and scrutiny, police and prison regimes and extensions of public order. Journalists and 'urban explorers', touring the East End of London to view the extent of the bleak and brutal poverty experienced by the new proletarian working class, brought back descriptions and images for consumption and analysis. The body was scrutinized with an increasingly intrusive and scientific intent, as lenses and microscopes admitted to the medical gaze the micro-levels of human being. Finally, as the century closed, this culture-wide and pathological obsession with looking was itself exposed, as scientific perspectives threw light on the mind itself, diving into the construction of subjectivity and the increasingly rationalized investigation of human culture, behaviour and motive. All of these found their place in the evolution of nineteenth-century performance forms: as architectures; in increasingly socially-oriented themes and topics of investigation; in the prolonged interest of the new urban audience for accurate and forensic representations of the world.

This chapter will take as its focus technologies of space and seeing on the Victorian stage, and the ways in which these impacted the interpretation of nineteenth-century performance culture. Of necessity, given the scope of the century and its innovations, a particular geographical limit must be imposed, and the focus here will be on London. Throughout the nineteenth century, this city was one of the key centres, not only of Western colonial expansion, but also of the development and imagination of a particular kind of power circulating around visuality and the gaze. Technological innovations served as central drivers in both of these interconnected and explicitly political projects.

Transformations in the mechanization of labour, transport and energy sponsored in the Western metropolitan centres were exported as means to shackle resources and labour power across the globe; developments in light and illumination permitted the expansion of both urban and colonial exploration, and laid the foundations for the commodity capitalism of modernity. The theatre, as always through its history, found itself intimately connected with particular nexuses of wider cultural change. Popular entertainment in London throughout the century evolved alongside, and in relation to, rapid urban change, sociologically driven improvements in public health, labour conditions and widening access to education and forms of visual display.

Reading these technologies of knowledge, inflected through technologies of theatrical representation and the mechanics of theatrical space, would certainly seem to support the narrative of a century moving towards the dominance of artistic realism and, beyond that, the rise of commodity capital and modernist subjectivity; nineteenth-century visual innovations extending the development of eighteenth-century panopticism by providing the technical resources for twentieth-century disciplines of surveillance. Yet, as Chris Otter points out in his cultural history of nineteenth-century light, the twin spectatorial fantasies of urban flâneurism and surveillant panopticism can both be understood more as inventions of late twentieth-century cultural studies than authentic experiences of nineteenth-century urban space. 'Factories, asylums, and workhouses were built at an impressive pace, but none of these structures were panoptic, despite the occasionally deceptive appearance of towers or annular rooms. Cities swelled, and their public spaces thronged with crowds, but *flânerie* remained a marginal practice, a luxury few could afford and still fewer desired'.[2]

Responding to this observation, this chapter will position the theatre as more than simply one among many evolving visual and spectacular cultural forms, all emerging throughout the century, all on a similar trajectory towards an increasingly scientific representation of the world enabled by the new possibilities offered by technology. Rather, it will propose that nineteenth-century theatre can be read as the site of a potential undertow, moving against the dominant tide, and producing a resistance to the dominant narrative of nineteenth-century visual culture by way of its particular exploitation of technological innovation; in particular, its invention, not of artificial light, but of artificial darkness.

The trend of the nineteenth-century stage towards enhanced realism certainly provided increasingly forensic and scientific representations of wider social life. Yet these reality-effects were achieved by obscuring a continuing practical reliance on technical illusion, and on the erasure from sight of particular forms of labour, of technologies of production and, finally, of the theatrical spectators themselves. By creating the appearance of clarity, illumination and realism, theatre and entertainment forms offered themselves as 'metaphors' for the wider description and interpretation of rapidly changing Victorian culture. But

FIGURE 9.1: The interior of the New Covent Garden, London, 1810. Rowlandson and Pugin, G00-740-1Dr. Theaterwissenschaftliche Sammlung, University of Cologne.

their management of technical production practices resisted and undermined this parallel between rationality and sight. The metaphors re-imported into the wider culture therefore could not help but contain ambiguities produced by the disjuncture between the appearance of clarity and the practice of concealment, and, arguably, these pre-empted the particular ambivalences of twentieth-century modernity in relation to the gaze, urban spectatorship and subjectivity. In order to investigate this proposal, the chapter will first examine the evolution of the scenic space of realism, and review some of the central technical innovations which allowed this to take place.

## TOWARDS THE SCENIC SPACE OF REALISM

The development of the English stage in the nineteenth century from, broadly, a two-dimensional space of representation to a three-dimensional one, is a familiar history and while it is important to provide some context for the arguments which follow, it does not need rehearsing in great detail here. The work of Richard Leacroft, for example, outlines the journey of the stage towards increasing scale and depth of illusion via the retreat of the action behind the proscenium arch, and the continual importing of mechanical devices, such as fly galleries, hydraulic lifts and trap doors, to manipulate and move both persons and pieces of set.[3] Edward Mayhew, in his 1840 *Stage Effects, or the Principles which Command Dramatic Success in the Theatre*[4] gave an insight into mid-century practice, as he observed that it was once desirable that 'an author should so construct his plot, that flats and set scenes might alternate the one the other'.[5] Richard Southern provides the description of such a change from a flat to a complicated set scene enabled by increasingly elaborate mechanics:

> Now the whole stage is put into action; the wings begin to slide off to the side, the normal straight borders to rise, and the backscene to open. The new borders descending from the grid may be high arch-borders. Each groove-arm has then to be raised out of the way as soon as the flats are freed, and lifted to the up-reared position against the fly-rail. Simultaneously with all this, further details of the new scene are beginning to be visible upon the stage; firstly sliders part to either side and through the cuts there rise up in their sloats the successive ground-rows running across the floor of the scene and giving the retreating planes of distance. Beyond these, through the opening flats at the back, are appearing still further vistas of successive set-pieces running away to the distant sky-cloth hung against the very wall of the theatre. And now to perfect the spectacle, the great bridges below begin to work, and into the dazzling picture growing before our eyes there rise grouped ranges of fairies, and, last of all [. . .] there descends from the skies a cloud-machine with an array of the celestial deities themselves.[6]

By 1881, Percy Fitzgerald was able to observe that the stage space itself had become a 'huge void, stretching upward to the roof and below into a mine, where the floor seems to be, and is really, a series of gratings or grid-irons supported on pillars'. The 'aspect of the whole', he noted, when cleared,

> is very much that of some great engine-house with its light galleries running round. All this is for the convenience of vast constructions and having a perfect 'clear' from top to bottom, so that the stage architect can build unobstructed. The floor, as we have seen, must be no floor, but opening whence and where, at will, he can call up his castles that must ascend or descend and have a clear passage. As these openings may be required at any part of the stage, the only mode was to make the entire stage an open frame covered with panels, which can be drawn away. A 'trap' can thus be opened at any spot, and one of these frames, containing the trap and its machinery be inserted.[7]

Thus, in a celebrated description, he observed,

> [t]he most complicated and familiar objects about us are fearlessly laid hold of by the property man, and dragged upon the stage. Thus, when we take our dramatic pleasure, we have the satisfaction of not being separated from the objects of our daily life, and within the walls of the theatre we meet again the engine and the train that set us down almost at the door; the interior of hotels, counting-houses, shops, factories, the steam-boats, waterfalls, bridges and even fire-engines.[8]

In *The World Behind the Scenes,* Fitzgerald spoke with a rare enthusiasm of the increasingly elaborate scenic abilities, noting that 'the English excel in all the mechanical arrangements of the stage'. He particularly mentioned the *trappe anglaise*, which comprised a number of elastic belts of steel or twigs, 'like two combs placed with their teeth together' and covered with painted canvas like any scenic door. This, which the actor must hurl himself towards, 'requires a sort of courage and daring, as the effect depends on it being, as it were, recklessly done'. The bravery of the performer seems to be a recurring theme in the successful use of many of the more dynamic traps. The 'star' trap, a circular hole in the stage, was controlled by a counterweight which, once let go, was not to be trifled with, as the performer must 'keep himself as straight as an arrow, and have exceeding nerve, and when the trap comes home must take his spring, or the jar will be tremendous.' Fitzgerald also mentioned 'a new agent'; the use of steam, which was 'supposed to give the vaporous effect of clouds in motion, hitherto attempted by gauzes and painted cloths', demonstrating how 'every resource is being enlisted in the service of the stage'.[9]

The familiar description of the new proscenium arch as a 'picture frame' represents again the tendency to read the nineteenth-century stage through visual paradigms. It does seem that the first managers to fully install the rich and elaborate borders, continuing around the whole frame of the stage and across the foot of the scene itself, were creating the illusion of a picture frame. The one installed by the Bancroft management at the 'New Haymarket' is described by Fitzgerald as 'two feet broad'. It caused the actors to seem entirely cut off from 'the domain of prose; there is no borderland or platform in front; and, stranger still, the whole has the air of a picture projected on a surface'.[10] However, there is, in addition to an aesthetic imperative, also a technological impulse at work: the continuing concern for public safety which encouraged the move to a more material division between the stage and the house. The London Fire Brigade had been established under the leadership of Eyre Massey Shaw by the passing of the Metropolitan Fire Brigade Act in 1865. Shaw, as part of his duties in that new role, prepared detailed reports between 1865 and 1876 on individual theatres, publishing *Fires in Theatres* that same year. To

FIGURE 9.2: Sketch of the *trappe anglaise*, date unknown. Drawing by Moyuel. Collection Friedrich Baumann. Theaterwissenschaftliche Sammlung, University of Cologne.

optimize the prevention of fire, Shaw advised dividing the building 'into as many distinct and separate risks as possible'. He paid particular attention to the point at which the curtain falls, as

> the opening on that spot is much reduced by the partial cross-walls and the supporting wall under the front of the stage. In short, at this point the whole house should be divided into two distinct parts by means of a firewall commencing in the basement and going through the roof and to a height of from 4 to 6 feet outside. This wall should be perforated at the sides on each landing, and at the bottom under the stage near the orchestra, and fitted at the perforation with wrought-iron doors; and it should, of course, have the usual large opening to the stage [. . .] and at the great opening an effectual protection could be obtained by means of a metal curtain which could be dropped at a moment's notice.[11]

Whether driven by aesthetics or pragmatics, or a combination of both, the division of stage and auditorium can be argued to have affected both the perception and experience of theatre space. It involved firstly the increasing materiality of stage space, by which is implied the literal use of material effects: machinery (albeit hidden from view), stage illusions built up from three-dimensional and physically (rather than graphically) present artefacts, real water, real horses, real trains; all 'the objects of our daily life' mentioned with such reluctant admiration by Percy Fitzgerald. Environments, too, were meticulously realized: the tea-garden featured in the opening scene of *The Ticket of Leave Man* (1863); the busy railway station in *London By Night* (1868); the Paris Opera and Forest of Fontainebleau in the 1880 Lyceum revival of *The Corsican Brothers*, described with fearful hyperbole by Clement Scott as realism being taken to the point of dangerous extreme. Even as the tastes of the century progressed, with the increasing presentation of bourgeois and domestic realism on a much smaller scale, it was the material aspects of the set and set dressing which continued to find comment: at the Olympic and the Haymarket, the likeness of the fictitious drawing rooms to their real-world counterparts was enhanced by the fact that the suppliers of furnishings and decor to the stage were often the very same firms that the audience itself would patronize. The wider question of the influence of scenic space on the imagination of the commodity will be revisited shortly.

Changes in architectural organization also served to separate the audience from the space of the action. As Martin Jay has noted, the withdrawal of the spectator from 'the seen (the scene)'[12] gives practical shape to what Alberti, on the Renaissance re-discovery of perspective, famously characterized as a 'window' on the world. In other words, the experience of space is conditioned by the perspective which one is able to take upon it. The incorporation of linear perspective and privileged viewpoints into theatre architecture, in addition to the well-documented enshrining of social stratification into the building forms, also transformed the relationship of the audience to the object of its gaze. The audience looked into an increasingly separate and three-dimensional scenic space; one made of real objects, with materials recognizable from the world, and in which human figures were able to sustain their scale without requiring an illusion-threatening proximity to the audience. Naturally, these shifts in the arrangement of perceptual space did not emerge from a void. Several key devices conditioned the re-imagining of scenic space, and, importantly, began to re-negotiate the representation of 'reality' which the work of the stage would later extend, not only through their pre-emption of perspective and other optical illusions, but crucially, through their manipulation of light.

## OPTICAL ENTERTAINMENTS: MODELS AND METAPHORS

Philippe Jacques de Loutherbourg developed the Eidophusikon, or 'Representation of Nature', in 1781, synthesizing focused light, transparent screens and clockwork technology. De Loutherbourg was of course already working with what might be understood as a theatrical imagination: as Garrick's scenic designer at Drury Lane, he had already pioneered several elements of set design that pointed towards an increasingly natural sense of perspective and representation, breaking up back flats and wings into more mobile pieces. His Eidophusikon further developed these innovations, crucially adding the element of changing light. The device was in the form of a box, ten-feet wide, six-feet high and eight-feet deep, into which the spectators looked. Theatrical back flats and wings created a frame for both two- and three-dimensional objects placed in the foreground, which created the depth of field. Battens mounted above the proscenium allowed, however, for lighting effects, especially with the changes and modulations of colour permitted by the addition of stained glass slips. Richard Altick, whose magisterial 1978 *The Shows of London* remains the key source for nineteenth-century visual culture, records a series of scenes with a particular emphasis on temporal changes: the effects of dawn, a sunset, the Mediterranean seen by moonlight, and the effects of violent weather. Altick points out that the Eidophusikon pre-empted with these aspects several elements that would become central to theatrical space, but which were as yet not possible for it to achieve. However, the device 'intensified interest in other forms of pictorial entertainment which created, above all, the illusion of reality'.[13]

As well as illustrating the growing appetite of the urban audience for visually-driven content, the panorama provides a further key example of experiments with the technology of vision. Robert Barker, an Edinburgh portraitist, developed in the mid-1780s a system of curved lines, which enabled the reproduction of an illusion of painted two-dimensional landscape on a cylindrical surface.[14] With the assistance of his son, Henry Aston Barker, he quickly began to exploit it as a form of entertainment, This 'instant history painting'[15] took the form most often of a large canvas, showing in great and realistic detail a geographical scene or current event. It was exhibited in natural light so as to maintain this illusion of reality, and, as it continued to be exploited commercially through the early nineteenth century, in buildings specially designed to prevent the viewer from seeing around or over the painted image, thus completing the impression that they gazed onto an actual scene. The panorama, demonstrating the educational imperative claimed as a motivating force in developing many of these new devices, specialized in geographic and historical scenes, and of course capitalized on the speed with which it could reproduce images of current events. Altick reports that within a week of a fire which occurred at the Houses of Parliament on 26 October 1834, a panoramic view of the same was on show at the Victoria Theatre.[16] As a form of cultural consumption, the panorama provided a somewhat more respectable (and cheaper) venue than the theatre, and, while the stage could outdo its capacity in terms of sheer ability to create depth of vision, its most profound influence on the development of scenic space was the continuing encouragement of the illusion of reality.

Occupying similar territory was the diorama; again, an immersive environment in which a seated audience looked under particular conditions at an optical illusion created with painted images and light. The original had been opened in Paris in July 1822 by the theatrical designer and later pioneer of photography, Louis Daguerre; the first in London opened shortly afterwards in September 1823, at the diorama in Regent's Park.[17] Although Daguerre was involved in this project, and had been assisted in Paris by his wife's brother, Charles Arrowsmith, it is not clear whether the John Arrowsmith who applied for a patent in 1824 claiming 'an improved Mode of publicly exhibiting pictures or painted scenery of every description, and of distributing or directing the daylight upon or through them, so as to produce many beautiful effects of light and shade' was also a relation. Like the panorama, the diorama required special architecture to be viewed properly: the audience was seated in a movable amphitheatre, the inner of two concentric rotundas, which enabled the whole seating area to be swivelled around to face in turn two forty-foot long tunnels. At the foot of the tunnels, they saw images which had been painted on translucent materials and were being lit by daylight from back and front. Notably, the success of the diorama show depended on a contrast between light and darkness. Altick records the discomfort of many eyewitnesses, being conducted to their seats in near-total darkness. The innovation allowed not only the available daylight to the images to be maximized, but also, as with the panorama, prevented as far as possible the audience being able to perceive other measures of distance, location and perspective, thus increasing the sense of the 'realism' of the illusion.

Although clearly influential in shaping the imaginary of the stage, none of these illusions had yet to deal with human scale, in the sense of accommodating the human figure in the creation of the image, and it would be the stage that would complete this work. Nevertheless, the impact of these new optical entertainments on the wider cultural imagination can be evidenced by the increasing use of the suffix '-orama', reported by Richard Altick as he lists the Georama, Cosmorama, Neorama and Uranorama among others.[18] More significantly perhaps, they began to enter the wider lexicon of cultural description, providing not only metaphors, but models for the alterations in perception of space and time being brought about by new technology. The phantasmagoria, another import from Paris at the turn of the nineteenth century, positioned a magic lantern behind a semi-transparent screen, and moved built pieces closer to and further away from the light source on sliders, giving the impression that the figures or objects were themselves drawing closer to or further away from the spectators. In 1830, a commentator at the opening of the Liverpool to Manchester railway wrote that 'the long continuous line of spectators [. . .] seemed to glide away, like painted figures swiftly drawn through the tubes of a magic lantern'. Of the trains themselves in their rapid movement, '[a] spectator observing their approach [. . .] can scarcely divest himself of the idea that they are not enlarging and decreasing in size rather than moving'.[19] In 1852, social investigator Henry Mayhew described his experience of a balloon flight: 'the buoyant machine bounded, like a big ball, into the air. Or, rather, let us say, the earth seemed to sink suddenly down as if the spot of ground to which it had been previously fastened had been constructed upon the same principle as the Adelphi stage, and admitted of being lowered at a moment's notice'. He spoke of 'that peculiar panoramic effect [. . .] which arises from the utter absence of all sense of motion in the machine itself', adding, 'the earth [. . .] seemed to consist of a continuous series of scenes which were being drawn along underneath us, as if it were some diorama laid flat upon the ground, and almost gave onto the notion that the world were an endless landscape stretched upon rollers, which some invisible sprites below were busy revolving for our especial amusement'.[20]

Theorists of visuality and power have observed that the capacity to see the world from different viewpoints radically changes experience of social space. Just as perspective subordinated the perception of space to the dominance of the eye, so speed and verticality produce a substantially reconfigured engagement with lived experience. How far contemporary commentators were utilizing descriptions of entertainment forms because they would be experiences with which their readers would have been familiar, and how far they were groping for a vocabulary within which to express a radically disrupted experience of space and time is, of course, difficult to determine. Nevertheless, there appears to be repeated use of descriptions of technologically-driven 'artificial' realities to capture the effects of 'real' experiences. The new modes of perception being pioneered in popular entertainment provided vivid descriptors for writers attempting to describe real life. In other words, dissociations of perception produced by the experience of reality itself were being captured through descriptions of the reality-effects produced by technologies – and technologies whose mechanisms were increasingly invisible and obscured.

All of these optical illusions were imported directly into theatres: the phantasmagoria in particular serviced the vogue for ghost effects and gothic themes in the early part of the century. What they also offered on a different scale was a model for what the stage itself might be capable of becoming: an enclosed space of representation, in which machines, screens, built elements and real (as opposed to pictorial) depth would allow for a rethinking of the scenic space in aesthetic, material and technical terms. What was also clear from the pioneering work evidenced by these new optical techniques was an increasing reliance on artificial light to enhance the illusion, and the artificial darkness which enabled it all to work.

## ARTIFICIAL LIGHT

Throughout the course of the century, the theatre adopted first gas and then electricity, both of which were to revolutionize dramatic representation and practice. The manufacture of gas had commenced in the very early years of the century and was to expand rapidly throughout the urban centres. Frederick Winsor, who would incorporate his London-based Gas Light and Coke Company in 1812, demonstrated gaslight at the Lyceum Theatre in 1804, and outdoors in Pall Mall in 1807.[21] As Chris Otter outlines, by 1823 there were forty-seven gasholders in London alone. Mains were laid throughout the city at huge speed: demand, both domestic and industrial, meant that among other resources, recycled water mains, hollowed-out tree trunks and old gun barrels were all pressed into service, and by 1875, over 5,000 miles of mains had been laid. As the distance between individual dwellings and the nearest gasworks could be several miles, fluctuations in demand and pressure led to the introduction of individual gas meters, all of which conditioned the experience of gas for domestic and other users.[22] There is evidence that domestic take-up of gaslight was somewhat slow: for many people, early encounters with mass-produced light would be in industrial or entertainment contexts. The introduction of gas into the theatre, however, was extremely swift: Terence Rees, in his extended study of nineteenth-century theatre lighting, describes the practice in place at Covent Garden in 1810, in which a mixed economy of lighting meant that the house was lit with 'glass chandeliers in front of each circle; two hundred and seventy wax candles are consumed in them every night. Three hundred patent (Argand) lamps light the stage and scenery, and nearly as many more are fixed in the corridors and staircases'[23]. The Argand, or 'patent' lamp was a key innovation in the use of gaslight in theatre buildings: it had been pioneered by the French designer and chemist François Pierre Ami Argand, who invented a new hollow type of wick, enabling double the amount of air to be available to the flame. Before Argand, the gas lamp was simply 'an orifice spewing fire into space'.[24] His additions, including a glass cylinder and a mechanism for raising and lowering the wick, completed the lamp, described by Wolfgang Schivelbusch as being 'to the nineteenth century household what the electric light bulb is to the twentieth century'.[25]

The new illumination provided a powerful marketing tactic for the theatres, especially as gas had yet to be extended on any scale into domestic contexts. The Covent Garden playbill for 11 September 1815 announced that 'The Exterior, with the Grand Hall and Staircase will be illuminated by Gas'.[26] The Lyceum presented the first gas-lit stage on 6 August 1817, as reported in *The Examiner*, which described the light it gave as being 'as mild as it is splendid – white, regular and pervading'. Drury Lane followed swiftly, and on 17 September, *The Times* wrote in praise of the flexibility of gas illumination, whose intensity could be regulated up or down.[27] There then occurred what appears to be a race between Drury Lane, the Lyceum and Covent Garden to install the most lavish and extensive provision of gas illumination across the entire stage and auditorium. As so often with the introduction of new technology into theatres, the new fittings themselves were presented for the admiration and approval of the public, who were assured that the 'great central light' and the 'clusters of glass ornaments' hanging from six circles of gas lamps above the Lyceum auditorium would not cast inconvenient shadows, nor block their views of the stage, 'even from the one shilling gallery'.[28]

In terms of the stage, gas lamps were fitted where the oil-lamps and candles had previously been, continuing the general trajectory of stage architecture to provide a coherent space of representation behind the proscenium. Bram Stoker, Henry Irving's business manager at the Lyceum, mentioned as late as 1878 that in addition to floats, battens and ground rows, gas lights were often hung on the back of the scenic piece immediately in front, and that the old grooves were still used as measures, as '[a]ll stage hands understand No. 1, No. 2, No. 3 and so on'.[29] The 'float', running across the foot of the proscenium, operated as footlights; these lamps were often still fitted as Argand burners, whose protective glass chimney reduced the risk of fire accidentally breaking out.[30] To these were added wing lights, oftentimes attached to the side scenes and set pieces, and battens which extended over the stage the entire width of the proscenium. While an 1819 account details the float and the side lights as 'permanent', there is no specific reference to lighting from above; an article on scene-painting from 1841 mentions gaslight 'occasionally thrown from above'.[31]

While there is no well-established date for the wider introduction of this mode of lighting 'from above', it was its introduction which ultimately allowed dramatic action to be moved significantly upstage. Rees raises explicitly the question of how far the withdrawal of dramatic action behind the proscenium arch was in fact enabled by the capacity to light actors from three sides following the introduction of the gas batten, and this speculation indicates that it may have been in part the technology of the stage which prompted the development of the 'picture frame', rather than purely aesthetic concerns.[32] In practical terms, an entire theatre's worth of gas lights were able to be managed from the gas-table in the prompt corner, thus obviating the need for individual snuffing out of the many hundreds of candles and Argand burners throughout the theatre. This adaptable and variable source of light permitted many special effects, not least the use of colour and changes in intensity of light, and was quickly incorporated into regular use in the theatres.

Several of the new technical innovations were first developed for social, industrial or military purposes, and were quickly exploited for entertainment novelty. One such was the introduction of limelight, a very intense white light produced by burning a small piece of quicklime in a mixture of oxygen and hydrogen. The discovery had been made in 1824 by Lieutenant Thomas Drummond of the Royal Engineers, who had been tasked with developing a light source able to burn with such an intensity it could be seen at great distances: Terence Rees mentions an experiment undertaken at Purfleet on 10 May 1830, in which the 'oxy-hydrogen limelight' created a light so bright that 'it produced the shadow of hand and fingers held before a dark brick wall on the wharf at Blackwall' more than ten miles away.[33] Initially, in the theatres, it seems to have provided a very bright floodlight (called 'open lime'), until a later addition of a focusing lens, credited to Charles Kean in 1855, enabled its use as a spotlight ('box lime'). Very shortly, it had contributed to the evolving divisions of labour which typified the development of stage practice in these years, supplying its own specialist expert, the 'consultant' limelight man, who 'might have two or more theatres and a large number of mere operators under his control at any one time'.[34] It was used, according to Bram Stoker for '[t]he moon, the lights from the windows of the "old home", the convenient ray which follows the hero about the stage, so that the audience may never forget that he is present'.[35]

Of course, from the early introduction of the new lighting technologies, there were significant health and safety considerations. The huge gas-driven 'sunburners' which now lit the auditoria had to be screened behind glass; had they not been, the heat would have been intense.[36] Strode's patent version contained 819 jets, burning with the strength of 12,000 candles.[37] The oxygen consumption relied on by gas also caused ventilation problems and issues with

FIGURE 9.3: Sketch of an experimental stage presented at the 3rd Internationale Elektrizitätsausstellung [International Fair for Electricity], Munich, 1883. Collection Friedrich Baumann. Theaterwissenschaftliche Sammlung, University of Cologne.

the air supply: R. E. B. Crompton, speaking on artificial lighting and its impact on health in 1881 noted, '[m]any of us are unable to go to the theatre [. . .] as the intense headache which invariably attends or follows our stay in such places actively prevents them'.[38] The risk of fire, too, was an ongoing and significant concern. Percy Fitzgerald, writing in 1881 of the Lyceum, observed,

> a row of jets, some thirty or forty feet long, and two or three hundred in number, are hoisted aloft, protected by a sort of curved metal screen. The lighting even of these jets, which is done from below with a light rod of enormous length, is a matter of danger, as a mere contact with the canvas might set all in a blaze.[39]

But the effects that were able to be achieved were evidently complex. This account, written by Phelps' scene painter, Frederick Lloyd, in 1875, captures the process of lighting a sunrise in some detail:

> The gas last alluded to being full on, let the cloth with the silks be slowly raised. While the yellow begins to appear, and the crimson is rising higher and higher in the sky, the gas behind must be gradually turned up to the full,

the mediums in front being worked round from blue to red, and then to yellow, in unison with the change at the back, and the green lights at the wings gradually turned down and the white lights partly up. The cloth with the silks will by this time have worked up out of sight and the whole of the painting at the back of the cloth will be seen, in consequence of the strong light at the back of it, to help which the white lights in front have been kept subdued. If lime-lights are used, the glasses will then change from blue to crimson, and the next to yellow, in unison with other changes of colour. By reversing the movement, the same painting and arrangements will serve to represent the change from sunset to moonlight.[40]

Electricity, as Chris Otter notes, was simply one among many innovations in lighting technology developed between 1870 and 1910, including 'acetylene, the regenerative gas lamp, the gas mantle, the Jablochkoff candle, the arc light, and the incandescent electric bulb'.[41] There is a question as to why electricity in particular took hold, especially given that new safety features such as the gas mantle produced a flameless gaslight. Furthermore, in addition to being too bright, too intense and 'casting unhelpful shadows', early electricity was

FIGURE 9.4:  Moon on stage, date unknown. Collection Friedrich Baumann. Theaterwissenschaftliche Sammlung, University of Cologne.

dangerous. It was not until Edison's invention of the incandescent bulb in 1880 that its use as a more widespread substitute for gas was seriously mooted. As Edison himself noted, the bulb was 'designed to serve precisely the same purposes in domestic use as gaslight [. . .] [it] can be gazed at without dazzling the eyes [. . .] It is also a purer light than gas, being white, while gaslight is yellow.'[42] In terms of wider social applications, this aspect of colour was one of its biggest selling points. Electricity, like daylight, is white, and the potential to accurately illuminate goods and other materials so that they appeared as they would in daylight was an important concern. Drapers advertised the fact that their stores were lit by this new light, which ensured that customers could buy their silks with no anxiety as to how the colour would appear by daylight, 'for daylight is here manufactured for them by the aid of Gramme and Jablochkoff'.[43] Chris Otter cites the experience of the fictional Mr Pooter, who orders cloth for a new suit 'by gaslight', and is alarmed to find, rather than the quiet 'pepper-and-salt mixture with white stripes down' which he believed himself to have selected, he has rather bought a pattern with a lot of green, and 'bright yellow-coloured stripes.'[44] Another key site where accuracy of colour and the capacity to see detail were important was in the organization of manufacturing labour. By the 1880s the clothing industry was using electricity extensively to enable night work, and the working day was able to be lengthened in many fields which required such clarity of vision: factories, operating theatres, and of course, in the entertainment industries.

In practical terms, in the theatres, electricity followed the pattern of existing installations adopted for gas, in particular retaining the pattern of the lighting rig, the focus on adjustability and the ability to be controlled from a central board. Schivelbusch in particular is very interesting on the ways in which new technologies imitate the best qualities of what is being superseded, and vice versa, for gas, in a short-lived attempt to extend its viability, also mimicked the incandescent qualities of the electric bulb.[45] Electric arc lighting, which had been used in theatres from the 1840s, usually for flood lighting, or external lighting for buildings, gave an exceptionally bright light. It would later be described by Robert Louis Stevenson as '[a] lamp for a nightmare! Such a light as this should only shine on murders and public crime, or along the corridors of lunatic asylums, a horror to heighten horror'.[46] Much milder was the incandescent carbon filament lamp pioneered by Joseph Swan in 1879. This received its theatre debut in the Savoy theatre auditorium on 6 October 1881, and on its stage on 28 December the same year.[47]

Although answering many of the issues which gas lighting raised, in particular some of the worst of the fire hazards, electricity was not universally popular. Percy Fitzgerald noted that pure electric light, though it had been a good deal displayed in pantomimes, seemed to be cold in its effects, and not likely to grow in favour. Ellen Terry spoke of 'the naked trashiness of electricity'[48] and Bram Stoker, perhaps unsurprisingly given his interest in fictions of horror, observed

FIGURE 9.5: Advertisement by the German company Siemens, date unknown: 'The electric Light on Stage. Against the cold that accompanies the electric light on stage, various measures and precautions have been taken'. Caricature by Siemens. Collection Friedrich Baumann. Theaterwissenschaftliche Sammlung, University of Cologne.

that its colour was not conducive to producing conditions of gloom, as it burned red and cheery instead of blue when lowered in intensity.[49] Indeed, at the Lyceum, Henry Irving continued the use of gas and lime-lighting, introducing lighting-rehearsals in order to fully exploit the capacity of well-directed light to enhance scenic effects. What was consistently enabled, however, was the increasing extension of the capacity of the stage, and the potential for action to be moved first upstage, and then fully behind the proscenium arch.

The forensic possibilities of light would also seem to echo the increasingly scientific impulses of dramatic realism towards accurate representations of the world. Yet, despite this seeming fit, the interests of presenting such 'realities' on stage were not unconditionally served. In *The Art of Acting*, Percy Fitzgerald drew attention to the limitations exhibited by the new lighting techniques, noting, 'the glare of light in which our stages are bathed is fatal to all illusion – it reveals everything, the rifts in the boards, the texture and creases in the canvas, the streaks of the paint'.[50] Further, he observed, '[n]othing looks less like water on the stage than *real* water [. . .] It is dark, even black, and can never be made to offer the charms of water sparkling in the sun. Gas or the electric light only bring out its opacity'.[51]

Fitzgerald was of course somewhat resistant to the new technology; in fact, he staged a series of complaints, including criticism of the use of real steam on stage, of which he reported that 'the general effect was of a literal kind, viz., that there had been an escape of steam'. Nonetheless, he provides a useful contemporaneous guide to the limitations of some of the new innovations. Rather than the dominant narrative of uncomplicated progress, in which the machines and inventions permit further and further verisimilitude, he identified a particularly theatrical problem, which is this: in the theatre, and under unforgiving electric light, real things do not resemble themselves. Rather, he insisted, the art of the stage consists in 'discovering what, *under the conditions of the stage*, would have the same appearance'.[52] In short, he concluded, to produce an appearance of reality, objects have to be made unlike reality, according to fixed rules. Artificial daylight was not enough.

## ARTIFICIAL DARKNESS

Bram Stoker reported that after the introduction of adjustable lighting into the Lyceum, Irving was able to carry out

a long-thought out scheme: that the auditorium should be darkened during the play. Up to this time such had not been the custom. Indeed, it was a general aim of the management to have the auditorium as bright as possible. The new order of things was a revelation to the public.

It had previously been necessary to drop the curtain for a 'full' scene change, so that the stage could be lit to allow the workmen to see what they were doing. But, continues Stoker,

> later on, when the workmen had been trained to do the work as Irving required it to be done, darkness itself became the curtain. The workmen were equipped with silent shoes and dark clothing, all of which were kept in the house and put on before each performance. Then, in obedience to preconcerted signals, they carried out in the dark the prearranged and rehearsed work without the audience being able to distinguish what was going on.[53]

In short, the very labour which enabled the illusion of reality to be constructed was rendered invisible in darkness, and it is this which enabled the ability of the spectacular stage to create the illusion of realism in its production of effects. Famously, Irving's Lyceum was able to exchange fully realized sets of the Paris Opera and the forest at Fontainebleau in their 1880 revival of *The Corsican Brothers* in under a minute. Yet while the swiftness of the effect was part of its impact, and there was, as Stoker has indicated, no intention to reveal how the illusion has been achieved, the audience remained fully aware of the means by which it has been done. Several contemporaneous accounts of the process were published. Moy Thomas, writing in the *Daily News*, described the expense which the theatre must surely be incurring in meeting the salaries of the army of men required night after night for the 'rapid and silent setting and changing of scenes', noting that,

> without minute division of the work, and almost military precision in the movements of the workers, 'waits' would become intolerably long. For this reason, no fewer than ninety carpenters, thirty gas-men and fifteen property men, in all 135 persons, are permanently engaged in the mere task of arranging and conducting the scenes. [Cost] £140 a night. Receipts £230 a night.

Fitzgerald, with less of an eye on expense, but no less for the amount of labour required, observed that,

> so soon as the 'curtains' are dropped the auxiliaries rush on; away to the right and left fly the portions of the Parisian drawing room; tables, chairs, piano, sofa vanish in an instant. Men appear carrying tall saplings fixed in stands; one lays down the strip of frozen pond, another the prostrate trunk of a tree – every one from practice knowing the exact place of the particular article he is appointed to carry. Others arrive with bags of sand, which are

emptied and strewn on the floor; the circular tree is put in position, the lime-light is ready. The transformation was effected, in what space of time will the reader imagine? In thirty-eight *seconds*, by the stage-managers watch.[54]

The sensation must have been, for the audience, partly a spatial dynamic: they knew themselves to be in the presence of an extraordinary feat of labour, but were not able, or enabled, to perceive it. In a sense, the theatre workers themselves here occupied the place of the invisible mechanisms of optical illusion in the diorama or Eidophusikon. The presence of the picture frame implies that it is the stage which must become a picture; a fictive, 'other' space, gazed into by the un-problematically 'present' viewer. Yet, the increasingly complex and sophisticated technologies and materialities of nineteenth-century scenic space suggest instead that it was the space of the stage which had concreteness and inhabitability. Increasingly, it would seem, a particular form of labour was being privileged and rendered visible: the labour of acting and representation. The labour of production, like the technologies of illusion, was not. The illusion of reality was therefore being managed, in part, through strategies of partial visibility, and strategic occlusion.

The extension of adjustable light throughout the auditorium had a further consequence for late nineteenth-century audiences, for not only does a darkened auditorium militate against particular sorts of communally experienced responses to the on-stage action, it also alters the nature of the spectator's own relationship to the image. As the space of the stage was increasingly operating less as a represented space, and more of a space in which representation was being made materially present, the question arises of precisely where the audience – shut off, as Schivelbusch puts it, from their own social context and relation to each other in the dark – might have imagined themselves to be. Their awareness of the scope and distance of their own physical location was being potentially reduced; they looked 'into' the space of representation, for whose benefit the optical and technical resources of the theatre had been organized. They were invisible to the actors, and invisible to each other. For Fitzgerald, they became almost phantasms, as 'the audience has a kind of power of being present in a sort of supernatural way, and are, as it were, in company with the figures. The scenery is for them but an indication [. . .] We are in the room, listening and looking on, but in no particularly defined locality'.[55]

Charles Kean's 1852 production of *The Corsican Brothers* manifested through technology this implicit invisibility of the audience. The character of Fabien saw a 'vision' of his brother Louis, dying in a duel in a far-away forest. This vision, enabled by upstage action, lighting effects and a sliding back wall, extended what had seemed to the audience to be the limit of scenic perspective, as it was further opened through technology into a space of fantasy. The narrative then re-started, following the story of Louis and leading up to the duel in the forest, at which point a vision was revealed upstage through the same technical means of Fabien watching in horror from his drawing room. Not only was this a technologically sophisticated rendering of scenic illusion, it also effectively performed a reversal of the entire scenic space: the perspective which the audience had been shown, they now shared. What was 'behind' the drawing room was the forest; what was 'beyond' the forest was the drawing room. But the 'reverse shot', so to speak, did not reveal any space where the audience might be supposed to be. The scenic space had closed and, even in its own space of fantasy, referred only to itself. This is the version of the stage which was exported into the imagination of commodity, and which endured into twentieth-century descriptions of the paradoxes and dissociations of modernity; one in which the space of representation floats, illuminated, behind a picture frame, with no apparent means of support: 'reality' made out of magic.

## TOWARDS MODERNITY

Most famously, it is Walter Benjamin who uses the image of the phantasmagoria to capture the experience of urban space and commodity capitalism, noting, 'the new forms of behaviour and the new economically and technologically based creations that we owe to the nineteenth century enter the universe as phantasmagoria.'[56] The original device was a magic lantern behind a screen, illuminating built pieces which moved closer to and further away from the light source. When understood as a machine of illusion which hides its mechanism, it serves, for Benjamin, as a perfect parallel for the presence in public space of gleaming commodities, separated to all intents and purposes from their contexts of production. This effect is, in part, derived from the assumed invisibility and anonymity of the urban spectator, as 'the crowd is the veil through which the familiar city is transformed for the flâneur into phantasmagoria'. This phantasmagoria, continues Benjamin, 'in which the city appears now as a landscape, now as a room, seems later to have inspired the decor of department stores, which thus put flânerie to work for profit'.[57] The mutability of the scene, dissolving from landscape to room, cannot also help but recall a transformation scene in the theatre.

Theodore Adorno, too, borrowed the phantasmagoria as an image for what he named as 'the occultation of production by means of the outward appearance of the product'.[58] This effect, of products without producers, had been captured half a century before in a more vernacular mode by Charlotte Brontë, who wrote of the goods on display at the Great Exhibition 'it seems as if only magic could have gathered this mass of wealth from all the ends of the earth – as if none but supernatural hands could have arranged it'.[59] The commodity spaces of modernity, in the cultural imagination, became what Martin Jay describes as 'a theatricalized "scenographic" space' which 'differentiated the dominant modern world view from its various predecessors'.[60] When John Berger refigures Alberti's 'shatterproof window' of perspective as rather 'a safe let into a wall, a safe in which the visible has been deposited', he summarizes not only alterations in the visual field, but also produces an image of both a shop window and an illuminated stage.[61]

Yet, these are not the same. As Chris Otter has noted, one of the most important motives for the illumination of public space was to make visible (or to deploy visibility within) contexts of production, in particular, enabling night work. The illumination of city streets did not produce completely darkened areas from which urban spectatorship could take place: both spectator and object were illuminated, producing, not so much a panoptic effect, but as Otter argues, an oligoptic one, in which social and cultural behaviours become self-regulated through shared visibility, not through policing by an invisible and surveillant 'eye of power'.[62]

The fantasy of the disembodied floating eye of the flâneur, and the 'magically' appearing 'image' which it observes, can thus be seen to derive, not from the experience of nineteenth-century *culture*, but from the experience of nineteenth-century *theatre*, with its dark auditorium and its invisible hands. Through the importing and advancing of technologies of vision, the nineteenth-century theatre transformed both its scenic and audience spaces. The stage became a three-dimensional box, within which representation was able to be fully, and materially, present. But the theatre retained its shadows: not on the stage, perhaps, but in its social spaces. It remained mutable. It could not annihilate time and space, for the time and space of the audience are experienced. It could only obscure them with sleights of hand and darkness; with the invisibility of the labour it required to fulfil itself, and the invisibility of its own social relations.

This is the new stage which re-entered the wider culture as a visual metaphor. The bright plate glass windows installed in shops and stores were described as the 'stage' on which the commodity made its appearance. Views from train windows were picked out as 'scenery'. Schivelbusch, in a chapter dedicated to the panoramic pleasures of rail travel, writes of the unspooling of landscape compressed by speed, in which views 'have entirely lost their dimension of depth and have become mere particles of one and the same panoramic world that stretches all around and is, at each and every point, merely a painted surface'.[63] He notes the blurring that takes place when scenery is viewed at speed through a train window:

> The foreground enabled the traveler to relate to the landscape through which he was moving. He saw himself as part of the foreground, and that perception *joined* him to the landscape [. . .] now velocity dissolves the foreground, and the traveler loses that aspect. He is removed from that 'total

space' which combines proximity and distance: he becomes separated from the landscape he sees by what Richard Lucae, speaking of ferrovitreous architecture, has called an 'almost immaterial barrier'.

He could almost be speaking of a fourth wall. For it is as the traveller is removed from having any direct connection to the scenic space that 'it becomes a stage setting [. . .] Panoramic perception, in contrast to traditional perception, no longer belongs to the same space as the perceived objects: the traveller sees the objects [. . .] *through* the apparatus'.[64] The nineteenth-century theatre spectator thus provides the model for the disembodied observer of an increasingly accelerating visually-driven culture. The technological ingenuity and the visual deceits of the nineteenth-century stage do not only create it as a space for presenting visions of nineteenth-century cultural forms. In their radical reframing of the experience of the spectator, they pre-empt, in important ways, the visual and cultural imagination of the century to come.

CHAPTER TEN

# Knowledge Transmission

## *Media and Memory*

DEREK MILLER

The nineteenth-century public consumed knowledge about theatre – from dramatic texts and staging practices to how to make a theatrical career – on a scale unimaginable by previous generations. Information about theatre hitherto acquired only through first-hand experience and informal networks became available for purchase by a general audience. New legal and institutional structures, expanded markets, shifting social configurations – in a word, industrialization – encouraged and facilitated the commodification of theatrical knowledge. The story of knowledge transmission in the nineteenth-century theatre is the story of theatre's status as property, and how theatre's commodification transformed the circulation of theatre in a rapidly industrializing and globalizing cultural economy.

Industrial capitalism, which requires mass reproduction achieved through economies of scale, magnified the importance of a fundamental question: how could theatre-makers transmit knowledge of a play or techniques of playing from the bounded space and time of production to other places and other times? In the eighteenth century, and in some cases well into the nineteenth century, knowledge about theatre moved from person-to-person, acquired through long experience in the business, and accessible almost uniquely to those in the profession itself. This process works well as long as the supply of theatrical knowledge adequately meets the demand for it. But demand for new plays and new performers, as well as for information about the theatre generally, grew astoundingly in the nineteenth century. This growth both spurred and benefited from the official end to weakened state theatre monopolies in places such as England (1843), France (1864) and Denmark (1889). Data from Charles Beaumont Wicks' catalogue *The Parisian Stage* show that in Paris alone new play production doubled and the number of theatre venues tripled between the first and the last quarter of the nineteenth century.[1] Theatre simply could not operate at such scale without clearly defined, externally verifiable methods for training new actors, buying and selling plays, and otherwise managing the system of production.

The solution to this problem required that theatrical knowledge cease being the private, implicit domain of informed professionals and become part of the public circulation of theatre itself. In other words, knowledge about theatre became an industrial commodity. Because nineteenth-century industrialization centred in Northern Europe and the United States, my examples draw particularly on developments there. (England plays a particularly large role in my discussion, in part because it industrialized first.) I address three major areas in which knowledge transmission took on a new form during the nineteenth century: copyright laws; social and cultural capital; and the organization of the theatre industry. In each area, theatrical knowledge moved from something generally held close to something widely distributed for sale. Industrial capitalism transformed theatrical knowledge into commodities suited to global, industrial commerce.

## COPYRIGHT LAWS

The most significant formal change in theatre's status as property was the expansion of copyright laws to encompass performance. Copyright dates to the previous century; the 1710 Statute of Anne in England was the first law to grant exclusive rights to print and sell texts, including (implicitly) plays. While theatre benefited from copyright laws that protected print, the later advent of performance rights – the right to perform, as opposed simply to print, a play – provided protections in the medium of theatre.

Performance rights emerged in Europe beginning in the 1790s and spread through the end of the nineteenth century. Key dates in the creation of performance rights (though often in some limited fashion) include:

- 1791, France
- 1833, England
- 1837, Prussia and Spain
- 1856, United States
- 1871, Germany[2]
- 1886, Berne Treaty (international accord that included performance rights)
- 1891, United States grants mutual protection for foreign authors.

The details of each nation's copyright system varied and national laws often changed significantly throughout the century, either through new legislation or through new legal interpretations and commercial practices. Indeed, while performance rights were created in the nineteenth century, the invention of those rights spurred creativity less through their establishment per se, than in the contests (legal and extra-legal) that the new rights inspired. In other words, while the status of theatrical knowledge as property transformed between 1800 and 1920, the process of transformation had as great an effect on theatrical knowledge as the final laws themselves. This section explores how copyright law affected theatre, both in print and in performance.

## Printing Drama

Officially, printed plays had received protection under the earliest copyright laws, but those laws 'had precious little effect so far as playwrights were concerned'.[3] Over sixty years separate the Statute of Anne's passage and the first recorded copyright decision involving a play. That opinion merely affirmed actor-playwright Charles Macklin's exclusive right to print the successful *Love-à-la-Mode*, of which a magazine had published the first act without authorization.[4] Changes in the form and style of printed drama were everywhere tied closely to enforceable performance rights.

Spain provides an excellent case study in what strong, well-policed performance rights could do to the published play text. Lisa Surwillo documents a comprehensive renovation of printed Spanish drama in the nineteenth century. After copyright protections for plays appeared in 1847, Spanish 'theatre evolved from a spectacle-based event to a textually grounded one'.[5] As a result, playwrights gained control over texts hitherto subject to wild interpretation by *autores de comedias* (similar to English theatre's managers). National censorship helped enforce central control, ensuring that provincial theatres observed the letter of the printed text and transforming Spanish theatre into a uniform system of performance.[6] Meanwhile, printed play collections called *galerías*, which gathered plays owned by a single publisher, 'transposed the theatrical performance into an alternate space for private readers through which the same gallery of national dramatic treasure could be found in all citizens' homes'.[7] The *galerías*' elaborate paratexts both asserted the authenticity of the dramas contained therein and offered advice on how to cast specific roles or on the proper set for a play. In the wake of copyright protections, Spanish citizens could claim uniform access to the nation's theatrical treasures, whether they witnessed those plays performed in the city or the countryside or read them in elegantly typeset *galerías*.

English drama presents a contrasting case. Despite the relatively early advent of performance rights in England, the absence of copyright protection for

British authors in the US kept many playwrights from taking much care with their printed works. Until the 1820s, high-quality printed plays had remained popular at competitive prices, published by a variety of prosperous publishers such as Longman, which offered forty-two volumes of plays, collected in three series by Elizabeth Inchbald in 1808 and 1809.[8] (High-quality refers, here, to the quality of the binding, paper, printed text, etc.) In the 1830s and early 1840s, expensive editions of plays by Sheridan Knowles, Thomas Noon Talfourd and Edward Bulwer Lytton – the latter two also prime movers behind revisions of the copyright laws – continued the previous decade's trend in play publication.[9] But from approximately 1841 to 1891, plays in finely bound, carefully printed reading volumes all but disappeared from the market, replaced by poorly printed, inexpensive acting editions. The high-quality printed play all but disappeared for fifty years.

Daniel Barrett attributes this change to a number of factors in addition to copyright: the rise of the novel (a safer commodity for publishers), the influx of translations and adaptations from France, the popularity of highly theatrical forms such as melodrama, burletta, pantomime, burlesque and comic opera, and the prevalence of acting editions.[10] Acting editions, published in cheap paperback by Thomas Hailes Lacy and other houses that the former eventually consolidated under his imprint, represent a transformation in the material quality of the printed English play.[11] As Barrett writes, 'The acting edition offers tangible evidence that playwrights in the nineteenth century wrote almost exclusively for a theatrical, not a literary, clientele.'[12] Julie Stone Peters offers a twist on this argument that echoes the function of the *galerías*, suggesting that 'published "promptbooks" were in fact crafted for the reader [. . .] hungry for both spectacle and the theatre in a state of undress'.[13] Acting editions, however, were literally written from the perspective of an actor. As a note in the Dicks' Standard Plays edition of *The Colleen Bawn* explains, 'The Reader is supposed to be on the Stage, facing the Audience.'[14] Such editions supported play production, complete with costume lists, stage directions and tableaux. In so doing, they transmitted far more knowledge about performance than the sparsely annotated, finely printed editions popular in the early part of the century.

When plays made it into print, then, those editions offered a surfeit of information about their performance. Yet the majority of most English dramatists' work never reached print at all. John Russell Stephens estimates that most playwrights in the period published between five and fifty per cent of their total output, which could amount to 200 plays or more.[15] Despite a few experiments with handsomely presented play collections in the 1870s, notably W. S. Gilbert's *Original Plays* of 1876, play publication for a general reading audience resumed in earnest only after the US granted copyright protection for foreigners in 1891. That same year, printed editions of Arthur Wing Pinero's *The Times* (published by Heinemann and sold in the theatre on opening night) and Henry Arthur Jones's *Saints and Sinners* put into practice the much-discussed project of reconnecting theatre to published literature.

In the wake of clearer copyright protections, Bernard Shaw was at the vanguard of a group of writers who would go on 'to make the white space of the page part of the play's semantic field of play'.[16] While the 'Shaw book' did not perform a print version of theatrical style as rigorously as a publication by Gertrude Stein or Samuel Beckett would in the following decades, Shaw's control over his printed texts anticipated how authors would go on to stage the page, as it were. Prefaces, careful use of fonts (roman for dialogue, italics for stage directions), spacing (extra spaces between letters indicated emphasis), and extensive attention to the layout of the page combined to create the Shaw book as an elegant, aesthetically pleasing object that simultaneously addressed readers and performers. Shaw also eliminated the technical language typical of acting editions (e.g. 'R. 2 E.' for second entrance, stage right) in favour of describing the play's environment in novelistic language. His control over punctuation and layout, like his careful use of dialect, 'scores the rhythm and emphasis of printed language in ways that bring the music of the play to book', as W. B. Worthen writes.[17] In some ways, the Shaw book transmits less knowledge about a play and its performance than cheaper acting editions. In place of that lost information (props lists, tableaux, costume designs) the Shaw book gave the public plays that spoke to their novel-reading habits, communicated a strong sense of authorial identity, and asserted the literary value of theatrical texts. The movement from the cheap editions printed by Lacy to the refined volumes sold by Shaw's publisher, Grant Richards, traces not only theatre's changing social status and its protection by copyright law, but also a reconsideration of what kinds of knowledge the play-script should transmit to its readers and in what form it should do so.

### Performance Rights

As a practical matter, performance rights granted playwrights the sole right to license performances of their works. This legal power should, in theory, give playwrights greater control over the theatrical realization of their texts and larger incomes. In practice, managers often reaped as much benefit as playwrights and the most valuable elements of the period's performances sometimes had little to do with the playwright's work. Considered more broadly then, performance rights had the potential to transform any valuable performance practices into property, at least insofar as creators and owners could convince courts that those practices were the proper domain of copyright laws.

In the 1860s in the United States, for instance, the manageress Laura Keene fought to assert some ownership over her blockbuster comedy *Our American Cousin*, by Tom Taylor. Keene won a partial victory in one such case, in a ruling that recognized actor Joseph Jefferson's interpolated gags as uniquely valuable to Keene's production. 'The judicious introduction of matter whose chief or only novelty consists in its happy adaptation to the production of stage effect', wrote a judge, 'may contribute more to that popularity of a light comedy, which secures profitable repetitions of its performance' than literary humour.[18] Keene, this judge found, had some exclusive rights to Jefferson's interpolations in her company's production of *Our American Cousin*. By contrast other courts, attuned to an aural culture that valued the free circulation of ideas, resisted the possibility of claiming ownership over performance. Keene's claims failed in another case in which the judge asserted that, absent an explicit indication to the contrary, audiences had a right to re-perform what they could memorize from watching a play. As one judge put it, restricting that right 'cannot be implied as one of the ordinary terms of admission to the performance, because remembering, to a certain extent, is the natural consequence of hearing, and using such recollection naturally flows from possessing it'.[19] This 'memory doctrine' survived almost twenty years in American law, revealing the complexities of transforming performance from evanescent event to tradeable property.

In spurring courts to define performance as a commodity, performance rights reshaped theatrical culture. Take, for example, the 'copyright performance', a uniquely English theatrical practice common from the 1860s to the 1910s that arose in response to domestic legal confusion and to market incentives for performing British plays in the US. 'Publication' was a key moment in the life of intellectual property in nineteenth-century Britain but copyright laws defined publication poorly, leaving uncertain whether print publication secured performance rights in a play. Many theatre professionals and lawyers came to believe that only a public performance could guarantee a playwright's performance rights. Thus developed the copyright performance, a one-time, pseudo-public performance of a play, staged usually in the morning for an almost-empty house, with no costumes, sets or rehearsal, solely to satisfy the perceived demands of English law. Contemporary descriptions suggest most copyright performances merely walked through the script. Though actors performed specific roles, plays were usually 'galloped through as fast as possible, amid no inconsiderable hilarity'.[20] The stripped-down style of those performances likely forestalled copyright disputes in the 1880s and after, and inadvertently established an aesthetic baseline copied by the minimal, under-rehearsed performances by non-profit societies such as the Independent Theatre Society and the Elizabethan Theatre Society.[21] Copyright performances became de rigueur among professional British theatre artists, a way to establish the bona fides of any theatrical property, no matter how negligible, that might someday be worth legally protecting. Thus, the playwright Hubert O'Grady, self-proclaimed '[a]uthor of some of the most Successful Plays of the Period', declared that a copyright performance of one play, 'although unaided by Scenery, Music, or Special Cast, caught on and held the audience from rise to fall of the curtain', and 'met with the decided approval' of that audience.[22] O'Grady made those claims in a newspaper advertisement seeking a producer for the play. Whatever legal force the copyright performance had – and its effectiveness seems never to have been tested in court – the practice became a hallmark of late Victorian theatrical life.

The copyright performance represents an extreme example of how performance rights influenced theatrical practice. More typically, performance rights inspired a scenario like that involving the famous melodramatic spectacle of the 'railroad scene', depicting the last-minute rescue of a man (though now imagined usually as a woman) from an oncoming train. In an 1868 American lawsuit, *Daly v. Palmer*, the court ruled that, despite no similarity in the dialogue of the disputed plays (by Augustin Daly and Dion Boucicault, respectively), Boucicault had no right to copy Daly's proprietary stage action.[23] That critical assessment made the contested scene (and potentially other sensation scenes) economically valuable, and Daly sold the right to perform the scenario to other managers around the United States.[24] Boucicault, meanwhile, continued to tweak and refine his adaptation until courts agreed that his version differed sufficiently from Daly's to be a non-infringing spectacle.[25] The lawsuit over a performance right thus made available a new form of theatrical market – in the spectacular scene, as well as in the drama as a whole – while spurring Boucicault to vary his stage effects.

After the advent of performance rights, transmitting theatrical knowledge frequently entailed transferring or licensing intellectual property rights. As the preceding examples demonstrate, debates over the proper form of such rights, over the nature and extent of performance as intellectual property, shaped both print and performance practices throughout the nineteenth century.

## SOCIAL AND CULTURAL CAPITAL

Knowledge about the theatrical event, circulating through scripts and performances, did not sate the public's hunger for knowledge about the theatre. Artists and audiences alike strove to understand how the theatre operated and what theatre meant to themselves and to their nation. This knowledge about theatre as a social practice and about theatre's cultural import disseminated through a wide variety of media including contracts, schools and handbooks, and critical essays. Contracts helped regularize and codify professional behaviour – particularly among actors, but also among other theatre workers – in the years before and after actors' unionization. Theatre schools articulated acting as a discrete sphere of knowledge and competed to determine how best to train the next generation of performers. Handbooks for professionals or amateurs provided key information about the art of theatre but also regularly included information about the theatre industry's operation. Finally, the vast critical literature on theatre throughout the century continued the tradition of promoting and building a dramatic canon through debates in print. While none of these media was new in the nineteenth century, all of them found an expanded audience eager to learn ever more about theatre's operation. They became increasingly important to transmitting theatrical knowledge to the rapidly expanding community of theatre's makers and consumers.

## Contracts and Unions

Just as copyright laws altered the balance of power among audiences, playwrights and managers, innovations in theatrical contracts caused a similar realignment of authority among theatrical artists. Contracts, legally enforceable agreements that create mutual obligations between two or more parties, help to define the terms under which managers employ artists and under which those artists commit to their employers. During the nineteenth century, as managers exerted more control, theatrical contracts increased in length and complexity. The expansion of contractual terms usually entailed making explicit in the contract what had previously been implicit practice. In other words, the contract became an increasingly important medium for the transmission of theatrical knowledge. New and more thorough contractual clauses marked transformations in the theatrical professions (manager, playwright, actor, etc.), those professions' relative power, the practice of making theatre, and the value of theatre in the marketplace. Eventually theatrical unions further equalized power both among theatre workers and between employers and employees. Theatre unions supported not only the growth of this contractual archive, but also standardized theatrical knowledge within the profession. Groups such as the Actors' Equity Association (AEA), with their modified guild systems, became gatekeepers of the stage and of the knowledge of professional behaviour.

In eighteenth- and early nineteenth-century repertory company, managers wielded some authority but often shared power with performers who, 'buttressed by traditional business, possession of parts, and lines of acting, enjoyed a large measure of autonomy'.[26] Such a system assumed that all parties understood their obligations to observe traditional practices and allowed leeway in enforcement. This structure is evident in a sample contract from the Theatre Royal at Drury Lane included in Leman Thomas Rede's *Road to the Stage* (1827).[27] The single clearest hallmark of the Drury Lane contract is the manager's discretion, particularly with regard to actors' privileges such as the benefit performance, from which actors collected part of the receipts from an evening's performance as a supplement to their salary. The contract gives prominent place to benefits, which feature in the second paragraph, suggesting performers' lingering authority. Benefits, however, are 'allowed' to actors deemed to have 'duly performed' the contract's articles, 'but not otherwise'.[28] Likewise, the date of the benefit is subject to managerial approval. Wherever the contract speaks to actors' rights and privileges – in cases of sickness; if the benefit fails to recuperate the house's expenses – 'the discretion' of the manager is the only hint of authority. The early-nineteenth century Drury Lane contract is, in short, vague and evasive, suggesting managerial authority while also conceding much to traditional practice.

British and American theatrical practice became more stringent as the theatrical markets in both countries grew more diverse. The American theatre in the late eighteenth century inherited its organizational practices from England via immigrant performers and companies such as those led by Lewis Hallam. If anything, early American 'managers were less exacting' than their counterparts in London.[29] The growth of the star system beginning around 1810 and the increasingly competitive and geographically expansive theatre scene in North America soon encouraged power to consolidate in the hands of stronger managers. As larger numbers of inexperienced artists entered a theatre business hungry for new talent, managers no longer relied on custom and tradition to control behaviour but turned instead to the contract. In the mid-1870s, Augustin Daly (who would reverse Hallam's journey, working first in New York, then in London) exemplified the dictatorial style. His contract epitomizes the expanded managerial authority and its explicit control of actors' behaviour.[30] Contracts were expected now to document appropriate decorum for actors, replacing an informal system policed solely among colleagues. For instance, Daly's contract explicitly forbids deviations from the play's text, a practice common among players during the period. A lengthy clause names such 'guying' or even 'aid[ing] or abet[ting] the instigator of any such misconduct by replying to or smiling thereat' as a violation warranting fines. Actors must observe even more stringent decorum offstage. The contract's ninth section, for example, forbids bringing 'intoxicating liquors' to the theatre, along with smoking, 'improper conduct' and 'oaths or questionable language, or conversations that would not be tolerated in polite society'. How to behave in Daly's company was not the subject of unwritten, informal rules: the employment contract itself transmitted a wide array of professional standards.[31]

By the end of the long nineteenth century, unions and their contracts began appearing in the US and Europe, providing further written documentation of practices previously left to local custom. Attempts at actor unionization in the US date at least to 1864, when William Davidge organized the first Actors' Protective Union; stagehands' unions date at least to 1886. Actors organized more intently in the 1890s, in configurations such as the Actors' National Protective Union, Hebrew Actors Union, and vaudeville's White Rats of America. The most successful union, the AEA, formed only in 1913, winning collective bargaining rights after a month-long strike in 1919.[32] Their first standard contract reveals how unionization, when successful, could transform the union and its contract into an important repository of knowledge for the profession.

In some ways, the AEA contract is vaguer than its predecessors.[33] Gone are the lengthy managerial stipulations, replaced by a general admonition to 'abide by all reasonable rules and regulations'.[34] In their place, the AEA contract offers extensive protections for the actor. For instance, the contract limits rehearsal periods to four weeks (five for a musical), sets rules for terminating employment and includes specific clauses about transportation back to New York when road companies close.[35] More fundamentally, the contract removes conflicts between actors and managers from the private sphere of the theatrical community by committing both parties in a contract dispute to arbitration. The two sides must come to an agreement – the initial arbitrators to be appointed one by the manager, one by the union – and, failing such agreement, a third arbitrator would be appointed, 'who shall not in any way be connected with the theatrical profession' (Section 18). This principle presumes that there exist mutually fair standards determined fully neither by the manager's discretion nor by the actor and the newly powerful union. The profession is no longer so insular that it must rely on internal authority. The rules are now comprehensible to all, and parsing them appropriately is merely a matter of fairness as such, rather than of justly interpreting implicit standards. In short, the contract is now so explicit that outsiders can arbitrate its enforcement. The AEA contract thus marks the beginning of a new phase in performance contracts, in which the contract's authority as a broker exceeds, in some sense, that of the agents who drafted it. Contracts became themselves not simply useful transmitters of knowledge about the culture of theatre, but their own authorities on theatrical culture.

## Handbooks and Training

Never had knowledge of that culture been so widely available. For instance, training in the theatre was no longer a matter simply of long apprenticeship. Professional knowledge moved, in the nineteenth century, from the stage and the rehearsal room into formal educational institutions and the pages of published books.

France contained one of the oldest acting training programmes in Europe. The Conservatoire National de Musique et de Déclamation taught musicians and actors alike since the Revolutionary period. An 1883 pamphlet summarized the goals of the institution as follows:

> to teach the pupils how to enunciate, how to act, how to bear themselves on the stage, and how to portray a character, i.e. how to present it logically and

harmoniously so that all its aspects are of a piece and nothing jars; and to encourage them to study, in accordance with the traditions, the classical masterpieces, the dynamism of each scene, the characters as they have been transmitted to us by past masters.[36]

*Sociétaires* from the Comédie Française taught the important courses in declamation. F. W. J. Hemmings assesses the training there as, for all its faults, 'varied, effective, and memorable', particularly after a reorganization in 1850.[37] The Conservatoire, in Hemmings' view, succeeded in its aim 'to preserve and transmit the traditions of the past' in a formal educational system.[38]

Michael Sanderson's history of acting training in Britain, though claiming an absence of serious acting education there until after the turn of the twentieth century, does document numerous opportunities for training in the nineteenth century, from company schools to formal academies. In the 1830s, Frances Maria Kelly ran a school in London dedicated to acting and elocution.[39] Thirty years later, Sarah Thorne filled out her professional company at the Theatre Royal Margate with paying pupils who trod the boards by night and took 'classes in acting voice production, gesture and mime, dialects and makeup' by day.[40] Hermann Vezin and Rosina Filippi taught students elocution; Henry Neville and Cairns James ran acting academies.[41] In 1904, Herbert Beerbohm Tree established the Royal Academy of Dramatic Art, which, along with Elsie Fogerty's Central School of Speech and Drama (1906), set a new standard for acting instruction in England. By creating clear curricula (elocution, pantomime, dancing, fencing, make up, rehearsal), these high-profile, well-funded organizations helped codify the set of skills an actor should possess and raised the profession's status.[42]

In the United States, a rich system of instruction arose during the nineteenth century, complete with competing theories of acting and competing methods for instructing actors. James H. McTeague has documented the 'hotbed of activity' aimed at educating and training actors between 1875 and 1925, including eleven schools, the work of which he traces.[43] While some institutions subscribed to the ideas of François Delsarte (particularly as adapted by Steele MacKaye), the schools pursued a variety of competing approaches, some favouring oratory, others (such as a short-lived experiment by Dion Boucicault) preferring practical lessons. Together, they opposed imitative methods like those exemplified by the Parisian Conservatoire. Yet these schools shared with their peers in Europe a firm belief that some aspects of acting could be taught, and constructed formal systems in which to teach them.

While acting schools helped establish acting as a profession, handbooks addressed the professional and amateur alike. Amateur theatricals, born first of private performances in aristocratic country houses, were exceedingly popular in England and the US during the nineteenth century. An entire corner of the theatrical publishing industry catered to these productions, with volumes that promised to explain the practical steps of putting on a play in one's drawing room while offering a small glimpse behind the curtain of the professional stage. For instance, W. J. Sorrell's *Amateur's Hand-Book*, printed by Thomas Hailes Lacy, disavows any intention 'to aid those ambitious aspirants who are satisfied with nothing less than a "real theatre"'.[44] Yet the same volume includes a full plate explaining stage shorthand, with a diagram and table translating such terms as R. 2 E. and L. C.[45] A similar guide offers chemical recipes for making coloured light effects.[46] In such handbooks, the theatrical knowledge made explicit ranged from such technical language and effects to more prosaic issues such as costuming, scene painting, and (inevitably) make-up: 'Making up the face and head is a great point, and for this purpose are required wigs, beards, and moustaches, rouge, pearl powder, and sepia or Indian ink, together with a hare's foot or two, for the proper application of the rouge.'[47] Amateur handbooks transmitted, along with a practical guide to theatre-making, some of the excitement of theatrical culture. If such volumes could not guarantee the roar of the crowd, they could at least encourage the purchase – and thus introduce the smell – of the greasepaint.

Handbooks about the professional theatre were not invented in the nineteenth century, of course. But the nineteenth-century books differ from their predecessors in that they often transmit not only knowledge of stage technique but also information about how the profession operates. Leman Thomas Rede's *Road to the Stage*, cited above, is an early example of this kind of volume. While the last clause of Rede's subtitle promises to reveal 'all the Technicalities of the Histrionic Art', the preceding clauses promise practical insights into 'Obtaining Theatrical Engagements'. The knowledge Rede transmits includes such essential facts as a list of provincial managers, along with standard salaries at their theatres. Even as Rede offers advice to the aspiring professional, he demystifies the life of an actor, putting the profession in layman's terms.

Later in the century, those eager to walk the boards could find similar advice in books such as *How to Become an Actor*, while young dramatists could turn to *The Art of Playwriting*.[48] The novelty in these nineteenth-century volumes lies not in their artistic content; advice about good play construction has existed since Aristotle; acting theories have nearly as long a lineage, particularly if one includes training in rhetoric. Rather, such handbooks add to the expected suggestions about gesture or scene construction detailed information about life as an actor or playwright, about the practical work of making a career in the theatre. *How to Become an Actor* includes one chapter recommending how to write to a manager to secure an engagement, another explains the stage manager's role. A chapter on stage slang humorously warns the would-be performer that the shout of 'beginners' refers to the curtain's imminent rise, not to novice actors.[49] Similar explanations appear in *The Art of Playwriting*, which was 'arranged in two principal divisions, the first dealing with the minutiae of the theatre, the second with the principles of dramatic construction', explains its author, Alfred Hennequin. 'In the first the reader is inducted into the twilight region which lies beyond the scenes, told the name and function of the pieces of stage machinery [. . .], initiated into the mysteries of stage conventionalities – in short, made acquainted with every feature of the modern stage which concerns him as a working playwright.'[50] Perhaps more sanguine about his or her reader's knowledge, the anonymous author of *Playwriting: A Handbook for Would-Be Dramatic Authors* does not supply as many definitions as Hennequin, but still devotes three-quarters of the volume to the process of production (from rehearsals to opening night) and to such important issues as monetary compensation and, for three chapters, legal protection.[51] All of these guides share the instinct not only to record the skills of dramatic artists but also to explain the practical tools necessary for a life in the theatre.

### Criticism and History

Among the ideas about theatre transmitted by handbooks and training programmes was a canon of theatre history. Consider the required course in theatre history at the Paris Conservatoire. As taught by Henry de Lapommeraye in the 1880s, the class moved chronologically, emphasizing French theatre: ancient and medieval drama; Corneille, Racine, and Molière; Shakespeare; Marivaux, Voltaire, Beaumarchais, etc.; drama from the Revolutionary period through the 1830s, including Goethe and Schiller.[52] The lectures themselves offered 'an appreciative commentary on the work itself from a perspective dramatic or literary, historical or moral'.[53] Outside of conservatories, education in theatre history as an academic discipline grew in stature in the late nineteenth century. For instance, the Gesellschaft für Theatergeschichte was founded in 1902, a key moment in establishing theatre history among the disciplines central to the modern research university. Brander Matthews at Columbia and George Pierce Baker at Harvard and later Yale helped legitimize and canonize the study of drama in American higher education.[54] By the eve of the First World War, the modern theatre classroom – where students hear a chronological survey of theatrical styles focused on the dramatic techniques and themes of a small canon of playwrights – was a common medium for transmitting knowledge about theatre history.

At the other end of the cultural hierarchy, amateur handbooks doubled as promotional materials for a publisher's catalogue of plays. The *Amateur's Hand-Book* sold by Lacy includes a lengthy supplement advertising plays well suited to the drawing room. One section divides plays by genre (comic, burlesque, fairy) and by character breakdown (all male, all female, etc.), followed by a section listing the eighteen volumes of Lacy's *Dramas for Private Representation*, each comprised of at least fifteen plays. A literary canon with an eye on aesthetic form this is not. But Lacy's functional, commercial canon offered a compelling (and, one must imagine, lucrative) vision of theatre that brought its audience out of the auditorium and onto the stage. The amateur dramatic canon advertised in Lacy's book and like volumes promulgated an alternative, amateur-oriented, commercially-minded theatrical canon for nineteenth-century consumers that regarded theatre as something both to observe and to do.

While classrooms and handbooks promoted competing visions of the canon, written theatre criticism featured intense debates about the nature and purpose of drama. Competing manifestos about the theatre asserted critical paradigms in which to receive contemporary drama and, necessarily, through which to renew assessments of older work. In France, Victor Hugo's Preface to *Cromwell* (1827) articulated the principles of Romantic drama much as Émile Zola's 'Naturalism on the Stage' (1880) advanced that genre's aims. Richard Wagner's essay on 'The Art-Work of the Future' (1849) offers another example of how nineteenth-century artists relied on prose manifestos to complement the dramaturgical visions promoted by and in their works for the stage. Even lesser artists contributed in this vein: English playwright Henry Arthur Jones published two volumes of collected essays during his lifetime, both of which advanced his vision of a literary drama.[55] In England, two great eras of criticism bookended the nineteenth-century. William Hazlitt and Charles Lamb helped rethink Shakespeare and the Elizabethan drama for the Romantic age, attempting to disentangle the poet's genius from the powerful performances of his leading roles by actors such as Edmund Kean and Sarah Siddons.[56] Two generations later, William Archer and Bernard Shaw painted a vision of Modern Drama with Henrik Ibsen as the focal point. Archer's writings and the private theatre societies that produced the Modern Drama not only built a contemporary canon, but also redefined the consensus about English theatrical history. By telling a consistent story of the English theatrical past, present and future, Archer and like-minded friends advanced a teleological narrative in which the literary, intellectual drama performed by the Independent Theatre Society or at the Court Theatre under Harley Granville-Barker triumphed over the uncouth spectacles of the Victorian period. As Cary Mazer argues, 'With the self-applied label "New," the advocates of the New Drama and New Theatre had declared the war; and, without even waiting for the battle to be over, they claimed victory; and then wrote the histories themselves.'[57] The knowledge of British theatre this group transmitted to the English-speaking public – in books, essays, criticism, plays and performances – favoured literary drama over spectacle and non-profit societies over commercial interests. They opposed the stage censor and advocated politically liberal (or even radically socialist positions) such as women's suffrage. Those priorities set the terms for the reception of nineteenth-century British theatre during the twentieth century, which Michael R. Booth summarizes as 'frequently dismissive and sometimes contemptuous' of the popular, commercial theatre.[58] Critics working in the nineteenth-century theatre have persistently shaped how later readers view the period's accomplishments. In particular, writings by revolutionaries – Hugo, Zola, Wagner, Archer – laid the groundwork for interpreting those revolutions' achievements and for denigrating the complex, multifaceted theatrical field in which those writers achieved their success.

# ORGANIZATION OF THE THEATRE INDUSTRY

The industrializing theatre industry within which the preceding changes took place also struggled, in the nationalist fervour of the period, through extensive debates about the quality of theatre as a mode of domestic production. By the end of the nineteenth century, the ostensibly local enterprise of theatre revealed its global face and developed new strategies for distributing itself internationally. This section looks at changing conceptions of and within the theatre industry, first as a national and then as an international phenomenon.

## National Theatres

Pleas for theatre as a vital national industry echoed throughout the nineteenth century. English debates about the Dramatic Literary Property Act in 1833, for instance, asserted that the patent theatres existed to promote 'the preservation of the dignity of the national drama'.[59] Observers felt that theatre expressed something fundamental about national identity, something only a domestic theatre industry could harness. In the 1890s, Henry Arthur Jones bemoaned 'the parallel degradation of English character and English speech which is rapidly taking place. For the degradation of the English tongue implies the correlative degradation of the national character.'[60] He blamed, in part, the stage for this failure: 'It could scarcely be asked without transparent irony how far the modern English drama has been a means of preserving the vigour and purity of the English language, and how far the English theatre has been a means of setting a standard of just accent and clear diction.'[61]

Like so many other aspects of national pride, theatre's national quality became evident only in an international context. In the 1833 debates, one Member of Parliament complained that the theatres' current spectacles 'made a greater display of depravity than any theatres in Paris, Naples, or Madrid, and, in this respect, were a reproach to the country'.[62] Critics, however, not only thought comparatively, but also actively sought out other nations' theatre practices as models for the home-grown theatre. That is, to fertilize theatre in any given national soil, writers sought to import theatrical knowledge from foreign lands. Nowhere was this process more apparent than in Britain and the US, where critics simultaneously expressed disgust with the constant importation of French plays and worked hard to encourage a domestic theatrical culture like that of France. Brander Matthews, for instance, attributed to Victor Hugo, Émile Augier, and Alexandre Dumas the 'returning vitality in the drama of our own tongue'.[63] When arguing for state arts funding, Jones not only refers to the French model, but even quotes – in untranslated French! – two full pages of a speech from the Chambre des Députés to support his own argument.[64]

Meanwhile, the non-profit theatres that helped grow Modern Drama throughout Europe – the Théâtre Libre, Freie Bühne, Tooneelvereeniging – modelled each other's practices.[65] J. T. Grein, for instance, founder of the Independent Theatre Society, published articles about a 'British Théâtre Libre' in 1889, two years after André Antoine had founded the seminal French institution, and the same year that Otto Brahm was organizing in Berlin.[66] These companies, each with a particular mission to facilitate a national drama, met that goal in large part by mimicking aspects of each other's organization and by performing the same emerging, international repertory of Modern Drama, particularly Ibsen. To create national theatrical cultures, in other words, for- and non-profit theatre-makers alike looked overseas, transmitting that knowledge from their European rivals back to their countrymen.

William Archer and his cohort famously advocated not only improvements in the quality of drama, but also a renovation in how Britain made its theatre. The most complete articulation of this ideal appeared in *Schemes and Estimates for a National Theatre*, a prospectus for a combined repertory company and training institute, composed by Archer and Harley Granville-Barker in 1908.[67] That document, like earlier essays, considered their proposed British model in relation to competing systems in Europe. In so doing, they took up a tradition dating back in its current incarnation to Matthew Arnold who, reviewing the Comédie Française's sojourn in Paris, concluded that Britons must 'organise the theatre', in a fashion inspired by and perhaps modelled on that in Paris.[68] By looking to Paris as a model for theatre-making in London, Arnold, Archer and others exemplified how the challenge of building a national theatrical tradition encouraged the international transmission of theatrical knowledge. In an era of fervent national feeling, theatre became one of the first global cultural phenomena. Making theatre global required that an array of production practices transcend the national boundaries within which many artists and audiences imagined theatrical creativity.

## International

Even as nations asserted unique theatrical identities, corporations became their own powerful theatrical brands and were essential media for the transmission of knowledge from centres of theatrical production to the rest of the globe. The English-speaking theatre industry, like so many other industries of the period, experienced a long period of consolidation in the late nineteenth century. Companies, usually led by one or two charismatic individuals, began to control both content (productions) and distribution networks (theatres). Control over productions was tied closely to performance rights laws, discussed above. Playwrights – and more frequently managers – who owned the rights to plays worked to ensure that authorized productions met a certain standard, thus maintaining the value of the play as a brand (although they would not have used that vocabulary). To maintain a strong brand identity, producers either had to transport productions wholesale or to find new ways to transmit knowledge of their production processes across increasingly vast distances. Henry Irving's American tours exemplify the former strategy. Irving, as Tracy C. Davis has carefully documented, used his Lyceum Theatre in London as a laboratory. He willingly (if not happily) lost money on developing new productions there, relying on American tours of those productions to recuperate his costs and account for his profits, profits he then poured into developing the next project in London.[69] Such a combination system was highly profitable with a successful show or a star performer like Irving or Bernhardt. Yet the process had its flaws, particularly the difficulty of transporting complex production materials (costumes, sets, lighting techniques) across oceans and continents. In the 1880s, foreign companies ran into protectionist concerns from American theatre manufacturers (seamstresses, drapery companies) over expensively fabricated goods the importation of which undermined American theatrical labour.[70] That conflict merely made visible the always complex logistics involved in moving theatrical productions within and across borders.

In the 1890s and, at an accelerated pace in the Edwardian Era, the material aspects of a production (costumes, sets) became less important as goods and more significant as ideas. That is, producers began to value less their productions' physical costumes and to value more their costume designs. Knowledge of how to stage a production became the key element transmitted from the metropole to the colony, rather than the physical goods that the company had used in its original production in the capital. Davis describes this as a 'conceptual [. . .] innovation':

> producers kept personnel and stock at home and simply exported designs and encrypted mise-en-scènes to authorized affiliates – usually in Australia, the Cape, or Asia – to produce full-scale duplicates of what audiences had seen in London. This significantly extended the lifetimes of West End shows by innovating in transportation and distribution of theatre as *a purely intellectual product*.[71]

In other words, content producers packaged their productions in ways that limited costs and risk to the metropolitan company while ensuring productions associated with the capital's name remained of high quality (i.e. did not devalue the brand). No longer would content owners depend on local producers to reinvent and somehow still maintain the creative vision cultivated in the metropole. Instead, creators could distribute the look and feel of the capital's productions without exporting any of the production's physical goods. Obviously, this drastically reduced costs while maintaining (theoretically) quality. By treating entire productions – and not only scripts or scores – as forms of knowledge to transmit around the globe, producers transformed theatre into a more efficient global product.

In the colonies, meanwhile, content distributors controlled access to the expensive knowledge from the metropole, translating that knowledge back into a physical production and then transporting that production around their distribution areas. Consider the example of J. C. Williamson, an American by birth, whose early acting career took him on tour across the Pacific where he saw first-hand the legal and financial challenges of managing theatrical production on a national and international scale. In 1879, he purchased the Australian performance rights to Gilbert and Sullivan's first smash hit, *H.M.S. Pinafore*. Fending off theatrical pirates, Williamson did well enough to secure rights to the next Gilbert and Sullivan work, *The Pirates of Penzance*, which he produced 'with costumes, wigs, swords and properties' imported from London and Paris.[72] Williamson's legal control over the wildly successful Gilbert and Sullivan catalogue secured him enough of an advantage with audiences to help him amass a fortune and gain control over theatres throughout Australia. The Firm, as his organization came to be known, relied on Williamson's ability to bring to Australia 'a wealth of technical skill from the great theatrical centres of the Old World'.[73] On the one hand, these assets appeared in the form of actual performers and productions: access to star actors – such as Sarah Bernhardt in 1891 – or the latest Gilbert and Sullivan shows and American hits (*Ben Hur*) passed through Williamson. But Williamson's expertise extended also to his ability to organize and transport productions around Australia, among his theatres in the country's leading cities. A somewhat hagiographic account of him summarizes: 'In colonial cities with limited audience potential, J. C. Williamson quickly realised the economic advantage to be gained from a system of alternating concurrent productions in the major cities. He organised each of his productions so that it was easily transportable.'[74] Williamson understood that entire productions were storehouses of cultural knowledge. Like his contemporaries, Maurice Bandmann, members of the American Theatrical Syndicate, or the Shubert Organization, Williamson knew how to transmit that knowledge from its origins in the metropolitan centre to the periphery, now along a distribution network owned and managed by the content-producer.[75]

Williamson sold his audiences not only productions, but also his own brand: the Williamson guarantee.

# CONCLUSION

The transmission of theatrical knowledge in the nineteenth century entailed primarily the explicit ordering of implicit knowledge into more public and more commercially viable forms, the commodification of theatrical knowledge. Whether they sought to learn acting techniques, copy costume designs, or read dramatic texts, theatre professionals and audiences in the 1920s had a far larger array of theatrical knowledge at their disposal than those at the turn of the previous century. As the theatre industry industrialized, professionalized and globalized, knowledge of theatre as a practice found its way into orderly channels that answered the demands of the complex and growing market for theatrical entertainment. Such a transformation generally entailed privatizing and commercializing theatrical knowledge. As a result, information previously accessible only to those within the theatrical profession was for sale to the public. Although theatrical performances remained very much the realm of disappearance and memory, everything else about theatre – particularly how theatre operated as an industry – was being transmitted to eager national and international audiences. Powerful commercial monopolies that facilitated and controlled the circulation of global hits, both in the popular and the elite theatre, supplanted the small circle of insiders who had previously monopolized access to theatrical knowledge. The new era that sold theatrical knowledge to a vast paying public made possible the growth of Modern Drama and new national theatre traditions, the extension of commercial theatre from capitals to colonies, and the entrenchment of theatre as an art suited to modern industrial capitalism.

# NOTES

*Introduction: Cartographing the Long Nineteenth Century*

1. Davis and Holland 2007.
2. Marx 2008.
3. It is important to distinguish between *modernity* as a social and cultural phenomenon rooting in the rise of capitalism, the division of labour, the emergence of the consumer society and the global exchange of goods and capital and *modernism* as an aesthetic movement. They both share the same space but are far from being synonymous.
4. Cf. Balme 2015, 19–20.
5. Benjamin 2015, 84.
6. Peter Gay states: 'In a less ominous sense, the modern movement was ripe as well. [. . .] There can be no doubt: the Weimar style was born before the Weimar Republic.'; Gay 2001, 5.
7. In his seminal study, *Wilhelm II. und die Moderne* Wolfgang König has shown to what extent the German Kaiser himself was an active agent in propagating new technologies while fashioning them in the decorum of tradition and chivalry. König 2007.
8. Osterhammel 2014, 422.
9. Greenblatt 2010, 252.
10. Osterhammel 2014, 423.
11. Cf. Volkov 2000, 13–36.
12. Roach 1996, 42.
13. Hunt 2014, 55.
14. Hunt 2014, 53.
15. Hunt 2014, 70.
16. Osterhammel 2014, 473.
17. Osterhammel 2014, 54.

18. Cf. Osterhammel 2014, 481–482.
19. Cf. Osterhammel 2014, 480–482.
20. Cf. Osterhammel 2014, 478.
21. Cf. Balme 2015.
22. It is in this light that we have to understand the famous legend that Napoleon took the crown out of the hands of Pope Pius VII to crown himself – the anecdotal gesture highlights the idea that his imperial authority is not granted by the pope – as the Holy Roman emperor – but is rooted in his political authority as leader of the French.
23. It is important to acknowledge that despite the general conservative tenor of the Congress of Vienna the newly created states were not simply absolutist political orders (cf. Schroeder 1994, 582); Napoleon had introduced a new legal system (*Code Napoléon*) to many European territories that could not be simply abolished. Paulmann argues: 'From the second half of the eighteenth century onwards the existential basis of the European states began to change. In the process dynasties lost their essential importance as binding forces for the state. They were supplemented and supplanted by other forces. Patriotism, nationalism, constitutions, bureaucracy, and civil society provided states with new, and at times contested, means of holding themselves together'; Paulmann 2001, 153.
24. For this concept as a leading principle of the Congress of Vienna cf. Schroeder 1994.
25. Cf. Anderson 1983.
26. Cf. Paulmann 2000, 398.
27. Cf. Hobsbawm and Ranger 1983.
28. Cf. Marx 2003, 368–70.
29. Cf. Kaynar 1998, 1–20.
30. Appadurai 2002, 177.
31. Cf. Biers and Marcus 2014, 2.
32. Cf. Biers and Marcus 2014, 6.
33. For an extensive discussion of this concept cf. Biers and Marcus 2014, 1–4.
34. For an expanded analysis of the incident cf. Cliff 2007.
35. To fully grasp the impact of Garrick, one has to keep in mind that his acting inspired a lot of writing about it that allowed for Garrick's presence even in countries and areas he never travelled to. Thus, it would be noteworthy to follow the echoes of his performances in various writings and languages, such as Diderot's *Paradox sur le comedien* or Lichtenberg's Letters from England.
36. Cf. Grünwald-Zerkowitz 1898/99, 509–12.
37. Cf. Roach 1998, 39–51.
38. For a detailed analysis cf. Haenni 2008.
39. Butsch 2000, 135.
40. Cf. Hoberman 1995.
41. Haenni 2008, 6.
42. Quoted in Osborne 1988, 55.
43. Cf. Erck 2006, 44.
44. Cf. Osborne 1988, 180.
45. Robert W. Rydell and Rob Kroes note: 'By the 1890s, what was popular in American culture was increasingly the product of culture industries that, like American corporations, required a great deal of capitalization and increasingly sophisticated

strategies for controlling resources and markets. The theater was one of the first arenas where these transformations became evident'; Rydell and Kroes 2005, 22.

46. Marline Otte has described to what extent American circuses served as a business model for German enterprises and how they imitated them; cf. Otte 2006, 72–4.

47. Rydell and Kroes 2005, 111.

48. Cf. for example the extended discussion of a German case by Otte 1999, 527–542.

49. Biers and Marcus 2014, 6.

50. Balme 2015, 20.

51. Cf. Vasold 2005, 52–4.

52. Cf. Faulstich 2004, 48–59.

53. Geyer and Bright 1995, 1047.

54. Cf. Schwartz and Przyblynski 2004, 9.

55. Cf. Schwartz and Przyblynski 2004, 9.

56. Cf. Schwartz and Przyblynski 2004, 7.

57. Cf. Faulstich 2004, 86–7.

58. Cohen and Higonnet 2004, 16.

59. Of course, the concept that realism depicts the world as it is – a postulate that was even taken to the extreme by naturalism – is rather naïve. As Dennis Kennedy has shown in his discussion of the work of André Antoine, the aspired precise reproduction of reality caused an irritating effect for the audience, creating what Kennedy calls an 'absolute symbol', cf. Kennedy 2009, 37–44.

60. Cf. Kocka 1987, 44.

61. 'The relationship of all to all, both before and outside convention and contract, can be seen as potential enmity or latent war – against which all those willed agreements stand out like so many pacts and peace treaties'; Tönnies 2001, 65. Tönnies references Thomas Hobbes – equating the modern society with the state according to Hobbes' *Leviathan*.

62. Stern 1979, xv.

63. Quoted in Zimmermann 2000, 16.

64. Hobsbawm 1983, 263.

65. Fritzsche 1998, 6–7.

66. Reif 2006, 4.

67. Cf. Carlson 1989, 112.

68. Carlson 1989, 105.

69. Far from being democracies in the modern sense of the word, most European societies saw the institution of civic laws following the *Code Napoléon*. Thus, stately authority was no longer tied to the prince's body but was executed through institutions that claimed a comparable authority, expressed, among others, through these new architectural types.

70. Carlson 1989, 151–2.

71. Cf. Veblen 2001.

72. Cf. Marx 2006, 129–144.

73. Simmel 2004, 53.

74. Kennedy 2009, 38–39.

75. Bennett notes: 'The institutions comprising "the exhibitionary complex", by contrast, were involved in the transfer of objects and bodies from the enclosed and

private domains in which they had previously been displayed (but to a restricted public) into progressively more open and public arenas where, through the representations to which they were subjected, they formed vehicles for inscribing and broadcasting the messages of power (but of a different type) throughout society'; Bennett 1995, 60–61.

76. Cf. Bennett 1995, 59–88.
77. Bennett 1995, 65–66.
78. Hoffenberg 2001, 3.
79. 'We contend that the very notion of "visual culture" was made possible by many of the changes in image production in the nineteenth century and we take seriously the notion that the technological reproducibility of lithography and, more significantly, photography, forever altered our connection to such fundamentals as materiality, experience, and truth.' (Schwartz and Przyblynski 2004, 3.)
80. Cf. Debord 1995.
81. Hoffenberg 2001, xiii.
82. Schwartz and Przyblynski 2004, 7.
83. Cf. Paquet 1908, 4.
84. Germany, for example, never hosted a World's Fair because the political class was divided over the question of its economic value and whether it was a feasible task; cf. Marx 2008, 320–323. It was eventually Wilhelm II, the Kaiser, who cancelled all plans and opted for a smaller exhibition that took place in Berlin in 1896.
85. Kennedy 2009, 34.
86. Hoffenberg 2001, xv.
87. Crossick and Jaumain 1999, 27.
88. Mitchell 1989, 233.
89. Bennett 1995, 62.
90. Bennett 1995, 69.
91. Richards 1990, 4.
92. Kennedy 2009, 17
93. Cf. Kennedy 2009, 63–69, discussing the clash of hats and matinees.
94. C.-F. Baumann points out that shading the auditorium required the technical capacities on the one hand but also an artistic program: first cases are reported from London 1821 and Paris 1863 but it was Richard Wagner in 1876 who for the opening of *Rheingold* in Bayreuth actually turned the auditorium in darkness; cf. Baumann 1988, 128–131.
95. Crary 2000, 33.

## Chapter One: Institutional Frameworks: Britain and Germany, 1800 to 1920

1. See Wilmeth and Miller 1993, 1.
2. See Weingärtner 2006. See also Heinrich 2007.
3. See Foulkes 2002, 4.
4. Adamson 1883, 29–30.
5. As listed, for example, in Calcraft 1839, 4. Calcraft was manager of Dublin's Theatre Royal and published his book as a reply to John Bennett's sermon.
6. Richards 2005, 66.

7. Foulkes 1997, 241.

8. Shepherd and Womack 1996, 219.

9. Although even to Victorians respectability was a bit of a slippery term most accounts of respectable behaviour included 'cleanliness, hard work, self-sufficiency, thrift, piety, deference to authority and even correct speech.' Schoch 2004, 331.

10. Brereton 1908, 297. Concerning changes in audience composition see Donohue 2004, 292–308.

11. Arnold 1882, 235. Even to Victorians respectability was a bit of a slippery term although most accounts of respectable behaviour include 'cleanliness, hard work, self-sufficiency, thrift, piety, deference to authority and even correct speech.' Schoch 2004, 331.

12. Letter to the editor of the *Daily Telegraph* by Charles Wyndham (published 26 March 1908). See also a similar letter by George Godwin in *The Theatre* ('The National Theatre Question', December 1878).

13. Quoted in Richards 2005, 89.

14. *The Era*, 8 June 1879.

15. Quoted in Foulkes 2002, 109.

16. See Foulkes 2002, 132.

17. Shaw 1948, 117. As late as the mid-1960s W. Bridges-Adams began his discussion of theatre in Edwardian England with financial considerations and stated that a successful West End management was determined by its economic achievements, with 'the prime distinction being that a play could pay its way'. He demonstrated how Edwardian managers could expect substantial returns on relatively modest investments: 'For a hundred pounds a week it was possible to rent a theatre of moderate size which had a nightly cash capacity of more than twice that sum.' Bridges-Adams 1966, 370.

18. Schiller 1993, 819. For an English translation of Schiller's 1785 treatise entitled 'The Stage Considered as a Moral Institution' see Brandt and Hogendoorn 1993, 217–221. Unless otherwise noted all translations from the German are my own.

19. See, for example, Sosulski 2007.

20. Quoted in Kaschuba 1995, 116.

21. Detering 2002, 117. See also Detering 2002, 123–168.

22. Quoted in Höpel 2007, 146.

23. Jelavich 1985, 8.

24. Möller 1996, 30.

25. Here relating to discourses in 1960s Britain. Cochrane 2011, 179.

26. Cochrane 2011, 8.

27. Foulkes 1997, 1.

28. Foulkes 1997, 145.

29. See Daniel 1995.

30. 'Wer also unwidersprechlich beweisen kann, dass die Schaubühne Menschen- und Volksbildung wirkte, hat ihren Rang neben den ersten Anstalten des Staats entschieden.' Schiller 1993, 819. See also Eduard Devrient's 1848 treatise 'Das Nationaltheater des Neuen Deutschland. Eine Reformschrift'. Devrient 1967, 393–424.

31. Dukes 1941, chapter II, 22 and Dukes 1941, chapter IV, 312.

32. Differences which are being remarked on today as well. Mark Ravenhill, for example, summarized the differences by asserting that in contrast to British theatregoers a 'German audience is used to having no points of empathy with the characters' and 'naturalism is frowned upon as intellectually unjustifiable' (quoted in Sierz 2001, 133.)

33. Engel 1921, 490.

34. Quote by A. M. Thompson who referred to an article published in *The Clarion*. See Wilson 1951, 167. See also Borsa, *The English Stage of Today* (London: Brendon and Son, 1908), quoted in Woodfield 1984, 19. It may be argued that it is due to these fundamental differences that research into Anglo-German theatrical relations and mutual influences is still relatively rare. Exceptions include Becker 2014 and Heinrich 2007.

35. Mill 1977, 219, 283, 288.

36. See, for example, an article entitled 'Mr Granville Barker's Gramophones', written by 'An Actor' and published in *New Age*, 9 January 1913. The author depicts Granville-Barker as a condescending bureaucrat. The article sparked a debate in the journal which lasted over two months. I thank Philippa Burt for making me aware of this article.

37. Bridges-Adams 1945, 405.

38. Craig 1911, 172.

39. Craig 1911, 134.

40. Lord Melbourne's response to the painter Benjamin Robert Haydon (1786–1846) who had petitioned the leading politicians of his day to grant support to national art education and asked Melbourne 'to establish a system for the public encouragement of High Art'. Haydon 1926, 572.

41. Garber 2008, 52–53.

42. Newey 2010, 119–134.

43. *Athenaeum*, 2 December 1843, 1073. It is worth noting that in reality there was significant cross-over concerning plays between, for example, London's East End and West End.

44. Daunton 2000, 57.

45. Hoppen 1998, 92.

46. Hoppen 1998, 91.

47. Hoppen 1998, 94.

48. Hoppen 1998, 94.

49. Although, interestingly, Kate Newey suggests that the development of the Lord Chamberlain's role in particular can also be seen as a constructive effort to provide a workable framework for theatrical production and 'indicates the seriousness with which policy makers regarded theatre as a national cultural institution'. Newey 2010, 121.

50. In his article on 'The French Play in London' Matthew Arnold called for subsidized theatres, a National Theatre and a civic theatre scheme. See Arnold 1892.

51. Hoppen 1998, 393.

52. Some financial details of the economics of the stage can be gleaned from a short summary in Hoppen 1998, 393. The key reference work on this subject is Davis 2000.

53. Martin 1874, 179–180.

54. One copy was read with intense interest and annotated throughout by William Gladstone, four times British Prime Minister, who took a great interest in the theatre. See Heinrich 2015.

55. The Select Committee under Bulwer Lytton also had distinct ideas about theatrical repertoires under an educational agenda, which favoured the literary drama as opposed to more popular forms of entertainment. They favoured 'literariness, the conventional forms of the five act verse tragedy and the three act "high" comedy' and sought 'an improving and educational purpose for the theatre'. See, in more detail, Newey 2010, 122–124.

56. In 1909 a joint committee of both houses of parliament was set up to look into the issue but – although some compromise was reached – the office of the Lord Chamberlain and its censorship powers were upheld. The most detailed study into British stage censorship is by Nicholson 2003.

57. Music hall entertainments included popular songs, comedy, variety, and speciality acts.

58. See Searle 2005, 565–566. The penalties the LCC could impose took the form of a non-renewal of a hall's licence in the worst case.

59. Jones 1913, 6–7, 17, 114.

60. Commentators also picked up on some of the smaller details and praised new regulations on improving comfort, safety and public health. In a letter to the editor of the *Pall Mall Gazette* Theodore Martin noted that 'we might then hope for houses in which we could see and hear, without being crammed and caged like travellers in a diligence, with blasts of cold air intermitting with suffocating heat, to distract us during the performance, and the certainty of impending over us of headache at least, if not of neuralgia, upon the morrow.' Martin 1874, 209–210.

61. See Arnold 1892, 240. Through 'virtuous' entertainment with Shakespeare and Molière as well as educational melodramas, Toga Plays and Pantomime theatre represented a powerful tool to 'better' the lower, middle and working classes.

62. See Schoch 2010, 241, 246.

63. Freydank 1995, 10.

64. Freydank 1995, 10.

65. For a fuller discussion of *Zirkus Busch* see Otte 2006, 38–41.

66. Ketelsen 1999, 60.

67. Devrient 1967, 389–390.

68. Quoted in Rühle 2007, 28.

69. For a detailed study of popular theatre in Berlin and London around the 'long turn of the century' see Becker 2014.

70. A claim incidentally which could also be heard in some Eastern European countries. See, for example, Stribrny 2000 or Klein and Davidhazi 1996.

71. Foulkes 2002, 71–73.

72. Carter 1925, 280.

73. Foulkes 2002, 115.

74. See, for example, Granville-Barker 1930.

75. Archer 1902, 153. Jones as quoted in the *Daily Chronicle*, 16 March 1908.

76. Vetter 1910, vii.

77. von Schleinitz 1910, 47.
78. Hauptmann 1915, xii.
79. Schiller was keen for the theatre to 'provide a channel through which the light of wisdom beams down from the thinking better half of the people' (Schiller 1993, 828).
80. Archer 1886, 272–273.
81. Granville-Barker 1922, 286.
82. Bridges-Adams 1945, 399.
83. In a development mirrored across pre-First World War Germany, increasingly wealthy upper middle class patrons offered capital investment if city councils agreed and equally contributed to the building of municipal theatres. See, for example, Pielhoff 2007, 10–45.
84. Bridges-Adams 1945, 400.
85. Kruger 1992, 97. See also Jones 1913, vii.
86. Quote from *The Parliamentary Debates* 1913, quoted in Kruger 1992, 126.
87. Guest 2006, 296.
88. In 1848 Effingham Wilson, one of the first commentators to call for a national playhouse, envisaged such an institution to educate the public through 'the standardization of the best'; quoted in Elsom and Tomalin 1978, 7.
89. *Parliamentary Debates* 1913, 454.
90. Quoted in Whitworth 1951, 101.
91. *Parliamentary Debates* 1913, 471.
92. See Lenk 1933, 17.
93. See Vogelsang 1994, 155. For Zürich see Kohler 2008. For Frankfurt see Schimpf 2007, particularly 255–354.
94. See Pielhoff 2007, 10–45.
95. Constitution of the German Reich, dated 11 August 1919, article 7, number 20.
96. Höpel 2007, 62, 146.
97. See *Theatre World* (January 1936): 3.

## Chapter Two: Social Functions: The Social Function of Theatre

1. See for instance Richards 1994, 161–236.
2. Berman quoted in Nead 2000, 4.
3. Nead 2000, 8.
4. Singer 2001, 21.
5. Singer 2001, 29.
6. Hill 1840, 17.
7. Robson 1969, 76–77.
8. Archer and Lowe 1894, 56–58.
9. *European Magazine* 58.
10. Vincent-Buffault 1991, 67.
11. Vincent-Buffault 1991, 237.
12. Thackeray 1869, 275–276.
13. See Figure 2.1.
14. Smyth 2014, 175.

15. See Figure 2.2.
16. Watt Smith 2014, 65.
17. Quoted in Watt Smith 2014, 66.
18. Watt Smith 2014, 67–68.
19. Balme 2014, 13.
20. Kennedy 2009, 25.
21. McConachie 2008, 187–188.
22. 'For the problem of the observer is the field on which vision in history can be said to materialize, to become itself visible. Vision and its effects are always inseparable from the possibilities of an observing subject who is both the historical product *and* the site of certain practices, techniques, institutions and procedures of subjectification'. Crary 1992, 5.
23. Crary 1992, 9.
24. Otter 2008, 74.
25. Nead 2000, 98.
26. Nead 2000, 100.
27. Donne 1858, 206.
28. Quoted in Booth 1981, 15.
29. Otter 2008, 185.
30. Otter 2008.
31. Otter 2008, 186.
32. Otter 2008, 210.
33. Flint 2000, 311. For an acknowledgement of the important relationship existing between the Victorian theatre and Victorian visual culture, see Heinrich, Newey and Richards 2009.
34. Watt Smith 2014, 36.
35. Cook and Wedderburn 1903–1912, 51.
36. Booth 1981, 3–4.
37. Emeljanow 1998, 112.
38. Schivelbusch 1980, 219 quoted in Emeljanow 1998, 112.
39. Charles Nodier in René-Charles Guilbert de Pixérécourt, *Théâtre Choisi* (Paris: 1841–1843), I, xvii quoted by J. Paul Marcoux, 'Guilbert de Pixérécourt: the people's conscience' in Redmond 1992, 54.
40. Quoted in Gabrielle Hyslop, 'Pixérécourt and the French melodrama debate: instructing boulevard theatre audiences' in Redmond 1992, 63.
41. Quoted in Richards 1994, 163.
42. *New Monthly Magazine* 19:1 (1827): 580.
43. *Tribune* (London: printed for the author, 1796), 526–527.
44. Simmel 1997, 61.
45. See Figure 2.3.
46. See Figure 2.4.
47. Davis 2000, 99.
48. See Figure 2.5.
49. Dickens 1996, 198.
50. *Porcupine* quoted in Wilson 1954, 192.
51. *Referee*, 3 February 1924.

52. See Davis and Davis 1991, 137–165.
53. Clipping, undated, Britannia Cuttings.
54. See J. Davis 1991, 369–389.
55. Hibbert 1916, 63–64.
56. See Figure 2.6.
57. See Figure 2.7.
58. Gould 2011, 1–2.
59. Bratton et al. 1991; MacKenzie 1986.
60. Waterhouse 1990, xii.
61. Waterhouse 1995,10.
62. Waterhouse 1995, 58.
63. Newspaper Cuttings, 'Mummer Memories'.
64. Mercer 1993, 77, quoting an advertisement for Her Majesty's Theatre in *Sydney Morning Herald*, 10 September 1887.
65. *Sydney Morning Herald*, 23 December 1901.
66. See Bland Holt Papers, MS. 2241.
67. See Figure 2.8.
68. 'A Perpendicular Interview with Mr Bland Holt' (typescript).
69. Bandmann 1885, 134–135. Balme 2015, 28, attributes similar views to his son, the manager and entrepreneur Maurice E. Bandmann.
70. Bandmann 1885, 141
71. Bandmann 1885, 174, 170.
72. Young, quoted in Foulkes 2002, 150.
73. Yajnik 1970, 244.
74. Forbes 2008, 78.
75. Newnham-Davies 1898, 230–231.

### Chapter Three: Sexuality and Gender

1. The commonplace in theatre histories is to contrast the burial of David Garrick with honours in Westminster Abbey with the relegation of Sophie Arnould to a potter's field.
2. Schidrowitz 1925, 206. Unless otherwise indicated, all translations are my own.
3. Moore 1923, 110.
4. *The Family Shakespeare*, intended for the use of women and children, was first published by Thomas Bowdler in 1807; it was itself bowdlerized, since his sister Harriet who had edited it was omitted from the title page. The idea that a woman could have recognized the inadmissibility of certain words and passages was itself inadmissible.
5. Schidrowitz 1925, 303.
6. Marx and Engels 1964, 478.
7. d'I***, 1864.
8. Fraxi 1962, 102–109. Davis 1989, 294–315. *Aus den Memoiren einer Sängerin* by 'Reginald Chesterfield' (*c.*1868, 1875) is allegedly the erotic memoirs of Wilhelmine Schröder-Devrient (1804–1860), the soprano who had enthralled Beethoven as Leonore and took part in the 1848 revolution in Dresden. It was translated into

English as *Pauline the Prima Donna* (*c*.1898) and into French in both a laundered and a complete version by Guillaume Apollinaire (1913).

9. Johnson 1975, 575–584. Gilfoyle 1992, 107–111, 365–366.

10. Schidrowitz 1925, 283–289.

11. Bauer 1927. The most reliable interpretation of the actress as prostitute in Great Britain is to be found in the writings of Davis 1988, 221–234 and T. Davis 1991. For France, see Fugier 2001 and Berianstein 2001. For Russia, see Gurevich 1939.

12. Ubersfeld 2002, 57, 89–89.

13. Sarcey 1900, 191–192. They were all French, of course. The other two were Labiche's vaudeville *Le Chapeau de paille d'Italie* and Offenbach's *opéra bouffe Orphée aux enfers*.

14. Dumas 1868, 22.

15. Allard 1955, 322–331.

16. *Débats*, 9 February 1852, quoted in Descotes 1964, 320.

17. Yates 1884, 245.

18. Davies 1983, 90–91.

19. In his 1867 preface to *La Dame*, Dumas pointed out that 'thirty years ago' no one used the Second Empire vocabulary for such females: kept woman, *lorette*, *biche*, *petite dame* or *cocotte*. Dumas 1868, 21.

20. Augier 1892, 3–4. In the same scene, Montrichard coins the term '*nostalgie de la boue*' for this taste for the gutter.

21. Vermorel 1860, 46.

22. Choler and Saint-Agnan 1859 quoted in Descotes 1964, 309.

23. Henri de Simeux in *Françillon* (1873), act I, sc.4.

24. Meilhac and Halévy 2003, 56.

25. 'Éloge du maquillage' in *Le peintre de la vie modern* (1863); Baudelaire 1961, 1184.

26. August Strindberg, *Tjänstekvinnans son*, quoted in Nordensvan 1918, 117, 226.

27. Senelick 1990, 455–467. Senelick 2016, 1–16.

28. *The Times of London*, 15 July 1869, 10.

29. *The Mask*, 'International compliments' (1868), 176.

30. Devrient 1964 [1869].

31. *The Theatrical Journal*, 27 July 1844, 236, quoted in Trudgill 1976, 109.

32. Goncourt 1964, 103. Mahalin 1862.

33. Deschamps 1888, 195–196.

34. *London Daily News*, quoted in Richardson 1969, 313.

35. Senelick 2006, 1289–1290.

36. Gasnault 1986.

37. Senelick 1991, 1–50. Davis 1990, 1–14.

38. Hudson 1974.

39. Mankowitz 1982, 175–178.

40. Fair hair was another fetish; since flaxen wigs (the so-called Gretchen model) were the most expensive, blondeness was achieved by peroxide. On American burlesque, see Allen 1991. For the European stage, see Witkowski and Nass 1909.

41. Quoted in Kracauer 1976, 242.

42. Mainardi 1989, 163.

43. The promiscuous mingling of the sexes in a theatre audience, long the custom in England, was slow in coming to France: women were not allowed in the parterre (or pit) of official theatres until 1819. Donnet and Kaufmann 1841.

44. The Théâtre Antoine was permitted by the police to hold only a reading for an invited audience. Alfred Jarry wrote a very funny notice of the event: 'À propos de "L'Avarie" [sic],' *La Revue Blanche*, 1 December 1901, reprinted in Jarry 1969, 137–140.

45. The situation can actually be traced back to Prince Hoare's *Indiscretion* (1800). The German equivalent is Hebbel's *Maria Magdalena* (1844).

46. 31 March 1858, quoted in Descotes 1964, 322.

47. Davies 1983, 95.

48. Dumas 1868, 38.

49. Clapp and Edgett 1902, 118.

50. *La Renaissance* 15 February 1873.

51. *Daily Telegraph*, 7 June 1875, 10, quoted in Eltis 2013, 107. Needless to say, Marguerite's use of a white camellia to indicate her sexual availability and a red one to signal her period of menstruation appears nowhere in the English-language adaptations.

52. Quoted in Davies 1983, 102.

53. Collins 1873, 58. He had based it on his novel of the same name.

54. Scott 1892, 99. Eltis 2013, 122–123.

55. Janin 1890.

56. Clapp and Edgett 1902, 167–168.

57. The play may have inspired Dürrenmatt's *The Visit*.

58. Tempest 1932, 17.

59. Ibels 1906.

60. Bloch 1907/1937, 343.

61. Ellis 1936, 215–216.

62. Hugländer 1914, 54–57.

63. McKenna 2012. Senelick 2000, chapters 12 and 13.

64. Davis 1998, 50–69. Senelick 2000, chapter 14.

65. Royle 1899, 487.

66. They were torn down by college boys, among them Winston Churchill. See Davis 1992, 111–131; Donohue 2005.

67. Titterton 1912, 116.

68. Strindberg's publisher made hundreds of alterations in *Miss Julie,* radically expurgating it. The original text was not made available until 1984. Hence, all editions, translations and productions, as well as criticism, before that date have been based on a corrupt version of the play. See Jacobs 1998, 80–88.

69. Senelick 2015, 25–28.

## Chapter Four: The Environment of Theatre

1.  Herrmann 1931, 271.
2.  Carlson 1989, 2.
3.  Harvie 2009, 25.
4.  Hall 1997, 300.

5. Osterhammel and Camiller 2014, 295; see also Lees and Lees 2007, 245–246; Driver and Gilbert 1999.
6. Olsen 1986, 12.
7. Osterhammel and Camiller 2014, 296. On London as imperial metropolis see Gilbert and Driver 2000; Schneer 1999.
8. Olsen 1986, 58–81.
9. See Hemmings 1993.
10. See Moody 2000, 10–47.
11. See Yates 1996; Linhardt 2006.
12. See Freydank 1988, 238–240, 271–290.
13. See Davis 2000, 18–19; Moody 2000, 206; Hemmings 1994, 4, 173; Freydank 1988, 286–312; Becker 2014, 29–36.
14. See Goldstein 1989.
15. See Hemmings 1993, 122–127.
16. Sims 1902, vol. 1.
17. See Howard 1970.
18. See Davis 1995, 214; Davis and Emeljanow 2011.
19. See Becker 2014, 132–9.
20. See Henderson 2004, 145–146.
21. See Becker 2014, 223–224.
22. Report from the Select Committee on Theatrical Licenses and Regulations, 191.
23. See Henderson 2004, 145.
24. Report from the Select Committee on Theatres and Places of Entertainment, 243.
25. 'Where it is never dull', F. P. Restall for Underground Electric Railway Company Ltd., London 1924, London Transport Museum (LTM), 1983/4/1601; 'To Central London for shops and theatres', J. L. Carstairs for London County Council Tramways, London 1927, LTM, 2005/15396; 'By tram in comfort to the theatres', von Charles Sharland for Underground Electric Railways Company Ltd., London 1910, LTM, 1999/31351.
26. Stevens 1964, 192; Simmons 1984.
27. Mander and Mitchenson 1968, 80–119, 193–195; Becker 2014, 141–142.
28. Woollan 1902, 297.
29. Huret 1997, 53.
30. Boyer 1985, 78–80; Scott and Rutkoff 1999, 11, 16, 19.
31. Satyr 1908, 10.
32. Rappaport 2000, 4; for New York see Boyer 1985, 87–129.
33. See Becker 2014, 379.
34. See Göhre 1907, 48.
35. See Göhre 1907, 78.
36. See Reinhardt 1991, 274.
37. See Lancaster 2000, 5.
38. Schweitzer 2009b, 182.
39. See Rappaport 2000, 179, 198, 107.
40. See Rappaport 2000, 204–205.
41. See Schweitzer 2009b, 76.
42. See Jelavich 1993, 113–117; Otte 2006, 234–276.
43. Janin 1843, 37.

44. Quoted in Latour 1958, 129; see there, 128–159, on the relationship between the theatre and the fashion industry as well as Steele 1998, 154.
45. Schweitzer 2009b, 65.
46. Duff-Gordon n.d., 68; see also Kaplan and Stowell 1995.
47. Schweitzer 2009b, 1–2.
48. Troy 2001.
49. See Otte 2006, 234–276.
50. See Jelavich 1993,113.
51. See Schweitzer 2009b, 186–187.
52. See Donohue 2005.
53. Allen 1980, 87.
54. See Blankenship 2012, 23–30.
55. Tibbetts 1985, 5.
56. See Ball and Sunderland 2001, 161; Müller 2001, 64; Erenberg 1984, 69.
57. Smith 1931, 45.
58. See Metzger and Dunker 1986, 102, 127.
59. Kessler and Lenk 2010, 64.
60. See Ball and Sunderland 2001, 161–162.
61. See Keim and David 2008, 14.
62. See Allen 1980.
63. See Becker 2014, 123–126.
64. See Ezra 2000, 129–131.
65. See Freisburger 1936; Guy 1998.
66. Tibbetts 1985, 10.
67. See Tibbetts 1985, 9.
68. Pückler-Muskau et al. 1833, 52.
69. See Donohue 2005.
70. See Donohue 2005; Walkowitz 2010.
71. See Castle 1982.
72. Ostwald 1907, 55.
73. See Johnson 1975.
74. On London's East End as theatre district see Davis and Emeljanow 2011.
75. Rappaport 2000, 183.

*Chapter Five: Circulation: Theatrical Mobility and its Professionalization in the Nineteenth Century*

1.  Hobsbawm 1987, 40.
2.  Mishkin 2006, 2–3.
3.  Dibner 1959, 5.
4.  Wallace 1959, 135.
5.  Wallace 1959.
6.  Greenblatt 2010, 250.
7.  Bayly 2004.
8.  These are ideoscapes, mediascapes, financescapes, ethnoscapes and technoscapes, Appadurai 1990, 7–10. For possible research approaches to 'Theatrescapes' see

http://www.theatrescapes.theaterwissenschaft.uni-muenchen.de/index.html as well as http://www.theatrescapes.gwi.uni-muenchen.de [accessed 17 January 2017].

9. Le Roux and Garnier 1890, 3.
10. *The Somewhat Different Magazine*, February 1905.
11. Grau 1909, 36.
12. Marbury 1923, 82.
13. Schweitzer 2009b, 5–6.
14. See Balme 2015, 19–36.
15. Grau 1909, 199–200.
16. Despite their enormous business success and influence though, they have been largely neglected by scholarly research. In Nic Leonhardt's current research project on transatlantic theatrical exchanges in the first decades of the twentieth century, she focuses on selected theatrical agents/managers/impresarios who were crucial for international and transatlantic theatrical business of the period. This project is part of the larger research project and Centre for 'Global Theatre Histories', at the LMU Munich, funded by the German Research Foundation (DFG) since 2010. www.gth.theaterwissenschaft.uni-muenchen.de. See also Leonhardt 2015, 140–155, and Leonhardt 2014, 2–23.
17. On the Shuberts, see Hirsch 1998; on D'Oyly Carte, see Joseph 1994.
18. See Wertheim and Blair 2000, 388.
19. Historians have only recently started to research the history of news agencies (see Barth 2011, 63–75, and Wenzlhuemer 2013) and image agencies.
20. Marbury 1923, 55.
21. Grau 1909, 33.
22. Le Roux and Garnier 1890, 10.
23. The business of theatrical agencies has also been a subject of study though in the context of legislature, labour and social movements for agents were often accused of unconscionability and breach of contract.
24. This causes a methodological challenge for researchers as this 'invisibility' correlates with a difficult access to source material and resources, as the work of agents has not been systematically archived.
25. During 1866–1867, at least five circus troupes toured abroad, some defying the death penalty stipulated by law for elopement.
26. The circuit linked London, Gibraltar, Malta, Egypt, India, Burma, the Straits settlements, Java, the Philippines, China, Japan and continued to Australia.
27. Invited by leading kabuki actors to the Shintomiza in Tokyo, the 'Opera scene', embedded in a modern kabuki play featuring a voyage round the world produced bafflement and hilarity among the local spectators.
28. Omitted in most Japanese theatre histories, the Gaiety Theatre is even erroneously related to Goethe, a confusion based on identical pronunciation in Japanese. To date, a single monograph has investigated the rich history of the theatre, Masumoto 1986.
29. On the exodus of fringe performers, see Miyaoka 1978. For the World Exhibitions, see Rydell 1993.
30. Groemer 2016 draws a vast historical panorama of Edo mountebanks, stressing their imbrication in the political and legislative system of Tokugawa Japan as well as their rapid decay in the phase of modernization.

31. Schodt 2012 offers a fascinating account of global and transnational circus, focusing on the exceptional acrobat and manager, 'Professor Risley'.
32. On Hanako, see Keene 1981; Sawada 1997; Sukenobu 2010.
33. A recent biography of Kawakami Otojiro by Murai 2012, 21–65. On the American tour see Anderson 2011; documents on the European tour are collected in Pantzer 2005.
34. Kushibiki had organized the Japanese contribution to the World Fairs in Chicago (1893) and Atlantic City (1896), where performers, craftsmen and geisha were a great attraction. Also, he must be credited with bringing the Vitascope to Kawakami's Tokyo theatre (1897).
35. After Kushibiki, who retired from the agreement, the Kawakamis relied on compatriots active in the US: Mitsuse Kôsaku (a dodgy entrepreneur, importer of cheap labour force from Japan, who eloped with the troupe's earnings), and the art brokers, Arai Tatsuya and Matsuki Bunkyo.
36. For studies on Loïe Fuller see Scholz-Cionca 2016, 60.
37. On Sadayakko, see Kano 2001; Downer 2003; Savarese 2010, 34–38.
38. See Scholz-Cionca 2016.
39. On Russian responses to Hanako, see Bannai and Kameyama 1987.
40. The list of personalities, who wrote about the Japanese shows read like a 'who's who' of the literati and artistic elites in the countries visited. Cf. Tschudin 2014.
41. The exceptions are Sadanji's kabuki performances in the Soviet Union in 1928, and Tsutsui Tokujirô's European tours in the 1930s.

## Chapter Six: Interpretations: The Interpretation of Theatre

1. Freud 1917, 135–144.
2. Bratton 2003, 125–126.
3. For more on the significance of family and dynasty in the organization of theatre, see Booth et al. 2003, 438–440.
4. Emeljanow 2003, 1342.
5. Williams 2003, 365–366. Cf. Niehaus 1956.
6. See Chapter 5 on Circulation in this volume.
7. For more on the German context, see Watzka 2006.
8. There had been training institutions founded earlier, such as the *Conservatoire d'Art Dramatique* in 1808, in 1812 a special class for the *Comédie Française,* or the London Academy of Music and Dramatic Art (1861) but arguably Stanislavsky was the first to have produced elaborate, professional method of training actors. Cf. Kershaw 2003.
9. Perkin 1989, 4; although Perkin in general refers to the twentieth century as the age of professionalism, he also explicitly mentions actors and playwrights as examples of professionals, who managed to turn 'human capital into visible wealth' (Perkin 1989, 6), as part of the industrial society.
10. Fritzsche 1998, 128.
11. Winds 1919, 7. My translation.

12. Bratton 2003, 34.

13. Bratton 2003. The field of German studies developed an interest in theatrical forms only as far as they were linked to written drama or as pre-literary forms, such as the Shrovetide plays. What was lacking from this discourse was any recognition of theatre/ performance as an art form in its own right. Max Herrmann, the pioneer of German theatre studies, focused on the early modern playwright Hans Sachs, who by then was very popular not the least because Richard Wagner had made him a leading protagonist in his *Meistersinger von Nürnberg* (1868), in order to gain legitimacy for his subject. For a more detailed analysis of this development, see Hulfeld 2007, 231–281.

14. In her seminal study, *Professing Performance* (2004), Shannon Jackson gives a comprehensive account of the emergence of theatre and drama in US academia around 1900; cf. Jackson 2004, especially 40–78.

15. For further discussion of the concept of the public sphere and its relation to theatre, see Balme 2014, 5–21.

16. Cf. Wagner 2013, especially 22–23.

17. Wagner 2013, 13.

18. Brockett et al. 2010, 209.

19. Zarrilli et al. 2006, 287–288.

20. Zarrilli et al. 2006, 282.

21. Frenzel 1892, 116–132.

22. Schönhoff 1897, 200.

23. Kirshenblatt-Gimblett 1998, 54.

24. Henry Mayhew produced a two-volume description of 'London labour and the London poor' in 1865 (cf. Mayhew 1865). In Berlin in 1905, Hans Ostwald commenced a series of essays called *Großstadt-Dokumente* [Documents of the metropolis] that covered various aspects of metropolitan life. His first volume is tellingly entitled *Dunkle Winkel in Berlin* [Dark Corners of Berlin]. Interestingly, theatre and theatrical enterprises appear regularly in this series; cf. Ostwald 1904/1905; Buchner 1905; Turzinsky 1906.

25. This can be even found in some of the protagonists' biographies. Hauptmann, as well as the playwright Johannes Schlaf, later sympathized with the Nazis.

26. Cf. Kruger 2003, 919–922.

27. Cf. Hart and Hart 1882, 3. During the Kaiserreich the date of this battle, 2 September, was celebrated as a national holiday, the *Sedantag*.

28. The nineteenth century is also the period in which the idea of language as a marker of national identity manifests itself in major enterprises of compiling dictionaries. Typical examples for these enterprises are the Brothers Grimm who started their *Deutsches Wörterbuch* in 1861, the *Oxford English Dictionary* (started in 1858), or the *Svenska Akademiens ordbok* (started in 1893). All these projects, which ran for decades and some of them are still under way, have to be seen as further evidence of this process of nation-building.

29. See Katie Gough's argument in Chapter 7 of this volume.

30. Cf. Raeck 1999.

31. Cf. Gerhard 1992 with respect to Verdi.

32. Wagner 1909, 277.

33. Wagner 1909, 287.
34. This anti-Semitism was also present in the reception of his work in the twentieth century and offered it to an appropriation by the Nazis in the 1930s. For further exploration of this topic see Weiner 1997, especially 256–259.
35. Wagner 1909, 271.
36. Wagner 1909, 274–275.
37. Wagner 1909, 282.
38. In his 2015 dissertation 'The Bayreuth Experience 1848–1924', Gero Tögl has closely investigated the international network of the Wagner Societies, forthcoming with Königshausen & Neumann (Würzburg, Germany).
39. Nietzsche 2000 [1872], 50.
40. Stone Peters 2009, 72.
41. Stone Peters 2009, 73.
42. Cf. Stone Peters 2008, 1–41.
43. Cf. for example Grosse 1894; Groos 1899; Wallaschek 1903; Wundt 1919; Hagemann 1919.
44. Matthews 1912, 8.
45. Stone Peters 2009, 74.
46. Stone Peters 2009, 80. Stone Peters relates this concept to the work of Jane Harrison. Stone Peters emphasizes Harrison's divergence from Nietzsche through her concept of the *methexis*; see also Fischer-Lichte 2005, 38–45.
47. Although he is rather critical of their theories, Richard Schechner acknowledges the works of the Cambridge Ritualists as one approach to the development of Performance Studies. Cf. Schechner 2003, 1–7.
48. Cf. Dreesbach 2005.
49. Fischer-Lichte 2005, 58.
50. The German word *völkisch* enters the public discourse in the nineteenth century as a translation of the word nation. But it holds specific associations to the concept of people – narrowing the concept of nation to an ethnically homogenous group. As it emerged in the late nineteenth century, it has also to be understood as containing an implicit anti-Semitic, even racist overtone. While the *völkisch* discourse is evidently pre-fascist, the two cannot be totally equated as there are considerable differences. The hallmark of the *völkisch* discourse is an anti-modern perspective, imagining an ethnically homogenous nation-state and emphasizing substantial differences between ethnic groups that cannot be overcome by behaviour, cultural training or even legislative measures.
51. Cf. Chambers 1903, 196, 191, note 9.
52. Chambers 1903, 202.
53. See therefore Chambers 1903, 183–188.
54. Erika Fischer-Lichte underlines to what extent Frazer's study was a substantial provocation in comparing (and thus almost equating) Western and 'primitive' cultures; cf. Fischer-Lichte 2005, 33–34.
55. Matthews 1912, 11; cf. also Matthews 1912, 7–15.
56. Mantzius 1903, 4–5.
57. For further discussion of Niessen's approach cf. Ellrich 2009, 175–192.

## Chapter Seven: Communities of Production

1. The term 'techno-primitivism' was first coined by Trotter 2011. The phrase 'Acting and Not-Acting' is taken from Michael Kirby 1972.
2. See Roche 2015, 19.
3. Balme and Davis 2015, 402.
4. Fay and Carswell 1935, 106.
5. For further details about these influences see Fay 1988; Fay and Carswell 1935; and Kelsall 1978.
6. Fay and Carswell 1935, 163.
7. Trotter 2011.
8. For a thorough study of media in Ireland see Morash 2010.
9. Auslander 1999, 58.
10. Roche 1995, 115.
11. Kelsall 1978, 190.
12. Bourgeois 1913, 129.
13. For further discussion of the move from Abbey stage to Hollywood screen see Fay 1988 and Frazier 2005.
14. The culmination of these studies appeared in print in Synge 1992 and Gregory 1970.
15. Discussions of America are ubiquitous in Synge's *The Aran Islands* and Gregory's *Visions and Beliefs in the West of Ireland*. In fact, 'America' is invoked no fewer than nineteen times in Synge's text and thirty-nine times in Gregory's study.
16. Bolter and Grusin 2000, 45.
17. Synge 1935, 60–61.
18. See Morash 2010, 107.
19. For a fuller discussion of the gendering of technology at this time see Gough 2012 and Gooday 2008.
20. See Diamond 1997 and Innes 2000.
21. Synge 1935, 61.
22. Synge 1935, 62.
23. Synge 1935, 94.
24. Quoted in Hunt 1979, 54.
25. Montague 1968, 50–51.
26. Montague 1968, 53.
27. Quoted in Fay and Carswell 1935, 168.
28. Gregory 1970, 15.
29. See Morash 2010, 98.
30. Quoted in Morash 2010, 97.
31. Fay and Carswell 1935, 134.
32. Fay and Carswell 1935, 33.
33. Gregory 1970, 57–58.
34. Synge 1935, 92–93.
35. Holloway 1967, 35.
36. Quoted in Hunt 1979, 54.
37. See Hobsbawm 1992, 50–53.

38. Hanák 1997, 9.
39. Sorba 2006, 282.
40. See Traubner 2003; Klotz 1991; Gál and Somogyi 1960; Gáspár 1960.
41. It is generally agreed that theatre is inter/cross-cultural in a sense that 'performance work necessitates the negotiation of cultural differences both temporally (across history) and spatially (across geographical and social categories)' (Lo and Gilbert 2002, 32). Inter- or cross-cultural theatre thus 'encompasses public performance practices characterized by the conjunction of specific cultural resources at the level of narrative content, performative aesthetics, production process, and/or reception by an interpretative community' (Lo and Gilbert 2002, 31). As a result, theatre can be defined as 'the meeting in the moment of performance of two or more cultural traditions' (Holledge and Tompkins 2000, 7). See also Pavis 1996; Balme 1999, 2005; and Knowles 2010.
42. Sorba 2006, 286.
43. Sorba 2006, 286.
44. Sorba 2006, 287.
45. See Saltz 2008.
46. In spite of its obvious intercultural and/or cross-cultural characteristics, 'Western' theatre has often been represented as a coherent cultural sphere in critical discourse and theatre history (see Hartnoll 1991; Simhandl 1998; Russell Brown 1995; Fischer-Lichte 1999). The exemplars of 'Western' theatre are usually chosen from 'the more or less well-documented theatrical events of the institutionalized (literary) spoken theatre' (Fischer-Lichte 2004, 3) in the metropolitan centres of (Western) Europe including London, Paris, Berlin, Vienna, Moscow and, from the late nineteenth century, New York. There are entire geographical–cultural regions (e.g. Eastern, Northern and Southern Europe) and entire (mostly popular) theatrical genres (operetta, vaudeville, pantomime, etc.), which are normally obscured by these theatre histories. Apart from the horizontal and vertical divides within the so-called unified 'West', there have always been exchanges among regions and/or highbrow and lowbrow theatrical cultures that are seldom mentioned in nationally focused theatre histories. But the history of Western theatre is better imagined if we treat it as 'meetings of performance of two or more cultural traditions' (Holledge and Tompkins 2000, 7) coming from both within and outside of Europe.
47. Grun 1970, 189.
48. Grun 1970, 122.
49. Grun 1970, 129.
50. Traubner 2003, 247.
51. See Postlewait 2007.
52. See Balme 2000; Balme 2005.
53. See Crittenden 1998; Crittenden 2000.
54. See Csáky 1999.
55. See Heltai 2007.
56. See Sorba 2006.
57. See Schweitzer 2008; Schweitzer 2009a.
58. Traubner 2003, 247.
59. Kálmán et al. 1916, 2.

60. Kálmán et al. 1916, 2.
61. Csáky 1999, 60.
62. Hermann 2011.
63. *Budapesti Hírlap* [*Budapest News*], 4 November 1916, 3.
64. Kálmán et al. 1917, 43.
65. For a detailed analysis of these productions see Imre 2013.
66. For a summary of the plot cf. *The Era*, 1 June 1921, 5.
67. Miller and Stanley 1912/13, 1.
68. Goldsworthy 1998, 51.
69. Goldsworthy 1998, 68.
70. *The Stage*, 2 June 1921, 16.
71. Jodie Matthews reminded us that 'Victorian children's literature is full of examples of "Gypsy" child-stealing myth' (Matthews 2010: 138).
72. See Dearing 2010.
73. Lyon 2009, 701.
74. Lyon 2009, 701.
75. Miller and Stanley 1912/13, 21, Act III.
76. The story appeared in various newspapers in the United States in 1916, and it was even reprinted in 1917 in the anthology of *True Stories of the Great War* (Miller 1917).
77. *The New York Times*, 23 May 1921, 6.
78. *The Stage*, 2 June 1921, 16.
79. Goldsworthy 1998, 64.
80. See Lawrence 1994, 151–168.
81. Anon. 1921e: *The Times*, 27 May 1921, 8.
82. Said 2005, 220.
83. Said 2005, 220.

## Chapter Eight: Repertoire and Genres

1. Davis 2012, 13.
2. Bratton 2003, 37.
3. Schanze 1973, 110–111; Nicoll 1959, see Appendix B, Hand-List of Plays, 230.
4. Report from the Select Committee on Dramatic Literature, with the Minutes of Evidence (1831-32) Paper No. 679, VII, 1, p.158. ProQuest, Parliamentary Papers (1831-32) Paper No. 679, VII, 1.
5. McCormick 1993, 6.
6. Carnwath 2013, 24.
7. Cannon 2012, 111.
8. For a thorough account British musical comedy and George Edwardes, see Gänzl 1986.
9. Davis Cordova 2007, 119.
10. Pickering 2008, 4.
11. Davis 2012, 270.
12. Jelavich 1985, 68, 329.
13. Faulk 2004, 1.
14. McCormick 1993, 114.
15. McCormick 1993, 125.

16. Mayer 2004, 148.
17. Brooks 1976.
18. Cited in the lemma 'melodrama, n.'. OED Online [accessed 9 September 2015]. June 2015. Oxford University Press. Source: Harris 1826, xviii.
19. Brooks 1976, 4.
20. McConachie 2006, 255.
21. Carli 2011, 105.
22. Mayer 2004, 159.
23. Davis 1914: 29. Quoted in Butte 2013, 123.
24. Mayer 2004, 21.
25. Fiske 1973, 76.
26. Altick 1978, 163.
27. Booth 1981, 10.
28. For a discussion of the term 'pictoral dramatury' in England see Meisel 1983, 47. For Germany see Leonhardt 2007.
29. Dobson 1992, 6.
30. *Locus classicus* of this discussion is Charles Lamb's 1811 essay, 'On the tragedies of Shakespeare, Considered with reference to their fitness for Stage-representation'. Lamb is best known, however, for his prose versions of selected Shakespearean plays, *Tales from Shakespeare* (1807) that he wrote with his sister Mary Lamb.
31. Moody 2000, 119.
32. Moody 2000, 146.
33. Levine 1988.
34. Teague 2006, 37.
35. Kahn 2008, 123.
36. Foulkes 2002, 150.
37. For an overview of the Parsi theatre see Gupta 2005.

## Chapter Nine: Technologies of Performance

1. Kern 2003.
2. Otter 2008, 7.
3. Leacroft 1973.
4. Mayhew 1840.
5. Mayhew 1840, 250.
6. Southern 1952, 323.
7. Fitzgerald 1881, 25.
8. Fitzgerald 1870.
9. Fitzgerald 1881, 59.
10. Fitzgerald 1881, 20.
11. Shaw 1876/1889, cited in Jackson 1989, 209ff. See also Davis 2015, 38–55.
12. Jay 1994, 54–55.
13. Altick 1978, 127.
14. Hyde 1988; Oettermann 1997; Oleksijczuk 2011.
15. Oleksijczuk 2011, 136.
16. Oleksijczuk 2011, 176.

17. See Hyde 1988, 208ff.; Oettermann 1997, 111–112.

18. Oettermann 1997, 176.

19. A Railer 1830, 825, cited in Altick 1978, 219.

20. Mayhew and Binny 1852, cited in Jennings 2012, 264–265.

21. Hunt 1907, 101, cited in Otter 2008, 137.

22. Otter 2008, 135–148.

23. Stockdale 1978, 6.

24. Otter 2008, 149.

25. Schivelbusch 1995, 14.

26. Rees 1978, 9.

27. Morgan 2005, 30.

28. *The Times*, 8 September 1817, 2, cited in Rees 1978, 10.

29. Bram Stoker cited in Jackson 1989, 188.

30. Rees 1978, 22.

31. Rees 1978, 34–35.

32. Rees 1978, 186.

33. Rees 1978, 43.

34. Rees 1978, 53.

35. Bram Stoker, cited in Jackson 1989, 189.

36. Schivelbusch 1995, 47.

37. Rees 1978, 102.

38. Crompton, n.d.[1881], 9, cited in Schivelbusch 1995, 51.

39. Fitzgerald 1881, 33.

40. Lloyd 1875, cited in Jackson 1989, 184.

41. Otter 2008, 173.

42. Edison 1880, 295–300, cited in Otter 2008, 181.

43. Hepworth 1879, 82, cited in Otter 2008, 184.

44. Grossmith and Grossmith 1965, 183, cited in Otter 2008, 184.

45. Schivelbusch 1995, 48.

46. Stevenson 1917, cited in Schivelbusch 1995, 134.

47. Rees 1978, 170.

48. Terry, cited in Otter 2008, 185.

49. Bram Stoker, cited in Jackson 1989, 190.

50. Fitzgerald 1892, 221.

51. Fitzgerald 1881, 66.

52. Fitzgerald 1881, 52.

53. Bram Stoker, cited in Jackson 1989, 190.

54. Fitzgerald 1881, 50–51.

55. Fitzgerald 1892, 176.

56. Benjamin 1999, 14.

57. Benjamin 1999, 21.

58. Adorno 1981, 85, cited in Crary 2004, 89.

59. Bronte 1907, cited in Jennings 2012, 262.

60. Jay 1994, 57.

61. Berger 1972, 109.

62. Otter 2008, 62–98.

63. Sternberger 1955, 57, cited in Schivelbusch 1980, 65.
64. Schivelbusch 1980, 66.

## Chapter Ten: Knowledge Transmission: Media and Memory

1.  Beaumont Wicks 1950–1979.
2.  The law was initially passed for the North German Confederation in 1870, but then adopted by the German Empire upon the latter's founding. See Kawohl n.d.
3.  Milhous and Hume 2015, 83.
4.  *Macklin v. Richardson*, 27 Eng. Rep. 451 (1770).
5.  Surwillo 2007, 18. The first legal protection of theatrical performances in Spain had been promulgated by royal decree a decade earlier.
6.  Surwillo 2007, 99–103.
7.  Surwillo 2007, 112.
8.  Stephens 1992, 119–124.
9.  Barrett 1999, 180.
10. Barrett 1999.
11. A complex sequence of mergers brought lists from Thomas Dolby, John Duncombe, John Cumberland and G. H. Davidson into Lacy's hands, from whence the plays became the property of Samuel French, whose eponymous firm publishes acting editions to this day. Stephens 1992, 125–126.
12. Barrett 1999, 178.
13. Stone Peters 2000, 85.
14. Boucicault n.d.
15. Stephens 1992, 118. Lacy published 1,485 plays in one series alone. Stephens' numbers suggest, even at the most conservative estimates, a lost repertoire of thousands of Victorian plays.
16. Worthen 2005, 13.
17. Worthen 2005, 56.
18. *Keene v. Wheatley*, 14 F. Cas. 180 (CCEDPA 1860), 190.
19. *Keene v. Clarke*, 5 Robt. 38 (New York Superior Court, General Term 1867), 60.
20. 'Before the Footlights', *The Saturday Review* 71, no. 1853 (2 May 1891), 531.
21. For a more complete version of this argument, see Miller 2012.
22. 'Advertisements & Notices', *The Era*, 19 September 1896.
23. *Daly v. Palmer*, 6 F. Cas. 1132 (CCSDNY 1868).
24. For instance, Frank Lawlor, managing a theater in Albany, NY, paid Daly for the right to perform both Daly's play *and* to interpolate the railroad scene in Boucicault's play. Frank Lawlor to Augustin Daly, 8 November 1869.
25. *Daly v. Webster*, 56 F. 483 (SC 1892), 487–488.
26. Schall 1956, 30.
27. Rede 1827.
28. Rede 1827, 70.
29. Schall 1956, 102.
30. The contract actually employs a Mr J. B. Wright as stage manager, but the form itself is the same as that used for actors. Where the printed contract says that Daly hires Wright 'to act and represent publicly', the Wright contract has inserted, in manuscript,

'as stage manager for'. 'Daly, Augustin', Theatre Autograph File, Box 24. Daly's contract represents a pinnacle of managerial control that appears in American theatrical contracts as early as 1815. See Schall 1956, Appendices, for evidence of changing contractual standards in the period.

31. Compare Goethe's suggestion that 'By making his behavior and movements in every-day life accord with his artistic profession, [the actor] will be greatly helped when on the stage.' Insofar as Goethe directs his actors' behaviour in public, he aims not to suppress vice (as Daly does) but to enhance and facilitate beauty in performance. Goethe 1894, 341.

32. Harding 1929 explains the early history of the union. Unions in Argentina, for example, followed a similar timeline. See Klein 1988. British Equity reached its current form in the 1930s, but has roots in the Actors' Association formed in the 1880s. See Macleod 1981. France saw abortive attempts at unionization starting in the 1890s, stabilizing around the Union des artistes dramatiques et lyriques des théâtres français starting in 1917. See Rauch 2006. Germany's union has greater seniority, dating to 1871 when it was founded under the leadership of Ludwig Barnay. See Rübel 1992.

33. *Producing Managers' Association-Actors' Equity Association Minimum Contract (Standard Form), 1919.* Printed in Fleming Gemmill 1926, 70–72.

34. Some of the most common rules and regulations still receive explicit mention, however. The same paragraph that notes the actor's general obligation to managerial rules lists specific requirements to 'be prompt at rehearsals', to behave 'in a competent and painstaking manner', and to 'render services exclusively' to the manager (Section 16).

35. Such 'strandings' were among the most important spurs to unionization, revealing how little obligation managers felt to their performers. See Harding 1929 and Holmes 2013 on AEA's early history.

36. De Meymarie and Bernheim 1883, quoted in Hemmings 1993, 176.

37. Hemmings 1987, 248.

38. Hemmings 1987, 251.

39. Bush-Bailey 2011.

40. Sanderson 1984, 34. Edward Gordon Craig was among Thorne's pupils.

41. Sanderson 1984, 35–37.

42. Sanderson 1984, 42, 47.

43. McTeague 1993, ix.

44. Sorrell 1869, 5.

45. Sorrell 1869, 2.

46. A Prominent Stage Manager 1900, 6.

47. Sorrell 1869, 34. Burton 1876 likewise offers ten pages of advice on make-up.

48. Buchanan n.d.; Hennequin 1890.

49. Buchanan n.d., 72.

50. Hennequin 1890, v.

51. A Dramatist 1888.

52. De Meymarie and Bernheim 1883, 30–31, my translation.

53. De Meymarie and Bernheim 1883, 32, my translation.

54. On theatre history in the United States, see Jackson 2004, particularly Chapter 2.

55. Jones 1895; Jones 1913.
56. See, for instance, Lamb's famous essay 'On the Tragedies of Shakespeare, Considered with Reference to their Fitness for Stage Representation.' *The Reflector* (1811).
57. Mazer 2004, 209.
58. Booth 1980, vii.
59. 13 Parl. Deb. (3rd ser.) 1832, 240.
60. Jones 1895, 181.
61. Jones 1913, x.
62. 13 Parl. Deb. (3rd ser.) 1832, 255.
63. Matthews 1906, 414.
64. Jones 1913, viii.
65. For a comparative study of these institutions, see Carlson 1961.
66. Schoonderwoerd 1963, 96–102.
67. Archer and Granville-Barker 1908. On the growth of national theatre cultures in the late-nineteenth century, see Kruger 1992.
68. Arnold 1882, 243.
69. Davis 2000, 222–223.
70. See Miller 2016, 20–33.
71. Davis 2000, 347–349.
72. Dicker 1974, 95.
73. Dicker 1974, 112.
74. Dicker 1974, 198.
75. On Bandmann, see Balme 2015, 19–36. On the Syndicate and the Shuberts, see Baker 1962.

# BIBLIOGRAPHY

## PRIMARY SOURCES

'A Perpendicular Interview with Mr Bland Holt' (typescript), Holt Papers Box 3, Series 3, Folder 2, MS. 2241, National Library of Australia.

Bland Holt Papers, MS. 2241, National Library of Australia; Coppin Collection MS. 8827, State Library of Victoria, Australia.

Clipping, undated, Britannia Cuttings, Theatre Collection, Victoria and Albert Museum.

Constitution of the German Reich, dated 11 August 1919, article 7, number 20.

Daly, Augustin, Theatre Autograph File, Box 24, Harvard Theatre Collection, Houghton Library, Harvard University.

*Daly v. Palmer*, 6 F. Cas. 1132 (CCSDNY 1868).

*Daly v. Webster*, 56 F. 483 (SC 1892).

Frank Lawlor to Augustin Daly, 8 November 1869, Folger Library, Washington, DC, Y.c.4117, item 5.

*Keene v. Clarke*, 5 Robt. 38 (New York Superior Court, General Term 1867).

*Keene v. Wheatley*, 14 F. Cas. 180 (CCEDPA 1860).

*Macklin v. Richardson*. 27 Eng. Rep. 451, 1770.

Newspaper Cuttings, 'Mummer Memories' (from *Sportsman*, 20 February 1907), Q 792.099/1 Vol. 23B, Mitchell Library, New South Wales.

Report from the Select Committee on Dramatic Literature, with the Minutes of Evidence (1831–32) Paper No. 679, VII, 1, p.158. ProQuest, Parliamentary Papers (1831–32) Paper No. 679, VII, 1.

*The Parliamentary Debates* (Official Report), 5th Series, vol. 52, Third Session of 30th Parliament of the United Kingdom of Great Britain and Ireland, House of Commons, Third Volume of Session 1913, Comprising Period from Monday, 21 April 1913, to Thursday, 8 May 1913 (London: HM Stationery Office, 1913), 454.

13 Parl. Deb. (3rd ser.) 1832.

*The Somewhat Different Magazine*, February 1905.

*Newspapers*

*Budapesti Hírlap* [*Budapest News*]. 4 November 1916, 3.
*European Magazine*. January 1805, XLVII.
*La Renaissance*. 15 February 1873.
*New Age*. 9 January 1913. 'Mr Granville Barker's Gramophones'.
*New Monthly Magazine*. 1827. 19 (1).
*Referee*. 3 February 1924.
*Sydney Morning Herald*. 23 December 1901.
*The Era*. 8 June 1879.
*The Era*. 19 September 1896. 'Advertisements & Notices'.
*The Era*. 1 June 1921, 5.
*The Mask*. 'International compliments'. 1868, 176.
*The New York Times*. 23 May 1921, 6.
*The Saturday Review*. 2 May 1891. 'Before the Footlights'.
*The Stage*. 2 June 1921, 16.
*The Times*. 8 September 1817, 2.
*The Times of London*. 15 July 1869, 10.
*Theatre World*. January 1936.
*Tribune*. 1796. London: printed for the author.


*Websites*

http://www.theatrescapes.theaterwissenschaft.uni-muenchen.de/index.html
http://www.theatrescapes.gwi.uni-muenchen.de


# OTHER SOURCES

A Dramatist. 1888. *Playwriting: A Handbook for Would-Be Dramatic Authors*.
  London: The Stage Office.
A Prominent Stage Manager. 1900. *How to Become an Actor: Giving Complete
  Instructions as to the Duties of the Stage Manager, Prompter, Scenic Artist, Property
  Man, and How to Make Out a Scene Plot, Property Plot, etc. Also, How to Make Up
  for the Various Characters Seen on the Stage*. New York: Frank Tousey.
A Railer. 1830. 'Opening of the Liverpool and Manchester Railroad'. *Blackwood's
  Magazine* 28 (173): 825–830.
Adamson, William. 1883. *The Theatre: Its Influence on Actors and Audience. A Lecture*.
  Edinburgh: Andrew Elliot.
Adorno, Theodor. 1981. *In Search of Wagner*. Translated by Rodney Livingstone.
  London.
Allard, Louis. 1955. 'La Dame aux camélias, Les Lionnes pauvres et la censure'. *Revue
  d'histoire du théâtre*, III–IV: 322–331.
Allen, Robert C. 1980. *Vaudeville and Film, 1895–1915: A study in media interaction*.
  New York: Arno Press.
Allen, Robert C. 1991. *Horrible Prettiness: Burlesque and American Culture*. Chapel
  Hill: University of North Carolina Press.
Altick, Richard. 1978. *The Shows of London*. Cambridge, Mass. and London: Harvard
  University Press.
Anderson, Benedict. 1983. *Imagined Communities. Reflections on the Origin and
  Spread of Nationalism*. London/New York: Verso.

Anderson, Joseph I. 2011. *Enter a Samurai: Kawakami Otojirô and Japanese Theatre in the West*. 2 vols. Tuscon: Wheatmark.

Appadurai, Arjun. 1990. 'Disjuncture and difference in the global cultural economy'. *Theory, Culture and Society* 7: 295–310.

Appadurai, Arjun. 2002. 'Here and Now'. In *The Visual Culture Reader*, edited by Nicholas Mirzoeff, 173–179. London/New York: Routledge.

Archer, William. 1886. *About the Theatre. Essays and Studies*. London: Fisher Unwin.

Archer, William and Robert W. Lowe, eds. 1894. *Dramatic Essays by Leigh Hunt*. London: Walter Scott Ltd.

Archer, William. 1902. 'The Case for National Theatres'. *Monthly Review* 8 (22): 140–155.

Archer, William and Harley Granville-Barker. 1908. *Schemes and Estimates for a National Theatre*. London: Duckworth.

Arnold, Matthew. 1882. 'The French Play in London'. In *Irish Essays and Others*, edited by Arnold, 208–243. London: Smith, Elder, & Co.

Augier, Émile. 1892. *Théâtre complet*, 7 vols. Paris: Calmann-Lévy.

Auslander, Philip. 1999. *Liveness: Performance in a Mediatized Culture*. London/New York: Routledge.

Baker, Dorothy Gillam. 1962. 'Monopoly in the American Theater: A Study of the Cultural Conflicts Culminating in the Syndicate and its Successors, the Shuberts'. PhD Thesis, New York University.

Ball, Michael and David Sunderland. 2001. *An Economic History of London 1800–1914*. London: Routledge.

Balme, Christopher. 1999. *Decolonizing the Stage*. Oxford: Oxford University Press.

Balme, Christopher. 2000. 'Sexual spectacles – Theatricality and the performance of sex in early encounters in the Pacific'. *The Drama Review* 4: 67–85.

Balme, Christopher. 2005. 'Selling the bird: Richard Walton Tully's *The Bird of Paradise* and the dynamics of theatrical commodification'. *Theatre Journal* 1: 1–20.

Balme, Christopher. 2014. *The Theatrical Public Sphere*. Cambridge: Cambridge University Press.

Balme, Christopher. 2015. 'The Bandmann Circuit: Theatrical Networks in the First Age of Globalization'. *Theatre Research International* 40 (1): 19–36.

Balme, Christopher and Tracy Davis. 2015. 'A Cultural History of Theatre: A Prospectus'. *Theatre Survey* 56 (3): 402–421.

Bandmann, Daniel. 1885. *An Actor's Tour or Seventy Thousand Miles with Shakespeare*. Boston: Cupples, Upham and Company.

Bannai, Tokuaki and Kameyama Ikuo. 1987. 'Roshia to Hanako' ['Hanako and Russia']. In *Kyôdô kenkyû Nihon to Roshia*. Tokyo.

Barrett, Daniel. 1999. 'Play Publication, Readers, and the "Decline" of Victorian Drama'. *Book History* 2 (1): 173–187.

Barth, Volker. 2011. 'Die Genese globaler Nachrichtenagenturen. Überlegungen zu einem Forschungsprogramm'. *WerkstattGeschichte* 56: 63–75.

Baudelaire, Charles. 1961. *Œuvres complètes*, ed. Y.-G. Le Dantec and Claude Pichois. Paris: Gallimard.

Bauer, Bernhard A. 1927. *Komödianten – Dirne? Der Künstlerin Leben und Lieben in Lichte der Wahrheit*. Wien/Leipzig: Fiba-Verlag.

Baumann, Carl-Friedrich. 1988. *Licht im Theater. Von der Argand-Lampe bis zum Glühlampen-Scheinwerfer. Die Schaubühne, 72*. Wiesbaden: Franz Steiner.

Bayly, Christopher. 2004. *The Birth of the Modern World, 1780–1914. Global Connections and Comparisons*. Oxford: Blackwell Pub.

Beaumont Wicks, Charles. 1950–1979. *The Parisian Stage*. 5 vols. University, Ala.: University of Alabama Press.

Becker, Tobias. 2014. *Inszenierte Moderne. Populäres Theater in Berlin und London, 1880–1930*. Oldenburg: de Gruyter.

Benjamin, Walter. 1999. *The Arcades Project*. Translated by Howard Eiland and Kevin McLaughlin. Cambridge, Mass. and London: Harvard University Press.

Benjamin, Walter. 2015. 'The Storyteller. Reflections on the works of Nikolai Leskov'. In *Illuminations*, edited by Hannah Arendt, 83–107. London: The Bodley Head.

Bennett, Tony. 1995. *The Birth of the Museum. History, Theory, Politics*. London/New York: Routledge.

Berger, John. 1972. *Ways of Seeing*. London: British Broadcasting Corporation and Penguin Books.

Berianstein, Leonard R. 2001. *Daughters of Eve: A Cultural History of French Theater Women from the Old Regime to the Fin de Siècle*. Cambridge, Mass.: Harvard University Press.

Berman, Marshall. 1983. *All that is Solid into Air: The Experience of Modernity*. London: Verso.

Biers, Katherine and Sharon Marcus. 2014. 'World Literature and Global Performance'. *Nineteenth Century Theatre & Film* 41 (2): 1–12.

Blankenship, Janelle. 2012. '1 November 1895: Premiere of Wintergarten Programm Highlights Traditional Nature of Early Film Technology'. In *A New History of German Cinema*, edited by Jennifer Kapczynski and Michael Richardson, 23–30. Rochester: Camden House.

Bloch, Iwan. 1903/1907. *The Sexual Life of Our Time. In its relation to modern civilization*, translated by Eden Paul. New York: Allied Book.

Bolter, Jay David and Richard Grusin. 2000. *Remediation: Understanding New Media*. Cambridge, Mass.: The MIT Press.

Booth, Michael R. 1980. *Prefaces to English Nineteenth-century Theatre*. Manchester: Manchester University Press.

Booth, Michael R. 1981. *Victorian Spectacular Theatre*. London: Routledge & Kegan Paul Ltd.

Booth, Michael R., Jonas T. Rimer and Rustom Bharucha. 2003. 'Families in the Theatre'. In *The Oxford Encyclopedia of Theatre & Performance*, edited by Dennis Kennedy, 438–40. London: Oxford University Press.

Borsa, Mario. 1984. *The English Stage of Today*. London: Brendon and Son, 1908 quoted in Woodfield, James. *English Theatre in Transition 1881–1914*. London: Croom Helm.

Boucicault, Dion. n.d. *The Colleen Bawn*, Dicks' Standard Plays. London: John Dicks.

Bourgeois, Maurice. 1993. *John Millington Synge and the Irish Theatre*. London: Constable & Co, Ltd.

Boyer, Mary Christine. 1985. *Manhattan Manners: Architecture and Style, 1850–1900*. New York: Rizzoli.

Brandt, W. and Wiebe Hogendoorn, comp. 1993. *German and Dutch Theatre 1600–1848*. Cambridge: Cambridge University Press.

Bratton, J. S. et al. 1991. *Acts of Supremacy: The British Empire and the Stage, 1790–1830*. Manchester: Manchester University Press.

Bratton, Jacky. 2003. *New Readings in Theatre History*. Cambridge/New York: Cambridge University Press.

Brereton, Austin. 1908. *The Life of Henry Irving*. Vol. 1. London.

Bridges-Adams, W. 1945. *The British Theatre*. London: Longman.

Bridges-Adams, W. 1966. 'Theatre'. In *Edwardian England 1901–1914*, edited by Simon Nowell-Smith, 367–409. London: Oxford University Press.

Brockett, Oscar G., Margaret Mitchell, and Linda Hardberger. 2010. *Making the Scene. A History of Stage Design and Technology in Europe and the United States.* San Antonio: Tobin Theatre Arts Fund.

Brooks, Peter. 1976. *The Melodramatic Imagination. Balzac, Henry James, Melodrama, and the Mode of Excess.* New Haven: Yale University Press.

Buchanan, R. C. n.d. *How To Become an Actor.* London: Samuel French.

Buchner, Eberhard. 1905. *Variété und Tingeltangel in Berlin, Großstadt-Dokumente.* 22. Berlin/Leipzig: Hermann Seemann Nachfolger.

Burton, C.E. 1876. *Burton's Amateur Actor.* New York: Dick & Fitzgerald.

Bush-Bailey, Gilli. 2011. *Performing Herself: AutoBiography & Fanny Kelly's Dramatic Recollections.* Manchester: Manchester University Press.

Butsch, Richard. 2000. *The Making of American Audiences. From Stage to Television, 1750–1990. Cambridge Studies in the History of Mass Communication.* Cambridge: Cambridge University Press.

Butte, Maren. 2013. *Bilder des Gefühls: Zum Melodramatischen im Wechsel der Medien.* Munich: Fink.

Calcraft, John William. 1839. *Defence of the Stage or an Inquiry into the Real Qualities of Theatrical Entertainments, their Scope and Tendency.* Dublin: Milliken.

Cannon, Robert. 2012. *Cambridge Introduction to Music. Opera.* Cambridge: Cambridge University Press.

Carli, Philip. 2011. 'Melodramatic spectacle on the English operatic stage'. In *Melodramatic voices. Understanding music drama*, edited by Sarah Hibberd, 103–120. Farnham: Ashgate.

Carlson, Marvin. 1961. 'The Théâtre-Libre, the Freie Bühne, the Independent Theatre: A Comparative Study,' PhD Thesis, Cornell University.

Carlson, Marvin. 1989 *Places of Performance. The Semiotics of Theatre Architecture.* Ithaca: Cornell University Press.

Carnwath, John Douglas. 2013. *The institutional development of municipal theatres in Germany, 1815–1933.* Ann Arbor: UMI.

Carter, Huntly. 1925. *The New Spirit in the European Theatre 1914–24.* London: Benn.

Castle, Charles. 1982. *The Folies Bergère.* London: Methuen.

Chambers, E. K. 1903. *The mediaeval stage.* 2 vols. Oxford: Oxford University Press.

Choler, Adolphe and Saint-Agnan. 1859. *Paris s'amuse.* Paris: M. Lévy.

Clapp, John Bouvé and Edwin Francis Edgett. 1902. *Plays of the Present.* New York: Dunlap Society.

Cliff, Nigel. 2007. *Shakespeare Riots. Revenge, Drama, and Death in Nineteenth-Century America.* New York: Random House.

Cochrane, Claire. 2011. *Twentieth-Century British Theatre. Industry, Art, Empire.* Cambridge: Cambridge University Press.

Cohen, Margaret and Anne Higonnet. 2004. 'Complex Culture'. In *The Nineteenth-Century Visual Culture Reader*, edited by Vanessa R. Schwartz and Jeannene M. Przyblyski, 15–26. New York/London: Routledge.

Collins, Wilkie. 1873. *The New Magdalen.* London: The Author.

Cook, E. T. and Alex Wedderburn, eds. 1903–1912. *The Works of John Ruskin.* Vol. 28. London: George Allen. New York: Longmans Green and Co.

Craig, Edward Gordon. 1911. *On the Art of the Theatre.* London: Heinemann.

Crary, Jonathan. 1992. *Techniques of the Observer: On vision and modernity in the nineteenth century.* Cambridge, Mass: MIT Press.

Crary, Jonathan. 2004. 'Techniques of the Observer'. In, *The Nineteenth-Century Visual Culture Reader*, edited by Vanessa R. Schwartz and Jeannene M. Przyblyski, 82–91. New York and London: Routledge.

Crary, Jonathan. 2000. *Suspensions of Perception. Attention, Spectacle, and Modern Culture*. 2nd edn. Cambridge, Mass./London: The MIT Press.

Crittenden, Camille. 1998. 'Whose patriotism? Austro-Hungarian relations and *Der Zigeunerbaron*'. *The Musical Quarterly* 2: 251–278.

Crittenden, Camille. 2000. *Johann Strauss and Vienna: Operetta and the Politics of Popular Culture*. Cambridge: Cambridge University Press.

Crompton, R. E. B. n.d. [1881]. *Artificial Lighting in Relation to Health, A Paper Read at Conference Held at the International Health Exhibition, South Kensington*. London.

Crossick, Geoffrey and Serge Jaumain. 1999. 'The World of the Department Store: Distribution, Culture and Social Change'. In *Cathedrals of Consumption. The European Department Store, 1850–1939*, edited by Geoffrey Crossick, 1–45. Aldershot: Ashgate.

Csáky, Moritz. 1999. *Az operett ideológiája és a bécsi modernség – Kultúrtörténeti tanulmány az osztrák identitásról [The Ideology of Operetta and Viennese Modernims – A Cultural-historical Analyses on Austrian Identity]*. Budapest: Európa.

Daniel, Ute. 1995. *Hoftheater. Zur Geschichte des Theaters und der Höfe im 18. und 19. Jahrhundert*. Stuttgart: Klett-Cotta.

Daunton, Michael. 2000. 'Society and Economic Life'. In *The Nineteenth Century*, edited by Colin Matthew, 41–82. Oxford: Oxford University Press.

Davies, Robertson. 1983. *The Mirror of Nature*. Toronto: University of Toronto Press.

Davis, Jim. 1991. 'The Gospel of Rags: Melodrama at the Britannia 1863–74'. *New Theatre Quarterly* VII (28): 369–389.

Davis, Jim and Tracy C. Davis. 1991. 'The People of the "People's Theatre": The Social Demography of the Britannia Theatre (Hoxton)'. *Theatre Survey* 32 (2): 137–172.

Davis, Jim. 1995. 'The East End'. In *The Edwardian Theatre. Essays on Drama and the Stage*, edited by Micheal Booth and Joel Kaplan, 201–219. Cambridge: Cambridge University Press.

Davis, Jim. 1998. 'Androgynous cliques and epicene colleges: gender transgression on and off the Victorian stage'. *Nineteenth Century Theatre* 26 (1): 50–69.

Davis, Jim and Victor Emeljanow. 2011. *Reflecting the Audience: London theatergoing, 1840–1880*. Hatfield: University of Hertfordshire Press.

Davis, Owen. 1914. 'Why I quit writing Melodrama'. *The American Magazine* 78 (3): 28–31.

Davis, Tracy C. 1988. 'Actress and prostitute in Victorian London'. *Theatre Research International* 13 (3): 221–234.

Davis, Tracy C. 1989. 'The actress in Victorian pornography'. *Theatre Journal* 41 (2): 294–315.

Davis, Tracy C. 1990. 'Sex in public places: The Zaeo Aquarium scandal and the Victorian moral majority'. *Theatre History Studies* 10: 1–14.

Davis, Tracy C. 1991. *Actresses as Working Women. Their Social Identity in Victorian Culture*. London: Routledge.

Davis, Tracy C. 1992. 'Indecency and Vigilance in the Music Halls'. In *British Theatre in the 1890s: Essays on Drama and the Stage*, edited by Richard Foulkes. Cambridge: Cambridge University Press.

Davis, Tracy C. 2000. *The Economics of the British Stage 1800–1914*. Cambridge: Cambridge University Press.

Davis, Tracy C. and Peter Holland, eds. 2007. *The Performing Century. Nineteenth-Century Theatre's History. Redefining British Theatre History*. Hampshire/New York: Palgrave Macmillan.

Davis, Tracy C., ed. 2012. *The Broadview Anthology of Nineteenth-Century British Performance*. Peterborough, Ont.: Broadview Press.

Davis, Tracy C. 2015. 'International Advocacy for Fire Prevention: Calculating Risk and Brokering Best Practices in Theatres'. *Popular Entertainment Studies* 6 (2): 38–55.

Davis Cordova, Sarah. 2007. 'Romantic ballet in France: 1830–1850'. In *The Cambridge Companion to Ballet*, edited by Marion Kant, 111–125. Cambridge: Cambridge University Press.

de Meymarie, Léo and Arnold Bernheim. 1993. *L'Enseignement Dramatique au Conservatoire*. Paris: Paul Ollendorff, 1883, quoted in F. W. J. Hemmings, *The Theatre Industry in Nineteenth-Century France*. New York: Cambridge University Press.

Dearing, Stewart. 2010. 'Painting the other within: Gypsies according to the Bohemian artist in the nineteenth and early twentieth centuries'. *Romani Studies* 2: 161–201.

Debord, Guy. 1995. *The Society of Spectacle [La Societé du Spectacle]*. New York: Zone Books.

Deschamps, Edmond. 1888. 'La déesse aux trétaux'. In *Le mal au théâtre*. Paris: E. Dentu.

Descotes, Maurice. 1964. *Le public du théâtre et son histoire*. Paris: Presses universitaires de France.

Detering, Heinrich, ed. 2002. *Thomas Mann. Essays I. 1893–1914*. 2nd edn. Frankfurt: Fischer.

Devrient, Eduard. 1964. *Aus seinen Tagebüchern*, edited by Rolf Kabel. 2 vols. Weimar: Boehlau.

Devrient, Eduard. 1967. *Geschichte der deutschen Schauspielkunst*. Vol. 2, edited by Rolf Kabel and Christoph Trilse. Munich: Langen Müller.

d'I***, M. le C. 1864. *Bibliographie des ouvrages relatifs à l'amour, aux femmes, au mariage*. 2nd edn, Paris: J. Gay.

Diamond, Elin. 1997. *Unmaking Mimesis: Essays on Feminism and Theater*. London and New York: Routledge.

Dibner, Bern. 1959. *The Atlantic Cable*. Norwalk: Burndy Library.

Dickens, Charles. 1996. *Dickens' Journalism Volume 2: The Amusements of the People and Other Papers: Reports Essays and Reviews 1834–51*, edited by Michael Slater. London: J. M. Dent.

Dicker, Ian G. 1974. *J.C.W. A Short Biography of James Cassius Williamson*. Rose Bay, N.S.W.: Elizabeth Tudor Press.

Dobson, Michael. 1992. *The Making of the National Poet: Shakespeare, Adaptation and Authorship, 1660–1769*. Oxford: Clarendon Press.

Donne, William Bodham. 1858. *Essays on the Drama*. London: John W. Parker & Son.

Donnet, Aléxis and Jacques-August Kaufmann. 1841. *Architectonographie des théâtres*. Paris: LaCroix & Baudry.

Donohue, Joseph. 2004. 'Theatres, Their Architecture and Their Audiences'. In *Cambridge History of British Theatre, Volume II: 1660 to 1895*, edited by Donohue, Vol. 2, 292–308. Cambridge: Cambridge University Press.

Donohue, Joseph. 2005. *Fantasies of Empire: The Empire Theatre of Varieties and the Licensing Controversies of 1894*. Iowa City: University of Iowa Press.

Downer, Leslie. 2003. *Madame Sadayakko: The Geisha Who Seduced the West*.
    London: Review.
Dreesbach, Anne. 2005. *Gezähmte Wilde. Die Zurschaustellung 'exotischer' Menschen
    in Deutschland 1870–1940*. Frankfurt am Main/New York: Campus.
Driver, Felix and David Gilbert, eds. 1999. *Imperial Cities: Landscape, display and
    Identity*. Manchester: Manchester University Press.
Duff-Gordon, Lucy Wallace. 1932. *Discretions and Indiscretions*. New York: Frederick
    A. Stokes Co.
Dukes, Ashley. 1941. 'Journey Through Theatre. Chapter II: Old Germany. And home
    Again via Zurich'. *Theatre Arts 25*
Dukes, Ashley. 1941. 'Journey Through Theatre. Chapter IV: Germany 1919'. *Theatre
    Arts 25*
Dumas, Alexandre. 1868. *Théâtre complet*, 14 vols. Paris: Michel Lévy.
Edison, Thomas. 1880. 'The Success of the Electric Light'. *North American Review*
    131: 295–300.
Ellis, Havelock. 1936. *Studies in the Psychology of Sex*, 4 vols. New York: Random House.
Ellrich, Lutz. 2009. 'Carl Niessens *Handbuch der Theater-Wissenschaft*. Versuch einer
    kritischen Lektüre'. *Maske und Kothurn 55* (1, 2): 175–192.
Elsom, John and Nicholas Tomalin. 1978. *The History of the National Theatre*.
    London: Cape.
Eltis, Sos. 2013. *Acts of Desire. Women and Sex on Stage, 1800–1930*. Oxford: Oxford
    University Press.
Emeljanow, Victor. 1998. 'Erasing the Spectator: Observations on Nineteenth-Century
    Lighting'. *Theatre History Studies* 18: 107–116.
Emeljanow, Victor. 2003. 'Terry Family'. In *The Oxford Encyclopedia of Theatre &
    Performance*, edited by Dennis Kennedy, 1342. London: Oxford University Press.
Engel, Eduard. 1921. *Geschichte der englischen Literatur von den Anfängen bis zur
    Gegenwart*. 9th rev. edn. Leipzig: Brandstetter.
Erck, Alfred. 2006. *Geschichte des Meininger Theaters, 1831–2006*. Meiningen:
    Südthüringisches Staatstheater.
Erenberg, Lewis A. 1984. *Steppin' Out: New York Nightlife and the Transformation of
    American Culture, 1890–1930*. Chicago: University of Chicago Press.
Ezra, Elizabeth. 2000. *Georges Méliès. The Birth of the Auteur*. Manchester:
    Manchester University Press.
Faulk, Barry J. 2004. *Music hall and modernity: the late-Victorian discovery of popular
    culture*. Athens, Ohio: Ohio University Press.
Faulstich, Werner. 2004. *Medienwandel im Industrie- und Massenzeitalter
    (1830–1900). Die Geschichte der Medien*. Göttingen: Vandenhoeck & Ruprecht.
Fay, Frank. 1988. 'Some Account of the Early Days of the INTS'. In *The Abbey
    Theatre: Interviews and Recollections*, edited by E. H. Mikhail, 71–77. London:
    Macmillan Press Ltd.
Fay, W. G. and Catherine Carswell. 1935. *The Fays of the Abbey Theatre: An
    Autobiographical Record*. London: Rich & Cowan, Ltd.
Fischer-Lichte, Erika. 1999. *Geschichte des Dramas. Epochen der Identität auf dem
    Theater von der Antike bis zur Gegenwart*. Tübingen-Basel: Francke Verlag.
Fischer-Lichte, Erika. 2004. 'Some critical remarks on theatre historiography'. In
    *Writing and Rewriting National Theatre Histories*, edited by S. E. Wilmer, 1–16.
    Iowa City: UIP.
Fischer-Lichte, Erika. 2005. *Theatre, Sacrifice, Ritual. Exploring Forms of Political
    Theatre*. London/New York: Routledge.

Fiske, Roger. 1973. *English Theatre Music in the Eighteenth Century*. London: Oxford University Press.

Fitzgerald, Percy. 1870. *Principles of comedy and dramatic effect*. London: Tinsley Brothers.

Fitzgerald, Percy. 1881. *The World Behind the Scenes*. London: Chatto and Windus.

Fitzgerald, Percy. 1892. *The art of acting in connection with the study of character, the spirit of comedy and stage illusion*. London: Sonnennschein.

Fleming Gemmill, Paul. 1926. *Collective Bargaining by Actors: A Study of Trade-Unionism among Performers of the English-speaking Legitimate Stage in America*. Bulletin of the Bureau of Labor Statistics, no. 402 Washington, D.C.: U.S. Government Printing Office.

Flint, Kate. 2000. *The Victorians and the Visual Imagination*. Cambridge: Cambridge University Press.

Forbes, Derek. 2008. 'Simla: Amateur Theatrical Capital of the Raj'. *Theatre Notebook* 62 (2): 76–120.

Foulkes, Richard. 1997. *Church and Stage in Victorian England*. Cambridge: Cambridge University Press.

Foulkes, Richard. 2002. *Performing Shakespeare in the Age of Empire*. Cambridge: Cambridge University Press.

Frazier, Adrian. 2005. 'From Abbey Tours to Hollywood Films'. In *Irish Theatre on Tour*, edited by Nicholas Grene and Chris Morash, 89–101. Dublin: Carysfort Press.

Fraxi, Pisanus. 1962. *Index librorum prohibitorum: being notes bio- biblio- icono-graphical and critical, on curious and uncommon books*. New York: Documentary Books.

Freisburger, Walther. 1936. *Theater im Film. Eine Untersuchung über die Grundzüge und Wandlungen in den Beziehungen zwischen Theater und Film*. Emsdetten: Lechte.

Frenzel, Karl. 1892. 'Die Berliner Theater'. *Deutsche Rundschau* 70: 116–132.

Freud, Sigmund. 1917. *A Difficulty in the Path of Psycho-Analysis*. In *The Standard Edition of the Complete Psychological Works of Sigmund Freud, Volume XVII (1917–1919): An Infantile Neurosis and Other Works*, 135–144. London: Vintage.

Freydank, Ruth, ed. 1995. *Theater als Geschäft. Berlin und seine Privattheater um die Jahrhundertwende*. Berlin: Hentrich.

Freydank, Ruth. 1988. *Theater in Berlin: Von den Anfängen bis 1945*. Berlin: Argon Verlag.

Fritzsche, Peter. 1998. *Reading Berlin 1900*. Cambridge, Mass./London: Harvard University Press.

Fugier, Anne Martin. 2001. *Comédienne. De Mlle Mars à Sarah Bernhardt*. Paris: Seuil.

Gänzl, Kurt. 1986. *The British Musical Theatre, vol.1 1865–1914*. Basingstoke: Macmillan.

Gál, S. G. and V. Somogyi. 1960. *Operettek könyve – Az operett regényes története* [*The Book of Operettas – The Long History of Operetta*]. Budapest: Zeneműkiadó.

Garber, Majorie. 2008. *Patronizing the Arts*. Princeton: Princeton University Press.

Gasnault, F. 1986. *Guinguettes et lorettes. Bals publics et danse sociale à Paris entre 1830 et 1870*. Paris: Aubier.

Gáspár, Margit. 1960. *A múzsák neveletlen gyermeke. A könnyűzenés színpad kétezer éve* [*The Spoiled Child of the Muses*]. The Two-Thousand-Year History of Musical Theatre. Budapest: Zeneműkiadó.

Gay, Peter. 2001. *Weimar Culture. The Outsider as Insider*. New York/London: W. W. Norton.

Gerhard, Anselm. 1992. *Die Verstädterung der Oper. Paris und das Musiktheater des 19. Jahrhunderts*. Stuttgart/Weimar: J. B. Metzler.

Geyer, Michael and Charles Bright. 1995. 'World history in a global age'. *American Historical Review* 100 (4): 1034–1060.

Gilbert, David and Felix Driver. 2000. 'Capital and Empire: Geographies of Imperial London'. *GeoJournal* 51 (1/2): 23–32.

Gilfoyle, Timothy J. 1992. *City of Eros. New York City, Prostitution, and the Commercialization of Sex, 1790–1920.* New York: W. W. Norton.

Godwin, George. 1878. 'The National Theatre Question'. *The Theatre*: 346–352.

Göhre, Paul. 1907. *Das Warenhaus.* Frankfurt am Main: Rütten & Loening.

Goethe, Johann Wolfgang von. 1894. 'Rules for Actors,' translated by Edgar S. Werner. *Werner's Magazine* 16 (10).

Goldstein, Robert. 1989. *Political Censorship of the Arts and the Press in Nineteenth-Century Europe.* Basingstoke: Macmillan.

Goldsworthy, Vesna. 1998. *Inventing Ruritania – The Imperialism of the Imagination.* New Haven and London: Yale University Press.

Goncourt, Edmond and Jules de. 1964. *Journal,* edited by Robert Ricatte. 3 vols. Paris: Robert Laffont.

Gooday, Graeme. 2008. *Domesticating Electricity: Technology, Uncertainty and Gender 1880–1914.* London: Pickering & Chatto.

Gough, Kathleen. 2012. 'Between the Image and Anthropology: Theatrical Lessons from Aby Warburg's "Nympha"'. *TDR: The Journal of Performance Studies* 56 (3): 114–130.

Gould, Marty. 2011. *Nineteenth-Century Theatre and the Imperial Encounter.* New York: Routledge.

Granville-Barker, Harley. 1922. *The Exemplary Theatre.* London: Chatto and Windus.

Granville-Barker, Harley. 1930. *A National Theatre.* London: Sidgwick & Jackson.

Grau, Robert. 1910. *The Business Man in the Amusement World. A Volume of Progress in the Field of the Theatre.* New York: Broadway Publishing Company.

Greenblatt, Stephen. 2010. 'A Mobility Studies Manifesto'. In *Cultural Mobility: A Manifesto,* edited by Stephen Greenblatt, 250–253. Cambridge: Cambridge University Press.

Gregory, Lady Augusta. 1970. *Visions and Beliefs in the West of Ireland.* Foreword by Elizabeth Coxhead, The Coole Edition. London: Colin Smythe.

Groemer, Gerald. 2016. *Street Performers and Society in Urban Japan, 1600–1900: The Beggar's Gift.* New York: Routledge.

Groos, Karl. 1899. *Die Spiele der Menschen.* Leipzig: Gustav Fischer.

Grosse, Ernst. 1894. *Die Anfänge der Kunst.* Freiburg/Leipzig: J. C. B. Mohr.

Grossmith, George and Weedon Grossmith. 1965. *Diary of a Nobody.* Harmondsworth: Penguin.

Grünwald-Zerkowitz, Sidonie. 1898/99. 'Toilettenkünstlerinnen auf der Bühne: Sarah Bernhardt'. *Bühne und Welt* 1: 509–512.

Grun, Bernard. 1970. *Gold and Silver. The Life and Times of Franz Lehár.* London: W. H. Allen.

Guest, Kristen. 2006. 'Culture, Class, and Colonialism: The Struggle for an English National Theatre, 1879–1913'. *Journal of Victorian Culture* 11 (2): 281–300.

Gupta, Somanatha. 2005. *The Parsi Theatre: Its Origins and Development.* Translated by Kathryn Hansen. Calcutta: Seagull Books.

Gurevich, Lyubov. 1939. *Istoriya russkogo teatral'nogo byta.* Moscow: Iskusstvo.

Guy, Stephen. 1998. 'Calling All Stars. Musical Films in a Musical Decade'. In *The unknown 1930s: an alternative history of the British cinema, 1929–39,* edited by Jeffrey Richards, 99–120. London: I. B. Tauris.

Haenni, Sabine. 2008. *The Immigrant Scene. Ethnic Amusements in New York, 1880–1920.* Minneapolis/London: University of Minnesota Press.

Hagemann, Carl. 1919. *Spiele der Völker. Eindrücke und Studien auf einer Weltfahrt nach Afrika und Ostasien.* Berlin: Schuster & Loeffler.

Hall, Thomas. 1997. *Planning Europe's Capital Cities: Aspects of Nineteenth-Century Urban development.* London: Spon.

Hanák, Péter. 1997. 'A bécsi és a pesti operett kultúrtörténeti helye'/'The Cultur-historical Position of the Viennese and Budapest Operetta'. *Budapesti Negyed*: 2–3, 9–30, http://epa.oszk.hu/00000/00003/00014/hanak.htm [accessed 10 June 2011].

Harding, Alfred. 1929. *The Revolt of the Actors.* New York: W. Morrow & Co.

Harris, H. 1826. Let. 7 Aug. In *Life & Times*, edited by F. Reynolds, vol. II., p. xviii

Hart, Henrich and Hart, Julias. 1882. 'Das "Deutsche Theater" des Herrn L'Arronge'. *Kritische Waffengänge* 4: 1–69.

Hartnoll, Phyllis. 1991. *The Theatre – A Concise History.* London: Thames and Hudson.

Harvie, Jen. 2009. *Theatre & the City.* Basingstoke: Palgrave Macmillan.

Hauptmann, Gerhard. 1915. 'Deutschland und Shakespeare'. *Jahrbuch der Deutschen Shakespeare-Gesellschaft* 51: VII–XII.

Haydon, B.R. 1926. *Autobiography.* Vol. 2. London: Peter Davies.

Heinrich, Anselm. 2007. *Entertainment, Education, Propaganda. Regional Theatres in Germany and Britain Between 1918 and 1945.* London: University of Hertfordshire Press/Society for Theatre Research.

Heinrich, Anselm, Katherine Newey and Jeffrey Richards, eds. 2009. *Ruskin, the Theatre and Victorian Visual Culture.* Basingstoke: Palgrave Macmillan.

Heinrich, Anselm. 2015. 'Performance for Imagined Communities: Gladstone, the National Theatre and Contested Didactics of the Stage'. In *Politics, Performance and Popular Culture: Theatre and Society in Nineteenth-Century England*, edited by Katherine Newey and Peter Yeandle, 96–110. Manchester: Manchester University Press.

Heltai, Gyöngyi. 2007. 'Az operett eredetmítoszai és a politika: egy "kitalált tradíció" a szocializmusban: 1949–1956' ['The Origin Myths of the Operetta and Politics. An "Invented Tradition" in Socialism: 1949–1956']. In *Hagyomány és eredetiség: tanulmányok [Tradition and Originality: Essays]*, edited by G. Wilhelm, 83–110. Budapest: Néprajzi Múzeum.

Hemmings, F. W. J. 1987. 'The Training of Actors at the Paris Conservatoire during the Nineteenth Century'. *Theatre Research International* 12 (3): 241–253.

Hemmings, F. W. J. 1993. *The Theatre Industry in Nineteenth-Century France.* New York: Cambridge University Press.

Hemmings, F. W. J. 1994. *Theatre and State in France 1760–1905.* Cambridge: Cambridge University Press.

Henderson, Mary C. 2004. *The City and the Theatre: The history of New York playhouses: A 250 year journey from Bowling Green to Times Square.* New York: Back Stage Books.

Hennequin, Alfred. 1890. *The Art of Playwriting: Being a Practical Treatise On the Elements of Dramatic Construction; Intended for the Playwright, the Student, and the Dramatic Critic.* Boston: Houghton, Mifflin and Co.

Hepworth, T. 1879. *The Electric Light: Its Past History and Present Position.* London: Routledge.

Hermann, Zoltán. 2011. 'Hajmási Péter & Tsai, avagy szabad-e újrakölteni a *Csárdáskirályn* dalszövegeit?' ['Péter Hajmási & Co., or Is It Possible to Revise the Lyrics of the *Csárdásqueen?*'] *Színház* 3. www.szinhaz.net/index. php?view=article&catid=52:2011-mar. Accessed 12 April 2011.

Herrmann, Max. 1931. 'Das theatralische Raumerlebnis'. In 'Vierter Kongreß für Ästhetik und Allgemeine Kunstwissenschaft'. Supplement, *Zeitschrift für Ästhetik und allgemeine Kunstwissenschaft* 25 (2): 152–163.

Hibbert, H. G. 1916. *Fifty Years of a Londoner's Life*. London: n.p.

Hill, Benson Earle. 1840. *Playing About: or Theatrical Anecdotes and Adventures*. Vol. I. London: W. Sams.

Hirsch, Foster. 1998. *The Boys from Syracuse. The Shuberts' Theatrical Empire*. Carbondale, Edwardsville: Southern Illinois University Press.

Hoberman, J. 1995. *Bridge of Light. Yiddish Film between Two Worlds*. Philadelphia: Temple University Press.

Hobsbawm, Eric, ed. 1983. 'Mass-Producing Traditions: Europe, 1870–1914'. In *The Invention of Tradition*. Cambridge: Cambridge University Press.

Hobsbawm, Eric and Terence Ranger, eds. 1983. *The Invention of Tradition. Past and Presence Presentation*. Cambridge: Cambridge University Press.

Hobsbawm, Eric. 1987. *The Age of Empire, 1875–1914*. London: Abacus.

Hobsbawm, Eric J. 1992. *Nations and Nationalism since 1780*. Cambridge: Cambridge University Press.

Höpel, Thomas. 2007. *Von der Kunst- zur Kulturpolitik. Städtische Kulturpolitik in Deutschland und Frankreich 1918–1939*. Stuttgart: Franz Steiner.

Hoffenberg, Peter H. 2001. *An Empire on Display. English, Indian, and Australian Exhibitions from the Crystal Palace to the Great War*. Berkeley/Los Angeles: University of California Press.

Holledge, J. and J. Tompkins. 2000. *Women's Intercultural Performance*. London: Routledge.

Holloway, Joseph. 1967. *Joseph Holloway's Abbey Theatre: Impressions of a Dublin Playgoer*. Carbondale/Edwardsville: Southern Illinois University Press.

Holmes, Sean P. 2013. *Weavers of Dreams, Unite!: Actors' Unionism in Early Twentieth-Century America*. Urbana: University of Illinois Press.

Hoppen, K. Theodore. 1998. *The Mid-Victorian Generation 1846–1886*. Oxford: Clarendon.

Howard, Diana. 1970. *London Theatres and Music Halls 1850–1950*. London: Library Association.

Hudson, Derek. 1974. *Munby man of two worlds: the life and diaries of Arthur J. Munby 1828–1910*. London: Abacus.

Hugländer, F. 1914. 'Aus dem homosexuellen Leben Alt-Berlins'. *Jahrbuch für sexuelle Zwischenstufen* 14: 54–57.

Hulfeld, Stefan. 2007. *Theatergeschichtsschreibung als kulturelle Praxis. Wie Wissen über Theater entsteht, Materialien des ITW Bern. 8*. Zürich: Chronos.

Hunt, Charles. 1907. *A History of the Introduction of Gas Lighting*. London: Walter King.

Hunt, Hugh. 1979. *The Abbey: Ireland's National Theatre 1904–1978*. New York: Columbia University Press.

Hunt, Lynn. 2014. *Writing History in the Global Era*. New York/London: W. W. Norton.

Huret, Jules. 1997. *Berlin um Neunzehnhundert*. Berlin: Tasbach.

Hyde, Ralph. 1988. *Panoramania!: the Art and Entertainment of the 'All-Embracing View'*. London: Trefoil Publications with Barbican Art Gallery.

Ibels, André. 1906. *La traite des chanteuses (moeurs de province)*. Paris: Felix Juven.

Imre, Zoltán. 2013. 'Operetta beyond borders: The different versions of Die Csárdásfürstin in Europe and the United States (1915–1921)'. *Studies in Musical Theatre* 7 (2): 175–205.

Innes, Christopher, ed. 2000. *A Sourcebook on Naturalist Theatre*. London and New York: Routledge.

Jackson, Russell, ed. 1989. *Victorian Theatre: a New Mermaid Background book*. London: A. and C. Black.

Jackson, Shannon. 2004. *Professing Performance. Theatre in Academy from Philology to Performativity, Theatre and Performance Theory*. Cambridge: Cambridge University Press.

Jacobs, Barry. 1998. 'Translating for the stage – the case of Strindberg'. *Tijdskrift voor Scandinavistik* 19 (1): 80–88.

Janin, Jules. 1843. *The American in Paris During the Summer*. London: Longman.

Janin, Jules. 1980. *Impressions du theatre*, V, 150 April 8.

Jarry, Alfred. 1969. *La Chandelle verte. Lumières sur les choses de ce temps*, edited by Maurice Saillet. Paris: Livre de Poche.

Jay, Martin. 1994. *Downcast Eyes: the denigration of vision in twentieth-century French thought*. Berkeley, Los Angeles and London: University of California Press.

Jelavich, Peter. 1993. *Berlin Cabaret*. Cambridge: Harvard University Press.

Jelavich, Peter. 1985. *Munich and Theatrical Modernism: Politics, Playwriting, and Performance*. Cambridge, Mass.: Harvard University Press.

Jennings, Humphrey. 2012. *Pandaemonium 1660–1886: The Coming of the Machines as seen by contemporary observers*. London: Icon Books.

Johnson, Claudia D. 1975. 'That guilty third tier: prostitution in nineteenth-century American theatre'. *American Quarterly* 27 (5): 575–584.

Jones, Henry Arthur. 1895. *The Renascence of the English Drama: Essays, Lectures, and Fragments Relating to the Modern English Stage, Written and Delivered in the Years 1883–94*. London: Macmillan and Co.

Jones, Henry Arthur. 1913. *The Foundations of a National Drama: A Collection of Lectures, Essays and Speeches, Delivered and Written in the Years 1896–1912*. London: Chapman & Hall.

Joseph, Tony. 1994. *The D'Oyly Carte Opera Company 1875–1892*. Bristol. Bunthorne Books.

Kahn, Coppelia. 2008. 'Forbidden mixtures: Shakespeare in Blackface Ministrelsy, 1844'. In *Shakespeare and the Cultures of Performance*, edited by Paul Yachnin and Patricia Badir, 121–144. Aldershot: Ashgate.

Kálmán, I., Jenbach, B. and L. Stein. 1916. *Die Czardasfürstin* (libretto). Vienna/ Frankfurt am Main: Joseph Weinberger.

Kálmán, I., Jenbach, B. and L. Stein. 1917. *Csárdáskirályné/The Queen Consort of Csárdás*. Budapest: n.p.

Kano, Ayako. 2001. *Acting Like a Woman in Modern Japan. Theatre, Gender and Nationalism*. New York: Palgrave.

Kaplan, Joe L. and Sheila Stowell. 1995. *Theatre and Fashion: Oscar Wilde to the Suffragettes*. Cambridge: Cambridge University Press.

Kaschuba, Wolfgang. 1995. 'Deutsche Bürgerlichkeit nach 1800. Kultur als symbolische Praxis'. In *Bürgertum im 19. Jahrhundert. Deutschland im europäischen Vergleich. Eine Auswahl*, edited by Jürgen Kocka, Vol. 2, 9–44. Göttingen: Vandenhoeck & Ruprecht.

Kawohl, Friedemann. n.d. 'Commentary on the German Imperial Copyright Act (1870)'. In *Primary Sources on Copyright (1450–1900)*, edited by Lionel Bently and Martin Kretschmer, www.copyrighthistory.org

Kaynar, Gad. 1998. 'National Theatre as Colonized Theatre. The Paradox of Habima'. *Theatre Journal* 50: 1–20.

Keene, Donald. 1981. *Appreciation of Japanese Culture*. Tokyo/New York: Kodansha.

Keim, Norman and Marc David. 2008. *Our Movie Houses: a history of film and cinematic innovation in central New York*. New York: Syracuse University Press.

Kelsall, Malcolm. 1978. 'Makers of a Modern Theatre: Frank and William Fay'. *Theatre Research International* 3 (3): 188–199.

Kennedy, Dennis. 2009. *The Spectator and the Spectacle: Audiences in Modernity and Postmodernity*. Cambridge: Cambridge University Press.

Kern, Stephen. 2003. *The Culture of Time and Space 1880–1918*. Cambridge, Mass.: Harvard University Press.

Kershaw, Baz. 2003. 'Training for Theatre'. In *The Oxford Encyclopedia of Theatre & Performance*, edited by Dennis Kennedy, 1379–1381. London: Oxford University Press.

Ketelsen, Uwe-Karsten. 1999. *Ein Theater und seine Stadt. Die Geschichte des Bochumer Schauspielhauses*. Cologne: SH-Verlag.

Kessler, Frank and Sabine Lenk. 2010. 'The French Connection. Franco-German Film Relations before First World War'. In *A Second Life. German Cinema's First Decades*, edited by Thomas Elsässer and Michael Wedel, 62–71. Amsterdam: Amsterdam University Press.

Kirby, Michael. 1972. 'On Acting and Not-Acting'. *TDR: The Drama Review* 16 (1): 3–15.

Kirshenblatt-Gimblett, Barbara. 1998. *Destination Culture. Tourism, Museums, and Heritage*. Berkeley: University of California.

Klein, Holger and Peter Davidhazi, eds. 1996. *Shakespeare and Hungary: The Law and Shakespeare*. New York: Edwin Mellen Press.

Klein, Teodoro. 1988. *Una Historia de Luchas: La Asociación Argentina de Actores*. Buenos Aires: La Asociación.

Klotz, Volker. 1991. *Operette. Porträt und Handbuch einer unerhörten Kunst*. Munich/ Zürich: Piper.

Knowles, Rick. 2010. *Theatre and Interculturalism*. London: Palgrave Macmillan.

Kocka, Jürgen, ed. 1987. 'Bürgertum und Bürgerlichkeit als Probleme der deutschen Geschichte vom späten 18. bis zum frühen 20. Jahrhundert'. In *Bürger und Bürgerlichkeit im 19. Jahrhundert*, 21–63. Göttingen: Vandenhoeck & Ruprecht.

König, Wolfgang. 2007. *Wilhelm II. und die Moderne. Der Kaiser und die technisch-industrielle Welt*. Paderborn: Ferdinand Schöningh.

Kohler, Christoph. 2008. *Wozu das Theater? Zur Entstehungsgeschichte der Theatersubventionen in Zürich (1890–1928)*. Cologne: Böhlau.

Kracauer, Siegfried. 1976. *Jacques Offenbach und das Paris seiner Zeit*, edited by Karsten Witte. Frankfurt am Main: Suhrkamp Verlag.

Kruger, Loren. 1992. *The National Stage. Theatre and Cultural Legitimation in England, France, and America*. Chicago: University of Chicago Press.

Kruger, Loren. 2003. 'National Theatre Movements, Europe'. In *The Oxford Encyclopedia of Theatre & Performance*, edited by Dennis Kennedy, 919–922. London: Oxford University Press.

Lancaster, William. 2000. *The Department Store. A Social History*. London: Leicester University Press.

Latour, Anny. 1958. *Kings of Fashion*. London: Weidenfeld & Nicholson.

Lawrence, Jon. 1994. 'The First World War and its aftermath'. In *20th Century Britain – Economic, Social and Cultural Change*, edited by Paul Johnson, 151–168. London and New York: Longman.

Le Roux, Hugues and Jules Garnier. 1890. *Acrobats and Mountebanks*. London: Chapman and Hall.

Leacroft, Richard. 1973. *The Development of the English Playhouse: an illustrated survey of theatre building in England from mediaeval to modern times*. London and New York: Methuen.

Lees, Lynn Hollen and Andrew Lees. 2007. *Cities and the Making of Modern Europe 1750–1914*. Cambridge: Cambridge University Press.

Lenk, Wolfgang. 1933. *Das kommunale Theater*. Diss., Universität Berlin.

Leonhardt, Nic. 2007. *Piktoral-Dramaturgie. Visuelle Kultur und Theater im 19. Jahrhundert (1869–1900)*. Bielefeld: transcript.

Leonhardt, Nic. 2014. 'Transatlantic Theatrical Traces. Sketches of Oceanic Trade Routes and Globe-Trotting Amusement Explorers'. In *The Passing Show 30,* edited by Shubert Archive, 2–23. New York: Shubert Archive.

Leonhardt, Nic. 2015. '"From the Land of the White Elephant through the Gay Cities of Europe and America" – Re-routing the World Tour of the Boosra Mahin Siamese Theatre Troupe (1900)'. *Theatre Research International* 40 (2): 140–155.

Leverton, W. H. 1932. *Through the Box-office Window*. London: T. Werner Laurie.

Levine, Lawrence W. 1988. *Highbrow/Lowbrow: The Emergence of Cultural Hierarchy in America*. Cambridge, Mass.: Harvard University Press.

Linhardt, Marion. 2006. *Residenzstadt und Metropole. Zu einer kulturellen Topographie des Wiener Unterhaltungstheaters 1858–1918*. Tübingen: Niemeyer.

Lloyds, Frederick. 1875. *Practical Guide to Scene-Painting and Painting in Distemper*. London: George Rowneys & Co.

Lo, J. and H. Gilbert. 2002. 'Toward a topography of cross-cultural theatre praxis'. *The Drama Review* 3: 31–53.

Lyon, Janet. 2009. 'Sociability in the metropole: modernism's Bohemian salons'. *English Literary History* 3: 687–711.

MacKenzie, John M., ed. 1986. *Imperialism and Popular Culture*. Manchester: Manchester University Press.

Macleod, Joseph. 1981. *The Actor's Right to Act*. London: Lawrence & Wishart.

Mahalin, Paul. 1862. *Ces petites dames du théâtre*. Paris: Tous les libraires.

Mainardi, Patricia. 1989. *Art and Politics of the Second Empire*. New Haven: Yale University Press.

Mander, Raymond and Joe Mitchenson. 1968. *Lost Theatres of London*. London: Hart-Davis.

Mankowitz, Wolf. 1982. *Mazeppa. The Lives, Loves and Legends of Adah Isaacs Menken, a Biographical Quest*. New York: Stein and Day.

Mantzius, Karl. 1903. *A history of theatrical art in ancient and modern times, with an introd. by William Archer, authorised translation by Louise von Cossel*. London: Duckworth & Co.

Marbury, Elisabeth. 1923. *My Crystal Ball. Reminiscences*. New York: Boni and Liveright.

Martin, Theodore. 1874. *Essays on the Drama*. London: n.p.

Marx, Karl and Friedrich Engels. 1964. 'Manifest der Kommunistischen Partei'. In *Werke*, vol. 4. Berlin: Institut für Marxismus-Leninismus.

Marx, Peter W. 2003. 'Diaspora'. In *The Oxford Encyclopedia of Theatre & Performance*, edited by Dennis Kennedy, 368–370. London: Oxford University Press.

Marx, Peter W. 2006. 'Consuming the Canon: Theatre, Commodification, and Social Mobility in Late Nineteenth-Century German Theatre'. *Theatre Research International* 31 (2): 129–144.

Marx, Peter W. 2008. *Ein theatralisches Zeitalter. Bürgerliche Selbstinszenierungen um 1900*. Tübingen: Francke.

Masumoto, Masahiko. 1986. *Yokohama Gêteza. Meiji, Taishô no seiyô gekijô*. [The Gaiety Theatre of Yokohama, The Westerners' Theatre During Meji and Taishô Years]. Yokohama: Iwasaki hakubutsukan shuppankyoku.

Matthews, Brander. 1906. 'On the Publishing of Plays'. *The North American Review* 182: 414–425.

Matthews, Brander. 1912. *The Development of the Drama*. New York: Charles Scribner's and Sons.

Matthews, Jodie. 2010. 'Back where they belong: Gypsies, kidnapping and assimilation in Victorian children's literature'. *Romani Studies* 2: 137–159.

Mayer, David. 2004. 'Encountering melodrama'. In *The Cambridge companion to Victorian and Edwardian theatre*, edited by Kerry Powell, 145–163. Cambridge: Cambridge University Press.

Mayhew, Edward. 1840. *Stage Effects, or the Principles which Command Dramatic Success in the Theatre*. London, n.p.

Mayhew, Henry and John Binny. 1852. 'The Criminal Prisons of London', *Illustrated London News*.

Mayhew, Henry. 1865. *London labour and the London poor: the condition and earnings of those that will work, cannot work, and will not work*. 2 vols. London: Ch. Griffin and Company.

Mazer, Cary. 2004. 'New Theatres for a New Drama'. In *The Cambridge Companion to Victorian and Edwardian Theatre*, edited by Kerry Powell, 207–221. Cambridge: Cambridge University Press.

McConachie, Bruce. 2006. 'Theatre and hegemony: comparing popular melodramas'. In *Theatre Histories: An Introduction*, edited by Gary Jay Williams, 254–260. New York and London: Routledge.

McConachie, Bruce. 2008. *Engaging Audiences: A Cognitive Approach to Spectating in the Theatre*. New York: Palgrave Macmillan.

McCormick, John. 1993. *Popular Theatre of Nineteenth Century France*. London, N.Y.: Routledge.

McKenna, Neil. 2012. *Fanny and Stella. The Young Men Who Shocked Victorian England*. London: Faber and Faber.

McTeague, James H. 1993. *Before Stanislavsky: American Professional Acting Schools and Acting Theory, 1875–1925*. Metuchen, N.J.: Scarecrow Press.

Meilhac, Henri and Ludovic Halévy. 2003. *La Vie Parisienne. Pièce en cinq actes*, edited by Jean-Christophe Keck. Paris: Boosey & Hawkes.

Meisel, Martin. 1983. *Realizations: Narrative, pictorial, and theatrical arts in nineteenth century England*. Princeton: Princeton University Press.

Mercer, Leah. 1993. '"A worthy scaffold": George Rignold's rewriting and staging of *Henry V*'. *Australasian Drama Studies* 23.

Metzger, Karl-Heinz and Ulrich Dunker. 1986. *Der Kurfürstendamm. Leben und Mythos des Boulevards in 100 Jahren deutscher Geschichte*. Berlin: Konopka.

Milhous, Judith and Robert D. Hume. 2015. *The Publication of Plays in London 1660–1800: Playwrights, Publishers and the Market*. London: The British Library.

Mill, John Stuart. 1977. 'On Liberty'. In *Essays on Politics and Society. Collected Works of John Stuart Mill*, edited by J. M. Robson. Vol. 18, 213–310. Toronto: University of Toronto Press.

Miller, Arthur and Arthur Stanley. 1912/13. *The Gipsy Princess* (libretto) Lord Chamberlain's collection at the British Library, 24 May, No. 3578, British Library.

Miller, Derek. 2012. 'Performative Performances: A History and Theory of the "Copyright Performance"'. *Theatre Journal* 64 (2): 161–177.

Miller, Derek. 2016. 'The Salve of Duty: Global Theater at the American Border, 1875–1900'. *Journal of Global Theatre History* 1 (1): 20–33.

Miller, Trevelyan, ed. 1917. *True Stories of the Great War*. New York: The Review of Reviews Company.

Mishkin, Frederic S. 2006. *The Next Great Globalization: How Disadvantaged Nations Can Harness Their Financial Systems to Get Rich*. Princeton: Princeton University Press.

Mitchell, Timothy. 1989. 'The World as Exhibition'. *Comparative Studies in Society and History* 31 (2): 217–236.

Miyaoka, Kenji. 1978. *Ikoku henro tabigeinin shimatsusho* [Itinerant Japanese Performers Abroad]. Tokyo: Chûô kôronsha.

Möller, Frank. 1996. 'Zwischen Kunst und Kommerz. Bürgertheater im 19. Jahrhundert'. In *Bürgerkultur im 19. Jahrhundert. Bildung, Kunst und Lebenswelt*, edited by Dieter Hein and Andreas Schulz, 19–33. Munich: C.H. Beck.

Montague, C. E. 1968. *Dramatic Values*. New York: Greenwood Press Publishers.

Moody, Jane. 2000. *Illegitimate Theatre in London, 1770–1840*. Cambridge: Cambridge University Press.

Moore, Eva. 1923. *Exits and Entrances*. New York: Frederick Stokes.

Morash, Christopher. 2010. *A History of Media in Ireland*. Cambridge: Cambridge University Press.

Morgan, Nigel. 2005. *Stage Lighting Design in Britain: The Emergence of the Lighting Designer 1881–1950*. Cambridge: Entertainment Technology Press Historical Series.

Müller, Corinna. 2001. 'Der frühe Film, das frühe Kino und seine Gegner und Befürworter'. In *Schund und Schönheit: populäre Kultur um 1900*, edited by Kaspar Maase and Wolfgang Kaschuba, 62–91. Cologne: Böhlau.

Murai, Ken. 2012. 'Zenryoku shissô no otoko Kawakami Otojirô' [The impetuous sprinter, Kawakami Otojiro]. In *Umi wo koeta enshutsukutuchi* [Theatre People Who Crossed the Ocean], edited by Nihon enshutsusha kyôkai, 21–65. Tokyo: n.p.

Nead, Lynda. 2000. *Victorian Babylon. People, Streets and Images in the nineteenth-century London*. New Haven/London: Yale University Press.

Newey, Katherine. 2010. 'Theatre'. In *The Cambridge Companion to Victorian Culture*, edited by Francis O'Gorman, 119–134. Cambridge: Cambridge University Press.

Newnham-Davies, Lieut.-Colonel. 1898. 'Amateur in Foreign Parts'. In *Amateur Clubs and Actors,* edited by W. G. Elliot, 221–246. London: Edward Arnold.

Nicholson, Steve. 2003. *The Censorship of British Drama 1900–1968. Volume I: 1900–1932*. Exeter: Exeter University Press.

Nicoll, Allardyce. 1959. *English Drama 1669–1900. Volume V. Late nineteenth century drama 1850–1900*, 2nd edn. Cambridge: Cambridge University Press.

Niehaus, Wolfgang. 1956. *Die Theatermaler Quaglio, ein Beitrag zur Geschichte des Bühnenbildes im 18. und 19. Jahrhundert*. Munich.

Nietzsche, Friedrich. 2000 [1872]. *The Birth of Tragedy*. Translated by Douglas Smith, *Oxford World's Classics*. Oxford: Oxford University Press.

Nordensvan, Georg. 1918. *Svensk teater och svenska skåspelere från Gustav III till våra dagar. Senare Delen 1842–1918*. 2 vols. Stockholm: Albert Bonnier.

Oettermann, Stephan. 1997. *The Panorama: history of a mass media*. New York: Zone.

Oleksijczuk, Denise Blake. 2011. *The First Panorama: visions of British Imperialism*. Minneapolis and London: University of Minnesota Press.

Olsen, Donald J. 1986. *The City as a Work of Art: London, Paris, Vienna*. New Haven: Yale University Press.

Osborne, John. 1988. *The Meiningen Court Theatre, 1866–1890*. Cambridge/New York: Cambridge University Press.

Osterhammel, Jürgen and Patrick Camiller. 2014. *The transformation of the world. A global history of the nineteenth century*. Princeton: Princeton University Press.

Ostwald, Hans. 1904/05 *Dunkle Winkel in Berlin. Großstadt-Dokumente*. Berlin/Leipzig: Hermann Seemann Nachfolger GmbH.

Ostwald, Hans. 1907. *Prostitutionsmärkte*. Leipzig: O. Müller.

Otte, Marline. 1999. 'Sarrasani's Theatre of the World: Monumental Circus Entertainment in Dresden, from Kaiserreich to Third Reich'. *German History* 17 (4): 527–542.

Otte, Marline. 2006. *Jewish Identities in German Popular Entertainment, 1890–1933*. Cambridge: Cambridge University Press.

Otter, Chris. 2008. *The Victorian Eye, A Political History of Light and Vision in Britain, 1800–1910*. Chicago: The University of Chicago Press.

Pantzer, P., ed. 2005. *Japanischer Theaterhimmel über Europas Bühnen. Kawakami Otojirô, Sadayakko und ihre Truppe auf Tournee durch Mittel- und Osteuropa 1901/1902*. Munich: Iudicium.

Paquet, Alfons. 1908. *Das Ausstellungsproblem in der Volkswirtschaft. Abhandlungen des staatswissenschaftlichen Seminars zu Jena. Vol. 2*. Jena: Gustav Fischer.

Paulmann, Johannes. 2000. *Pomp und Politik. Monarchenbegegnungen in Europa zwischen Ancien Régime und Erstem Weltkrieg*. Paderborn: Ferdinand Schöningh.

Paulmann, Johannes, ed. 2001. 'Searching for a "Royal International". The Mechanics of Monarchical Relations in Nineteenth-Century Europe'. In *The Mechanics of Internationalism. Culture, Society, and Politics from the 1840s to the First World War*, 145–176. New York/Oxford: Oxford University Press.

Pavis, Partice, ed. 1996. *The Intercultural Performance Reader*. New York and London: Routledge.

Perkin, Harold. 1989. *The Rise of Professional Society: England since 1880*. London: Routledge.

Pickering, Michael. 2008. *Blackface Minstrelsy in Britain*. Burlington: Ashgate Publishing Company.

Pielhoff, Stephen. 2007. 'Stifter und Anstifter. Vermittler zwischen "Zivilgesellschaft", Kommune und Staat im Kaiserreich'. *Geschichte und Gesellschaft* 33: 10–45.

Postlewait, Thomas. 2007. 'George Edwardes and musical comedy: The transformation of London Theatre and Society, 1878–1914'. In *The Performing Century: Nineteenth-Century Theatre's History*, edited by Tracy C. Davis and P. Holland, 80–102. New York: Palgrave Macmillan.

Pückler-Muskau, Hermann, Henri Monnier and Eugène-Louis Lami. 1833. *Tour in England, Ireland, and France in the Years 1828 and 1829. With Remarks on the Manners and Customs of the inhabitants, and Anecdotes of Distinguished Public Characters*. Philadelphia: Carey, Lea & Blanchard.

Raeck, Kurt. 1928. *Das Deutsche Theater zu Berlin unter der Direktion Adolph L'Arronge. Beiträge zu seiner Geschichte und Charakteristik*. Berlin: Verlag des Vereins für die Geschichte Berlins.

Rappaport, Erika D. 2000. *Shopping for Pleasure. Women in the Making of London's West End*. Princeton: Princeton University Press.

Rauch, Marie-Ange. 2006. *De la cigale à la fourmi, histoire du mouvement social et syndical des artistes interprètes 1840–1960*. Paris: Editions de l'Amandier.

Rede, Leman Thomas. 1827. *The Road to the Stage; or, the Performer's Preceptor. Containing Clear and Ample Instructions for Obtaining Theatrical Engagements; with a List of All the Provincial Theatres, the Names of the Managers, and All Particulars as to their Circuits, Salaries, &c., with a Description of the Things Necessary on Outset in the Profession, where to Obtain Them, and a Complete Explanation of all the Technicalities of the Histrionic Art!.* London: J. Smith.

Redmond, James, ed. 1992. *Themes in Drama 14: Melodrama.* Cambridge: Cambridge University Press.

Rees, Terence. 1978. *Theatre Lighting in the Age of Gas.* London: The Society for Theatre Research.

Reif, Heinz. 2006. 'Metropolen. Geschichte, Begriff, Methoden'. In *CMS Working Paper Series* 1, 1–20. Berlin: CMS.

Reinhardt, Dirk. 1991. *Von der Reklame zum Marketing. Geschichte der Wirtschaftswerbung in Deutschland.* Berlin: Akademie-Verlag.

Richards, Jeffrey, ed. 1994. *Sir Henry Irving: Theatre, Culture and Society, Essays, Addresses and Lectures.* Keele, Staffordshire: Ryburn Publishing/Keele University Press.

Richards, Jeffrey. 2005. *Sir Henry Irving. A Victorian Actor and his World.* London: Hambledon.

Richards, Thomas. 1990. *The Commodity Culture of Victorian England. Advertising and Spectacle, 1851–1914.* Stanford, Cal.: Stanford University Press.

Richardson, Joanna. 1969. 'Offenbach'. *History Today*, 1 May: 310–316.

Roach, Joseph. 1996. *Cities of the Dead. Circum-Atlantic Performance. The Social Foundations of Aesthetic Forms.* New York: Columbia University Press.

Roach, Joseph. 1998. 'Barnumizing Diaspora: The "Irish Skylark" Does New Orleans'. *Theatre Journal* 50 (1): 39–51.

Robson, William. 1969. *The Old Play-goer.* 1846, reprinted Fontwell, Sussex: Centaur Press Ltd.

Roche, Anthony. 1995. *Contemporary Irish Drama: From Becket to McGuiness.* New York: St Martin's Press.

Roche, Anthony. 2015. *The Irish Dramatic Revival 1899–1939.* London: Methuen Drama.

Royle, Edwin Milton. 1899. 'The vaudeville theatre'. *Scribner's Magazine* (October).

Rübel, Joachim. 1992. *Geschichte der Genossenschaft Deutscher Bühnen-Angehörigen.* Hamburg: Bühnenschriften.

Rühle, Günther. 2007. *Theater in Deutschland 1887–1945. Seine Ereignisse – seine Menschen.* Frankfurt: Fischer.

Russell Brown, John, ed. 1995. *The Oxford Illustrated History of Theatre.* Oxford: Oxford University Press.

Rydell, Robert W. 1993. *World of Fairs: The Century-of-progress Expositions.* Chicago: University of Chicago Press.

Rydell, Robert W. and Rob Kroes. 2005. *Buffalo Bill in Bologna. The Americanization of the World, 1869–1922.* Chicago/London: The University of Chicago Press.

Said, Edward W. 2005. 'Orientalism and after'. In *Power, Politics and Culture – Interviews with Edward W. Said*, edited by G. Viswanathan, 208–232. London: Bloomsbury.

Saltz, David Z. 2008. 'Popular culture and theatre history'. *Theatre Journal* 4: X–XII.

Sanderson, Michael. 1984. *From Irving To Olivier: A Social History of the Acting Profession in England, 1880–1983.* London: Athlone Press.

Sarcey, Francisque. 1900. *Quarante ans de théâtre. Feuilletons dramatiques*. Paris: Bibliothèque des Annales politiques et littéraires.

Satyr [Richard Dietrich]. 1908. *Lebeweltnächte der Friedrichstadt*. Berlin: Seemann.

Savarese, Nicola. 2010. 'La création d'un monstre sacré'. *Théâtre/Public* 198: 34–38.

Sawada, Suketarô. 1997. *Petite Hanako. L'étrange histoire du seul modèle japonais de Rodin*. Frasne: Canevas.

Schall, David George. 1956. 'Rehearsal-Direction Practices and Actor-Director Relationships in the American Theatre from the Hallams to Actors' Equity'. PhD Thesis, University of Illinois.

Schanze, Helmut. 1973. *Drama im Bürgerlichen realismus (1850–1890). Theorie und Praxis*. Frankfurt am Main: Klostermann.

Schechner, Richard. 2003. *Performance Theory, Routledge Classics*. London/New York: Routledge.

Schidrowitz, Leo, ed. 1925. *Sittengeschichte des Theaters. Eine Darstellung des Theaters, seiner Entwicklung und Stellung in zwei Jahrtausenden*. New, enlarged edition. Vienna/Leipzig: Verlag für Kulturforschung.

Schiller, Friedrich. 1993. 'Was kann eine gute stehende Schaubühne eigentlich wirken?' In *Sämtliche Werke*. Vol. 5. 9th rev. ed. Darmstadt: Wissenschaftliche Buchgesellschaft.

Schimpf, Gudrun-Christine. 2007. *Geld Macht Kultur. Kulturpolitik in Frankfurt am Main zwischen Mäzenatentum und öffentlicher Finanzierung 1866–1933*. Frankfurt am Main: Kramer.

Schivelbusch, Wolfgang. 1980. *The Railway Journey*. Translated by Anselm Hollo. Oxford: Basil Blackwell.

Schivelbusch, Wolfgang. 1995. *Disenchanted Night: The Industrialisation of Light in the Nineteenth Century*. Berkeley and London: University of California Press.

Schleinitz, Otto von. 1910. 'Londoner Brief'. *Zeitschrift für Bücherfreunde*, n.s., 2 (1):

Schneer, Jonathan. 1999. *London 1900: Imperial Metropolis*. New Haven: Yale University Press.

Schoch, Richard W. 2004. 'Theatre and mid-Victorian Society'. In *Cambridge History of British Theatre, Volume II: 1660 to 1895*, edited by Joseph Donohue. Vol. 2, 331–351. Cambridge: Cambridge University Press.

Schoch, Richard. 2010. 'Shakespeare in the Music Hall'. In *The Performing Century. Nineteenth- Century Theatre's History*, edited by Tracy C. Davis and Peter Holland, 236–249. Houndmills: Palgrave.

Schodt, Frederik L. 2012. *Professor Risley and the Imperial Japanese Troupe*. Berkeley: Stone Bridge.

Schönhoff, Leopold. 1897. 'Das berlinische Publikum und seine Schaubühnen'. *Die Zeit* 10 (130): 200–202.

Scholz-Cionca, Stanca. 2016. 'Japanesque Shows for Western Markets: Loie Fuller and Early Japanese Tours through Europe (1900–1908)'. *Journal of Global Theatre History* 1: 46–61.

Schoonderwoerd, N. H. G. 1963. *J.T. Grein, Ambassador of the Theatre, 1862–1935: A Study in Anglo-Continental Theatrical Relations*. Assen, Netherlands: Van Gorcum.

Schroeder, Paul W. 1994. *The transformation of European politics, 1763–1848. Oxford history of modern Europe*. Oxford: Clarendon Press.

Schwartz, Vanessa R. and Jeannae M. Przyblynski, eds. 2004. 'Visual Culture's History. Twenty-First Century Interdisciplinarity and its Nineteenth-Century Objects'. In *The Nineteenth-Century Visual Culture Reader*, 4–14. New York/London: Routledge.

Schweitzer, Marlis. 2008. 'Patriotic act of consumption: Lucile (Lady Duff Gordon) and the vaudeville fashion show craze'. *Theatre Journal* 4: 585–608.

Schweitzer, Marlis. 2009a. '"Darn That Merry Widow Hat": The on- and offstage life of a theatrical commodity, circa 1907–1908'. *Theatre Survey* 2: 189–221.

Schweitzer, Marlis. 2009b. *When Broadway was the Runway. Theater, Fashion, and American Culture.* Philadelphia: University of Pennsylvania Press.

Scott, Clement. 1892. *Dramatic Table-talk in Thirty Years at the Play.* London: The Railway and General Automatic Library.

Scott, William and Peter Rutkoff. 1999. *New York Modern. The Arts and the City.* Baltimore: Johns Hopkins University Press.

Searle, G. R. 2005. *New England? Peace and War 1886–1918.* Oxford: Clarendon.

Senelick, Laurence. 1990. 'Offenbach and Chekhov, or La belle Yelena'. *Theatre Journal* 4 (2): 455–467.

Senelick, Laurence. 1991. 'Eroticism in early theatrical photography'. *Theatre History Studies* 11: 1–50.

Senelick, Laurence. 2000. *The Changing Room. Sex, drag and theatre.* London and New York: Routledge.

Senelick, Laurence. 2006. 'Le Théâtre érotique de la rue de Santé'. In *Encyclopedia of Erotic Literature 2 vols.*, edited by Gaëtan Brulotte and John Phillips. London: Routledge.

Senelick, Laurence. 2015. 'Lesbians, please leave the stage!' *Gay and Lesbian Review Worldwide* (May–June): 25–28.

Senelick, Laurence. 2016. 'Offenbach, Wagner, Nietzsche: The Polemics of Opera'. *New Theatre Quarterly* (February): 1–16.

Shaw, Bernard. 1948. *Our Theatre in the Nineties*, vol. 3. London: Constable and Company.

Shaw, Eyre Massey. 1876/1889. *Fires in Theatres.* London.

Shepherd, Simon and Peter Womack. 1996. *English Drama: A Cultural History.* Oxford: Blackwell.

Sierz, Aleks. 2001. *In-Yer-Face Theatre: British Drama Today.* London: Faber.

Simhandl, Peter. 1998. *Színháztörténet [Theatre History].* Budapest: Helikon.

Simmel, Georg. 2004. 'The Metropolis and mental life'. In *The Nineteenth-Century Visual Culture Reader*, edited by Vanessa R. Schwartz and Jeannene M. Przyblynski. New York/London: Routledge.

Simmons, Jack. 1984. 'Railways, Hotels and Tourism in Great Britain, 1839–1914'. *Journal of Contemporary History* 19 (2): 201–222.

Sims, George R. 1902. 'In London Theatre-Land'. In *Living London. Its Work and its Play; its Humour and its Pathos; its Sights and its Scenes*, edited by Sims, Vol. 1, 248–253. New York: Cassell and Company.

Singer, Ben. 2001. *Melodrama and Modernity: Early Sensational Cinema and its Contexts.* New York: Columbia University Press.

Smith, Hubert Llewellyn. 1931. *The New Survey of London Life & Labour.* Vol. 9, Life and Leisure. London: King.

Smyth, Patricia. 2014. 'Performers and Spectators: Viewing Delaroche'. In *Art, Theatre, and Opera in Paris, 1750–1850: Exchanges and Tensions*, edited by Richard Wrigley and Sarah Hibberd, 159–184. Farnham: Ashgate Publishing Ltd.

Sorba, Carlotta. 2006. 'The origins of the entertainment industry: The operetta in the late nineteenth-century Italy'. *Journal of Modern Italian Studies* 3: 282–302.

Sorrell, W. J. 1869. *The Amateur's Hand-book and Guide to Home or Drawing Room Theatricals, Etc. (by W. J. Sorrell.) to which is added How to 'Get Up' Theatricals in a Country House. (by Captain Sock Buskin.) and a Supplement Containing a List of Suitable Plays, Etc. (by T. H. Lacy.)*. London: T. H. Lacy.

Sosulski, Michael J. 2007. *Theater and Nation in Eighteenth-Century Germany*. Aldershot: Ashgate.

Southern, Richard. 1952. *Changeable Scenery, its origin and development in the British theatre*. London: Faber and Faber.

Steele, Valerie. 1998. *Paris Fashion: A Cultural History*, 2nd edn. Oxford: Berg.

Stein, C. 1869. *Die Todsünden der Bühne*. Dresden: L. Wolf.

Stephens, John Russell. 1992. *The Profession of the Playwright: British Theatre, 1800–1900*. Cambridge: Cambridge University Press.

Stern, Fritz. 1979. *Gold and Iron. Bismarck, Bleichröder, and the Building of the German Empire*. New York: Vintage Books Edition.

Sternberger, Dolf. 1955. *Panorama, oder Ansichten vom 19. Jahrhundert*. Hamburg: Claassen.

Stevens, D.F. 1964. 'The Central Area'. In *Greater London*, edited by J. T. Coppock and Hugh C. Prince, 167–201. London: Faber and Faber.

Stevenson, Robert Louis. 1917. 'A Plea for Gas Lamps'. In *The Travels and Essays* vol. 13. New York: n.p.

Stockdale, John Joseph. 1810. *The Covent Garden Journal*. London.

Stone Peters, Julie. 2000. *Theatre of the Book, 1480–1880: Print, Text, and Performance in Europe*. Oxford: Oxford University Press.

Stone Peters, Julie. 2008. 'Jane Harrison and the Savage Dionysus: Archaeological Voyages, Ritual Origins, Anthropology, and the Modern Theatre'. *Modern Drama* 51 (1): 1–41.

Stone Peters, Julie. 2009. 'Drama, Primitive Ritual, Ethnographic Spectacle: Genealogies of World Performance (ca. 1890–1910)'. *Modern Language Quarterly* 70 (1): 68–96.

Stribrny, Zdenek. 2000. *Shakespeare and Eastern Europe*. Oxford: Oxford University Press.

Sukenobu Isao. 2010. *Roda nto Hanako* [Rodin and Hanako]. Theatre. A Western Theatre in Meiji and Taishô Japan. Yokohama.

Surwillo, Lisa. 2007. *The Stages of Property: Copyrighting Theatre in Spain*. Toronto: University of Toronto Press.

Synge, J. M. 1992. *The Aran Islands*. London: Penguin Books.

Synge, J. M. 1935. 'Riders to the Sea'. In *John M Synge: The Complete Plays*. New York: Random House.

Teague, Frances. 2006. *Shakespeare and the American Popular Stage*. Cambridge: Cambridge University Press.

Tempest, Marie. 1932. Preface to W. H. Leverton, *Through the Box-office Window*. London: T. Werner Laurie.

Thackeray, William Makepeace. 1869. *The Paris Sketch Book of Mr. M. A. Titmarsh*. London: Smith, Elder.

Tibbetts, John C. 1985. *The American Theatrical Film: Stages in Development*. Bowling Green: Bowling Green State University Press.

Titterton, W. R. 1912. *From Theatre to Music Hall*. London: Stephen Swift.

Tönnies, Ferdinand. 2001. *Community and Civil Society. Cambridge Texts in the History of Political Thought*. Cambridge: Cambridge University Press.

Traubner, Richard. 2003. *Operetta. A Theatrical History*. New York and London: Routledge.

Trotter, David. 2011. 'Techno-Primitivism: A Propos of Lady Chatterley's Lover'. *Modernism/modernity* 18 (1): 149–166.

Troy, Nancy J. 2001. 'The Theatre of Fashion: Staging Haute Couture in Early Twentieth Century France'. *Theatre Journal* 53 (1): 1–32.

Trudgill, Eric. 1976. *Madonnas and Magdalens. The origins and development of Victorian sexual attitudes.* New York: Holmes & Meier.

Tschudin, Jean-Jacques. 2014. *L'Éblouissement d'un regard. – Découverte et réception occidentales du théâtre japonais de la fin du Mpyen-Âge à la seconde guerre mondiale.* Toulouse: Anacharsis.

Turzinsky, Walter. 1906. *Berliner Theater, Großstadt-Dokumente. 29.* Berlin: Hermann Seemann Nachfolger.

Ubersfeld, Anne. 2002. *Victor Hugo et le théâtre.* Paris: Livre de poche.

Vasold, Manfred. 2005. 'Reisen zur Postkutschenzeit'. *Kultur & Technik* 2: 52–54.

Veblen, Thorstein. 2001. *The Theory of the Leisure Class. Introduction by Alan Wolfe.* New York: The Modern Library.

Vermorel, A. 1860. *Ces dames,* 2nd edn. Paris: Charles Noblet.

Vetter, Theodor. 1910. Main address. In *Deutsche Shakespeare- Gesellschaft 1909. Jahrbuch der Deutschen Shakespeare-Gesellschaft* 46, XIV–XXXII.

Vincent-Buffault, Anne. 1991. *The History of Tears: Sensibility and Sentimentality in France.* Basingstoke: Macmillan.

Vogelsang, Bernd. 1994. 'Die Moderne in der "Theaterprovinz". Bühne und Bühnenbild rheinischer Theater 1908–1928'. In *Die Moderne im Rheinland. Ihre Förderung und Durchsetzung in Literatur, Theater, Musik, Architektur, angewandter und bildender Kunst 1900–1933,* edited by Dieter Beuer, 53–200. Cologne: Rheinland-Verlag.

Volkov, Shulamit, ed. 2000. 'Antisemitismus als kultureller Code'. In *Antisemitismus als kultureller Code. Zehn Essays,* 13–36. Munich: C. H. Beck.

Wagner, Meike. 2013. *Theater und Öffentlichkeit im Vormärz. Berlin, München und Wien als Schauplätze bürgerlicher Medienpraxis, Deutsche Literatur. Studien und Quellen. 11.* Berlin: Akademie Verlag.

Wagner, Richard. 1909. *Art Life and Theories. Selected Writings,* translated by Edward L. Burlingame. New York: Henry Holt & Company.

Walkowitz, Judith R. 2010. 'Cosmopolitanism, Feminism, and the Moving Body'. *Victorian Literature and Culture* 38 (2): 427–450.

Wallace, Irving. 1959. *The Fabulous Showman. The Life and Times of P.T. Barnum.* New York: Alfred A. Knopf.

Wallaschek, Richard. 1903. *Anfänge der Tonkunst.* Leipzig: Johann Ambrosius Barth.

Waterhouse, Richard. 1990. *From Minstrel Show to Vaudeville.* Sydney: New South Wales University Press.

Waterhouse, Richard. 1995. *Private Pleasures/Public Leisure: A History of Australian Popular Culture since 1788.* Melbourne: Longman.

Watt Smith, Tiffany. 2014. *On Flinching: Theatricality and Scientific Looking from Darwin to Shell Shock.* Oxford: Oxford University Press.

Watzka, Stefanie. 2006. *Verborgene Vermittler. Ansätze zu einer Historie der Theateragenten und -verleger. Kleine Mainzer Schriften zur Theaterwissenschaft.* Marburg: Tectum.

Weiner, Marc A. 2006. '1903. Gustav Mahler launches a new production of *Tristan and Isolde*'. In *The Arts as a Weapon of War. Britain and the Shaping of National Morale in the Second World War,* edited by Jörn Otto Weingärtner. London: I. B. Tauris.

Weiner, Marc A. 1997. '1903. Gustav Mahler launches a new production of Tristan and Isolde, Otto Weininger commits suicide shortly after his Geschlecht und Charakter is published, and Max Nordau advocates the development of a "muscle Jew"'. In *Yale Companion to Jewish Writing and Thought in German Culture, 1096–1996*, edited by Sander L. Gilman, 255–261. New Haven/London: Yale University Press.

Wenzlhuemer, Roland. 2013. *Connecting the nineteenth-century world: the telegraph and globalization*. Cambridge: Cambridge University Press.

Wertheim, Arthur and Barbara Blair. 2000. *Wild West and Vaudeville. The Papers of Will Rogers*. Norman: University of Oklahoma Press.

Whitworth, Geoffrey. 1951. *The Making of a National Theatre*. London: Faber.

Williams, Simon. 2003. 'Devrient Family'. In *The Oxford Encyclopedia of Theatre & Performance*, edited by Dennis Kennedy, 365–366. London: Oxford University Press.

Wilmeth, Don B. and Tice L. Miller, eds. 1993. *Cambridge Guide to American Theatre*. Cambridge: Cambridge University Press.

Winds, Adolf. 1919. *Quer über die Bühnen*. Berlin: Schuster & Löffler.

Wilson, Albert Edward. 1951. *Edwardian Theatre*. London: Barker.

Wilson, Albert Edward. 1954. *East End Entertainment*. London: Arthur Parkes Ltd.

Witkowski, G.-J. and L. Nass. 1909. *Le nu au théâtre depuis l'antiquité jusqu'à nos jours*. Paris: H. Daragon.

Woollan, J. C. 1902. 'Table Land in London'. In *Living London. Its Work and its Play; its Humour and its Pathos; its Sights and its Scenes*, edited by Sims, Vol. 1, 297–300. New York: Cassell and Company.

Worthen, W. B. 2005. *Print and the Poetics of Modern Drama*. Cambridge: Cambridge University Press.

Wundt, Wilhelm. 1919. *Völkerpsychologie. Eine Untersuchung der Entwicklungsgesetze von Sprache, Mythus und Sitte. Bd. 3: Die Kunst*. 3 ed.

Yajnik, R. K. 1970. *The Indian Theatre*. 1934, reprinted New York: Haskell House Publishers Ltd.

Yates, Edmund. 1884. *Edmund Yates: His Recollections and Reminiscences*. London: Richard Bentley and Son.

Yates, William E. 1996. *Theatre in Vienna. A Critical History, 1776–1995*. Cambridge: Cambridge University Press.

Zarrilli, Phillip B. et al. 2006. *Theater Histories. An Introduction*. London/New York: Routledge.

Zimmermann, Clemens. 2000. *Die Zeit der Metropolen. Urbanisierung und Großstadtentwicklung*. 2nd edn. *Europäische Geschichte*. Frankfurt am Main: Fischer.

# INDEX